# A DAILY DEVOTIONAL

## Developing Your Relationship with the Holy Spirit

**Grow in Fellowship with God our Father and the Lord Jesus Christ through a dynamic relationship with the Holy Spirit.**

By George Runyan

"The grace of the Lord Jesus Christ, and the love of God, and the fellowship of the Holy Spirit, be with you all"
(2 Corinthians 13:14).

# A Daily Devotional

# Developing Your Relationship with the Holy Spirit

## By George Runyan

Copyright © 2012 George Runyan

ISBN 978-1-61529-052-9

Vision Publishing
1672 Main Street E 109
Ramona, CA 92065
1 800–9-VISION
www.booksbyvision.com

Quotations from the Bible are in the New American Standard Version unless otherwise stated.

# WHAT OTHERS ARE SAYING

The most neglected member of the Trinity is the Holy Spirit. Jesus stated that it was good for him to go to the Father, so the Comforter, the Holy Spirit could come, to guide, strengthen, convict and convince the believer. Further, Paul stated that the Kingdom of God is righteousness, peace and joy...all in the Holy Spirit. George Runyan has always been an apostle of prayer, with a special gift of caring for pastors, and laying a foundation for healthy Christian living. Recognizing the "often neglected member" as his and our source of life on earth, he has written a daily devotional guide to focus our attention on the wonderful gift which is the Holy Spirit. Daily guidance is provided in each devotional, wisdom for difficult decisions, and comfort in our daily grind. Be blessed as you read and devote yourself more completely to the Lord, the Spirit.

Dr. Stan DeKoven
Founder and President
Vision International University


Jesus promised His disciples that He would not leave us as orphans, but would send another Helper or Comforter to be with us (John 14:16-18). The Christian life is a wonderful ongoing discovery of what it means to have the Holy Spirit walk with us as our Helper and Comforter. George Runyan takes you on a one year adventure through the Scriptures to deepen our walk in the Spirit. This book is a rich experience in growing in the knowledge and power of the Holy Spirit.

Mark Hoffman, Sr. Pastor
Foothills Christian Church
El Cajon, California


I have read George Runyan's book and encourage you to do so. It is loaded with Biblical truth and helpful counsel. George focuses on God's will for us as the Body of Christ with a deep sensitivity to the Holy Spirit. Each chapter closes with a prayer for the Lord to complete His work in us.

Charles Simpson
CSM

In this daily devotional George Runyan challenges you daily to be filled and led by the Spirit of God. Each daily devotional concludes with a prayer of commitment to continue to grow as a disciple of Jesus Christ. I highly recommend this devotional to anyone who wants to further their understanding of the Holy Sprit's work in their daily life.

David Hoffman, Sr. Pastor
Foothills Christian Church


The IronMen Ministry Foundation wants to thank Pastor, Teacher and Author George Runyan for his obedience to Father God in completing this writing. It is filled to overflowing with applicable truths of God's Word that are inspirational and encouraging to the reader. George's heart felt thoughts and his transparency fold out of each day. He expresses the gift of an apostolic message to the body of Christ through God's word that is specific, and it clearly equips and edifies the saints.

Trusting in the Lord,
Ronnie L. Holderby
CEO, IMF
Richard D. Holderby
CFO, IMF
IronMen Ministry Foundation


George Runyan's book "Developing Your Relationship with the Holy Spirit"combines the Word, the Spirit, and church history tying it to everyday life. It is a book to be read and re-read. George has been a faithful friend and pastor's pastor in my life for 25 years.

Nathan Daniel, founder of Freedom Through Forgiveness Ministries San Diego, California

# ACKNOWLEDGMENTS

Thank you to my parents George and Shirley Runyan, who have always given to me and my brothers' wonderful support and encouragement. I will always be grateful to the Lord for the parents He gave to me. They are now with the Lord and rejoicing in His presence.

John Seymour – Father God used John to lay in my life the foundation for a love of God's Word. He was instrumental in leading me into a relationship with the Holy Spirit. He taught me the importance of rightly dividing the Word of God. Because of Brother Seymour my teaching ministry was launched in San Diego at the Berean Bible College.

Charles Donhowe, who pastored me in the seventies and helped me to learn how to navigate through the rough waters of life. Brother Donhowe is a man of principle and he taught me the importance of covenant relationship and integrity.

George Kouri – Brother Kouri was used of the Lord to stir up the apostolic calling on my life. He brought further clarity concerning the kingdom of God and the recovery of apostolic teachings. Brother Kouri continues to teach leaders as the Chancellor of the Apostles Theological Seminary.

Charles Simpson – For forty years Brother Charles Simpson has been impacting my thinking as he has with multitudes. He has helped me to understand the kingdom of God and culture. I highly recommend Brother Simpson's book – "The Covenant and the Kingdom."

Thank you to all those who have helped in the editing of the manuscript and in producing this devotional book. Thank you; John Barry, Mick McCoy, Richard Niessen of Expert Proofreading and Editing, and Kathy Smith of Vision Publishing.

Thank you men of God for writing endorsements. Each of you has sown into my life over the years. I respect and appreciate your contributions in advancing God's kingdom purposes: thank you Charles, Mark, Dave, Stan, Nathan, Rick and Ronnie.

A special thank you Dick Dungen for the encouragement as I wrote this devotional and for taking your valuable time to write the forward, you are a blessing!

Thank you to my mother in-law, Vanlora Scott, for the picture of the dove featured on the cover. She painted the picture for a church she was attending in Sweetwater, Texas. Thank you mom for your years of faithfulness in prayer and your artwork dedicated to God's Kingdom.

Thank you to my good friend Steve Parks who graciously allowed me to use their family's mountain home for the writing of Developing Your Relationship with the Holy Spirit.

Thank you to my friends Jim and Linda Bell and their large contribution making it possible to publish this book. Thank you so much!

I must mention my good friend Julie Kirk who has helped me over the years with becoming a better communicator both in speaking and writing.

Dr. Stan DeKoven, President of Vision International University. I thank you Stan for your abiding friendship and all of the valuable help that you have offered me in so many areas for the past twenty years.

There are so many others that should be mentioned. All my fellow elders in the San Diego region who have been a part of building strong committed relationships in order to advance God's kingdom purpose in this local area. And my many friends across the nation and throughout the world who have had a part in the development and ministry effecting the advancement of God's kingdom.

Thank you to all my children for their love and support over the years. Each one of you is a real encouragement to me. I always pray for your success and growth in the knowledge of our Lord and Savior Jesus Christ. I pray that the truths and lessons written in this book will serve you and your children in the years to come.

Last, but not least, thank you to my wife Becky. I thank you Becky for your love and patience with me over these many years. You, more than anyone, have impacted my life for good. Thank you for all your patience and the sacrifices made in support of my calling in Christ and the raising of our children. Thank you for your input and help in learning to live out the principles of God's word in marriage, family, and covenant relationship.

# FOREWARD

## Developing Your Relationship
## with the Holy Spirit

What a privilege it is to introduce you, the reader, to this anointed devotional that is so timely in helping us to recognize the person and work of the Holy Spirit throughout the Scriptures. The author, my esteemed friend, George Runyan, has done an excellent work in challenging us to recognize and embrace this often neglected third person of the Godhead.

While holding fast to the integrity of sound doctrine, the author urges and invites the reader to see the Holy Spirit at work throughout the pages of God's Holy Word; while acknowledging the importance of how we can trust the Spirit of God to speak to us in our daily journey.

George's insightful grasp of how absolutely critical it is for each of us to walk intimately with our Lord Jesus Christ by recognizing and obeying the voice of the Holy Spirit is tragically overlooked in many Christian circles today. Wasn't it Jesus who told His disciples that *"And I will pray the Father, and He will give you another Helper, that He may abide with you forever the Spirit of truth, whom the world cannot receive, because it neither sees Him nor knows Him; but you know Him, for He dwells with you and will be in you."* (John 14:16-17) and *"These things I have spoken to you while being present with you. But the Helper, the Holy Spirit, whom the Father will send in My name, He will teach you all things, and bring to your remembrance all things that I said to you."* (John 14:25-26).

As I have had the opportunity to read and reflect upon these daily devotionals during the authors 'labor of love' I've been profoundly amazed at the rich insights that are shared each day. I have been blessed with not only knowing the author since 1996, but also with the privilege of traveling internationally as well as serving on the same apostolic team. I am honored to call George my friend, brother and co-laborer in our Father's vineyard. He is truly a faithful, humble and trustworthy servant of the Lord who is recognized as a 'pastor to pastors' by those who know him.

As you open the pages of this devotional book, it is my prayer that the Spirit of God will invade your life in ways you have never known. As the Scriptures teach us, we will overcome by the blood of the Lamb, the Word of our testimony and by not loving our lives unto death (Revelation 12:11). This can and will only be accomplished in our lives as we are willing to allow the Holy Spirit to be our teacher, guide and interpreter of the Scriptures thus establishing sound doctrine as the foundation of our faith.

I trust that you will encounter not only the transforming power of the Word of God, but also His sweet, embracing, life-giving Presence!

Enjoy!

Richard (Dick) Dungan
Founder/Director
Rejoice Ministries International
Norfolk, Nebraska

# INTRODUCTION

While I was in India during 2008, the Holy Spirit gave me an assignment to write a devotional focused on developing a daily relationship with Him. He is the Spirit of the Father and the Spirit of the Son. He is God's gift to every believer as they trust in Christ's redemptive work which He accomplished on the cross and in His burial and resurrection. The Father promised the Son that He would give Their Holy Spirit to all who trusted in Christ (see Luke 24:49).

Jesus told His disciples "wait in Jerusalem until you are given power to go with the message of the Gospel" (Acts 1:7-8). In Acts 2, we read of the mighty Holy Spirit being poured out on the 120 disciples waiting in the upper room and the overflow into the streets of Jerusalem. Three thousand men were added to the Lord's church that day. We do not know how many over the three thousand may have been women and children.

Acts 8 tells of the multitude of Samaritans who believed the word preached by Philip the Evangelist and confirmed by miracles he performed. When the disciples heard that Samaria had received the Word, they sent Peter and John who laid hands on the Samaritan believers and they too received the promised Holy Spirit.

Acts 9 tells of Saul's conversion on the road to Damascus with authority to arrest Christians. He encountered the living Christ and was given orders that redirected his entire life. Soon after, a man named Ananias found Saul. After laying his hands on him, Saul was filled with the Holy Spirit. He also was healed of blindness that had overtaken him from the glory of the Lord on the Damascus road.

Acts 10 records how the Gentiles received the Father's promise when Peter preached to all of Cornelius household. Before he had finished his sermon, the Holy Spirit fell on all the Gentiles listening to the message. They were all filled with the Spirit, speaking in tongues just like what the Jews had experienced on the Day of Pentecost. Peter, in amazement, turned to his Jewish friends saying "Surely no one can refuse the water for these to be baptized who have received the Holy Spirit just as we did, can he?" (Acts 10:47).

Acts 19 records about some disciples of John the Baptist who believed, but had not heard that the Holy Spirit had come to fill their life with His presence. Paul laid his hands upon these disciples, and they too received God's Spirit in power and spoke in tongues and prophesied (Acts 19:1-7).

Jesus has been giving the Holy Spirit to believers down through history. Many have received the Holy Spirit with supernatural evidences. There has been an increase of the Spirit's presence in the Church throughout the Twentieth Century. He continues to make Himself known throughout the world as multitudes give witness to their experiences with the Holy Spirit. He wants believers to have much more than just an experience; He wants a deep relationship with each person.

This book is dedicated for the purpose of helping God's people develop a closer walk with God's Spirit. To learn how to be led by the Spirit, to recognize His promptings, and to be used in His power to bear witness of God's great love revealed in the Lord Jesus Christ.

When I completed this devotional book, I found that the Lord had given three powerful helps which I call the (Three I's): Inspirational, Informational, and Instructional. All three are necessary for developing a healthy balanced walk in the Spirit of God.

All of us need to be inspired in order to live out the relationship God has given us because of Christ' sacrifice and the coming of His promised Holy Spirit. The Scriptures inspire us to persevere as others who have gone before. The Spirit and the Word are the dynamic duo of our faith.

Inspiration is not enough. We must also have (information) in order to know how to apply the inspiration received. Learning of God's purpose, plans, and how others lived a "Spirit filled life" is extremely important. Knowing all that is available to the believer is a must in fulfilling God's plan for one's life.

We must be (instructed). The Word of God, the Bible, is our instruction book. It is the manual to know how to live out the will of God. It reveals that you and I cannot live out His will without His divine power working through us. It shows us that we need to be filled with the Holy Spirit daily. Our body is the temple of the Holy Spirit. His dwelling place in the earth is in each believer to work His divine plan and purpose. He is the one building the Lord's church. He is the one sent to administrate the Lord's Kingdom and His will on earth as it is in Heaven.

"You are a chosen race, a royal priesthood, a holy nation, a people for God's own possession, so that you may proclaim the excellencies of Him who has called you out of darkness into His marvelous light" (1 Peter 2;9). Be blessed as you daily read His Words of Life!

In His Grace,
George Runyan

# January 1 – FROM CHAOS TO LIGHT

Genesis 1:2-3 – The Earth was formless and void, and darkness was over the surface of the deep, and the Spirit of God was moving over the surface of the waters. Then God said, "Let there be light" and there was light.

As the earth was "formless and void," so too are we before God speaks. Darkness was over the surface of the deep. Is your life without form and void? Do you feel void of purpose, trying to understand why you exist? Many wrestle with who they are and why they exist. Many feel a sense of purposelessness.

As it was in the natural creation, the Spirit of God is moving over the surface of people's lives. He has come to speak the Word of God into the life of individuals and nations. The same Word of God that brought order out of chaos and light to the natural creation in the beginning wants to bring order to our lives and reveal God's purpose in us. He has come to bring forth a new creation out of the old. This is what Paul meant when he said, "Therefore, if anyone is in Christ, he is a new creature; the old things passed away; behold new things have come" (2 Corinthians 5:17).

Today, many are full of confusion, emptiness, and without purpose. The darkness of sin rules in their life choices. Each area can be brought into the light of God's Word through the life-giving presence of the Holy Spirit. God gave His Word in human form when He sent His Son, the Lord Jesus Christ. The Spirit of God is waiting for individuals to receive the spoken Word. God's word can be made flesh in our lives as well. Jesus said, "I am the Light of the world; he who follows Me will not walk in darkness, but will have the Light of life" (John 8:12). The Holy Spirit is present, helping men and women come to the Light of God revealed in His Word and manifested through the Lord Jesus Christ. Some need to receive the initial salvation of forgiveness and the new birth. Others have come to Christ, yet they still have areas in their lives that are bound by darkness. The Holy Spirit came to set the captives free and bring fruitfulness in lives that are surrendered to God's plan. Let us be fruitful by fulfilling God's plan in our life.

Ask the Holy Spirit to remove chaos from your life and replace it with His order. Give Him permission to search all parts of your life and reveal any darkness by exposing it to His light.

## January 2 – BE FILLED WITH THE SPIRIT

Genesis 2:7 Then the Lord formed man of dust from the ground, and breathed into his nostrils the breath of life; and man became a living being.

In the beginning, it was God that formed man. God is the divine architect of life. His purpose was not to have a design to look upon and admire as an art form, but to have a "living" man who would do His will on the earth. It was God's "breath" that gave man life. The word "spirit" means "breath." God breathed into man and man came to life.

The divine creator is still breathing into mankind. In the first creation, man became a "living soul." Man's disobedience in the Garden of Eden brought sin, separation, and darkness. God has chosen to create a "new creation" out of the sinful chaos of the fallen creation. It is what the apostle Paul was speaking concerning the new self when he states, "Put on the new self, which in the likeness of God has been created in righteousness and holiness of the truth" (Ephesians 4:24).

If you are "in" Christ, you are a "new creation." The work of God's Spirit is to breathe upon all those that receive God's Word and recreate Christ in them. Paul said, "We once knew Christ after the flesh, but now we know Him no more that way, rather we now know Him after the Spirit" (2 Corinthians 5:16). The first disciples walked with Christ as He lived in an earthly body. We have believed in Him as the Son of God in the flesh that died on the cross. The Spirit of God raised Him from the dead and He is now alive through the Spirit. We can only know Christ by the Spirit of God. Let Him breathe new life into you today. God's will is for us to daily receive a new infilling of His Holy Spirit. Sometimes we need to be filled many times in a day.

Father, reveal to me if I am allowing the Holy Spirit to fill me as much as You desire. I know that I need a fresh infilling of Your power and presence each and every day. I invite the Holy

Spirit to fill me today and throughout this year for the glory of God.

## January 3 – BECOMING AWARE OF HIS PRESENCE

John 3:5 – Jesus answered, "Truly, truly, I say to you, unless one is born of water and the Spirit he cannot enter the kingdom of God."

The key to entering the kingdom of God is the Spirit of God. It is the Holy Spirit who carries the mandate to bring forth in the earth a "new creation." The natural man does not receive the Spirit of God because the kingdom is spiritual and not natural. Many try reasoning in their minds how to be accepted by God. This is the height of folly because God will not allow any to know Him and His ways simply through natural reasoning. All of the world religions are based upon self-effort in trying to reach God. The basis of the "faith once delivered to the saints" is rooted in God reaching out to us. He has done this through His Holy Spirit. The Spirit caused the Christ child to be formed in Mary's womb. It was the Spirit who came upon Jesus at His baptism. It was the Holy Spirit that empowered Jesus to heal the sick and cast out demons. The Holy Spirit strengthened the Lord Jesus to endure the cross for each of us. Finally, the Father promised Jesus that the Holy Spirit would be given to all who would believe in Him.

Nicodemus, a religious leader in Israel, came to Jesus in the dark of night. He knew in his heart that Jesus had been sent by God, confirmed by the signs that followed Jesus' life. Nicodemus only knew the Law as a way to God. Jesus began to share that the true way of entrance into the kingdom of God was through a new birth, and not by attempting to keep the Jewish Law. Jesus told Nicodemus that it is by water and the Spirit that one must be born again. Water speaks of the natural birth process. Baptism was not a new thought to the Jews, for they had many kinds of baptisms. Being born of the Spirit was a new dimension for this Pharisee to grasp.

Many try entering into a relationship with God through various kinds of religious works. But Jesus' words help us understand that only by the Spirit of God can one be "born into the Father's Kingdom." Are you resting fully upon a relationship with the Holy Spirit for your entrance and life in the Kingdom of God today? Or is it self-effort and natural reasoning which drives you toward spiritual things?

Our greatest need is to increase our dependence upon God's Spirit. He wants us to let go of all self-effort and fully embrace a relationship of intimacy with Him. God, as promised to Jesus, has sent His Spirit to be received by all those who have chosen to put their trust in the Lord Jesus. If you have been "born of the Spirit," then get to know Him in ever deepening ways. Always inquire of His will and direction in your life. Learn to discern His voice in your inner man.

Father, I ask for an increase in my awareness of the need for Your Holy Spirit's presence. I ask that I might be led more by Your Spirit and less by my own natural reasoning in my day-to-day life.

## January 4 – FLESH AND SPIRIT

John 3:6 – That which is born of the flesh is flesh and that which is born of the Spirit is spirit.

Jesus explained to Nicodemus the two types of birth. One is a birth that is generated by the flesh or through the human reproductive process that God initiated at the creation. Because of sin, man lost his standing of righteousness before God, and came under the judgment of God. Man had a desperate need for something to save him from his lost condition.

Jesus came to provide a way of salvation for mankind. Through the Holy Spirit man could be born again. A "new" creation would begin through Christ. Jesus told Nicodemus this second birth would be a work of the Spirit. Through the new birth, we are once again brought back into a relationship with God. When born again, we have a "right standing with God." It is a birth that the Holy Spirit initiates. As we allow His work in our lives, He matures us into the image of Christ. His mandate is to empower believers to grow up in Christ so that He might be revealed in everything we do.

Paul speaks both about the man of the flesh and the spiritual man when writing to the Corinthians in 1 Corinthians 3:1-2. The man of the flesh is the person who tries to serve God from his own reasoning. Paul says that this one is an "infant in Christ." Paul goes on to say that he had to give them "milk" rather than solid food because "they could not receive it." The "new birth" is not unlike the natural birth as it relates to babes and mature individuals. We begin as an infant, but the hope is that we will grow up into Christ by becoming a "spiritual man," in other words, one that is led by the Holy Spirit. This can only come about as we develop a relationship with the Spirit of God. He leads us to the Word of God with the purpose of washing our minds from the fleshly way of thinking to a "spiritual" way of thinking and biblical application in our daily life.

Where are you in the process of change? Are you still fleshly in your thinking and practices or are you developing as a spiritual man or woman? Is Christ being revealed in your thoughts and practices?

## January 5 – THE SPIRIT WILL NOT CONVICT FOREVER

Genesis 6:3 – Then the Lord said, "My Spirit shall not strive with man forever because he also is flesh; nevertheless, his days shall be one hundred and twenty years."

This pronouncement of God is prior to the flood that destroyed all mankind except for Noah and his family. God saw Noah as a righteous man. God reveals in our scripture for today that His Spirit had to deal with sin at some point. The sixth chapter of Genesis reveals how God determined that man had 120 years to repent and begin to serve God's purpose. He chose to use Noah as His instrument to call man to salvation by the construction of the ark. Men laughed at Noah, but when the ark was finished, God's judgment came quickly.

Paul helps us understand that God is still dealing with mankind's rebellion. "God is now declaring to all men that all people everywhere should repent because He has fixed a day in which He will judge the world in righteousness through a Man whom He has appointed" (Acts 17:30-31). That man is God's own Son who came to bear the sins of the world and take on Himself the wrath of God. Jesus' atoning work is what caused God the Father to make this statement through Paul. There is a day which God has fixed to judge all those who refuse to repent by changing their mind and submitting to God's Spirit who has come to transform all those who trust in Christ.

Jesus is God's ark of safety for mankind from God's judgment when it finally comes. That judgment will not be by water, but a rain of fire as God has declared. "By His Word the present heavens and earth are being reserved for fire, kept for the Day of Judgment and destruction of ungodly men" (2 Peter 3:7). Repentance is a lifestyle that allows the Holy Spirit to point out areas where God wants us to change our thinking and actions. Allow the Spirit to reveal Christ in your thinking and how you might live life before God and this generation.

What does the Spirit of God desire to speak with you about in regard to your thinking and the way you live as a son or daughter of God? He is always close to bring fresh insights, so our minds might be renewed after His.

## January 6 - I WOULD THAT ALL GOD'S PEOPLE WERE PROPHETS

Numbers 11:29 – I would will that all the Lord's people were prophets, that the Lord would put His Spirit upon them!

God took of His Spirit which rested upon Moses and placed Him upon the seventy elders. When the Spirit rested upon them, they prophesied. Two of the seventy remained in the camp and were not present, but they too received the Spirit and prophesied. Joshua did not think this was right because those men were not present with the others. Moses thought that Joshua was jealous for Moses' sake, but Moses revealed the heart of God with his response in verse 29.

God desires for His people to have such a relationship with Him that He can reveal His will to them so that they can voice God's will to others. "God is no respecter of persons" (Acts 10:34). He reveals His desire that all of His people would "prophesy." In 1 Corinthians 14:31 Paul wrote, ". . . for you can all prophesy one by one." Paul went on to reveal that prophecy has purpose; that it is ". . . for learning and the exhorting of God's people." Prophecy is not the attempt of the natural man trying to figure out God's will, but the Spirit making known God's will to the spirit of a person. What one believes the Spirit of God has revealed to them is subject to others who are hearing God as well. No spirit of prophecy is "private," but is to be confirmed by what others are hearing God say. "The spirits of the prophets are subject to the prophets;  for God is not a God of confusion but peace as in all the churches of the saints" (1 Corinthians 14:32-33).

Confusion and the lack of peace are produced by a person holding onto a private interpretation of God's Word. The man or woman that possesses the true spirit of prophecy is the one who spends time with God listening carefully for what the Spirit desires to speak. They freely submit what they are hearing to others for discernment of accuracy. The Spirit never contradicts the Word of God, nor does He limit what He is saying to one individual. The Spirit of God does not bring new "revelation" that is outside of God's revealed Word, but helps us to apply God's Word in our present world and culture. Wisdom is necessary to work with revelation. That is why Paul prays "that the God of our Lord Jesus Christ, the Father of glory, may give to you a spirit of wisdom and of revelation in the knowledge of Him" (Ephesians 1:17).

Ask God every day for the spirit of wisdom and revelation in the knowledge of Christ. Not only read God's Word and pray, but become a listener for what the Spirit would say to you. Be prepared to speak, so others may learn and be exhorted.

## January 7 – FELLOWSHIP OF THE HOLY SPIRIT

2 Corinthians 13:14 – The grace of our Lord Jesus Christ, and the love of God, and the fellowship of the Holy Spirit, be with you all.

In ending his letter to the Corinthians, Paul includes the community of the Godhead. The grace of Jesus speaks of the one who is a gift from God. The love of God addresses the Father's heart. The "fellowship" of the Holy Spirit reveals how the Spirit is the part of the Godhead with whom we develop intimacy. Out of God's love, Jesus came as the Father's gift so we might have the continual fellowship in the Holy Spirit. Many times we hear of receiving Jesus into our hearts, but the only way we can receive Jesus and know the Father is through the Holy Spirit. The Holy Spirit, who is the Spirit of the Father and the Spirit of the Son, has come as the "promise" of the Father for each one who would receive God's gift, Jesus. Jesus said to His disciples, "Behold, I am sending forth the promise of My Father upon you; but you are to stay in the city until you are clothed with power from on high" (Luke 24:49).

The Holy Spirit has been the "neglected" part of the Godhead. In the Apostle's Creed, all we find is the statement "I believe in the Holy Spirit." Part of the message of the gospel is that Jesus came so that true fellowship with God could be restored to all mankind through faith in Jesus as the "sin bearer." That fellowship is found in the Holy Spirit. Many of God's people have not been taught to nurture their relationship with the Holy Spirit. One reason is a misunderstanding of Jesus' statement in John 16:13 (KJV) ". . . for He will not speak of himself . . . "A better translation is ". . . or he will not speak on His own initiative . . . ." Just as Jesus Himself, did nothing out of His own initiative, the Holy Spirit only does the Father's bidding.

Our great need is to spend time in fellowship with the Spirit. This means that we must become familiar with His voice and learn how to follow His leading. Only fellowship with the Holy Spirit can bring us into an ever-increasing relationship with the Father and the Son.

How much of our time and energy is spent in the natural realm trying to develop our relationship with God? We can only know Him by the Spirit. Today, ask the Father and the Son to fill you afresh with their Holy Spirit and begin to nurture a daily fellowship with Him.

## January 8 – THE SPIRIT'S PURPOSE IS TO WORK ALL THINGS AFTER HIS WILL

1 Corinthians 12:8-11 – For to one is given the word of wisdom through the Spirit, and to another the word of knowledge according to the same Spirit; to another faith by the same

Spirit, and to another gifts of healing by the one Spirit, and to another the effecting of miracles, and to another prophecy, and to another the distinguishing of spirits, to another various kinds of tongues, and to another the interpretation of tongues. But one and the same Spirit works all these things, distributing to each one individually, just as He wills.

The Apostle helps the Corinthian believers understand the work of the Holy Spirit in the life of an individual believer within the community of the church gathering. Some have wrongly interpreted this passage as saying that the Holy Spirit gives one gift to each believer as He wills. Paul had concern because the Corinthian believers were misusing the gifts by making them personal rather than for the edifying of the body. When believers gather together in an assembly, it would be confusing if everybody spoke in tongues or tried to prophesy at the same time. Within the corporate body the Holy Spirit gives to each as He wills for the edification of all.

In our daily walk and fellowship with the Holy Spirit, we live out our life around others who do not know God. The Holy Spirit desires to reveal the love of God through us by releasing His gifts. He chooses what He deems beneficial in helping our witness. It is possible that one might find a few particular gifts of the Spirit working regularly in their life, but all are available to the believer as the Holy Spirit leads. In the corporate body, He distributes to each one individually just as He wills, but outside the gathering of the body, all His gifts are available to the believer at any given time.

Father, I ask for the Holy Spirit to use me today as you so desire. I am Your servant and cannot effectively share Your love with others unless You empower me. Be free to release Your gifts through my life to assist me in ministering to those You chose to bring across my path.

## January 9 – IF ANYONE IS THIRSTY

John 7:37 – If anyone is thirsty, let him come to Me and drink.

There are two different kinds of thirst that human beings experience. The natural thirst for water and the spiritual thirst for God. A person can go without food for many days. The body will begin to draw from its own resources until they are depleted and they begin to die of starvation. This is not true of our need for water. In a very short time the body dehydrates from a lack of water. The body does not store water like a camel which has a reservoir that holds water for long periods.

Jesus begins to reveal that He is their source which can satisfy spiritual thirst. Only by coming to Jesus can one be refreshed with a supply of living water. He goes on to explain in verse 38 that the one who believes in Him will experience this living water flowing like a river from one's innermost being. The spiritual water that Jesus is referring to is not from an outside source, but the source will be within the believer. Literally, this means from the person's "belly". Jesus states that this is the promise of Scripture. He is referencing Isaiah 58:11, "You will be like a watered garden, and like a spring of water whose waters do not fail."

John 7:39 explains that Jesus was referring to the coming work of the Spirit in the life of those who believed. First, Jesus had to be raised from the dead, glorified, and seated next to the Father. The Spirit was manifested on the day of Pentecost when the promised Holy Spirit came with a number of manifestations, as revealed in Acts 2. Every believer needs to have their personal Pentecost. The disciples believed on Jesus, but they needed to receive the Holy Spirit. Have you asked to receive the Holy Spirit? Can you relate to Jesus' words "that from your innermost being will flow living water"? If not, why not ask Him today to give you the Holy Spirit and the promised "living water." Perhaps you have received, but you need to be filled again with the Spirit. The Bible teaches that there are many fillings that one might experience.

Today, receive the Holy Spirit and let Him release the living waters from your innermost being! Why not pray right now? Father, I ask today that Jesus would fill me with the Holy Spirit. I recognize I need to be filled daily and sometimes more than once in the period of a day.

# January 10 – GO AND WAIT FOR THE PROMISE OF MY FATHER

Luke 24:49 – Behold, I am sending forth the promise of My Father upon you; but you are to stay in the city until you are clothed with power from on high.

Everything the Lord does, He does with purpose and in the context of His own timing. The disciples had experienced the Holy Spirit's power while Jesus was with them. Now, our Lord was going back to the Father, taking His place at the Father's right hand. He was about to receive the Promise of the Father and send the Holy Spirit to earth. The Spirit came to empower believers for the work which God has appointed in establishing His kingdom on earth.

The disciples waited for the promise. After ten days, He fell upon them with a great blast of wind and mighty manifestations. Today, He is here with us, but we still need to wait before the Lord with expectation for the empowerment of the Spirit's presence. Many times, we read the Scriptures and assume the promises of God are automatic. This is not an accurate understanding of how God works in fulfilling His promises. "Without faith it is impossible to please Him, for he who comes to God must believe that He is and that He is a rewarder of those who seek Him" (Hebrews 11:6). Seeking the Lord is foundational to receiving His promises.

Many believers depend upon others who have sought the Lord. Some depend upon their pastors to study and seek God for understanding of His Word. Some depend on the faith of others in receiving the promises of God. The Father desires that all His children would seek Him personally. As believers, we should be thirsty for righteousness. It is only through our relationship with the Holy Spirit that we can receive all that the Lord has for us to fulfill His will in our lives.

If you have not committed yourself to wait upon the Holy Spirit, why not begin today? Ask the Father for the Holy Spirit to reveal Himself in increasing ways. Expect Him to manifest His presence to you and open up your understanding to the Word of God and its application in and through your life.

# January 11 – RECEIVING THE DOVE OF HEAVEN

Luke 3:21-22 – Jesus was also baptized, and while He was praying, heaven was opened, and the Holy Spirit descended upon Him in bodily form like a dove.

Jesus is the perfect man before God and sets the pattern for all of us. Thirty years before His baptism, Jesus was born from a divine act of God through the person of the Holy Spirit as Mary conceived. Now, thirty years later, Jesus came to John, his cousin, to be baptized in water. The Jews understood baptism as a cleansing, but Jesus was baptized in witness of His coming death, burial, and resurrection. For Jesus, it was His public testimony of His commitment to the will of His Father. The Father's response was to open heaven and send the Holy Spirit in "bodily form" to anoint Jesus for His ministry. After Jesus' ascension, the Father poured out His Spirit upon those who believed in the Lord Jesus Christ.

Today, the Holy Spirit is here with us. He is not only with each believer, but He has come to indwell each one who is trusting Christ. Have you allowed the Holy Spirit to come on you and indwell you? Just as with Jesus, every believer that has trusted Christ has been born of the Spirit of God. In the same way that Jesus came to the waters of baptism submitting Himself to the will of God, we too must yield to the full will of the Father as we consider the rest of our life on earth. This will take the power of God through His indwelling Spirit. Many believers, once they trust Jesus for their salvation through forgiveness of sin, do not go on to being filled daily with the Holy Spirit. We need empowerment to live the life of a disciple, to witness with power, and to overcome the evil one who ever waits to tempt and distract us from the Father's will.

Many times, in the book of Acts and throughout the apostle's letters, we are instructed to be filled with the Holy Spirit. On one occasion, Paul says "… be filled with the Spirit, speaking to one another in psalms and hymns and spiritual songs, singing, and making melody with your heart to the Lord" (Ephesians 5:18-19).

Today, let us yield to the Father as Jesus did. Receive the gift of the Holy Spirit to empower you for the call of God in your life. Ask Him to fill you with the Holy Spirit every day. Then open yourself to receive of the Spirit's presence and guidance.

## January 12 – LED BY THE SPIRIT

Luke 4:1-2 – Jesus, full of the Holy Spirit, returned from Jordan and was led around by the Spirit in the wilderness for forty days, being tempted by the devil.

Jesus had to be temped, as it was written, "One who has been tempted in all things as we are" (Hebrews 4:15). Being directed by the Holy Spirit and using the Word of God, He overcame the evil one. God does not *tempt* anyone (James 1:13), but temptation will come to all, especially after we have determined to follow Jesus.

The Holy Spirit has been given to enable us to follow, obey, overcome, and help others experience God's amazing grace. The Holy Spirit is always present to empower each believer to be led by the Spirit (Romans 8:14). He will establish us in the Word of God, He will lead us to divine appointments, He will guide us to overcome temptation, and He will release His gifts so that we can effectively give witness to Christ as the Risen Lord. So many believers try to work out salvation in their own strength and understanding. This has brought many to a place of discouragement and infancy rather than "growing up into the full measure of the stature of Christ" (Ephesians 4:13).

One distinctive change which is meant to take place when we become believers and followers of Christ is a life led by the Spirit. Paul shares in 1 Corinthians 2:14-15 that the natural man does not accept the things of the Spirit. It is only the spiritual man which can appraise all things.  Are you led by your natural reasoning most of the time or have you become a spiritual man, one led by the Holy Spirit?

Father, I want to be the spiritual individual You will me to be. I choose to surrender my thoughts and my ways to You. I invite the Holy Spirit to take control of all areas in my life. Father, fill me daily with your Holy presence and lead me through the wilderness of this life, into Your purpose of ministering to others Your wonderful grace.

# January 13 – THE SPIRIT OF THE LORD IS UPON ME

Luke 4:18 – The Spirit of the Lord is upon Me because He Anointed Me to preach the Gospel.

It is one thing to be born of the Spirit and entirely another to be anointed of the Spirit. Jesus was both born of the Spirit and thirty years later anointed to preach the good news of the kingdom of God. The preaching of the gospel is not something that an individual decides one day. Only the Holy Spirit has the authority to call a person to preach the gospel. Only the Holy Spirit can commission one to go with the good news of the kingdom. Only the Holy Spirit can convey on us the authority that produces eternal results.

There are many people who, for one reason or another, try to do the work of God by their own initiation. Jesus addresses this in Matthew 7:22-23 when he speaks of those who went in His name but were not sent by Him. He calls them *lawless* because they went without His authority. When the Lord calls a person, it can be years before that person is ready to fulfill the call placed upon their life. The Holy Spirit spends the majority of the time preparing the one He has called through many trials and tribulations. He has to put to death the natural ambition that we all possess. The call of God emerges through much pain and disappointment. This can include rejection from family and close friends.

When Jesus was anointed of the Holy Spirit, He had already experienced the rejection of family and friends. His brothers thought He had a demon. He was known as *Mary's boy*, in other words *illegitimate*. This carried into His ministry life. Isaiah declares, "He was despised and forsaken of men, a man of sorrows and acquainted with grief" (Isaiah 53:3).

The Holy Spirit is calling many today. He has come to rest upon believers and anoint them as He did with God's only begotten Son. Jesus could stand and declare, "The Spirit of the Lord is upon Me" (Luke 18:4) because He had chosen to submit to His Father's desires as He lived a human life. Only a few are willing to go through the disciplines it will require. God is looking for willing sons and daughters who will say, "Here I am, send me."

Inquire of the Lord what He might say to you regarding His call and anointing in your life. Will you be part of that few?

Pray, asking the Father to anoint you for the call He has in your life. Father, I choose to do Your will in all that I do for the rest of my life, regardless of the cost, as You supply me with grace.

## January 14 – HANGING WITH THE PROPHETS

1 Samuel 10:10 – The Spirit of God came upon him mightily, so that he prophesied among them.

Saul was sent by his father to find some lost donkeys. Saul sought to find the Prophet Samuel to see if he could help in finding the donkeys. Instead Saul encountered the Word of the Lord spoken through Samuel. Samuel told Saul that "he had been chosen to rule over God's people." As Saul left Samuel, he met a group of prophets who were prophesying. Then the Spirit of the Lord came upon Saul mightily and he prophesied with them. Saul was changed into another man.

Revelation 19:10 states "the testimony of Jesus is the spirit of prophecy." Prophecy is directly related to testifying of God's will and purposes. Samuel prophesied God's will regarding Saul. When Saul got close to the prophets, he too prophesied and was counted among the prophets. All the Scriptures point to Jesus as God's one and only King. When we declare the Lordship of Christ, we are prophesying. God wants all His people to have the spirit of prophecy. Moses declared, "Would that all the Lord's people were prophets, that the Lord would put His Spirit upon them" (Numbers 11:29)! Paul taught that we can all prophesy in 1 Corinthians 14:31.

A prophet is a spokesperson for God. We are all called to be led by the Spirit to speak for God. The Scriptures are abundantly clear of how God has willed for His sons and daughters to be filled with His Holy Spirit and be His voice to a lost and dying world. In summary, Jesus is the Prophet Moses spoke of in Deuteronomy 18:15-18. Prophecy is the "testimony of Jesus" (Revelation 19:10). "You can all prophesy one by one" (1 Corinthians 14:31).

Let me encourage you to spend time in the presence of God asking Him for the spirit of prophecy. It is one of the gifts of the Spirit God desires for all His people to embrace and use to testify of Jesus and His will. The gift is not motivated by emotions or individual opinions. The Father desires for His people to be able to hear His voice and testify of all He has given through His Son.

Father, fill me with the Holy Spirit and cause me to speak with a prophetic voice of the Lordship of Jesus Christ for Your glory.

## January 15 – LIFTED UP BY THE SPIRIT OF GOD

Ezekiel 11:24 – The Spirit lifted me up.

Ezekiel was a prophet of the Lord with many experiences in the Spirit of God. The Spirit of the Lord led him to act out much of what he saw and heard. The Holy Spirit is still lifting up men and women dedicated to doing God's bidding. Testimonies are received from around the world of visions and dreams God's people are having. Testimonies of healings and miracles are becoming common place throughout the body of Christ. The Lord is speaking to His people through unusual events and experiences. As in Ezekiel's time, the Lord wants to draw near to His people.  He wants to lift His people into realms of the Spirit and show them how to accomplish His work.

The Spirit of the Lord does not bring revelation that is contrary to God's Written Word, but confirms the Word of God by supernatural means. The writer of Hebrews addresses this issue when he asks the question, "How will we escape if we neglect so great a salvation? After it was at first spoken through the Lord, it was confirmed to us by those who heard, God also testifying with them, both by signs and wonders and by various miracles and by gifts of the Holy Spirit according to His own will" (Hebrews 2:3). The Holy Spirit breathes life on the Word of God. Many try to use the Word without the life-giving power of the Spirit and are left with legalism and death. Paul said in 2 Corinthians 3:6, "who also made us adequate as servants of a new covenant, not of the letter, but of the Spirit; for the letter kills, but the Spirit gives life."

Some important questions to consider are: Is there life in the word you carry for God? Has the Spirit of God lifted you into places of fellowship and revelation to hear what the Spirit would say to you? Do you minister out of your head knowledge or by the Spirit of God quickening you with a message and deeds that produce life in the ones to whom you are ministering?

Take time to seek the Holy Spirit and ask Him to release His life in and through you. Prepare to allow the Holy Spirit to do unusual things through you. Expect Him to confirm the Word of God that you speak to others with His signs and wonders according to His will.

Father, I pray that your Holy Spirit would be free to speak words to me that are filled with Your life. I pray that I may hear your voice guiding me and that You would confirm your Word through me with Your life-giving power. Protect me and others from the "letter of the law which kills" and fill me with the knowledge of Your Holy Spirit.

## January 16 – LETTING THE SPIRIT REIGN IN YOUR HEART

1 Samuel 16:14 – Now the Spirit of the Lord departed from Saul, and an evil spirit from the Lord terrorized him.

This is a difficult passage in that it conveys the thought that both the Spirit of God and an evil spirit were sent from the Lord to Saul. God put His Spirit on Saul when he was anointed as King of Israel. Saul even prophesied when he was among the prophets. Saul turned from the Lord's commands to his own plans during his reign. His heart became cold and selfish. The Lord withdrew His Spirit because Saul chose to do evil before the Lord. Afterwards, the Lord sent an evil spirit to terrorize Saul.

The God of Heaven is in control of both the good and the evil. Satan and his kingdom of darkness have restrictions placed on them by the Lord. They are confined to the earth in their ability to have influence. As believers, we wrestle against these powers (Ephesians 6:12). Satan and the kingdom of darkness have already been judged by Jesus according to John 16:11

declaring that "the ruler of this world has been judged." Many Christians are still in bondage to the kingdom of darkness because their hearts have not been fully cleansed and released (1 John 1:5-10). The Spirit of God comes to convince of sin (John 16:8). He also comes to produce righteousness (John 16:10).

Many of God's people battle continually with evil spirits because they refuse to allow the Holy Spirit complete control in their lives. They remain king of their own circumstances, rather than allowing the Holy Spirit His rightful place of rule in their hearts. Unforgiveness is one of the main bondages giving the enemy a right to control, confuse, and bind up our walk with Christ and our relationship with others. Jesus addresses this in the parable of the unforgiving servant in Matthew 18:21-3). The King was angry that the servant He had forgiven failed to forgive a fellow servant a much smaller debt. The King turned over the unforgiving servant to the tormentors in jail until the debt was fully paid. Jesus stated in Matthew 18:35, "My heavenly Father will also do the same to you, if each of you does not forgive his brother from the heart." The tormentors are evil spirits. The debt can only be paid through *forgiveness* from the heart.

Today, ask the Holy Spirit to search your heart and reveal to you any unforgiveness that would give Satan's demonic tormentors rights in your life. Ask the Holy Spirit to give you a heart of forgiveness for anyone who has hurt you. Ask God for grace to forgive anyone He shows you. Then bind the evil one and be filled with the Holy Spirit. The Spirit of God has come to fully establish God's kingdom reign through the Lord Jesus Christ in each of our hearts today and every day.

## January 17 – SPIRIT LED SONS OF GOD

Romans 8:14 – All who are being led by the Spirit of God, these are the sons of God.

Sonship with God is only possible through the Holy Spirit. Children are born to their parents, but a true son is one that obeys his father by following his instructions. The same is true in the kingdom of God. Many have been given power to become children of God (John 1:12), but sonship is a matter of maturity. A father trains his child with the hope and desire for that child to grow up and become a responsible individual. As a father of six boys and one daughter, my great joy was to watch them grow and become mature, able to handle the affairs of life with the values instilled by their mother and me.

Our Heavenly Father is bringing forth sons and daughters with the character of His only begotten Son. The work of the Holy Spirit in the earth is to create a new creation out of the old. He is producing a spiritual race that has the *spiritual* DNA of God's only begotten Son. The Holy Spirit is ready to help you as Paul states, "know the love of Christ which surpasses knowledge, that you may be filled up to all the fullness of God" (Ephesians 3:19). You cannot gain this understanding through human reasoning. Only the Holy Spirit can reveal *the love of Christ* and only the Holy Spirit can fill us with the fullness of God.

Only in the love of Christ and the fullness of God can we become mature sons and daughters of God. As sons and daughters, we are to carry out the Father's will and not our own will. There is no male or female in the matter of sonship. Every person who has surrendered their life to Christ has been called to reflect Christ in and through their life. It is in men and women throughout the nations that God is revealing His kingdom purpose in the earth. The Written Word is being lived out in their lives. These are lives which have been recreated in Christ by the power of the Holy Spirit. God's purpose is for the nations to come to know Him and do His will. This can only happen through sons and daughters of God that are led by the Holy Spirit.

Today, ask the Holy Spirit to help you know the love of Christ in an ever-deepening way. Ask Him to fill you with the fullness of God so that Christ may be revealed in every facet of your life. Ask that you might have a part in helping others come to know God and to do His will.

## January 18 – WALK BY THE SPIRIT

Galatians 5:16 – I say, walk by the Spirit, and you will not carry out the desire of the flesh.

Walking by the Spirit is our great challenge! Our human tendency is to trust in our humanness. Our human nature is made up of our natural senses and our human reasoning, which some call common sense. Paul teaches us that "a natural man does not accept the things of the Spirit of God, for they are foolishness to him" (1 Corinthians 2:14). The natural creation is always battling with the spiritual creation. Daily, we must ask the Holy Spirit for His help. The Lord Jesus called the Holy Spirit "the Helper." Jesus said, "I will ask the Father, and He will give you another Helper, that He may be with you forever" (John 14:16). God answered His Son's request when the Holy Spirit was given on the day of Pentecost.

A mistake that many believers make is to assume that all the promises of God are *automatic*. They are not! He has given us His promises, but He wants us to seek Him for their manifestation in our lives. This truth is no different concerning the Helper. We must ask for His help. Do not assume that the Holy Spirit's help will automatically be there. He desires us to develop a relationship with Him.

Daily, and many times throughout the day, ask the Holy Spirit for His help. We do not have to be limited to our natural senses, but can receive *supernatural* help by simply learning to ask the Helper. He has helped me many times by solving problems that were beyond my scope of understanding. Nurture a consistent discipline of asking for the Spirit's help day or night. Do not leave Him behind in your devotions, but make Him first place in all of your life's activities (Matthew 6:33).

Father, I thank You for sending the Helper. I ask forgiveness for how often I have trusted in my own reasoning and for how I have failed to invite the Holy Spirit' help in my life. I commit myself to depend more and more on Your-ever present help in my times of need.

## January 19 – THE FRUIT OF THE SPIRIT IS LOVE

Galatians 5:22 – The fruit of the Spirit is love, joy, peace, patience, kindness, goodness, faithfulness, gentleness, self-control; against such things there is no law.

This is a mouthful to chew all at once. As we devote ourselves to this meditation, we want to consider each aspect of the fruit of the Spirit, one at a time. It should be understood that these are not nine individual fruits. Notice that Paul says, "The fruit" singular, not plural. The Holy Spirit does not distribute only one of these qualities, but these attributes are the very character of the Spirit of God in us. All should be the character of God's children when they allow the Holy Spirit to control their lives. Each attribute needs to be considered on its own merit, but at the same time, they are interdependent.

We begin with love. God is love! The entire verse states, "We have come to know and have believed the love which God has for us. God is love, and the one who abides in love abides in God, and God abides in him" (1 John 4:16). To know does not mean simply knowledge, but experience. The love of God through the Holy Spirit is revealed to us as we experience His forgiveness and acceptance.

We begin to grow into belief by accepting God's offer of salvation through forgiveness. As we receive His promises, beginning with the reception of the Holy Spirit, we come to have many experiences of His love for us. Some have only known salvation, but have not pressed on into the love of the Father because of hurts and unforgiveness that yet controls their heart toward others. Not only do we receive God's love of forgiveness, we must forgive others. The key to abiding in God is abiding in His love. Forgiveness is the first step toward that abiding life.

Today, if you cannot testify of the abiding love of God in your life, ask the Holy Spirit to examine your heart and see if there is any unforgiveness which you are holding. Allow the Holy Spirit to reveal hurts that have been covered up over time. Let Him bring those hurts to the surface. Although it might be painful for the moment, He will give you the power of the love of God to forgive and to let go so you can experience the fullness of God's love in your life.

Father, I pray that You would reveal any unforgiveness I might have. Give me grace to forgive anyone against whom I have been holding a grudge. I ask for the Holy Spirit to fill me afresh to overflowing with the love of God for that individual. This is a great time to ask the Lord if there are any others you need to forgive.

## January 20 – THE FRUIT OF THE SPIRIT IS JOY

Galatians 5:22 – The fruit of the Spirit is joy.

Joy follows love. When we have experienced the love of God and His love begins to take root in our inner man, the natural outflow is joy. "The joy of the Lord is your strength" (Nehemiah 8:10). His joy is promised to all those who serve Him as Lord. "Enter into the joy of your Master" (Matthew 25:23). Paul wrote to the church at Thessalonica, reminding them, "You also became imitators of us and of the Lord, having received the word in much tribulation with the joy of the Holy Spirit" (1 Thessalonians 1:6). After David had sinned greatly and sought the Lord with a heart of repentance, his one request was "Restore to me the joy of Thy salvation, and sustain me with a willing spirit" (Psalm 51:12). When God's salvation and rule over the whole earth is finally established, His rule becomes the "joy of the whole earth" (Psalm 48:2). The Psalmist is exalting the Lord and declaring His ultimate purpose.

It is joy that attracts others to the believer who has truly embraced God's love. The work of the Holy Spirit becomes manifest in a believer's life when righteousness and peace are established. Joy comes from these two works of the Spirit (Romans 14:17). Joy is not external, but flows from the innermost being of a person. It is part of what Jesus is saying when He declared, "If any man is thirsty, let him come to Me and drink. He who believes in Me, as the Scripture said, 'From his innermost being shall flow rivers of living water'" (John 7:37-38). Although the word joy is not used here, it is there by implication as one reads the references from which Jesus drew His teaching. The literal translation reads "let him keep coming to Me, and let him keep drinking." It does not take much to lose one's joy, so we must keep coming to Jesus through the Holy Spirit and keep drinking of this spiritual water that only He can supply.

The joy of the Lord is a supernatural joy and not the happiness that the world promises. Earthly happiness fades ever so easily, but the Lord supplies a continual reservoir of His joy. If you need to repent for anything, do it now. Ask for the righteousness of Christ to rule in you, receive His peace and let the joy that is in the Holy Spirit flow from your life.

Today, why not take a deep drink of the Holy Spirit? Allow Him to establish you in His righteousness and then let the peace of Christ rule in your heart. The result will be to be strengthened in the joy of the Lord! Ask the Holy Spirit for His joy.

## January 21 – THE FRUIT OF THE SPIRIT IS PEACE

Galatians 5:22 – The fruit of the Spirit is peace.

In Romans 14:17, Paul puts peace before joy, but here in Galatians he lists joy before peace. In Romans14:17, righteousness is mentioned preceding peace. Peace comes as a result of becoming righteous in Christ Jesus. Joy flows from that peace. In Paul's letter to the Galatians, he is speaking of the attributes of the Holy Spirit. The Spirit brings His joy out of His love. When that joy is experienced, supernatural peace becomes the result.

The world is constantly trying to find peace, whether individually or among the nations. The efforts are futile, if they are not predicated upon God's righteousness. Only God's righteousness can produce lasting peace. The Scriptures declare that "the peace of God that surpasses all comprehension shall guard your hearts and your minds in Christ Jesus" (Philippians 4:7). Peace is not static but dynamic in nature. The peace of God guards our hearts from the intrusion of the subtle deceptions of the enemy and allows us freedom to live freely in Christ.

A number of questions are worth considering: Do you enjoy the peace of your salvation? Do you have peace in your life that the righteousness of Christ is sufficient to cause you to be accepted in the beloved? Do you experience the peace of God guarding your heart? If you have that supernatural peace, rejoice in the Lord and give Him thanks because many people do not have what you have. Make sure you share God's love with those you meet who do not enjoy the peace you enjoy.

Give them opportunity to receive and experience the peace you have received.

If you do not have the peace of which the Scriptures speak, that can change today. Invite the Holy Spirit to show you what you must do to receive the peace of God's kingdom. Wait upon Him for His counsel. Give up whatever He shows you and receive what He desires to give you.

My confession is that, though I walk through the valley of the shadow of death, I will not fear any evil; for the Lord is with me, His rod and His staff they comfort me (Psalm 23). Father, I thank You for Your peace that is available to me in the Holy Spirit. Teach me how to daily enter into Your peace that surpasses all comprehension and guards my heart and mind through Christ Jesus. Help me to be able to lead others to that peace.

## January 22 – LET THE SPIRIT OF THE LORD PRODUCE PATIENCE

Galatians 5:22 – The fruit of the Spirit is patience.

Patience is a direct result of peace. In fact, you really cannot have patience unless you're walking in peace. We begin to see how the fruit of the Spirit is singular and cumulative. In other words, one part of the fruit leads to another.

James said, "Count it all joy when you encounter various trials" (James 1:2). True character is formed in the trenches. An older friend who is a minister was listening to a younger man talk about his own ministry experiences. The older minister was intently looking at the younger man. The young minister asked, "What are you looking at?" My friend answered, "I am looking for the scars."

The Scriptures teach, "The testing of your faith produces endurance" (James 1:3). In the King James Version, endurance is translated patience. I am grateful for all the difficult times I have known in my life although, at the time, I did not like it one bit. Today, I can see how the Lord used tests beyond my strength, and wounds too deep to heal without His grace.  Each trial became a new challenge to overcome, an instrument of the discipline of God's great love.  I now know each trial and wound helped to form Christ in me.  I like what Paul said, "Brethren, I do not regard myself as having laid hold of it yet; but one thing I do: forgetting what lies behind and reaching forward to what lies ahead, I press on toward the goal for the prize of the upward call of God in Christ Jesus" (Philippians 3:13-15).  In this verse, Paul captures the essence of what patience is about.

Paul was a man who knew rejection, prison, and beatings.  He was misunderstood and was even left for dead.  Yet, he never lost sight of the goal; he never turned back and gave up.  He cried out to the Lord three times for help.  After the third time, Jesus spoke to Paul and assured him that His grace was sufficient.  The Lord told Paul that "His power is perfected in weakness" (2 Corinthians 12:8-9).  Today, those words are for us as well.  Determine to be a man or woman of patience.  Ask the Holy Spirit to strengthen you as you walk through the various trials of your faith. Ask the Holy Spirit to give you grace sufficient for each situation that comes your way.

Pray, thanking the Holy Spirit for being your helper in all things.  Verbalize that you submit your weaknesses to Him.  Ask Him to help you receive patience out of every trial so that His character would be manifested in your life.


## January 23 – REMEMBER THE KINDNESS OF OUR GOD

Galatians 5:22 – The fruit of the Spirit is kindness.

Out of patience flows kindness.  Impatience always produces unkindness, whether it would be in in words or in attitude.  The Lord has shown great kindness in Christ to all humanity.  Throughout the Scriptures, we are reminded of God's kindness toward His people.  I love what the Psalmist wrote:  "He is gracious and compassionate and righteous.  It is well with the man who is gracious and lends" (Psalm 112:4-5).  Kindness speaks of graciousness and compassion.  It is so easy to forget the needs of others and get caught up with our own situation and circumstances.  The kind person not only has a pleasant attitude, but is aware of other people's needs, always ready to help when possible.

The Spirit of God is never harsh.  At times, He may be stern in His correction, but it is always in the spirit of kindness.  The Holy Spirit desires to help us control our words.  Have you noticed how easy an unkind word can slip from your mouth? This is especially true with family members or people with whom we have a close relationship.  Familiarity causes one to speak before we think.  The apostle James provided a good understanding concerning the use of words. "Everyone must be quick to hear, slow to speak, and slow to anger" (James 1:19). Again in James 1:26 we are warned that we are "deceived" if we think ourselves to be religious and do not bridle our tongues.  This type of deception is a deception of the heart.

The Psalmist David experienced the kindness of God.  David declared that God's kindness is better than life itself.  "Because Your loving kindness is better than life, my lips shall praise You. So I will bless You as long as I live; I will lift up my hands in Your name" (Psalm 63:3-4).

Celebrate the kindness of God as David did.  Meditate on His kindness.  How many ways has He been gracious and compassionate toward you?  How often have you not responded with kindness toward others?  Will you let your lips praise Him and will you bless the God of your salvation? Will you allow Him to release His kindness through you to others as you encounter people in your daily walk?  Many experience unkindness on a daily basis.  Let kindness rise up in you and give another this part of God's character through the power of the Holy Spirit.

Pray and ask the Holy Spirit for kindness to be developed in you all the days of your life.  Share the kindness which your Heavenly Father has extended to you.  Ask for His help to express kindness to others.  Set a watch, O Lord, before my mouth and keep the door of my lips!

## January 24 – GOODNESS AND MERCY SHALL FOLLOW ME

Galatians 5:22 – The fruit of the Spirit is goodness.

Goodness is the result of the righteousness of Christ established in one's life through the goodness of God. "It is the goodness of God that leads us to repentance" (Romans 2:4) KJV. The NASB says "It is the kindness of God." Goodness and kindness are very closely related. Paul told the Church at Rome that he was convinced they were full of goodness. He related goodness to what they knew in Christ for the purpose of admonishing one another (Romans 15:14).

Taking the time to encourage others comes from "goodness." Paul says that "the fruit of light is rooted in goodness" (Ephesians 5:9). Paul links goodness to a desire God has for the life of a believer. "To this end, we pray for you always, that our God will count you worthy of your calling, and fulfill every desire for goodness and the work of faith with power" (2 Thessalonians 1:11). Paul links goodness with free will: "Without your consent I did not want to do anything, so that your goodness would not be, in effect, by compulsion, but of your own free will" (Philemon 1:14).

Goodness begins with God's love toward us. Goodness continues as it becomes part of our nature through the work of the Holy Spirit. The Spirit of God is always at work to manifest the nature of Christ in every believer. He desires to see us filled and full of the goodness of God. This can only happen as we grow in our knowledge of Christ. This knowledge is not only about Him, but what He desires for us to impart to others. He has called each of us to admonish and encourage one another in our walk as believers in the Lord Jesus Christ.

The manifestation of goodness in our daily walk is evidence that we have embraced God's light. Two areas that reveal God's goodness are our strong desire for goodness and how goodness flows out of our free will without any compulsion on the part of others.

Father, I thank You for Your goodness in leading me to repentance. Thank You for helping me turn from my old ways of thinking. Thank You for giving me Your supernatural way of thinking which comes from Your Holy Word. Father, help me be aware of any darkness which may still be in my life. I desire to be full of goodness and to freely encourage others to receive the goodness of God.

# January 25 – UNBELIEF DOES NOT NULLIFY GOD'S FAITHFULNESS

Galatians 5:22 – The fruit of the Spirit is faithfulness.

The fruit of the Spirit flows out of God Himself. Faithfulness originates with our Heavenly Father, as do all of these attributes. When Jesus judged the religious leaders of His day, as recorded in Matthew 23, He pointed out their neglect of the weightier matters of the law recorded in Micah 6:8. He accused them of neglecting justice, mercy, and faithfulness. Faithfulness is associated with humility. Faithfulness relates to another person's interest. It takes humility in order to be faithful. Our first priority in faithfulness is toward God. We need to be faithful in His interests, faithful to His will, faithful to other believers, and faithful to share with those still separated from God's love revealed in Christ, the Lord.

We begin to learn about faithfulness as we make reading God's Word a priority. Through the Word of God, we learn of His desire to reveal Christ in us. The Word of God is the primary way the Spirit of God instructs each of us. He will give us power to be faithful to His instructions as we allow Him to control our thinking and actions. At times, He will reprove us in order to bring our thoughts into alignment with His own. He brings correction as needed, to establish our life in Christ's righteousness.

Our life of prayer is as important to our relationship with our Father as His Holy Word. We need to hear God's still, small voice. Every believer is called to be faithful in praying for others. Jesus has invited us to participate with Him in His ministry of intercession. The Scriptures declare, "He ever lives to make intercession for us" (Hebrews 2:17; 7:25). It is our responsibility to pray faithfully as well. There are two specific areas the Lord Jesus commanded us to ask the Father. First, we pray for His kingdom to come and His will to be done on earth as in heaven. Second, we must pray faithfully for God to send laborers into the Harvest.

Father, I ask for the Holy Spirit to strengthen me in faithfulness. I ask for a greater commitment to Your interests. I ask for faithfulness toward my brothers and sisters in Christ

Jesus. I ask for faithfulness to bear witness of Your kingdom to those around me.

## January 26 – YOUR GENTLENESS HAS MADE ME GREAT

Galatians 5:22-23 – The fruit of the Spirit is gentleness.

King David gave this testimony of the Lord in 2 Samuel 22:36, "Your gentleness has made me great" (NKJV). In 2 Samuel 22, David wrote a song to the Lord in gratitude for God's deliverance from the hands of his enemies, including King Saul. David began by declaring that the Lord is his rock, his fortress, and his deliverer. In verse 36 (KJV), David spoke of God's "gentleness." In the NASB, the word gentleness is translated "help." Gentleness speaks of the Lord's help. Our God is an ever-present help in the time of need for He said, "I will never desert you, nor will I ever forsake you, so that we confidently say, 'The Lord is my helper, I will not be afraid. What shall man do to me?'" (Hebrews 13:5-6). The writer of Hebrews also exhorted us by saying, "Let us therefore draw near with confidence to the throne of grace, that we may receive mercy and may find grace to help in time of need" (Hebrews 4:16). In all these exhortations, we find the gentleness of the Lord revealed.

The Scriptures repeat David's conviction of God's help in Psalm 18:35. "You have also given me the shield of Your salvation and Your right hand upholds me; and Your gentleness makes me great." In this verse, the translators use the word gentleness. Paul, as he instructed the church at Corinth, spoke about the attitude in which he handled them. "Now I, Paul, myself urge you by the meekness and gentleness of Christ, I who am meek when face to face with you, but bold toward you when absent!" (2 Corinthians 10:1). Paul strongly depended upon Christ and His meek and gentle spirit to be manifested in and through him as he ministered to God's people. Before Paul's encounter with Jesus, he was hard and legalistic in his dealings with God's people. Later, as Christ's apostle to the Gentiles, he was the representative of Christ. He understood that it was Christ's Spirit in him ministering to the Lord's people.

The fruit of the Spirit in the believer is gentle. He administers the salvation of God with gentleness and meekness. God does not come with the attitude, "I am the Lord, and you had better obey me"! Rather, He draws us to Himself through His mercy and grace. He takes His time ministering His salvation to each of us. At times, He cries for the lost through an intercessor. Other times, He lays His burden for the salvation of a person on the heart of a believer. The Spirit of God is gentle in His dealings. The testimony of David should be ours as well.

Father, I pray for the Holy Spirit to give me the shield of salvation for every problem I face. I ask You to uphold me with the nature of Jesus and then to strengthen me with Your gentleness. Make me great for Your Glory. Your right hand upholds me, and Your gentleness makes me great.

## January 27 – MANIFEST YOUR SALVATION BY GIVING ME SELF-CONTROL

Galatians 5:22-23 – The fruit of the Spirit is self-control; against such things there is no law.

The last attribute Paul mentions to the Galatians is self-control. The word temperance used in KJV is translated self-control in the NASB. Paul shared Christ with Felix in Acts 24:25. He discussed righteousness, self-control, and judgment. God's desire for every believer is self-government. That was God's plan in the beginning for Adam and Eve. Out of a relationship with God, Adam was expected to govern his own life within the surroundings where the Lord had placed him. Jesus, whom Paul calls "the last Adam, who is a life giving spirit" (1 Corinthians 15:45), governed Himself out of His relationship with the Father through the Holy Spirit. It is possible for each believer to be self-governing if one is fully surrendered to the Spirit of God.

Self-control is very important in the marriage bond. Consider Paul's instruction to "Stop depriving one another, except by agreement for a time, that you may devote yourselves to prayer, and come together again lest Satan tempt you because of your lack of self-control" (1 Corinthians 7:5-6). Paul also gave instructions concerning the unmarried. "If they do not have self-control, let them marry; for it is better to marry than to burn" (1 Corinthians 7:9-10). Peter also dealt with the subject of self-control by writing, "in your knowledge, self-control, and in your self-control, perseverance" (2 Peter 1:6). Peter gave his own list of disciplines for the Christian life, and self-control is right in the center. Are there areas in your life that are out of control and need the power of this attribute? Can you list areas in your life in which self-control operates freely?

I want to be clear that I am not speaking about a person by their own strength or effort living a life of self-control. I am addressing an attribute of the Holy Spirit. We can live a life of self-control by surrendering our lives to the Lord Jesus Christ, through the power of His Spirit.

Father, I ask for the Holy Spirit to show me areas of my life needing Your power for self-control. I ask for the Spirit to strengthen me with this attribute in specific areas in which You make me aware. Lord, I want to live under Your governmental rule and demonstrate a lifestyle of self-control in all I do. Thank you, Holy Spirit, for this part of Your nature in me!

## January 28 – THEN THE SPIRIT LIFTED ME UP

Ezekiel 3:12 – Then the Spirit lifted me up, and I heard a great rumbling sound behind me, "Blessed be the glory of the Lord in His place."

The Spirit of God comes with a single purpose, to declare the glory of the Lord. Ezekiel's commission is described in Ezekiel chapter 3. The Lord commanded him to go to his people which are in exile and speak to them whether they listen or not (Ezekiel 3:11). The Spirit of God is not dissuaded by those who do not listen. He still proclaims God's will and purpose. The Spirit speaks through any individual willing to be a servant. Once, when I was overseas, I was a speaker for a large evangelistic meeting. The minister that had invited me, in my view, was not handling the meeting properly on the first night. He was elevating himself and not listening to the Spirit's desire. That evening as I laid in bed, the Holy Spirit spoke to me. "Tell the brother he is not handling the meeting properly, that he is making it about himself and the promotion of his ministry." I told the Lord that I did not want to confront the man.  The Lord spoke to me in no uncertain terms that I was of no use to Him unless I obeyed and did what He was instructing me to do. Well, I repented and obeyed the Spirit.

What the Spirit of God was commanding Ezekiel to do was not easy.  The Spirit of God lifted Ezekiel up so He could hear what the Lord wanted done.  He then gave Ezekiel the ability to declare the Word of the Lord and perform all that God instructed.  The same Spirit that lifted up the prophet lifted up the Lord Jesus. Jesus said, "And I, if I be lifted up from the earth, will draw all men to Myself" (John 12:32).  God lifted up His Son to draw men into a relationship with Himself. The Spirit of God has come to lift us up too.  The Holy Spirit lifts us up before the Father and presents us as righteous and holy through the blood of Jesus.  He also wants to lift us up before men, that they might see what God has done in our lives and magnify the Lord.  "Humble yourselves therefore, under the mighty hand of God, that He may exalt you at the proper time" (1 Peter 5:6-7).

Father, I ask for the Holy Spirit to create in me a great desire to obey all You have commanded.
I ask for grace to walk in humility so You can lift me up at Your choosing.  I want to make myself available to the Holy Spirit. Father, I am Your servant and You have the right to command me.  Give me grace to obey whatever You command.


## January 29 – I WILL PUT MY SPIRIT UPON HIM

Matthew 12:18 – Behold My Servant whom I have chosen, My beloved in whom My soul is well pleased; I will put My Spirit upon Him.

The Spirit of God does not come upon us out of our choosing, but rather God Himself has chosen us.  God chose to send His only begotten Son and redeem us from all unrighteousness. The Spirit of the Lord is the one who draws us to the Father through Christ. Jesus said that "No one can come to Me, unless the Father who sent Me draws him" (John 6:44). It is the Father, who works by His Spirit to draw an individual to Christ. The Father initiates and the Spirit responds. It is the Holy Spirit, who convicts of sin, righteousness and judgment (John

16:8). God's great joy is to put His Spirit upon all those who will embrace His Son, embracing Him as God's Anointed One, and accepting all Jesus did through His earthly ministry.

Matthew 12:18-21 fulfills what the prophet Isaiah spoke (hundreds of years before Christ) when the Father promised "His Spirit would be upon His Servant." The Father promised the Son that He would give the Holy Spirit to all those who believed on the Son. Jesus' instruction to His disciples was, "I am sending forth the promise of My Father upon you; but you are to stay in the city until you are clothed with power from on high" (Luke 24:49).

Many are still following Jesus' instructions to wait for the promise of His Father. Multitudes today have received the Lord's salvation and this promise of the Holy Spirit. The Holy Spirit is still being poured out today in general church gatherings, in house meetings, and even in the privacy of one's own home. Unfortunately for some, it has only been an experience. Many of the Lord's precious people have not waited on the Lord for the empowerment of His Holy Spirit. Please don't only seek an experience, but rather seek the person of the Holy Spirit that you might be filled and empowered to do the Father's will.

Ask the Holy Spirit to create in you a desire to wait for His empowerment to do God's will. Waiting on the Lord is not a natural response, but a desire which comes from God Himself. As you wait upon Him, the Spirit of God will manifest His transforming presence. His power will reveal God's will in your life. His power will release the fruit of the Spirit. His power will be the key to His gifts operating through you.

## January 30 – IMMEDIATELY, HE SAW THE HEAVENS OPEN

Mark 1:10 – Immediately coming up out of the water, He saw the heavens opening, and the Spirit like a dove descending upon Him.

As Jesus stood in the waters of baptism, He saw the heavens open. Jesus was standing in the very center of God's will. The water spoke of His coming death, burial, and resurrection. By His action, publically and before heaven, He was declaring, "I am committed to do the Father's will! I am dead to Myself and alive to the Father's purpose." He stood as a man, in the weakness of His flesh, in the same way we are weak. He could only accomplish what He had been sent to do with the Father's help. Seeing His only begotten Son's surrender, the Father immediately responded by opening the heavens and sending the Holy Spirit. The Spirit of God descended in the form of a dove, his wings spread, and ready to land. The Holy Spirit came to fully cover the Lord Jesus during His earthly ministry. Jesus was totally under the wings of His Heavenly Father's love and grace. The Spirit of God knew that earth would be His home until the full purpose of the Father was completed. Jesus was the first man whom the Spirit came to rest and remain, but many more would follow.

In like manner, the disciples obeyed their Lord when He instructed them to "wait in Jerusalem for the promise of the Father" (Luke 24:49). They truly did not know what to expect, but they obeyed. Ten days later, the Holy Spirit came "like a violent rushing wind" (Acts 2:2). He came upon them just as Jesus had promised. One hundred and twenty were waiting in that upper room. This was the same room where the disciples, fifty days earlier, had shared their last meal with Jesus before His crucifixion. Now, God was about to anoint with His Spirit all those who obeyed Jesus' instructions to wait. The disciples waited to be empowered to do all that Jesus had commanded. We must surrender, as Jesus did, with determination to do the will of the Father. We too, must do what the disciples did, and wait for the promise of the Father. It is one thing to experience the Holy Spirit in a meeting, and quite another to be anointed in order to fulfill the call of God in one's life.

Ask the Holy Spirit to reveal if you have only known an experience of His presence or if you have truly been anointed to fulfill God's will. An experience is made up of feelings, whereas an anointing comes with power and authority to carry out a command. Heavenly Father, I ask You for power to live fully in Your will and be Your witness in my sphere of influence.

# January 31 – IN YOU I AM WELL PLEASED

Mark 1:11 – A voice came out of the heavens: You are My beloved Son, in You I am well pleased.

The Father loves to confirm the faithfulness of His sons and daughters. Jesus is the One who made it possible for us to be reconciled to the Father. He is the One who gives us "the right to become the children of God" (John 1:12). Every believer stands accepted before God because Jesus was fully accepted by the Father. In Mark 1:11, the Father audibly declared His pleasure from the heavens over Jesus. Many believers have a hard time receiving the love of our Heavenly Father because of bad experiences with an earthly father. Many people have not heard their earthly father speak words of acceptance and affirmation, but rather judgments and condemnation. Jesus came for the specific purpose of revealing the Father. "He who has seen Me has seen the Father" (John 14:9). The disciples experienced how Jesus treated them and saw how He treated others. Through this, the Father's love was revealed. The disciples had known of God through the Law, but now they were learning of Him through God's love and grace.

The Scriptures make it clear how much the Father loves humanity. The three letters recorded in the Bible, written by John the Beloved, express the Father's focused love for every believer. The Gospel of John declares that "God so loved the world that He gave His only Begotten Son" (John 3:16). Paul wrote that "He hath made us accepted in the beloved" (Ephesians 1:6 KJV). The Holy Spirit has come to reveal the Father's love. He is grieved when we have barriers to receiving His love. Those barriers can be broken if you will allow the Spirit of Grace to open your heart to the Father's love. He will give you a spirit of forgiveness toward an earthly father who wounded you. He will give you courage to trust and believe your Heavenly Father's word of acceptance. He will help you not only to know His love, but to be empowered to share His love. Ask the Holy Spirit to search your heart and expose any area hindering you from hearing the Father say, "You are my beloved one, in whom I am well pleased through my Son, Jesus."

Father, today, I open my heart to the fullness of Your love. Please give me grace to forgive anyone I need to forgive. I realize that my unforgiveness stands in the way of receiving Your love. By faith, I receive Your love made possible through Your Son in the power of the Holy Spirit.

## February 1 – I AM FILLED WITH POWER

Micah 3:8 – I am filled with power—With the Spirit of the Lord—And with justice and courage to make known to Jacob his rebellious act, even to Israel his sin.

We know little about the prophet Micah. He shared two specific messages with God's people by the Spirit of the Lord. On one hand, he dealt with a word of judgment against Israel's rebellion. On the other hand, he promised God's help for restoration and blessing. Micah brought God's Word against the false seers and diviners. Many today represent themselves as God's messengers. Different messages are being declared to God's people. Many run after the hype and glitter of modern day prophets. Micah declared, "On the other hand, I am filled with power—with the Spirit of the Lord." Only the Power of the Lord can make the difference. The Power of the Lord brings judgment into the life of a believer. The Power of the Lord establishes peace and security.

The wise individual allows God's judgments to work a deepening sense of God's presence in them. They become increasingly aware of what God is after in their life. If someone refuses to submit to the correction of the Lord, increasingly severe results will follow. God loves His children and therefore disciplines them through His Holy Spirit in order to bring them to a place of sharing in His Holiness. Read Hebrews 12:4-11 for a clear perspective of this point.

God's dealings with His people always have a redemptive purpose. He does not discipline His children out of anger as an earthly father might, but out of love, looking toward their future and their success. Any individual that is charged with caring for the people of God must possess a strong sense of justice and courage. Making sin known is not a light matter. Skill is required to administer justice and mercy to the offender. It requires compassion with a view toward restoration. The Spirit of God has not only come to judge, but also to restore. The individual who claims to have the Word of the Lord, but does not have courage to deal with sin, is a false prophet. A prophet who deals with sin must do so with a view toward God's redemptive purpose. This is clearly seen throughout the Old Testament story and is established in the cross of Christ.

Ask the Holy Spirit to give to you a deepening sense of God's presence and what He wants to judge in your life. Ask Him to fill you with power, both to deal with sin and to encourage righteousness. Father, I thank You for Your judgments of my sin and for Your redemptive purpose in my life.

## February 2 – THE SPIRIT OF THE LORD GAVE THEM REST

Isaiah 63:14 – As the cattle which go down into the valley, the Spirit of the Lord gave them rest. So You led Your people, to make for Yourself a glorious name.

It is in the valley where the meadows are found that the cattle find rest. It is a place of grazing and the place of chewing their cud. The Spirit of the Lord desires to lead us *into green pastures* for His name's sake. For the child of God, it is the place of eating the Word of the Lord. The Word of God is not just meant to be read, but eaten and digested. Part of the digesting process is to ruminate on the Word. This means to meditate and think upon God's Word repeatedly. The Word of God is meant to go down and then come back up for more chewing. This process is similar to what a cow experiences in the chewing of its cud.

In this valley, during the times of eating, meditating, and memorizing God's Word we find our greatest rest. Isaiah 63:14 references the fulfillment of God's Word to Abraham, Isaac, and Jacob through the people of Israel, when He gave them the land He had promised. The Scripture says that "the Lord gave them rest on every side . . . the Lord gave all their enemies into their hand" (Joshua 21:43-44). God's purpose was to make a glorious name for Himself.

Through the Lord Jesus Christ, He is continuing that purpose. The Father is working by His Spirit through His *glorious body*, His church. "For as many are the promises of God, in Him they are yes; therefore also through Him is our Amen to the glory of God through us" (2 Corinthians 1:20). Our rest is truly found in receiving God's Word, speaking God's Word, and in finally doing the will of God, all of which brings glory to His name.

Ask the Holy Spirit each day to lead you to the place of His rest. Ask Him to give you grace to receive all His promises that are yes, and to help you decree the Amen, so that your life may bring glory to His Holy Name. Father, thank You for the place of rest You have provided for me in Christ Jesus.

## February 3 – ACCORDING TO THE SPIRIT OF HOLINESS

Romans 1:4 – Declared the Son of God with power by the resurrection from the dead, according to the Spirit of holiness, Jesus Christ our Lord.

Paul begins his letter to the Romans by establishing the purpose of his Apostleship. This purpose was to preach the gospel promised beforehand through God's prophets, as recorded in the Holy Scriptures. The promise was concerning God's Son, who was born as a descendant of David. This is what Paul meant by writing, "according to the flesh" (Romans 1:3). Jesus' birth line could be traced back to King David, 1000 years prior. Paul is declaring that Jesus is who He said He was, by the power of the resurrection. God's holiness was satisfied in the sacrifice of His Son's life. The Spirit of God raised Christ Jesus up and seated Him on the highest throne. Heavens throne!

At the end of verse 4, Paul includes the name of God's Son, "Jesus Christ." Jesus means Savior, and Christ means Messiah. Paul identifies Jesus Christ as *Our King* when he says "our Lord." What Paul is describing is the work of the Holy Spirit in raising Christ from the dead. Those who believe and have put their trust in the work of Christ will also be raised from the dead. "If the Spirit of Him who raised Jesus from the dead dwells in you, He who raised Christ Jesus from the dead will also give life to your mortal bodies through His Spirit who indwells you" (Romans 8:11). We presently walk by faith since the Father promised resurrection, "Even when we were dead in our transgressions, made us alive together with Christ (by grace you have been saved), and raised us up with Him, and seated us with Him in the heavenly *places*, in Christ Jesus" (Ephesians 2:5-6).

Everything God has done in the Lord Jesus Christ has been accomplished by the Spirit of holiness. The contrast is stark between God's holiness and His fallen creation man, between His Holiness, and our depravity. You cannot get farther apart than that. Our total hope in this present evil world and in the world to come is rooted in the *Holiness of God*.

The Holy Spirit is the Administrator of the kingdom of God, directing what the Father has commanded. The Father thought through His redemptive purposes before time began. The Son came as the Logos or the Living Word of God to give us redemption. The Holy Spirit is executing God's plans through the Work of the Son. The Spirit is working in the life of believers who have put their complete trust in God's redemptive plan.

Father, I thank You for Your King who died that we might live. I pray for the Spirit of holiness to lead and direct my life. I yield to your redemptive purpose through me.

## February 4 – WE HAVE THIS TREASURE IN EARTHEN VESSELS

2 Corinthians 4:7 – We have this treasure in earthen vessels, so that the surpassing greatness of the power will be of God and not from ourselves.

At the beginning of this chapter, Paul is defending his apostolic ministry. He declared the gospel, which the true apostles preach. In verse 7, he wrote that the treasure we have as believers is in earthen vessels, in other words, our human body. Although the Holy Spirit is not mentioned in this verse, it is clear Paul wrote concerning the treasure of the Spirit of God. The Holy Spirit is the power of God who gives us salvation. We can never claim the power originates with us. This surpassing greatness of the power originates in God.

An earthen vessel can easily be broken. The enemy tries to defeat us on many fronts. Our earthen vessels give Him great advantage. As humans, our fleshly appetites easily control our thinking. In the beginning, this is how the enemy of our souls got an upper hand. In the Garden, he attacked a weakness in Eve. Through Eve, he went after a weakness in Adam. In the wilderness, as recorded in Matthew 4 and Luke 4, the devil tried to use the same tactics when he tempted Jesus. Jesus did not cave in to the appetites of the flesh, but rather relied completely on the Holy Spirit by using the Word of God to overcome the tricks of the enemy.

In every area of His life, Jesus sought to glorify His Father. He chose the Father's desires over the appetites of His earthen vessel. Even on the cross, as He drew close to the final moments in His fully human body, He cried out to His father and said, "Into Your hands I commit My spirit." He then gave up His spirit which returned to the Father. Paul wrote, "To those who are the called, both Jews and Greeks, Christ the power of God and the wisdom of God" (1 Corinthians 1:24). It is clear that the apostle understood the truth regarding the power of God. Jesus became weak by taking on human form. He totally relied upon God to supply the power. There is nothing weaker than our flesh, but God has chosen to indwell these human vessels so that all the praise and all the glory might belong to Him.

Ask the Holy Spirit to be free in you to reveal His surpassing greatness so that the power might be of God and not of you. Relinquish control once again to Him in all things. Father, into Your hands I commit my life to be used as You see fit.

## February 5 – HAVING THE SAME SPIRIT OF FAITH

2 Corinthians 4:13 – But having the same spirit of faith, according to what is written, "I believed, therefore I spoke," we also believe, therefore we also speak.

Paul used the word "spirit" with a small "s" because it is referring to the "spirit of faith". One could say it is the spirit of "belief." True faith is given to an individual by the Spirit of God.

The same Holy Spirit that caused the prophet to believe and speak also caused the apostles to believe and speak. The same Holy Spirit is at work in believers today. It is the spirit of faith within me that produces a need to speak. My speaking stems from the faith that is within me given by the One behind my faith.

When a person is filled with the Spirit of God, they will be led to speak about the Lord. This should be the experience of every believer in Christ Jesus who is being led by the Spirit. The Spirit has come to speak of Christ. "When the Helper comes, whom I will send to you from the Father, that is the Spirit of truth, who proceeds from the Father, He will bear witness of Me" (John 15:26). The King James Version says, "He will speak of Me." Every believer is called to speak or testify of Christ. This is not simply the preacher's assignment, but of every child of God. Testifying to others of Christ is a vital part of our Christian development. Many of God's people are stunted in their growth because they keep their faith to themselves rather than sharing what Christ has done for them.

Paul stated in Romans 1:16, "I am not ashamed of the gospel of Christ." This was not limited to the apostles, but was meant to be a model for believers in Rome. It should be an example for every believer in the 21st century. Why? The Gospel remains *the power of God unto salvation*. The good news tells of Jesus the Christ, who was put to death for our sins, whom God raised up by the power of His Holy Spirit and seated at His own right hand in Heaven. The Gospel is the only answer to the human condition. The world is looking for salvation, most of the time in the wrong places. This is why we must declare by the Spirit of God "The faith which was once for all handed down to the saints" (Jude 3). As you trust the Spirit of God, you will be astonished at how the Lord will use you for His glory.

Father, help me to speak from the faith I have received of Jesus. Holy Spirit, fill me with boldness to speak to others about my faith in Christ Jesus, concerning what He has done for me.

# February 6 – THE SPIRIT SEARCHES ALL THINGS

1 Corinthians 2:9-10 – "Things which eye has not seen and ear has not heard, and which have not entered the heart of man, all that God has prepared for those who love Him." For to us God revealed them through the Spirit; for the Spirit searches all things, even the depths of God.

When 1 Corinthians 2:9 is quoted alone, the full thought that Paul is communicating does not come through. Paul is quoting from a passage in Isaiah 64:4. 1 Corinthians 2:10 is the key to understanding what the Spirit wants communicated. "For to us, God revealed *them* through the Spirit; for the Spirit searches all things, even the depths of God." The Isaiah passage finds its ultimate fulfillment in Christ, who gave us the Holy Spirit as promised by the Father (Luke 24:45-49). We can know the thoughts of God through our relationship with the Holy Spirit. He reveals God's intent through the Scriptures as well as God's will in our personal lives.

The Holy Spirit desires to bring each of us a personal great awakening. Paul expressed it this way, "All things become visible when they are exposed by the light, for everything that becomes visible is light. For this reason it says, Awake, sleeper, and arise from the dead, and Christ will shine on you" (Ephesians 5:13-14). The Holy Spirit always works to keep us awake and give us light. As God's light enters into our lives, we are able to discern what is transpiring around us. News reports are not sufficient to keep us informed; instead, our source is the Holy Spirit. He searches the depths of God and brings to the people of God revelation.

The Holy Spirit has raised the level of prayer in the Lord's church, which is a "clue" that God is getting ready to do some extraordinary things in our day. Many are sensing that God is currently preparing His church for *revival*. I prefer to call it a *Great Awakening*. As we hear reports of many challenges throughout the world, it would be easy to become discouraged and apathetic. For those that are seeking God, it is a time of great expectation. The Spirit of the Lord envisions numerous believers preparing for His presence to break in and give opportunity for multitudes to turn to Christ. "God acts in behalf of one who waits for Him" (Isaiah 64:5b).

Ask the Holy Spirit to awaken you to what He desires to share with you today. He loves for God's people to press into Him, to know God's will in their lives. Father, I pray for a great awakening to take place in me. I desire to know Your thoughts and to be aligned with Your will.

## February 7 – WE ARE ONE SPIRIT WITH HIM

1 Corinthians 2:11-12 – Who among men knows the thoughts of a man except the spirit of the man, which is in him? Even so, the thoughts of God no one knows except the Spirit of God.

According to scientists, billions of thoughts go through our brain daily. We process an amazing amount of simultaneous information. Think of it! Your brain assimilates all the colors and objects you see. It takes in the temperature around you, the pressure of your feet against the floor, the sounds around you, and even the dryness of your mouth. Your brain holds and processes all your emotions, thoughts, and memories. Most of your thoughts are undetected by the conscious mind. There are signals that control all your bodily functions.

Paul tells us in these Scripture verses, that it is our spirit man that knows our thoughts. In the same way, the Holy Spirit knows all the thoughts of God. It is extremely important for us to develop a daily relationship with the Holy Spirit, because He is the only One who can help us know God in a deepening way. The Holy Spirit is the Spirit of the Father and of the Son. This is why Paul prayed, "that the God of our Lord Jesus Christ, the Father of glory, may give to you a spirit of wisdom and revelation in the knowledge of Christ" (Ephesians 1:17).

The Father's desire is that our spirit be united with His Spirit, making it possible to grow in our knowledge of God. In Paul's letter to the Corinthians, he taught that we have been joined with the Lord. Paul spoke about being led by the Spirit in his letter to the Romans. Paul wrote of the fruit of the Spirit in his letter to the Galatians. As we fellowship with the Holy Spirit, He will reveal more and more of Christ to us and we will become increasingly aware of the Holy Spirit's abiding presence. As we increase in our knowledge of Christ Jesus, we will also increase in our knowledge of the Father. Through this working of the Spirit, we are able to fulfill God's desires and experience God's rest. We will also be able to share God's will with others, which has been revealed in Christ Jesus.

Ask the Holy Spirit to reveal God's plans to you on a daily basis. He is always much more willing to share than we are willing to receive. This is usually because we are so caught up with our own agenda, hindering us from hearing His voice. Father, today I call upon You to take greater control of my life. I pray to increase in the wisdom and knowledge of Your Son. Help me share with others what You have shown to me.

## February 8 – DRINKING FROM THE SPIRITUAL ROCK

1 Corinthians 10:4 – All drank the same spiritual drink, for they were drinking from a spiritual rock which followed them; and that rock was Christ.

It is vitally important to understand how God has chosen to reveal Himself to His triune creation man. His choice was to reveal "Divine Community": Father, Son, and Spirit living as perfect unity, the One and True God. The Son existed as the pre-incarnate Christ in the Old Testament. God's purpose was that the Son would take on human form. He was the Messiah before the incarnation through the virgin birth, God's appointed King.

God has always been the King. He intended to be Israel's King as revealed in 1 Samuel 8:8. As He led Israel out of Egypt, He proved Himself to be their sustainer. In the wilderness, when they needed water, He supplied water out of the rock. It was not just a natural drink, but a spiritual one as well. Paul taught that it was "a spiritual rock that followed them and that rock was Christ." The Lord Jesus Christ made it possible for us to drink of that spiritual drink as well.

Consider what Jesus said in John 7:37-39. "Now on the last day, the great day of the feast, Jesus stood and cried out, saying, 'If any man is thirsty, let him come to Me and drink. He who believes in Me, as the Scripture said, from his innermost being shall flow rivers of living water.' But this He spoke of the Spirit, whom those who believed in Him were to receive; for the Spirit was not yet given, because Jesus was not yet glorified."

Water is necessary in order for life to be sustained. Throughout the Old Testament, Christ is seen as the life-giving water that God has provided. The spiritual rock is pointing to this very moment of which Jesus was speaking. The same Holy Spirit that caused water to flow from the rock and supplied Israel's need has now come to cause rivers of living water to flow from your innermost being. Today, you can drink deeply from the Rock, Christ Jesus, by receiving the Holy Spirit's power in your life.

Go ahead and drink! Just say, Holy Spirit, come and fill me with Christ. Say to Him, Cause Your living water to flow from my innermost being. Begin to worship Him, yield your tongue to His control, and let the spiritual water flow! Do not be surprised if the Holy Spirit gives you a new language to help you in your worship of God.

## February 9 – PURSUE LOVE AND DESIRE SPIRITUAL GIFTS

1 Corinthians 14:1 – Pursue love, yet desire earnestly spiritual gifts.

Paul clearly taught in 1 Corinthians 13 that a significant work of the Spirit is to help us be established in love. Certainly, we all fall short of the biblical mandate in this area at times. Paul builds a bridge between the 12th and 14th chapters with the admonition to "pursue love," but he also says to "desire earnestly spiritual gifts." There are some in the faith who persist on setting love against spiritual gifts, but this is a total misrepresentation of what Paul is teaching the church. It is important to understand, the Holy Spirit gives *gifts* because they are intended to be the vehicle by which love is conveyed to all those in need of receiving God's grace. Unfortunately, the Corinthian believers were using the Gifts of the Spirit in a selfish way. Paul did not say to stop using the gifts, but rather *change your mind* about how you are viewing these gifts that the Spirit is so willing to bestow.

Before we can fully grasp what Paul is teaching in the chapters about the gifts, we must become rooted in love. I like the NASB translation that tells us to "pursue love." Love does not just materialize; it must be pursued in order for us to experience its development in our lives. A close walk with the Holy Spirit is required for this attribute of God to become evidenced in an increased way in our lives. As we devote ourselves to thinking about the gifts of the Holy Spirit, let us begin by requesting His help in pursuing the love of God. I am personally convicted of how far short I fall from allowing His nature to be revealed through me. My flesh is weak but with the Holy Spirit's help, my spirit is willing to become a greater lover towards all.

Father, help me to be enlarged in my capacity to activate Your love in serving others. Make me more of a vehicle of Your love towards others through an increased operation of Your gifts in and through my life. Let me be used to benefit others in their need, and to help them come to know You by the gifts You choose to give and release through me.

## February 10 – BE MATURE IN YOUR THINKING

1 Corinthians 14:20 – Brethren, do not be children in your thinking; yet in evil be babes, but in your thinking be mature.

Paul brought correction to the saints at Corinth over the mishandling of the gifts of the Spirit. As a spiritual father, he wanted the Corinthians to grow up in Christ and not be like children concerning *spiritual gifts.* He was especially speaking about the use of the gift of tongues. In verses 21-22, Paul quoted Isaiah 28:11 where God declared that He would speak to His people Israel with "stammering lips and another tongue, but they would not hear."

Paul taught tongues as a sign gift to Israel as well as a sign gift to the unbeliever (verse 22). The passage in Isaiah goes on to say, "Here is rest for the weary." It is interesting that Paul uses this quote from Isaiah to make His case for tongues as a sign gift. This supernatural ability to speak in an unknown tongue is like the refreshing water that flowed from the rock in the wilderness, when God supplied water to refresh His people. Paul's teaching in 1 Corinthians 14:4 instructs us that the gift of tongues is meant to edify. The unbelievers hear the Gospel in their own language, while the individual believer is edified as the tongue is interpreted. In one's personal prayer life speaking in tongues refreshes the saint of God and builds up the inner man.

Again, Paul's strong encouragement is not to be *children in your thinking, but be mature*. Paul encourages the use of spiritual gifts, while encouraging a mature perspective. Many respond negatively to tongues as a result of misreading Paul. He is not against the use of tongues, nor does he set tongues against anything else such as love. Paul said, "I thank God I speak in tongues more than you all" (1 Corinthians 14:18). The gift of tongues is healthy, for it is one way the Spirit of God refreshes the believer. Corporately, when a message in tongues is given, an interpretation needs to be given so others can be edified.

Allow the Holy Spirit to release your spirit to speak in a new language. He wants to give you the ability to pray and sing in the Spirit. Allow your worship and prayers to be controlled by the Spirit of God. As the Scriptures declare, it will be refreshing to you just as He has promised. Father, I yield my entire self to You, especially my tongue. As the Palmist David said, "Set a guard, O Lord, over my mouth; keep watch over the door of my lips" (Psalm 141:3).

## February 11 – DESIRE TO PROPHESY

1 Corinthians 14:1 – Pursue love, yet desire earnestly spiritual gifts, but especially that you may prophesy.

Paul stresses the importance of prophecy throughout chapter fourteen. He does this for a number of reasons. The Bible makes it clear that "the testimony of Jesus is the spirit of prophecy" (Revelation 19:10). Moses cried out, "I would that all of the Lord's people were prophets, that the Lord would put His Spirit upon them" (Numbers 11:29)! All of God's people can prophesy because the promise of the Father to send the Holy Spirit has been fulfilled. The Spirit of God is present and He wants to release His gift of prophecy. Paul declares that all prophecy in the church is for the purpose of "edification, exhortation, and comfort" (1 Corinthians 14:4).

The Lord delights in speaking His Word through His chosen vessels. Men and women throughout the Old Testament spoke of the great things God planned to do through His people in Messiah's Day. The Lord Jesus Christ is the Anointed One who has opened the way for all God's people to be used of the Lord. The Father promised His Son that He would give the Holy Spirit to all who believed on Christ. The same Spirit who spoke the Word in the Old Testament is now indwelling believers with the purpose of speaking and confirming the Word of God to a lost world.

Paul teaches that we "can all prophesy, one by one, so that all may learn, and all may be exhorted" (1 Corinthians 14:31). It pleases the Father when His children desire spiritual gifts, especially the gift of prophecy. The choice belongs to us, because God has already expressed His will in the matter. Prophecy is a gift that is meant to be expressed in the local church setting. It can also be quite effective when ministering to an individual through prayer or even counseling.

Today, ask the Holy Spirit to activate the gift of prophecy in your life. Pray about the gift of prophecy on a regular basis. Expect God to begin to speak to you and give you words to minister to others as you open your mouth for His glory.

## February 12 – CONCERNING SPIRITUALS – DON'T BE IGNORANT

1 Corinthians 12:1 –Concerning spiritual *gifts*, brethren, I do not want you to be unaware.

Notice, the word "gift" is italicized by the translators for clarification. This is because the word "gift" is not found in the original manuscript. Paul's expression is "spirituals" which refers to spiritual graces. Many have interpreted Paul to be saying that the gifts are like a personal gift that one now possesses. This is far from what Paul had in mind. Today, there is much ignorance regarding these spiritual gifts, just as in Paul's day. The enemy especially enjoys confusing God's people regarding *spiritual gifts* because he knows that if we lay hold of what God has provided in the work of the Spirit, great harm will come to his plans of resistance against the kingdom of God.

Ignorance is one of the enemy's great weapons to bind up God's people in their effort to pull down demonic strongholds. The Holy Spirit has been poured out so that we might receive the Father's plans for taking back what the enemy has stolen. Paul makes it clear throughout his writings that God has provided grace in giving spirituals or *grace gifts* in order to help us with the tasks He has assigned. All the spirituals are available in the Holy Spirit. They are initiations of the Spirit, so if one has the Spirit of God inside, then all of these spiritual gifts are there and available.

The Holy Spirit chooses when and where the gifts are to be released. Remember that Jesus said "He would not leave us as orphans" (John 14:18). You are in a family surrounded by others who stand with and support you. They encourage you to move into deeper waters in the things of the Spirit. Do not be afraid to let the Holy Spirit have complete control in your life. Step out in faith and trust Him to give you the exact grace you need when the opportunity presents itself.

Simply ask the Holy Spirit what it is that He wants to do at any given time. Begin right now by asking Him for a great sensitivity to His work in and through you. "Father, please guide me in the exercise of spiritual gifts. I need Your help daily to accomplish Your will. I want to experience Your love and power being released through me to others. I yield my life to the Holy Spirit to have complete control." Pray this every day until it is a part of your daily experience.

## February 13 – SPEAKING BY THE SPIRIT

1 Corinthians 12:3 – I make known to you that no one speaking by the Spirit of God says, "Jesus is accursed"; and no one can say, "Jesus is Lord" except by the Holy Spirit.

An interesting scripture follows Paul's expressed desire for believers not to be ignorant of spiritual gifts. The Corinthians had come from a pagan religious background of idolatry. Idolatry, by its very nature, brings people under the curses of the particular religion with which it is associated. Jesus, on the other hand, has delivered us from the curse. "Christ redeemed us from the curse of the law, having become a curse for us" (Galatians 3:13). Jesus became a curse for us by bearing our sins. The good news is that He is alive from the dead, having carried our sins to hell and He now lives to bless those who put their trust in Him. He is a King who blesses, not a king that curses. The Holy Spirit has come to enable us to say, "Jesus is Lord!" In these chapters, Paul is contrasting the believer's former life lived under curses and our new life found in blessings from our risen King.

The Holy Spirit is God's agent in the earth to help God's people overcome and throw down all idolatry. The Holy Spirit exalts the Lord Jesus through the people of God as they proclaim Jesus' Lordship. They do works of power demonstrating the kingdom of God is present and the enemy's kingdom has been defeated. There is a continual process of judgment taking place through the Lord's people until the final Day of Judgment before God. "This is the day which the Lord has made; Let us rejoice and be glad in it" (Psalm 118:24). We think in terms of days, but the Lord is thinking in terms of *a day*. God sees this period for the Church as the day He is raising up a people who are judging the world by the Lord Jesus through the gifts of the Holy Spirit. Captives are set free by being "delivered from the kingdom of darkness and translated into the kingdom of God's dear Son" (Colossians 1:13).

Ask the Holy Spirit to empower you with His gifts so that you can share the good news of the gospel of the kingdom, not only with words, but in demonstration of power by the work of the Holy Spirit. Let those gifts declare to others that Jesus is Lord!

## February 14 – THE FRUIT OF LOVE

Galatians 5:22 – But the fruit of the Spirit is love.

Many today will be celebrating what is called Valentine's Day, a day that has been set aside to remember those we love. The love of the world has deep roots in the natural and the sensuous dimensions of love. This is not wrong when kept in the context of God's designs for a man and woman. Paul contrasts love with the deeds of the flesh. This is why Paul uses the conjunction "but" as he begins his statement about the fruit of the Spirit, which consists of nine parts. Paul begins with "love."

Love is the singular action that connects us to God and to one another. Jesus summed up the law with the word "love" in Matthew 22:37. In the upper room, Jesus gave His disciples a New Commandment, "Love one another as I have loved you" (John 15:12). Love is central to the work of the Spirit because it comes from the very nature of God Himself, who is love. God's love is like light, revealing the darkness of the works of the flesh.

Whether speaking of redemption or operating in the gifts of the Spirit, love must always be the motivating force. Agape love is the Father's love, a love which is always putting others first. The Holy Spirit always leads with others in mind. He came because of others, He convicts because of others, and He saves because of God's love for others. In everything you do, think, "How does this affect others?" Become one who is thinking about the *other person*. You can only do this by the power of the Holy Spirit. Our basic nature is a self-nature, but the Holy Spirit wants to produce in us *Christ's nature*. His nature is a *love nature*. He cannot help Himself because He is Love.

Today, ask for Christ's nature to be revealed and fully matured in you. Ask the Holy Spirit to fully accomplish the work of maturity in your life. Celebrate this day with a choice to yield to the Holy Spirit and let Him release the love of God through you to all those you touch.


## February 15 – THE VARIETY OF THE SPIRIT

1 Corinthians 12:4 – Now there are varieties of gifts, but the same Spirit.

The Holy Spirit chooses many ways to manifest His presence. In 1 Corinthians 12, Paul discusses nine spiritual gifts that are manifestations of the Spirit. In verse 4, he lays the foundation for discussing the gifts of the Holy Spirit. He begins by helping us know that it is the same Spirit regardless of the individual gift operating in the believer. The Holy Spirit chooses through whom He will manifest a particular gift. He chooses when and what gift to release. He is doing this everywhere in the earth through many different believers. He indeed is the Omnipresent God.

The Holy Spirit is manifesting His gifts through the various ministries our Lord Jesus has operating in the earth. The Spirit anoints individuals as Apostles, Prophets, Evangelists, Pastors and Teachers. He operates through the Deacons and all those who have Help ministries in the body of Christ. He expresses His gifts through the Administrators in the body of Christ. In fact, every believer can be used of the Spirit to express Christ's love to His body the Church and through His body to the world. If you are a believer, you then are a candidate to be used of the Spirit of God in any variety of ways.

Our part in the operation of the Holy Spirit's gifts is to allow Him to impart the gifts He chooses at any particular time. The rationalization of our minds is our biggest problem. God does not call us to give up our mind, but rather to yield our thinking to God's Word. God's promise is the indwelling presence of the Holy Spirit who produces God's divine nature in the believer. This is what Paul meant when he said, "We have the mind of Christ" (1 Corinthians 2:16). His divine nature which was manifested in Jesus Christ is now revealed in His children by the presence of His indwelling Holy Spirit.

Ask the Holy Spirit to help you turn your mind over to Him. Ask Him to help you let the gifts of God operate when He so chooses. Ask Him to cause you to be sensitive to the Spirit's leading and to be filled with the faith of the Son of God in every situation. Father, thank You for Your reservoir of gifts made available in the Holy Spirit. I am Your servant to be used as You choose.

## February 16 – THE COMMON GOOD

1 Corinthians 12:7 – Each one is given the manifestation of the Spirit for the common good.

It is important to realize that Paul wrote to all the believers at Corinth and not just to a select few. As it relates to the gifts of the Spirit, many think a special few are able to operate in this realm. This could not be farther from the truth. God has no favorites! The Apostle Peter understood this when he said, "I most certainly understand now that God is not One to show partiality, but in every nation the man who fears Him and does what is right is welcome to Him" (Acts 10:34-35). We should rejoice over the fact that any believer can be used of God in regard to these supernatural gifts. The problem is never with God, but with us. The problem is rooted in our thinking and expectation. How do you expect God to use you? Do you trust in the Lord for His gifts to operate through your life? Some think that they are not worthy to be used, while others believe that the Lord does not manifest Himself through the gifts any longer. Whatever the blockage, let it go today. Allow the Holy Spirit to use you in releasing God's kingdom through your life to another in need today.

Notice, Paul says, "The manifestation of the Spirit is for the common good." The Lord intends for the gifts to be manifested regularly, not every once in a while. We should expect "Divine" appointments daily, where a gift of the Spirit freely operates through our lives. As we fellowship with other saints who have similar expectations, faith is increased to trust the Lord for His gifts. We do not want to breed familiarity with the work of the Spirit, but we should expect His manifestations regularly and always for the good of those in need. Be ready to be used of God by letting the Holy Spirit work though you. The needs are great and the Lord is calling His people to be workers with Him. Choose today to be an instrument of blessing to others wherever you may be, in the church assembly, at work, or even seated on an airplane. The Spirit of God is ready to use us. Are we ready to be used?

Father, I make myself available to be used by the Holy Spirit for the common good of others. I open my heart to You and yield all of me to the Holy Spirit's control. I pray to be an instrument of righteousness for the common good of all those I meet today.

## February 17 – THE WORD OF WISDOM

1 Corinthians 12:8 – To one is given the word of wisdom through the Spirit.

It is important to understand from this verse of Scripture that Paul is addressing order in the public gathering. As the Spirit directs the meeting, a number of individuals may be chosen to be used in a variety of the gifts. This is the reason, Paul specified, "to one is given." Believers should have an expectation for the manifestation of these gifts in their gatherings. A few people may be used to speak a "word of wisdom" while others may be used in another gift. Please take note; it is important for leadership to be listening carefully for the Spirit's promptings in the gathering as we learn to be led by the Spirit.

Any and all of the gifts are readily available to believers, relating to their individual walk with the Lord. Many times, I have experienced the gift of wisdom in counseling. I may receive a thought that did not come from my natural reasoning, but rather the prompting of the Holy Spirit as He guides me in the counseling session. In past years, I experienced the Holy Spirit guiding me through a word of wisdom to solve problems while working a secular job. How honored the believer is to have a close relationship with the Holy Spirit! We can ask Him to release the word of wisdom as needed in any given situation.

The Scriptures place a great deal of emphasis on the importance of wisdom in one's life. We find this especially true in the book of Proverbs. By studying and applying God's Word, one will move in wisdom on a regular basis. Please understand, there is a difference between gaining wisdom from studying God's Word and the gift of the "word of wisdom" which is an immediate word from heaven given by the Spirit of God. Paul encourages each of us to seek after the best gifts. Truly, *the word of wisdom* is to be highly sought after.

Begin to ask the Holy Spirit for the gift of the word of wisdom every day. Ask Him to give you a great desire for the word of wisdom and to cause you to be sensitive to His promptings when He wants to speak to you and release this awesome gift.

## February 18 – THE WORD OF KNOWLEDGE

1 Corinthians 12:8 – To another the word of knowledge according to the same Spirit.

Paul reminds us that the same Spirit, who gives the word of wisdom to one, gives the word of knowledge to another. Paul is addressing the public gathering of believers and the need for godly order in the meeting. The Holy Spirit, who is charged with distributing the gifts, is also residing in each believer. He can release a gift through any believer at His will. The "word of knowledge" is not the knowledge one receives by diligent study or from a teacher in the classroom, but rather a supernatural word the Holy Spirit imparts. It is information the Spirit is privy to know, He chooses to share this information to accomplish His particular purpose. The word of knowledge can be very helpful in assisting when ministering to another. At times, the Spirit of the Lord will give a needed word of knowledge to assist a believer in problem solving.

I have experienced this gift operating when I had come to the end of my natural reasoning in a matter. I had exhausted my own resources of information and needed a word which the Holy Spirit held. Other times, while an individual is sharing with me their perspective, I will be praying, "Lord, give me Your supernatural knowledge of what this one needs." Shortly, a word would come into my mind, or a picture that usually does not make sense to me, but communicated exactly what the other person needed. Our God is great! He is close to us by His Holy Spirit, and so willing to share His gifts with all His children. Develop a discipline of asking the Holy Spirit for a "word of knowledge" and see if He begins to share with you what you need to know. On a personal note, when I have lost something, I have asked the Holy Spirit to give me a word of direction to find the lost item. Many times, He has. It is not magic, but His word of knowledge freely given.

Go ahead. Begin to ask the Holy Spirit for the word of knowledge to operate in your life. Thank Him for the times this gift has operated, even though you did not recognize the knowledge you had received actually came from Him. He is closer than most of us realize. Nurture the relationship we have been so blessed to have with the Living God!

## February 19 – THE SPIRIT OF GOD RELEASES FAITH

1 Corinthians 12:9 – To another faith is given by the same Spirit.

Faith is always being exercised in the public gathering of the saints. Each believer exercises their faith simply by assembling with other believers. At times, special faith is required. There are times when the Holy Spirit will impart to an individual believer a special gift of faith. In the public meeting, the Spirit may choose to use one or two individuals in the "gift of faith" to meet a particular need. The Scriptures declare, "We walk by faith" (2 Corinthians 5:7). Our daily walk is an exercise of our personal faith in our Lord. There are also times when we must operate in faith through the application of particular Scriptures in various circumstances we face. Perhaps you are trusting for healing, believing for a certain financial need, or facing some impossible situation. We all face these times.

In every believer's life there are times when a special gift of faith is required. These are times when the Holy Spirit will impart a special gift of faith to meet a need or answer the cry for help as we come to the end of our own operation of faith. Paul operated in special times of exceptional faith. "God was performing extraordinary miracles by the hands of Paul, so that handkerchiefs or aprons were even carried from his body to the sick, and the diseases left them and the evil spirits went out" (Acts 19:11-12).

I have personally had times when the Holy Spirit imparted special faith for a job to be done. I found this to be most often true when traveling into a foreign country and facing certain dangers. I knew, in these times, I was not operating in my normal walk of faith, but in special grace the Holy Spirit was supplying for a specific task. I do not experience the "gift of faith" daily, but over the years I have found the Lord to be so faithful to give me the grace of faith so I could accomplish what He had purposed for me to do.

Father, I pray that You will grace my life with special, even extraordinary measures of faith as needed. I pray to be reminded of Your ever-present help in time of need. I open up my spirit to the Holy Spirit, who is full of grace and gifts. Father, I thank you for the faith You have given me. I also thank You for the gift of faith available to me in those special times of need.

## February 20 – THE SPIRIT OF GOD GIVES MANY GIFTS OF HEALING

1 Corinthians 12:9 – To another, gifts of healing by one Spirit.

The Holy Spirit is the giver of healing, but He has many gifts or manifestations of healing. Our God is a God of restoration! In order for restoration to take place, it requires some kind of healing. It may be physical, mental, emotional, or relational healing. Mostly spiritual issues are at the core of all healing. Today, let us consider the physical side of healing. There are multitudes of diseases in this world that oppress people's lives. Peter spoke of "how God anointed Jesus with the Holy Spirit and with power, and how He went about doing good and healing all that were oppressed by the devil, for God was with Him" (Acts 10:38). Jesus demonstrated His delight and willingness to heal, even on the Sabbath day, when He healed the Hebrew woman whom Satan had bound. Jesus asked the religious leaders, "Should not this woman, whom Satan had bound for eighteen years, be released from this bond on the Sabbath day" (Luke 13:16)?

God appointed the Sabbath as a day of rest. What better way to demonstrate God's purpose of the Sabbath than to heal one whom the enemy had bound for many years? God gives "gifts of healing" to individual believers because He loves us and wants to help us enter into all forms of His rest. Whether we are addressing the healing of a broken spirit, a tormented soul or perhaps a broken body in some form, Jesus is still the healer today. He uses the body of believers to bring about healing for the masses, just as in His earthly ministry 2,000 years ago. The Holy Spirit will use all who yield to Him and are willing to receive wonderful gifts of His healing power.

Today, ask the Holy Spirit to use you to bring about healing in broken lives. They are all around us, beloved. All we must do is be available for the Holy Spirit to give us a healing gift for another. Father, I ask You to use me as an instrument of healing as often as You would choose.

# February 21- TO ANOTHER THE EFFECTING OF MIRACLES

1 Corinthians 12:10 – To another the working of miracles.

Many believe that the days of miracles are over. It has always seemed strange to me that anyone could come to this conclusion. God is the author of miracles. He is supernatural and we are natural by virtue of how He created us. God is unlimited and we are limited. Paul gave us an order for church life recorded in 1 Corinthians 12:28. He lists a number of ministries we should expect in the Lord's church. He begins with apostles, second prophets, third teachers, then "miracles," and then healing. The list goes on. It seems Paul understood miracles were to be a regular part of God's order in His church. Just like the other gifts, not everyone operates in the gift of miracles, but all believers have the gift available by virtue of the Holy Spirit living inside them.

Some believe miracles stopped after the original apostles died. Those who hold to this view believe we have the finished Canon of God's Word and have no need of any of the gifts. Nothing could be farther from the truth! The gift of miracles confirms the Word of God by the Lord's Holy Presence existing in the believer. Jesus, Paul, and the disciples were used by the Spirit in the miraculous, confirming the Word of God that they preached. In fact, in Mark 16:18, Jesus told us that miracles would be part of the ministry of the Great Commission. The writer of Hebrews makes this statement: "How will we escape if we neglect so great a salvation? After it was at the first spoken through the Lord, it was confirmed to us by those who heard, God also testifying with them, both by signs and wonders and by various miracles and by gifts of the Holy Spirit according to His own will" (Hebrews 2:3-4).

"Jesus Christ *is* the same yesterday and today and forever" (Hebrews 13:8). Do you believe that? Then He is still the miracle worker and He has not removed this vital gift from His church. Rejoice! Be courageous and ask the Holy Spirit to use you in this realm of the Spirit's work. Yield to the Holy Spirit and expect the gift of miracles to become a part of your life and ministry to others.

Father, I yield to Your miracle power. Use me according to Your will to help others come to know Your miraculous power manifested in the resurrection life of Your Son through Your indwelling Holy Spirit.

## February 22 – YOU CAN ALL PROPHESY ONE AT A TIME.

1 Corinthians 12:10 – To another the gift of prophecy is given.

Prophecy is one of the greatest gifts the Holy Spirit gives to God's people. Paul encouraged the Corinthians with the words "all may prophesy" (1 Corinthians 14:31). I believe what makes this a great gift is the fact that *all can prophesy*. Individuals learn and are exhorted through this gift. God's people are encouraged to go forward and enter into all the Lord has appointed for them. Many times, the words are very specific and help in guiding a person in a particular direction. Prophecy is supernatural in its nature because it comes by the inspiration of the Holy Spirit. Prophecy is not the natural words of encouragement or teaching, which can be beneficial. The prophetic gift operates as the Holy Spirit stirs up a believer to speak. Sometimes the Holy Spirit will speak one word to a person in order to "prime the pump" for speaking more. Other times it might be a vision that one sees. Most of the time, it is by inspiration and one does not know what will follow the initial word or words the Spirit has given. The Bible connects "faith" to the gift of prophecy. "Prophesy, according to the proportion of faith you have" (Romans 12:6).

The gift of prophecy is a great way to become familiar with the Holy Spirit's leading and directing. The gift can operate while praying for another, while sharing the gospel, or just encouraging someone in the natural. All of a sudden, the Holy Spirit releases a supernatural word of learning and encouragement. The gift of prophecy can be helpful in leading to the operation of other gifts as the Spirit leads.

I have had prophetic words spoken over my life for the last forty-seven years. Many of these words were very accurate in the detail they contained. This has been helpful for me to continue in the Lord's direction for my life. At times, these words called me to specific areas of ministry. The Lord had already placed the call in my heart, but others were used to confirm His leading. I have been honored to be used by the Holy Spirit to provide the same ministry to others.

Ask the Holy Spirit to heighten your sensitivity to His presence and to begin to use you in an ever-increasing way in the "gift of prophecy." You will be astonished how often you begin to share under the anointing of the Spirit of God. How blessed people will be as the Lord uses you to be an instrument of encouragement and learning!

## February 23 – TO ANOTHER, THE DISCERNMENT OF SPIRITS

1 Corinthians12:10 – To another, the distinguishing of spirits.

The Bible reveals four areas relating to the subject of "spirit." The first is the Holy Spirit, for whom this devotional is dedicated. Next, the human spirit, which becomes regenerated by the power of the Holy Spirit when one repents and is converted. The third is angels, who are called ministering spirits. The fourth is demonic spirits, who are associated with the realm of darkness.

In the Gospels, these spirits of darkness are referred to in a number of ways. They are called devils, evil spirits, and unclean spirits. The gift of discernment, translated in the NASB as "distinguishing of spirits," is a gift the Holy Spirit gives so the body of Christ knows with what realm of the spirit world it is dealing. This is a necessary gift in helping to bring freedom to those bound by evil spirits. It is also beneficial to help an individual find God's eternal purpose for their lives as they learn to be led by the Holy Spirit.

Because of the influence of the occult in society, both in Bible days and in ours, the problem of spirits is a real issue. Many people come to Jesus, but have not received ministry regarding their past, when evil spirits attached to their lives. The early church understood the spiritual battle in which they were engaged and ministered "deliverance" from evil or unclean spirits so that the new believers could walk in freedom in their new faith in Christ.

The gift of discernment is a powerful tool that the Holy Spirit wants to impart to willing believers. It can be used to discern spiritual realms in the corporate gathering, in times of ministry to an individual, and in our personal walk with the Lord. God wants us to know how the enemy is battling against our success in Christ. The Bible is clear about our warfare not being with flesh and blood. "For our struggle is not against flesh and blood, but against the rulers, against the powers, against the world forces of this darkness, against spiritual forces of wickedness in the heavenly places" (Ephesians 6:12).

Ask the Holy Spirit today to heighten your discernment of the enemy's territories. Yield yourself to the Holy Spirit and allow Him to show you the battle in which you are engaged. Ask for discernment as you minister to others. Father, I thank You for Your Word that tells of our spiritual battles. Cause me to be discerning as I fight the good fight of faith.

## February 24 – TO ANOTHER, THE SPIRIT GIVES VARIOUS KINDS OF TONGUES

1 Corinthians 12:10 – To another, various kinds of tongues.

The subject of tongues and prophecy are at the heart of this part of Paul's letter to the Corinthians. The gift of tongues was being misused in the corporate gatherings. The purpose for the gift was to convince the unbelieving foreigner, in their own language, their need of salvation. Through the supernatural gift of tongues, the unbeliever was convicted and won to Christ. If believers were speaking in tongues at the same time in church gatherings, it brought confusion to both unbelievers and other believers. Read 1 Corinthians 14 for a complete discussion of the matter. Paul wanted believers to understand that this gift is specifically for the common good. Many are confused about this gift and have a tendency to neglect its importance to the body of Christ.

In the fourteenth chapter, Paul made a distinction between the gift given for utterance in the meeting place and the practical use of tongues in the believer's personal life. In our devotional today, I want us to think about Paul's admonition in 1 Corinthians 14:5, "Now I wish that you all spoke in tongues." I know that not all spoke in tongues, for if they did, Paul would not have needed to wish that all did. Paul explained that for tongues to edify, the language must be interpreted. Paul wrote, "If I pray in a tongue, my spirit prays, but my mind is unfruitful" (1 Corinthians 14:14). Paul went on to say in verse 15, "What is the outcome then? I will pray with the spirit and I will pray with my mind also." Do not set your natural mind against your spirit. Both need to make expression to God, whether by prayer or by worship. The Lord has given this wonderful gift of tongues so our spirits, as well as our minds, may pray and worship our Lord. It is very helpful to be able to express our worship and prayers with our natural minds as well as our spirits.

If you have not received the "gift of tongues" from the Holy Spirit, why not simply ask Him now? Continue to ask with the view toward being strengthened in your prayer life and worship to the Lord. It will not make you more spiritual. It is added grace to help you pursue your relationship with the Lord.

## February 25 – INTERPRETATION OF VARIOUS KINDS OF TONGUES

1 Corinthians 12:10 – To another, the interpretation of tongues.

The gift of interpretation was very important in the early church. There were many languages spoken throughout the Roman Empire. In Acts 2, we read about all those from around the empire that had come to Jerusalem for the Feast of Pentecost. They spoke the language of their homeland. Those speaking in tongues were speaking of the kingdom of God in the many languages represented. Tongues were a sign gift to the Jews that the Spirit had come and the Kingdom was being established. In Acts 10, we see this sign gift of tongues given to the Gentiles. As the Gentiles received the Holy Spirit with the evidence of tongues, it was a sign to the Jews that God had accepted the Gentiles in His kingdom. Supernaturally, the message of the Gospel was given in an understood tongue by some but needed interpreting for those who did not understand the language by which the Spirit was speaking.

Today, the gift of interpretation is still relevant. There are testimonies from the mission field of tongues and interpretations being helpful in the sharing of the Gospel. From time to time, a message in tongues will come in a gathering of believers. If only the gift of tongues is exercised, there will be no edification for those who do not understand the language spoken. Interpretation provides others an opportunity to be encouraged as understanding is brought to the hearers. Paul encouraged tongues in the corporate gathering, but only if the gift of interpretation is exercised. Paul went on to say, some speak in tongues, some interpret, but all can prophesy. The Holy Spirit has made provision for the many languages spoken in the nations to hear the Gospel and has given an opportunity to receive Christ's offer of forgiveness and life.

Rejoice today in your time of devotion with the Lord, in how He has made provision for all people to hear and understand the good news of the Kingdom of God. If the gift of tongues is exercised in a public meeting, maybe the Lord would use you to interpret what was spoken for the edifying of the body of Christ.

## February 26 – THE HOLY SPIRIT IS AT WORK DISTRIBUTING HIS GIFTS.

1 Corinthians 12:11 – One and the self-same Spirit works all these things, distributing to each one individually just as He wills.

We have spent a number of days in our devotion considering the work of the Holy Spirit. We have especially considered His work as it relates to the gifts He gives in the body of Christ. Paul wrote that the one Spirit works everything according to what He wills. As believers, it is not necessary to strive over the gifts the Holy Spirit distributes. We must learn how to rest in His provisions. As our relationship with the Holy Spirit matures, we will become more available for Him to work through us for the sake of others.

A considerable challenge for a believer is to traverse the relationship between the spirit and the soul. The spirit of a person is drawn to the mystical side. This embraces areas outside the natural realm and focuses on the unseen realm. Paul calls this "spiritual" and not natural. At the same time, it is important that we do not throw our reasoning out the door. A key is to consistently bring our natural thought process to the Holy Spirit and invite Him to affect how we reason. This means that we need to study the Word of God. The Word of God reveals God's viewpoints. The Spirit of God will help affect our reasoning through His Word. At the same time, be bold to ask the Holy Spirit to allow His supernatural gifts to be given to you as He wills. I have prayed for over forty years, "Lord, give me heaven's point of view, and help me see things from Your perspective." I have asked many times for the Holy Spirit to help me by giving me an operation of His gifts. He has been so faithful to help me!

Father, I surrender my natural mind to the Holy Spirit. I ask You to open my understanding of Your Word and freely distribute Your gifts as You choose through my life. Holy Spirit, I give You complete control of my life. I pray that I may be a faithful steward of what You entrust to me.

## February 27 – THE LORD'S ONE BODY HAS MANY MEMBERS

1 Corinthians 12:12-13 – Even as the body is one and yet has many members, by one Spirit we were all baptized into one body, we were all made to drink of one Spirit.

The Apostle Paul uses the illustration of the human body to illustrate Christ's spiritual body. The human body is one, but it has many members. Paul is saying that by one Spirit we have all been baptized into Christ's body. He expands his thought by mentioning Jews, Greeks, slaves, and free men. Every person that has put his or her trust in Christ is drinking of the one Holy Spirit. Our unity is not by all having the same understanding, nor is it in our form of worship, but in the fact that we are all drinking of the same Spirit. The Holy Spirit is the unifying factor in the body of Christ.

Are you drinking of the one Spirit the Father and the Son have given? He is the Spirit of the Father and He is the Spirit of the Son. The Godhead remains a mystery because we are speaking of God. All we know and experience of God is through the Holy Spirit. In Corinthians, Paul spoke of the water that flowed from the rock in the wilderness. He called it "a spiritual drink" which was Christ. Paul taught that our spiritual drink is the Holy Spirit through Christ our Rock. The Holy Spirit ministers all that Christ has provided for us. Drink deeply of the spiritual water that you have been given! Receive all that the Holy Spirit has for you! Remember, it is spiritual, but it becomes manifested in tangible ways. Whether it is righteousness, peace, joy, or a particular gift that the Holy Spirit chooses to release, it all comes from Him.

Today, drink of the Spirit! The Lord Jesus, by His sacrifice, has made it possible for us to receive all that the Holy Spirit has to give. Receive your portion today.

## February 28 – A MORE EXCELLENT WAY

1 Corinthians 12:31 – Earnestly desire the greater gifts. And yet I show you a still more excellent way.

All that God has done for us comes from His personal attribute of love, for God is love! Any gift He imparts to a believer comes from a motivation of His love. He expects His children to be operating with the same motivation as His. Desire for spiritual gifts is good and proper. The question becomes, "What is our motivation?" For some, it may be a need to feel accepted by God. For others, it may be the need for attention, and for others perhaps a sense of power. Our motivations must be measured up against the love of God.

Paul the apostle spent a great deal of time addressing the use of spiritual gifts. The subject is not a small one, nor should it be quickly glossed over. He bridges the believers' instructions in 1 Corinthians twelve and fourteen with chapter thirteen. This chapter is known as the "love chapter." We must be careful not to make the mistake so many have made setting the subject of love against the gifts of the Spirit or thinking that love is *superior* to the gifts, thus dismissing the need for these gifts. That view completely misses Paul's point of writing these chapters. The gifts are an important part of our relationship to Christ. They are also our resource to more effectively share the good news of the kingdom. When our motivation is born out of love, the gifts become what God intended, conduits of His love. The same Holy Spirit who imparts His gifts to believers is the One who supplies the love of God through every believer.

Allow the Holy Spirit to examine your heart. Ask the Lord to reveal your true motivation. Ask the Holy Spirit to make your motivation pure. Ask for His supply of grace to move you into greater degrees of His love for others.

## March 1 – HAVING GIFTS THAT DIFFER

Romans 12:6 – We have gifts that differ according to the grace given to us.

The promise of the Father as recorded in Luke 24:49 was that the Holy Spirit would be given to everyone who put their faith in the Lord Jesus Christ. When we speak of grace, we are speaking of God's gift. We receive the grace of God when we receive the gift of the Holy Spirit. The Holy Spirit brings with Him everything the Father has made available in Christ. Paul is helping us understand that we are given different gifts according to the grace in our life. Romans 12:6 list some of those gifts. Each gift operates according to the measure of grace the Holy Spirit gives to an individual believer.

As we develop our relationship with the Holy Spirit, we should become increasingly aware of how the Spirit of God chooses to use our lives. We should become aware of the individual grace given to us to help others in their need. The Holy Spirit desires for us to receive His grace that has been freely made available to each believer. Some think, when the grace of God is given to a believer, the gift operating in and through them is complete and fully developed. Grace is simply God's gift, whether it is our initial salvation, the receiving of the Holy Spirit in power, or one of the gifts of the Spirit spoken of here in the Romans passage and throughout 1 Corinthians 12-14.

Each gift of the Spirit must be nurtured and developed. We grow in our salvation, learning how to apply what the Lord gives us on a daily basis. A particular gift such as prophecy must be exercised in order for us to learn how to become effective in the gift's operation. The *gifts of healing* are another example. One must begin to pray for the sick in order for the gift to be imparted. The more people for whom we pray, the more experience we will gain in exercising this beautiful grace of God. Our daily walk with the Lord should be one of learning and growing in His grace.

Ask the Lord to make clear to you the grace He has and wants to give you. Ask Him to guide you in the operation of His gifts. Ask Him to help you grow in the application of His grace in your life. Pray to become increasingly effective in ministering His power to those in need of His wonderful grace.

## March 2 – EXERCISE THE GIFTS GOD HAS GIVEN YOU

Romans 12:6 – Each of us is to exercise our gifts.

In our devotion yesterday, I spoke of *exercising the gifts*. Paul makes the point that we are to exercise or use the gifts given to us by the Holy Spirit. The Spirit of God gives us gifts, but we must receive them and put them to use. Many believers have received gifts from God, but do not use them regularly, if at all. I know of those who were prayed for to receive the gift of prophecy and then prophesied, but did not continue to exercise the gift and it fell dormant. What is the purpose of receiving a gift if the one receiving the gift never uses it?

The gifts of God are meant to be used. In most cases, they are used to benefit others by revealing God's love for them. Not exercising the gifts which the Holy Spirit chooses to give, denies others an experience of God's grace through our life. It is important that we seek God for how He wants to use our lives. It is equally important to develop a personal relationship with the Holy Spirit, the helper, so we learn to be sensitive to His leading and gifting through us. As we increase our devotion to God, we will become increasingly sensitive to the Spirit's leading and to His empowerment.

Father, I make myself available to Your Holy Spirit. Lord, show me the gifts You desire to give and release through my life. I ask to be used effectively in ministering Your love to others. I desperately need Your presence and Your gifts to be operating in my life.

## March 3 – PRAYER IS THE KEY TO ALL WE HAVE FROM GOD

Matthew 6:8 – Your Father knows what you need before you ask Him.

Spirit-led prayer is not informational. Our Father in heaven already knows our needs. Prayer is not about words as much as it is about a relationship with our creator, redeemer, and the lover of our souls. The religious leaders of Jesus' day uttered many words in prayer. They truly were not praying to God. They prayed to impress those watching them go through their religious act. Some take prayer to the extreme of only meditating. It is good to meditate! The Holy Spirit will lead us at times to what the Psalmist taught: "Be still and know that I am God" (Psalm 46:10). Waiting and listening is a very essential part of prayer. Some have gotten so mystical they separate themselves from family and culture. They isolate themselves to meditate, trying to touch God. The Holy Spirit will lead, from time to time, to get alone with our heavenly Father. Jesus regularly spent private time with His Father. He brought back to His disciples what He had received.

As we allow the Holy Spirit to teach us the Word of God, He will instruct us how to be an instrument in God's hands by coming to know God's *will*. Christian prayer is meant to be relational. It is spending time in our Father's presence. Prayer is using the views of Scripture in our communication with the Lord. Prayer is sharing your heart's burden. Prayer is making our requests known to God. Spirit-filled and Spirit-led prayer comes out of *righteousness and relationship* with the heavenly Father. "The effective prayer of a righteous man can accomplish much" (James 5:16).

Many more things could be said about prayer, but nothing takes the place of simply praying. Start today with these few thoughts I have shared. Regularly have your Bible with you in your dedicated prayer time. Let the Scriptures guide you in knowing God's will. Ask the Holy Spirit to lead you to portions of God's Word which He would have you consider.

## March 4 – OUR FATHER IN HEAVEN

Matthew 6:9 – Pray then, in this way.

As Jesus continued His teachings on the mountain, He began to instruct about prayer. Jesus gave us a pattern of prayer and the Holy Spirit uses this pattern to guide us as we pray. Many know this prayer as *The Lord's Prayer.* It was not meant to be recited, but to be a pattern of critical areas for which we are to seek God.

The first area the Spirit of God wants to help us with is the fact that God is our Father. The Jews knew of God as a Father, but Jesus revealed Him as *Our Father.* What a revelation the Spirit of God has given! He is not a father who is distant, but the Father who is personal and close! Spirit-led prayer is meant to develop *intimacy* with our heavenly Father. Many believers confess a relationship with Christ, but still do not know a relationship with their heavenly Father. In many cases, it is because they have not known a true relationship with their earthly father.

In the upper room at the Last Supper, Phillip asked Jesus "to show them the Father" (John 14:8). Jesus was disappointed in the request because the purpose of His time with the disciples was to reveal His Father. They had missed one of the most important reasons of His mission. We too, can be blessed by Jesus' presence in the gifts and His nature, but miss what the Holy Spirit wants us to know. The Father! Jesus said to His disciples, "Have I been so long with you, and yet you have not come to know Me, Phillip? He who has seen Me has seen the Father; how can you say, 'Show us the Father' (John 14:9)? Could it be that the Holy Spirit might say the same thing to us?

To know the Holy Spirit, who is the spirit of the Father and the spirit of the Son, is to know the Father. Every day, speak to God as Your Father and make it even more personal by relating to Him as *your* Father. I want to know Him more and more as my Father who is my all in all. If that is your desire, begin to ask the Holy Spirit to reveal the Father to you. He desires to be known as *Daddy,* in the original language, "Abba." By His power, He has made you His child. "As many as received Him, to them He gave the right to become the children of God, even to those who believe in His name" (John 1:12).

## March 5 – OUR FATHER IN HEAVEN

Matthew 6:9 – Pray then, in this way, Our Father who is in heaven.

In the beginning, God intended that earthly fathers would reflect the nature of His Father's heart. Unfortunately, disobedience got in the way and man was separated from the heavenly Father through sin. Adam lost the ability to convey God's true nature to his wife and his children. Jesus came with the purpose of revealing the Father to humanity. He promised His disciples that "He would not leave them as orphans" (John 14:18). The fourteenth chapter of the book of John is about the coming of the Holy Spirit. Again, Jesus said to His disciples, "The Helper, the Holy Spirit, whom the Father will send in My name, He will teach you all things, and bring all things to your remembrance, all that I said to you" (John 14:26).

A major portion of our salvation is rooted in getting to know our Father in Heaven. What a blessing we have in our developing relationship with the Holy Spirit as He helps us to know the Father. We will soon be ushered into our Father's Holy Presence to stand before His throne in heaven. In the present moment, we are invited to "draw near with confidence to the throne of grace, so that we may receive mercy and find grace to help in time of need" (Hebrews 4:16). Prayer is a work of the Holy Spirit as He guides us to know how to pray. "We do not know how to pray as we ought, but the Spirit helps our weaknesses" (Romans 8:26).

An old hymn says, "I am weak, but Thou art strong." I come to the Lord in my natural weakness, but my heavenly Father meets with me and gives me strength as I grow in my relationship with Him. Let the Holy Spirit lead you into increasing knowledge and fellowship with your heavenly Father. He loves you so much! He proved it by sending Jesus and then sending the Holy Spirit to indwell your life.

Ask the Holy Spirit to increase your revelation of the Father. Ask Him to show you how much He loves you. Ask for more of the Father's nature to be manifested in your life. Finally, ask to be one who reveals the Father to others.

## March 6 – YOUR NAME IS HOLY

Matthew 6:9 – Hallowed be Your name.

"Like the Holy One who called you, be holy yourselves also in all your behavior, because it is written, you shall be holy, for I am holy."

God's *holiness* is a difficult attribute for humans to understand. I am sure that if you asked ten people to describe God's holiness, you would receive ten different answers. Each answer would be limited by an individual's fallen human understanding. Jesus' life is the only real valid representation of the holiness of God that we have in human form. We know God the Father by the life our Lord Jesus Christ lived here on earth. His *holy life* became our pattern for how we should live as children of God.

Jesus gives believers His Holy Spirit as promised by our heavenly Father. One of His divine purposes for giving the Holy Spirit to a believer is to supply power to overcome sin and live a holy life. Paul's statement to the believers in Corinth says it all. "I am jealous for you with a godly jealousy; for I betrothed you to one husband, that to Christ I might present you as a pure virgin (2 Corinthians 11:2-3). Our heavenly Husband is holy. As His bride, we are to be holy as well.

"For this is the will of God, your sanctification" (1 Thessalonians 4:3). The meaning of the word sanctification is "to be set apart." We have been set apart unto God by His Word and by the work of the Holy Spirit. We belong to God in every respect: spirit, soul and body. Paul dealt with the church at Corinth over sexual immorality. In Thessalonians, Paul specifically addressed the issue of idolatry and immorality. Both these evils cause culture to fall from a foundation which was to be established in God's moral law. The result has been for many of God's people to be drawn away from seeking after God and His holiness and drawn into idolatry and immorality.

Today, make the choice to be holy and ask the Holy Spirit for His help in your sanctification. He knows the weakness of our flesh and will help all who call upon Him. God the Father desires a pure bride for His Son. Today, and every day, ask the Holy Spirit for the grace to be able to present your body to God as a living sacrifice, holy and acceptable to your heavenly Father.

## March 7 – COME, KINGDOM OF GOD

Matthew 6:10 – Your kingdom come.

Jesus is calling the disciples into His ministry of declaring the kingdom of God. The first advent of the kingdom after our Lord was crucified, descended into hell, and on the third day rose from the dead, was the Holy Spirit poured out on the Day of Pentecost. He is the one who brought the kingdom to earth. He is the one that causes the will of God to be accomplished. Many believe the kingdom is a future event, but Jesus said to His disciples, "Behold, the kingdom of God is in your midst" (Luke 17:21). The KJV translates it this way, "the kingdom of God is within you." The kingdom was present because the king was present. Jesus is ruling from heaven. He sent the Holy Spirit to indwell each believer. The kingdom of God is present in the believer here and now.

Paul wrote, "The kingdom is in the Holy Spirit" (Romans 14:17). The kingdom of God came to earth when the Holy Spirit arrived. The will of God is being worked out through the Spirit even unto this day. We are to continue to pray for the kingdom to come, but with an emphasis of increase in the earth. From the days of the apostles to the present, one purpose of the Spirit has been to increase the kingdom of God in the earth until the whole earth is full of the glory of the Lord (see Habakkuk 2:14).

It is important to evaluate the increase of the kingdom of God in our own lives. Many receive Christ as their Savior, but neglect to receive Him as Lord in the present. We first ask for God's kingdom to come into us. We ask the Holy Spirit to take control in every area of our life. We then begin to share the kingdom of God with others, giving them an opportunity to receive God's grace. If they respond to the invitation, they too may have the kingdom of God reigning in their life through the power of the Holy Spirit. Each person who repents of their sins and invites the Holy Spirit to fill them receives the promise of the Father. When someone does this, they are receiving God's kingdom. What a wonderful gift the Father has given us through His Son!

As you pray "Your kingdom come, Your will be done," pray for the Holy Spirit to enlarge the kingdom of God in your life. Pray for the power to live a life fully committed to our great king and His kingdom purpose in the earth. Thank Him, for calling you into the kingdom of God and a relationship of service.

## March 8 – WILL OF GOD BE DONE

Matthew 6:10 – Your will be done

There is nothing more important than the will of God. His will reigns supreme above all else. God the Father has invited humanity to cooperate with His purposes.    The will of God is rooted in His purpose. Jesus is the full revelation of that purpose, *a new man*. Jesus completely fulfilled His Father's will through His human life. He was led by the Holy Spirit to represent God the Father and lay down His own life for the lost. In His redemptive work, He made it possible for all to be reconciled to the Father. Jesus has made it possible for each believer to also do God's will through the power of His Spirit.

Just as Jesus intercedes on our behalf, we have been invited to intercede on behalf of those yet needing redemption. Peter writes, "The Lord is not slow about His promise, as some count slowness, but is patient toward you, not wishing for any to perish but for all to come to repentance" (2 Peter 3:9). God's will is that each believer be matured in Christ and give testimony of God's salvation to others. Just think, if every believer was praying for the lost and sharing their faith, how many might be saved.

The Lord Jesus did the will of His Father when He walked on earth. He finished the work when He died for the sins of the entire world. The Father raised Him up through His surpassing power and seated Him in the highest authority at His own right hand. The purpose of our salvation is to be joined with the Lord in doing the Father's bidding on earth. Yes, we will go to heaven and be with Him throughout eternity, but for now, it is about doing His will.

God's will was accomplished through the Lord Jesus Christ, who is the only acceptable sacrifice for sin. He redeemed all of mankind once and for all. No other sacrifice is needed, only the blood of Jesus. The Holy Spirit was given to each believer to help us to be able to do God's will. He brought conviction for sin, righteousness, and judgment. He is bringing forth a *new man* in the earth. This new man is known as the corporate body of Christ. He made it possible *for the will* of God to be done in and through each believer's life.

Today, examine yourself and see if you are doing His will. Allow the Holy Spirit to reveal any areas of your life that fall short of the will of God. Quickly repent and renounce any of those areas He shows you. Receive the Holy Spirit in a fresh infilling of power and do the work of the Father in your life.

## March 9 – ON EARTH AS IN HEAVEN

Matthew 6:10 – On earth as it is in heaven.

God's will is for heaven's influence to be brought to earth. His plan from the beginning was that His creation man would fill the earth with the righteousness of heaven. He began by creating man in His own image. Because of man's disobedience in the Garden, sin entered the scene. In God's dealings with Adam and Eve, He looked down the annals of time and said, "I will put enmity between you and women, and between your seed and her seed; He shall bruise you on the head, and you shall bruise him on the heel" (Genesis 3:15). We have come to understand that the Lord was speaking about the battle between Satan and Christ.

Jesus came to provide redemption for all mankind. In the process, Satan bruised Him through the crucifixion, but Christ the Lord crushed Satan's ability to stop the advancement of the Lord's kingdom purpose in the earth. One day, the old earth and heaven will be destroyed and a new heaven and earth created. "The day of the Lord will come like a thief in the night, in which the heavens will pass away with a roar and the elements will be destroyed with intense heat, and the earth and its works will be burned up" (2 Peter 3:10). This is a prophetic mystery about which the Scriptures speak. We should not get hung up in mysteries and things which are not altogether clear. We need to trust God about the future, while in the present we seek His face to know His will for our daily lives. As long as we draw breath, we are called to affect the earth with heaven's perspective and heaven's authority.

Worship and praise must be a continual throughout my life, for this is a part of bringing heaven to earth. My daily walk should include intimate fellowship with the Godhead. This is bringing heaven to earth. As I observe needs in the lives of people, I am a ready servant to help meet those needs as God enables me. This is bringing heaven to earth. As I allow the Holy Spirit to fill me and release His gifts through me to others, this is bringing heaven to earth. God's love for me and God's love in me released to others in my daily walk, most assuredly helps bring heaven to earth. Keep this phrase in your mind "on earth as in heaven" it will help you to be more sensitive to the Holy Spirit and His plans.

Father, I pray that my life will be used to manifest heaven's will here on earth. Please continue to change me into Christ's likeness. Help me put on the mind of Christ in all that I do and in everything that I say. Lord, You are faithful, so please cause me to be faithful in doing Your will consistently.

## March 10 – GIVE US TODAY, TOMORROW'S SUPPLY

Matthew 6:11 – Give us this day our daily bread.

Our God is the God of today just as He was the God of yesterday and will be the God of tomorrow. It is today that our need is greatest. God takes from His eternal storehouse to supply us on a daily basis. The writer of Hebrews tells us, "Draw near to God with confidence to the throne of grace, so we may receive mercy and find grace to help in time of need" (Hebrews 4:16). James reminds us that "every good thing given and every perfect gift is from above, coming down from the Father of lights, with whom there is no variation or shifting shadow"(James 1:17).

God just does not change. He is our Rock and our fortress. The Holy Spirit is the Spirit of the Father and He shows us the Father's will. For every need we may possibly have, we can receive the Father's resources by the Holy Spirit. Shadows change as the sun moves across the sky, but God never changes. God spoke through the prophet Malachi stating, "I the Lord do not change; therefore you, O sons of Jacob, are not consumed" (Malachi 3:6). God supplied all of Israel's needs even as they demonstrated stubbornness and rebellion through disobedience. How much more will He give us our daily need because of what Jesus has established for us in a better covenant? Jesus fulfilled His Father's will on earth and made it possible for each of us to receive our portion from the Father's supply.

Come with confidence, asking the Father for bread. It may be natural food or it may be the bread of healing as with the Canaanite woman in Matthew 15. It may be a passage the Holy Spirit gives in order to help bring you through a tough time. We call this "the bread of His Word." Jesus is the bread which came down from heaven to feed the whole world.

Father, I thank You for the promise that you will supply all of my needs according to Your riches in glory by Christ Jesus, the Lord. Please grant me an increasing grace to trust You daily. As I trust in You, help me to be an inspiration to others in their time of difficulty.

## March 11 – OUR DAILY BREAD

Matthew 6:11 – Give us today our daily bread.

In the Old Testament, the priests were required to bake fresh showbread every day. The showbread spoke of *His Presence*. God's presence was made flesh in the person of the Lord Jesus Christ. He is the Bread that came down from Heaven. Jesus said to the multitudes, "I am the Bread of life; he who comes to Me will never hunger" (John 6:35). Eating of this Bread fills us up, eating of this Bread satisfies, eating of this Bread will sustain us when everything else seems to be lacking.

The Holy Spirit of God has come as the comforter. He is the one who indwells us. He is the spirit of the Father and of the Son. He is the one who supplies us with the spiritual food necessary for our daily existence. He is the promised "daily bread." He feeds us with God's Word, He releases God's gifts through us for others, and He builds up our inner man so we might mature in the Lord. Whenever I turn to the Holy Spirit, He brings refreshment which cannot be compared to anything else in this world. The Psalmist expresses it like this, "Because Thy loving-kindness is better than life, my lips will praise Thee. So I will bless Thee as long as I live; I will lift up my hands in Thy name. My soul is satisfied as with marrow and fatness, and my mouth offers praises with joyful lips" (Psalm 63:3-5).

Allow the Comforter to have His full way in your life today. He has Bread for you right now that will nourish and sustain you. Every day, turn to Him and say, "Give me this day the Bread you have for my life. I ask for my spirit, soul, and body to feed daily upon the presence of Your life.

Father, You are my resting place. I feed at Your table and drink from Your cup. I want to thank You for being my source and supply. It is You that sustains me.


## March 12 – FORGIVE US OUR DEBTS

Matthew 6:12 – Forgive us our debts.

We are born as debtors. This view is an offense to many who refuse to accept their fallen condition before God. As an infant we are innocent, but it is an innocence that comes from a lack of knowledge. As we develop, we become aware of our guilt before the creator. The beginning point for our relationship with the Father is when we accept our condition and ask for His forgiveness through Jesus Christ.

When we are born again through the work of God's Holy Spirit, our sins are forgiven and removed. The Scriptures tell us that He removes our sins "as far as the East is from the West" (Psalm 103:12). We still have to deal with the challenge of sin which is in our members. Study Romans 5 for a more complete understanding of this truth. With the Father's forgiveness, we receive a responsibility and obligation to forgive the debt of others. We remain debtors made free by the blood of Christ. We are humbled by the fact that the Father loved us in spite of the enmity that existed between Him and mankind. When we are filled with the Holy Spirit, we are delighted to have been given power to forgive others their debt toward us.

For the individual who is living their life by the leading of the Spirit, unforgiveness ceases to be a problem. Forgiveness of others is at the core of the foundation we have in the cleansing of the blood of Christ. Because He has forgiven us, we must forgive others! The Scriptures are emphatic about this topic. When we fail to forgive as we have been forgiven, a door is opened for the enemy to attack us. Jesus' cleansing blood is our defense against the devil, but this fact is rooted in our willingness to forgive. Study Matthew 18 for a larger understanding of the importance of forgiveness.

Ask the Holy Spirit to show you areas in your life where you have not yet surrendered to God's rule. Ask forgiveness and commit all He shows you to His authority. Ask Him to show you anyone that you need to forgive. Pray for His power to live a life that is above reproach for His glory.

## March 13 – WE HAVE FORGIVEN OUR DEBTORS

Matthew 6:12 – Forgive us our debts, as we also have forgiven our debtors.

The power to forgive is one of the greatest gifts the Father has given His children. Forgiveness is a lifestyle that we grow into while walking with the Lord. Offenses are a regular part of life. Forgiveness is an ebb and flow that we learn how to practice. As the Father consistently forgives us, so we are to forgive those who sin against us. We have been given the power to forgive by His indwelling Spirit.

Matthew 18:15-35 contains some of the most powerful passages in all of Scripture. The whole chapter basically deals with the subject of offenses. Here is a summation of what Jesus taught. If your brother sins against you, go to him alone and confront him. If he listens, you have won your brother. If he does not listen to you, take one or two others. If he refuses to listen then tell the church. If he refuses to listen to the church, let him be to you as a sinner. This led Peter to ask, how often should one forgive? Jesus clearly teaches us that forgiveness is ceaseless for the child of God. Jesus then gives the parable of the unforgiving servant and the results of unforgiveness. Jesus uses some very strong language when He says, "My heavenly Father will also do the same to you, if each of you does not forgive his brother from your heart" (Matthew 18:35).

This implies that Satan, our enemy, is able to imprison and torment those who do not forgive. Forgiving others is the key to real victory in the Christian life. Through many years of ministry, I have learned how unforgiveness is at the root of most problems in an individual's life. It is one of the greatest avenues for the enemy's access to our lives.

Ask the Father, "Is there anyone I have not forgiven?" If so, ask for grace and power to forgive them. Yield to the Holy Spirit and be filled with forgiving grace for those who have hurt you or wronged you in anyway.  Experience the liberty of walking in true forgiveness as a son or daughter of God.

## March 14 – REMEMBERING THOSE THAT ARE OFFENDED WITH YOU

Matthew 5:24 – If you are presenting your offering at the altar, and there remember
your brother has something against you, leave your offering there before the altar and go; first be reconciled to your brother, then come and present your offering.

Wow! Jesus is raising all religious activity to a new level of personal reconciliation. It all began with the heart of God. He became one of us in the person of Christ Jesus, so He would be able to reconcile the world to Himself. He did this while we were still in our trespasses and sins. This is the reason the Father puts such high priority on *reconciliation* and *forgiveness*.

In Matthew 18, we see how important it is to forgive any that sinned against us. Here in Matthew 5, Jesus makes it clear that we must first become right with any person holding an offense toward us, before our offering is accepted by God. The Father has given each believer His nature of *reconciliation* through the power of the Holy Spirit. "God was in Christ reconciling the world unto Himself, not counting their trespasses against them, and He has committed to us the word of reconciliation" (2 Corinthians 5:19).

The letters of the apostles are filled with admonitions concerning relationships among the believers. Here are a few examples: "Be devoted to one another in brotherly love; give preference to one another in honor (Romans 12:10-11), "Be kind to one another, tender-hearted, forgiving each other, just as God in Christ also has forgiven you" (Ephesians 4:32-5:1), "Therefore, confess your sins to one another, and pray for one another, so that you may be healed" (James 5:16). As believers, we are to walk out the reconciliation God has given us by being reconciled to one another, in the fear of God, whether it be forgiving another their offense toward us, or asking forgiveness of one against whom we have sinned.

Father, thank You for extending Your reconciling love to my life. Fill me with Your Holy Spirit to walk in the power of reconciliation. Help me to fulfill Your will to be a minister of reconciliation in this world.

## March 15 – LET NOT TEMPTATION OVERCOME ME

Matthew 6:13 – Lead us not into temptation.

Why would Jesus teach us to pray this way when Scripture clearly teaches, "God tempts no man" (James 1:13)? Jesus was modeling for His disciples how to be led by God. Jesus knew that He was being led into temptation for our sakes. Jesus was aware that He would stand between heaven and hell for all mankind. As He contemplated the cross with all the sufferings He was about to endure, He knew that the enemy would come one more time to tempt Him. Jesus was teaching His disciples to yield completely to the Father. If the Father chose for them to go through temptation, He would keep them in that hour. God Himself does not tempt any man, but life is full of temptation. Our prayer should be for God to lead us around or through those times of temptation.

Scriptures declare, "I will never leave you nor forsake you, that you can boldly say the Lord is my helper, in Him will I trust" (Hebrews 13:5-6). Is that your testimony in the Holy Spirit? Do you know He is always with you? There may be times when you do not sense His presence, but will you trust His Word of promise? The Holy Spirit is the promise of the Father and of the Son. Jesus said, "I will pray the Father and He shall give you another Comforter, that He may abide with you forever" (John 14:16).

Today, look to Jesus who is the author and the finisher of our faith. He authored and finished the work for you. He was tempted in every way, yet He did not sin. Temptation surrounds us beloved, but Jesus has overcome on our behalf. Pray for His overcoming life to fill you and to guide you in all that you do.

Are you presently facing temptation? Call on the Father and ask Him to lead you through this time. Ask Him to use the hour of temptation to strengthen you. Ask Him for grace to overcome the evil one. Give the reins of your life to the Holy Spirit and watch Him work the mighty works of God in and through you.

## March 16 – BEING DELIVERED FROM THE EVIL ONE

Matthew 6:13 – Deliver us from evil.

Evil surrounds us in the world system. Paul teaches in Ephesians 2:2 that the devil is the prince of the power of the air. He is the prince of this world and the world's systems. The phrase "the prince of this world" speaks about the world's systems and governments. Evil forces are behind the world's systems. The good news is that this prince has been judged (John 16:11). The prince of the world killed the Prince of Life, whom God has raised from the dead (Acts 3:15). This was the beginning of deliverance and freedom for the inhabitants of the earth. Today, a man reigns from heaven, the man Christ Jesus.

We too, have power over the evil one because of Jesus. Jesus told His disciples, "I give you power to tread on serpents and scorpions, and over all the power of the enemy, and nothing shall by any means hurt you (Luke 10:19). Through faith and obedience we are more than conquerors in Christ Jesus. Our deliverance from evil began with Jesus' sacrifice, resurrection, and ascension to the right hand of the Majesty on High. The Father and Jesus poured out their Holy Spirit to bring refreshing from their presence. Jesus instructed the disciples to "wait in Jerusalem, until they were given power from on high" (Acts 1:8). The word "power" in the original language meant authority. Jesus gave His disciples authority to proclaim to the nations the good news of the kingdom of God. Jesus is now reigning as King! Speaking to the philosophers on Mars Hill, Paul proclaimed, "God is now declaring to men that all people everywhere should repent, because He has fixed a day in which He will judge the world in righteousness (Acts 17:30).

The power or authority which the Lord released on the Day of Pentecost is still being released today. We cannot overcome the evil one without the power of God. It is the Holy Spirit who gives believers power and authority against the kingdom of darkness.  Prayer was the beginning of the early believer's preparation. The work of God continues today through the prayers of God's people. God's grace of power is released through faithful, obedient sons and daughters. Our deliverance is not automatic, but effectual through righteous prayer. See James 5:16.

Father, I ask to be delivered from evil. Strengthen me with the spirit of obedience. Thank You for giving to me Your faith and authority to obey and live Your life of righteousness.  Thank you for giving me the overcoming life of Christ in the power of the Holy Spirit.

## March 17 – KINGDOM POWER AND GLORY ARE HIS FOREVER

Matthew 6:13 – For Yours is the kingdom, and the power, and the glory forever.

What a powerful declaration of truth! Jesus directs everything back to the Father. The Holy Spirit was poured out on believers to work the works of the Father in the earth. The first thing the Holy Spirit established was God's reign in the earth. On the Day of Pentecost, the Holy Spirit came on those waiting for Him in the upper room. He began to rule in the lives of individuals. From this place of His ruling flowed power, power to transform and govern in the lives of those who have trusted in Christ. "The kingdom of God is not coming with signs to be observed; nor will they say,' Look, here it is!' or, 'There it is!' For behold, the kingdom of God is in your midst" (Luke 17:20-21).

The Lord revealed how He was working in the earth through the apostles and the early church. The same Holy Spirit power continues today. The productivity of His rule and power is a manifestation of His glory. Ultimately, we will share in the fullness of His glory when Christ returns, but for now, the glory is revealed through committed, Spirit-filled lives. Jesus said, "It is your Father's good pleasure to give you the kingdom" (Luke 12:32). Paul instructed the church to "Walk in a manner worthy of the God who calls you into His own kingdom and glory" (1 Thessalonians 2:12). This is the work of the Spirit, releasing the kingdom of God to those who believe and using each believer for the glory of God.

The kingdom of God is now and is yet to be some day. I say now, because the Holy Spirit lives in the believer and helps us do the will of God. It is in the future, because there is yet a day when Christ Jesus will gather to Himself all that are His. Together with Christ, we will judge this world and the angels. The Scriptures declare that we will rule with Him in eternity. The writers of the New Testament continually establish a balance between *then and now*. Our responsibility is to examine our lives and determine if the Lord is indeed ruling. This is a daily process in our thoughts and actions toward others. Our calling is to present to the world a lifestyle that is led by the Lord. Corporately, we are to be a people that demonstrate the goodness of God. We are to bring to bear an influence, first by prayer and then by our actions. The direct influence of God's kingdom in the earth is because of the Holy Spirit's presence. Consider the testimony of the apostles and the early believers in Acts 15:3-4.

Father, help me examine my life and honestly determine where Jesus is reigning as Lord. Help me see those areas I have yet to surrender to Your rule. I pray for Your kingdom rule in every part of my life, for Your glory.

# March 18 – THE POOR IN SPIRIT ARE BLESSED

Matthew 5:3 – Blessed are the poor in spirit, for theirs is the kingdom of heaven.

The poor in spirit are all those who have suffered under this world's system. These are the oppressed, neglected, and underclass who are the majority of people in the world. Jesus came for such as these. "The Spirit of the Lord is upon Me, because He anointed Me to preach the gospel to the poor. He has sent Me to proclaim release to the captives, and recovery of sight to the blind, to set free those who are downtrodden, to proclaim the favorable year of the Lord" (Luke 4:18-19). The kingdom of God goes to the deepest areas of an individual's life, to heal the broken spirit. The good news is that there is a King who reigns in heaven and cares about the hurting of this world. Christ redeems those who have been made captive in their circumstances through a system controlled by Satan's kingdom. Although they might suffer in this life, they are to rejoice in the *promise* that the kingdom of God "belongs to them."

There is a change coming! Even if one's circumstances are oppressed, the Holy Spirit has come to first make the human spirit alive. To the one who is born again, He makes available the experience of a deep abiding joy which the world cannot steal. All of this begins in the spirit and finds its way into the chambers of the soul. Paul's prayer for the church at Thessalonica was "Now may the God of peace Himself sanctify you entirely; and may your spirit, soul, and body be preserved complete, without blame at the coming our Lord Jesus Christ" (1 Thessalonians 5:23).

This explains why so many persecuted believers are able to have such joy in the midst of oppression which comes through the systems of the world. This also explains why believers are able to stay afloat through the many struggles that take place in life. Even during financial setbacks, sickness, or relational difficulties, they still remain strong. One who is strong in their spirit, knowing they have been given the kingdom, is able to rise up in this life and demonstrate God's provision. God makes them rich in their spirit and strong in their kingdom lifestyle.

Today, allow the Holy Spirit to establish you in His grace regardless of your circumstances. Claim your portion in Christ and rest in all He has promised for the future. Father, thank You for all of Your promises, beginning with this promise of Your blessing to my spirit.

## March 19 – THOSE THAT MOURN WILL BE COMFORTED

Matthew 5:4 – Blessed are those who mourn, for they shall be comforted.

Multitudes throughout the ages have known what it is to mourn. We may mourn the passing of a loved one, the loss of a child, a war casualty, calamities, or the loss of property such as a house or finances. Consider the oppression people suffer throughout the world. Modern day news coverage allows us to observe people weeping and lamenting their present day circumstances. Because of these first-hand observations, many become moved with compassion to share their resources with those who are suffering. Many times believers have experienced the prompting of the Holy Spirit to reach out in practical ways to those in need. There is a good reason why Jesus called the Holy Spirit "the Comforter." Only the Spirit of God can comfort completely those who are mourning. True comfort can only be brought by what Jesus promised in Matthew 5:4.

Have you ever been hindered by your lack of words or ability to comfort another? Have you ever felt helpless during times when a person has experienced the death of a loved one, a calamity of some kind, or when their life is being oppressed by some difficult circumstance? At these times, it can be humanly impossible to bring comfort. As a believer, we have received the necessary grace from the Holy Spirit, to come alongside an individual and speak a word of comfort through the inspiration He gives. There will be a day in which we will know the totality of the Spirit's comfort. The Scriptures speak of the day in which all our tears will be wiped away. "He shall wipe away every tear from their eyes; and there shall no longer be any death, there shall no longer be any mourning, or crying, or pain; the first things have passed away" (Revelation 21:4).

The only answer for the conditions found in a fallen world, is found in Christ. The believer has the answers dwelling within through the person of the Holy Spirit. All His fruit, His gifts, and His power is available to those who have put their faith in Christ. Allow the Holy Spirit freedom and total access to use you for the glory of God.

As the old gospel song declares, "The Comforter has come, the Holy Ghost from heaven, the Father's promise given." Today, allow His comfort be your portion. He will give you peace and assurance in every situation. He will use you to minister comfort to another.

## March 20 – THE EARTH BELONGS TO THE LORD AND TO HIS PEOPLE

Matthew 5:5 – Blessed are the gentle for they shall inherit the earth.

Gentleness demands humility. The arrogant do not practice gentleness or meekness. One evidence of a Spirit-filled life is the fruit of gentleness (Galatians 5:22). There are many who try to move ahead in life with an arrogant attitude. Usually, this person is filled with selfishness, only thinking about their success no matter how it may affect others. This character flaw is especially seen in the business world, the entertainment industry, and the political arena. A drive for power and control is behind arrogance and selfishness. It can be observed that most of these people end up losing in life. Many times their dreams are dashed by heartbreak and loss.

The Scriptures teach, and many lives demonstrate, that gentleness is the way to success. Jesus is teaching a key to life's success in Matthew 5:5. Humility, which demonstrates gentleness, will help bring success. Through gentleness the Holy Spirit touches the hearts of people and opens opportunities. Individuals are moved to reach out and help the gentle person. Opportunities come, doors open, and a way is made for the gentle person to be received as their reputation begins to be spread.

Some people are gentle by nature. This is a human quality which is rare and honorable. As Jesus brings into focus His Kingdom, He is anticipating those that would be filled with His Holy Spirit, demonstrating the fruit of the Spirit in all of their relationships. Paul said, "All things are ours. So then let no one boast in men, for all things belong to you" (1 Corinthians 3:21). All things belong to the child of God, but we must see this corporately. As an individual, I cannot claim all things at all times, but the Lord blesses His body throughout the earth. Remember Paul's teaching when he said, "There are many members, but one body" (1 Corinthians 12:20). As members of the body of Christ, we enter into His promised inheritance through humility and gentleness, not arrogance or pride.

Ask the Holy Spirit to increase growth in you regarding gentleness. Ask Him to show you what He has set aside in the earth as your inheritance. Father, I thank You for Your promise that the gentle shall inherit the earth.

## March 21- HUNGER AND THIRST FOR RIGHTEOUNESS

Matthew 5:6 – Blessed are those who hunger and thirst for righteousness, for they shall be satisfied.

As humans, we find ourselves in an impossible situation from a natural perspective. We are slaves to sin. The righteousness of the Law of God continually declares us to be guilty. The Scribes and Pharisees perverted the Law and brought the people under religious bondage by human means. Jesus said, "Unless your righteousness surpasses theirs, you will not enter the kingdom of heaven" (Matthew 5:20). Even the keeping of their strict application of the Law fell short of the requirements of God.

There is a void in every human, a void of the righteousness of God. This void can only be filled by the righteousness of Christ Jesus. "There is none righteous, not even one" (Romans 3:10). People deal with this condition in different ways. Some pervert the need to fill the void by feeding the unrighteousness with increasingly unrighteous acts. Others try to satisfy their need through religion, trying to get to God on their terms. The Scripture says, "We all have sinned and fallen short of the glory of God" (Romans 3:23). Throughout the ministry of Jesus, He taught how to satisfy this hunger and thirst. We learn that Jesus is the Way in John 14:6. Each person who has received the Lord, by giving their life to Him, knows firsthand that He alone satisfies the longing for the void to be filled. We must continually draw on the righteousness of Jesus Christ to know and experience the true *satisfaction* He alone can bring.

It is not by our performance that we find satisfaction, but through relationship alone. A relationship rooted in Christ Jesus fulfilling the entire requirement of the Father. A relationship filled with the acceptance of our heavenly Father. The true satisfaction comes from knowing that God loves me and in His love I am fully accepted.

Father, I ask for a deepening hunger and thirst for Your righteousness. Release the Holy Spirit to draw me closer to Jesus. I join in the writer of Hebrews' prayer that we may fix "our eyes on Jesus, the author and perfecter of our faith" (Hebrews 12:2).

## March 22 – BE MERCIFUL, EVEN AS YOU HAVE RECEIVED MERCY

Matthew 5:7 – Blessed are the merciful, for they shall receive mercy.

Sir Isaac Newton first presented his three laws of motion in 1686. His third law states "that for every action (force) in nature there is an equal and opposite reaction." In other words, if object A exerts a force on object B, then object B also exerts an equal and opposite force on object A.

Newton was given revelation by God relating to a law of physics, but we have been given revelation by God in the spiritual realm. When you are merciful, it sets up a spiritual law of receiving mercy. This is true about all the Beatitudes. God's life exerts a spiritual force of mercy upon us. We in turn exert a spiritual force upon others by showing *mercy*. They in turn become open to receiving mercy from God and give mercy back. In the law of the Spirit, the Scripture says, "Give, and it shall be given to you" (Luke 6:38). One of the evidences of the new birth in an individual is their desire to give to others.

Let us consider a few biblical statements that bear witness to this truth. Consider what the Psalmist said, "Those who sow in tears shall reap with joyful shouting" (Ps 126:5). Brokenness over others and their condition carries the promise that God will honor your brokenness with a day when the watering from your tears will give a crop of salvation that will produce in you a joy that cannot be contained.

Again consider what Paul said, "If we sowed spiritual things in you, is it too much if we should reap material things from you? (1 Corinthians 9:11). This is a Principle or Law in the New Testament. When God sends those who carry spiritual things that are imparted to our lives, we in turn should respond by supporting that person through financial gifts. The spiritual person gives from his heart. He does it freely.  A right response in *mercy* is to give what we have to help others who cannot repay us at all.

Mercy is manifested in a variety of ways. Ask the Holy Spirit to show you increased avenues to give mercy. You can be confident that there will be numerous occasions when you will also receive mercy from God and others.

## March 23 – IT IS THE PURE IN HEART THAT WILL SEE GOD

Matthew 5:8 – Blessed are the pure in heart, for they shall see God.

When the Scripture speaks of purity of heart, it is addressing motivations. The subject of the heart is a large topic in God's Word. Here are some samplings. God searches the heart (Jeremiah 17:10). Unbelief comes from a hardened heart (Mark 8:17). Jesus knew what they were thinking in their hearts (Luke 9:47). The heart is where one's treasure is (Luke 12:34). The heart is where secrets are kept (1 Corinthians 14:25). Paul prayed for the eyes of the heart to be enlightened, so that we may know what is the hope of His calling (Ephesians 1:18). Consider Paul's admonition in Colossians 3:12-13. "So, as those who have been chosen of God, holy and beloved, put on a heart of compassion, kindness, humility, gentleness and patience; bearing with one another, and forgiving each other, whoever has a complaint against anyone; just as the Lord forgave you, so also you forgive." The pure in heart have received forgiveness and forgiven all those who have sinned against them.

The heart is what I call "the seedbed of our emotions." It is the deepest area in a person's being. Some connect the heart to our human spirit. The pure in heart are those who have opened to God every secret they hold. The pure in heart have repented of unbelief. Although they do not understand everything yet, they trust completely in God. The pure in heart are becoming a treasure house of godliness. This new heart of purity must be received. Paul said to "put on a heart of compassion, kindness, humility, gentleness, and patience" (Colossians 3:12). These qualities are not the fruits of a good idea, but of a pure heart!

Today, why not join in Paul's prayer for the church at Ephesus "that the eyes of your heart may be enlightened to know the hope of His calling". It is in that seeking of God's will and purpose that our hearts are changed and purity begins to form. Ask the Holy Spirit for a pure heart. Allow Him to identify areas in your life in need of His cleansing power.

## March 24 – CALLED TO LEAD THE PROCESSION OF PEACE

Matthew 5:9 – Blessed are the peacemakers, for they shall be called sons of God.

Jesus said, "Do not think that I came to bring peace on the earth; I did not come to bring peace, but a sword" (Matthew 10:34). This statement seems to be in direct contrast to what Jesus said in the Sermon on the Mount. Is He contradicting himself? Jesus is the Prince of Peace. At His birth, the angels announced, "peace on earth, good will to men" (Luke 2:14). In Matthew 10:34, Jesus is describing the separation of those who belong to His Father from those belonging to this world's systems. Many families and nations have divided over Jesus Christ, the Son of God. Jesus made it possible to have peace inside oneself, with one's neighbors, and even among the nations. The hardness of men's hearts keeps peace from being a reality. Many today pray for the peace of Jerusalem, not understanding the answer to that prayer was a person and not a city. The Prince of peace entered the city, but they received Him not.

Jesus reconciled us to God through His sacrificial death on the cross. "Therefore having been justified by faith, we have peace with God through our Lord Jesus Christ" (Romans 5:1). He made peace possible for all those who would believe on Him. This has enraged the world's systems against those who are the sons of God. We are peace carriers as Jesus was, but many reject the peace we carry and in doing so, reject becoming a son of God. Peace is in the Father's DNA. That same peace is in every true son and daughter of God. Those who will not harden their hearts can become peacemakers. To those whose hearts are hardened in unbelief, Christ's peacemakers will be a problem. This is what the sons of God do. On one hand they offer peace, on the other, they cause division. There have been many times when the Lord sent me to stir the pot. In doing so, I found out who really wanted the peace of God.

Ask our Father to make you a peacemaker, while realizing there will be some that will reject you as "a son of God." Ask the Holy Spirit for His strength to help you be faithful in your role as a peacemaker. The world still rejects the "Prince of Peace," but those who receive Him have peace beyond comprehension.

## March 25 – PERSECUTION FOR RIGHTEOUNESS SAKE

Matthew 5:10 – Blessed are those who have been persecuted for the sake of righteousness, for theirs is the kingdom of heaven.

Most in the western world do not have an appreciation for Jesus' statement. We might receive some rejection from folks, but for the most part, Christianity has been accepted. This is not at all true in many places in the world. A Jewish convert may be rejected by their own family. In the Islamic world, a price can be put on one's head. A family member would be honored for killing the Christian convert. In places like Pakistan, the Christian is paid the lowest of wages and has a difficult time getting ahead. In China, many are in prison for not being part of the so-called state-run church.

When the church in the West begins to stand up against unrighteousness, it will draw persecution. Today, many have suffered financially and even gone to jail for trying to protect the life of innocent babies in the womb. In our government, there are those who want to silence those who are crying out against the injustices in today's society. The Scriptures command us to obey the laws of the land. There are those who are calling on the government to enforce laws that were implemented to protect us. Many are persecuted for their righteous positions by a government that is sworn to uphold the law and provide protection for each member of society.

Today, in America, preachers have to make a choice between easy street and persecution for righteousness sake. The true believer must be willing to be persecuted, but one must be sure it is for *righteousness* and not one's individual morality. It must be a righteousness that comes from God, rooted in Jesus Christ, and clearly supported by the Word of God.

Ask the Lord to make clear what He considers "righteousness." Surrender to His will for your life and ask Him for strength to endure hardship for righteousness' sake. Then enter into your Lord's kingdom reign by allowing the Holy Spirit to lead you.

## March 26 – PERSECUTED LIKE THE PROPHETS

Matthew 5:11-12 – Blessed are you when people insult you and persecute you, and falsely say all kinds of evil against you because of Me. Rejoice and be glad, for your reward in heaven is great; for in the same way they persecuted the prophets who were before you.

It is amazing how some Christians expect everyone to like and honor them for good works on behalf of Jesus. As we stand against all that is represented in this world's system, we draw fire from those who love the system. The Psalmist asks the question, "Why are the nations in uproar and the peoples devising a vain thing? The kings of the earth take their stand

and the rulers take counsel together against the Lord and against His anointed, saying let us tear their fetters apart and cast away their cords from among us" (Psalm 2:1-3). In a few parts of the world, there has been a higher tolerance for Christ's people, but in most places He and His people are hated. We know why from the Scriptures! Satan influences their minds through demonic strongholds. The apostle Paul spoke to this subject in detail in his writings to the churches (2 Corinthians 10:1-5; Ephesians 1:15-23; 6:10-20; Colossians 2:8-15).

The Holy Spirit was sent to fill God's people with the life of Christ and His power over Satan's domain. Whenever the church has been persecuted, it seems to advance. In Matthew 5:11, the Lord promised blessing when we are insulted or persecuted. Our flesh wants to run from the pressure of resisting evil, but Paul encourages us to be strong in our spirit, "Only conduct yourselves in a manner worthy of the gospel of Christ; so that whether I come and see you or remain absent, I may hear of you that you are standing firm in one spirit, with one mind striving together for the faith of the gospel; in no way alarmed by your opponents—which is a sign of destruction for them, but of salvation for you, and that too, from God" (Philippians 1:27).

The great testimony of Christ in us is the ability to conduct ourselves in a fashion which honors our Lord. His Holy Spirit gives us power to live above the world's system. Standing firm is standing strong. It is a corporate action, that is, we need others who are also standing firm in the faith. Together, we resist demonic strongholds, knowing their destruction is assured.

Ask the Holy Spirit to show you areas in your life where He can help you live in a manner worthy of the gospel. Ask Him for strength to stand firm in your spirit and give to you others that are also standing firm with the same mind.

## March 27 – REJOICE AND BE GLAD, FOR YOUR REWARD IN HEAVEN IS GREAT

Matthew 5:13 – Rejoice and be glad, for your reward in heaven is great.

Although there are many challenges in this life, we are passing through to a greater time where rewards will be given for faithfulness in the kingdom of God. Jesus promises a "great" reward to those who have suffered insults and persecution for His sake. "He who receives a prophet in the name of a prophet is promised a prophet's reward" (Matthew 10:41). "When you receive a righteous man in the name of a righteous man, you receive a righteous man's reward" (Matthew 10:41). Even the giving of cold water qualifies one for a reward (Matthew 10:42). "When you lend, expecting nothing in return, your reward is great" (Luke 6:35). Paul says, "Each one will receive their own reward according to their own work "(1 Corinthians 3:8). Works that are built upon an imperishable foundation will receive a reward according to 1 Corinthians 3:14.

Don't throw away your confidence, because it has a great reward (Hebrews 10:35). John the apostle said, "Watch yourselves that you might not lose what we have accomplished, but that you may receive a full reward" (2 John 8). The Lord Jesus Christ promised that He "is coming quickly and His reward is with Him, to render to every man according to what he has done" (Revelation 22:12).

Finally, diligence carries the promise of reward "But without faith it is impossible to please Him, for he who comes to God must believe that He is, and that He is a rewarder of those who diligently seek Him" (Hebrews 11:6 NKJV). One does not have to wait for heaven to begin receiving rewards from our gracious Savior. Faithful diligence releases God's favor throughout one's life.

Ask the Holy Spirit to show you about His reward for you. The Father loves to give to His children. Don't be bashful about expecting to receive rewards from Him. The Holy Spirit loves to honor the sons and daughters of God in this life. So be in a receiving mode now and in an expectant mode about the future.

# March 28 – YOU ARE THE PRESERVATIVE OF THE EARTH

Matthew 5:13 – You are the salt of the earth; but if the salt has become tasteless, how can it be made salty again? It is no longer good for anything, except to be thrown out and trampled underfoot by men.

As Jesus addresses the multitudes, He is speaking to the people of the Nation that God had chosen to impact all the other nations by pointing them to Jehovah, the redeeming God. They started out as "salt" when God made the promise to Abraham, Isaac, and Jacob. Moses led the enslaved people out of Egypt to receive God's Law at Mount Sinai. Joshua then led them into the land of promise to be God's hand of judgment and an example to the nations of what it is like to serve the living God and not idols. The Holy Spirit of God made the people of Israel "salt" to the nations.

They were still called to be the salt of the earth when their Messiah came to revive them by becoming the sacrifice for their sins and healing their land. All they needed to do was receive and believe on their Messiah and then receive the promise of the coming Holy Spirit. Only a remnant of Israel trusted Christ by believing the scriptures through preaching. On the Day of Pentecost, a handful believed and received the Holy Spirit which Jesus poured out upon them. This was the beginning of a revived Israel whom Jesus called "My Church" (Matthew 16:18). Through the preaching of the Gospel of the kingdom, many Gentiles also believed and were included in this work of the Holy Spirit. The whole book of Acts tells the story of this great revival of God and the salty people He raised up by the work of the Holy Spirit.

The work of the Spirit continues today, as both Jewish people and Gentiles are coming to Christ. We are called the salt of the earth. As it was then, so it is today. We need a revival of our saltiness. Ask the Holy Spirit to make you salty so you can be the preservative He has ordained you to be.

Father, I ask you to show me any areas of my life that are not salty as you have purposed. Keep me from being "good for nothing." Fill me with your Holy Spirit, allowing Your life to overflow in all I do.

# March 29 –SALT THAT IS TASTELESS IS GOOD FOR NOTHING

Matthew 5:13 – It is no longer good for anything, except to be thrown out and trampled underfoot by men.

Jesus is warning the multitudes of Israel. For centuries this people had been "stiff-necked and stubborn" (Acts 7:51). For the next forty years, from the time Jesus returned from the desert to the destruction of Jerusalem and the Temple, the gospel was preached throughout Israel and the Roman Empire. That preaching reached out to the nations where the children of Israel had been scattered many years prior. Although only a remnant of Israel believed, many Gentiles turned to the Lord and became the salt God was seeking.

Over time, the church began to lose its saltiness and God would have to send the reviving power of the Holy Spirit. There comes a time when people won't receive what God the Holy Spirit is doing. I call this "becoming crystallized" in doctrine and form. God moves by His Spirit to revive His church and a remnant receives the present work of the Holy Spirit. Many that accepted the previous move of God become stuck and reject what God is currently doing. The last move becomes "tasteless" and "good for nothing" in effecting God's purpose.

We are presently in what some have called a "post-denominational" time. That means "denominationalism" is becoming less and less important. Each of the denominations served a purpose at a particular time in history, but when they crystallized, they began becoming salt less. I respect the denominations and their respective contributions to God's restoration plan for His church. Many precious saints are part of a particular denomination, but are also embracing the larger work of the Spirit in the whole of His Church. Paul helps us understand the Lord's view when he says, "He gave some as apostles, and some as prophets, and some as evangelists, and some as pastors and teachers for the equipping of the saints for the work of service, to the building up of the body of Christ; until we all attain to the unity of the faith, and of the knowledge of the Son of God, to a mature man, to the measure of the stature which belongs to the fullness of Christ" (Ephesians 4:11-13).

Ask the Holy Spirit to enlarge your view of His work in the earth. Ask Him to protect you from being tasteless. Ask Him to fill you afresh with Himself, that you might share with others the wonderful news of His salvation.

## March 30 – THE COVENANT OF SALT

2 Chronicles 13:5 – Do you not know that the Lord God of Israel gave the rule over Israel forever to David and his sons by a covenant of salt?

Salt in the Scriptures speaks of covenant. Offerings in the Old Testament were made with salt. As 1 Chronicles 13:5 states, God made a covenant of salt with David that "his sons would rule over Israel forever." God fulfilled His word to David when David's greater Son was seated at the right hand of the Majesty on High. The Lord Jesus Christ is the one who is now reigning as "the King of kings and Lord of lords."

On the mountain, Jesus taught His disciples, and now teaches us that we are to demonstrate the quality of salt. If we lose that divine attribute, we will be like sand, trodden under foot. Sand looks like salt, but is not cohesive like salt. Because the nation of Israel lost its saltiness, it was trodden underfoot. In like manner, the church has lost its ability to influence society as it once did. All is not lost though, because God desires to revive His people. He revived the nation of Israel throughout the Old Testament. His purpose was fully completed in Christ, the son of David. Jesus had in mind the restoration of the House of Judah and Israel, who became divided after the reign of Solomon. His message of repentance was to the nation of Israel to repent and receive the New Covenant sealed in His blood. The majority refused and thus was trodden underfoot in 70 AD, when Jerusalem along with their Temple was destroyed.

Today, God is reviving His church which, like Israel of old, has lost her saltiness. Jesus' words ring strong and true as they did when He spoke on the mountain. Today, He is calling His church to be revived and be the salt of the earth. His message is also going out to Jewish people. "Come to your Messiah, the son of David, and He will revive you and place you in the "household of God." In the same way He spoke to the seven churches of Asia Minor, He speaks today, "He who has an ear, let him hear what the Spirit says to the churches" (Revelation 3:22).

Father, I pray for Your revival power to be manifested in my life. Thank You for the covenant of salt made with David. Thank You for the covenant's fulfillment in Christ Jesus our Lord. Father, make me salty to my generation. Fill me with Your Holy Spirit and use me to lead others to Your covenant promises.

## March 31 – YOU ARE THE LIGHT OF THE WORLD

Matthew 5:14 – You are the light of the world. A city set on a hill cannot be hidden. Nor does anyone light a lamp and put it under a basket, but on a lamp stand, and it gives light to all who are in the house.

The light in the world is the Lord's church. Imagine what it would be like if the church was non-existent in the earth. Try to imagine America without the effect of the gospel on the Constitution and her laws. In fact, America would not exist as we have known her. As Jesus produces light in individual lives, whole nations are changed for the glory of God. "You" are the light of the world. Your world is where you have the opportunity to influence others for righteousness. Somebody asked the question, "If you were arrested for being a Christian, would there be enough evidence to convict you?" I hope so! If so, it would mean that you are a shining light for the Lord.

As the oil of the Holy Spirit is poured into our lives, it fuels the flame that emits the light from within. That light is manifested through your personality, the way you take care of yourself, and reaching out to others in the name of the Lord. His light is demonstrated by your unwavering conviction and obedience to God's Word, and your faithfulness to God's people through committed relationship. A life of service and humility demonstrates the work of the gospel in your inner man. Through the ministry of "Halloween Harvest," which was created by my friend, Mick McCoy, a pumpkin would be used to illustrate the need to first repent and allow the Lord to remove the sinfulness in our hearts, so the Holy Spirit can "light our candle."

Ask the Holy Spirit for fresh oil. We are leaky vessels and need to be filled afresh regularly, in fact many times in a day. He is present to fill you with His oil so you can keep the light burning brightly.

## April 1–BE A LIGHT TO ALL MEN BY LETTING THEM SEE YOUR GOOD WORKS

Matthew 5:16 – Let your light shine before men in such a way that they may see your good works and glorify your Father who is in heaven.

What a clear word from our Lord! "Let your light shine." We have to cooperate with the Holy Spirit in this matter of letting our light shine. He has placed the light in us, but we must choose to shine. Many times I have heard God's people say, "I know what I should do," but then they struggled in doing it. I remember one time I was very angry at an individual. My dad reminded me of my responsibility to forgive. I told my dad, "I know, but right now it feels good to be angry." Our emotions can snare us and keep us from being the kind of light God has ordained us to be.  A few hours later, I chose to forgive that person and be *a light of forgiveness* to him.

Jesus taught His disciples to pray in secret. There is a time to do business with God in secret, but here He says let your light shine before all men so they might "*see* your good works and glorify your Father who is in heaven." Witnessing is not simply about speaking words, but it is more about how we live our lives. The first week I was in the Army, I asked God, "How can I live for you in this place?" He spoke a surprising word to me. "Be you!" That meant, continue to serve the Lord, pray, read the Word of God and share when I can. That is what I did. I had the privilege of leading many men to Christ with the evidence of changed lives. Letting our light shine is a *lifestyle* lived out. It is in the living out of our faith on a daily basis that others will glorify our Father in heaven. When people begin to acknowledge there is something different about you, they are recognizing the light that is shining. God is glorified!

Ask the Holy Spirit to give you good works that cause the people around you to glorify your Father in heaven. Ask Him to quicken your mind regarding how you should respond in any given situation. He will show you your responsibility and give you the ability to reflect His nature. He will give you of His wisdom and His power in order for you to carry out His good pleasure.

## April 2 – THE LAW AND PROPHETS ARE FULFILLED IN CHRIST

Matthew 5:17 – Do not think that I came to abolish the Law or the Prophets; I did not come to abolish, but to fulfill.

Some teach that the Law has been done away with in the sacrifice of Christ. Some teach that the Old Testament is not relevant because we are now living in New Testament times. "Fulfilled," does not mean done away with, but to accomplish the purpose. The Ten Commandments are eternal truths. That means they cannot be put aside and neglected. It took the righteousness of Christ to fulfill all of the intent of the Law of God. Under the Law, the Sabbath was kept on prescribed days that were sanctified by God. Jesus fulfilled the Sabbath by becoming our Sabbath. Our rest is found in His Work, "For the one who entered His rest has himself also rested from his works as God did from His" (Hebrews 4:10). The writer of Hebrews goes on to say, "Therefore let us be diligent to enter that rest ..." (Hebrews 4:11).

God began His Sabbath rest in Genesis. He then established it in the Law and the Prophets, and found its completion in the Lord Jesus Christ. This is why Paul told the early churches not to let anyone act as your judge concerning food, drink, festival, new moon or Sabbath days (see Colossians 2:16). The whole second chapter of Colossians addresses this freedom that Christ purchased for all of us. The Holy Spirit has been sent from Heaven to be our Comforter and to bring forth the life of Christ in us. He enables us to enter into God's Sabbath Rest and live out the life of Christ fulfilling the Law and all that the Prophets had envisioned. Today, the people of God can live in obedience to God's commandments, not through religious works, but by the grace and rest of Christ in the power of the Holy Spirit.

If you are burdened with religious works and guilt, release them today to the Holy Spirit. In faith receive the rest of Christ. Be free to obey the Word of God, not by your works, but by His grace and power supplied by the Holy Spirit.

## April 3 – RIGHTEOUSNESS THAT SURPASSES THAT OF RELIGIOUS LEADERS

Matthew 5:20 – For I say to you that unless your righteousness surpasses that of the scribes and Pharisees, you will not enter the kingdom of heaven.

This is a powerful statement by our Lord that draws a line in the sand regarding righteousness. Jesus came to establish righteousness as God intended. The Holy Spirit was sent to produce His righteousness in each one that puts their faith in the work of Christ. Titus reminds us, "He saved us, not on the basis of deeds which we have done in righteousness, but according to His mercy, by the washing of regeneration and renewing of the Holy Spirit" (Titus 3:5). The "surpassing righteousness" of which Jesus is speaking became established in the work of the cross as He bore our sins. Our Father in heaven accepts the righteousness of Christ on our behalf. A believer is accepted by God as one fully fulfilling the Law of God, and its entire requirement for dealing with the penalty of sin. The Holy Spirit raised Christ from the dead (Romans 8:11), and He is now given as God's gift to all who trust Christ. He washes us, causing "regeneration" that is, He makes alive what was dead. The Holy Spirit "renews" us to the original purpose of God when He had created man.

As soon as we receive the work of Christ we are ushered into the kingdom of God. Some think that the kingdom is a future event. The scriptures make it clear "the kingdom is now, in the Holy Spirit" (Romans 14:17). In the future, there will be a greater manifestation of God's kingdom. Presently, each believer is to live under the reign of King Jesus through the Holy Spirit. Jesus was teaching two important principles. First, it takes a righteousness which exceeds the attempt of keeping the Law. This righteousness is connected to entering Jesus' Kingdom. Second, in the Romans passage above, Paul teaches that we enter the kingdom by receiving the Holy Spirit. Only the Spirit of God can supply the grace of righteousness and only the Spirit of God can usher us into the kingdom where Christ Jesus reigns as Lord.

Be renewed today in the righteousness of God. Let go of your own attempts to please God. Fully trust in Christ in all that He has done. Enjoy His kingdom rule, and walk in His righteousness in the power of His Spirit.

## April 4 – JESUS LIFTS THE BAR FOR LIFE LIVED IN HIS KINGDOM

Matthew 5:48 – Therefore you are to be perfect, as your heavenly Father is perfect.

In Matthew 5:21- 47 Jesus deals with relationships on many different levels. The Law forbade murder, but Jesus said, don't be angry with your brother. If you remember when giving your offering someone has something against you, leave your offering and go get reconciled to your brother. Read through these laws of the kingdom of God and ask the Holy Spirit to help you rise up to the life that our Lord has called us to live. The higher bar is what Jesus calls us to, even the perfection of our heavenly Father. This sounds impossible, but we have the Holy Spirit to help us.

The word perfect translates "mature." The Lord is looking for mature sons and daughters, those that will allow the life of Christ to be released in them by yielding to the Holy Spirit. We have been led by our flesh for so long that it is strange to think about being led by the Spirit. The only way we can consider being "perfect" is as the Holy Spirit takes control of our mind and we submit to him in everything.

My experience is that I have to take one situation at a time. This means I must pray about every relationship and submit it to God. Through the Spirit's empowerment, choose to keep short accounts with people, forgiving quickly, not letting the sun go down on my anger. These things are not easy, but the Holy Spirit will help us if we will stop and ask for His involvement.

In 1 Corinthians 14:20 the apostle says, "Brethren, do not be children in your thinking; yet in evil be babes, but in your thinking be mature." Paul is communicating the same view that Jesus is declaring in Matthew 5:48, "be perfect, as your heavenly Father is perfect." The New Creation is all about a new way of thinking, God's way of thinking. It is possible to be mature and live in righteousness, because we have been redeemed from our sin condition to a life of righteousness in the Holy Spirit.

Let the Holy Spirit search you heart and reveal any areas that are childish and not mature. Repent of childish views and attitudes. Then receive His infilling power to grow as a son or daughter of God.

## April 5 – BE A GIVER, BUT DO NOT PUBLISH YOUR GIVING HABITS

Matthew 6:2 – So when you give to the poor, do not sound a trumpet before you, as the hypocrites do in the synagogues and in the streets, so they may be seen by men.

Finances, for the most part, have been seen as a private affair. Typically, you do not ask a person "How much do you earn" or "How much money do you give to charity?" In this passage, Jesus is dealing with the "religious heart," a heart that is more interested in the praise of others than the need before them. In America, because our Founders gave us laws that were built upon eternal laws, they chose to reward people for "charitable giving." There is a time to report giving to the government and receive a break on your taxes. This is wisdom, because it gives you more to give.  On the other side of this subject, I have watched pastors parade hundred dollar bills in front of God's people so that all know how much they are giving. Some believe this helps the people be inspired to give more money.

Many times it is the work of the Holy Spirit that leads one to give. It is also the evidence of a good heart. What another does or does not do in this regard should have no bearing on my giving practices. Jesus states clearly in verse 2 that a show of our giving is "hypocrisy." Jesus used the word hypocrisy, because it was not a motivation of a good heart in their giving, but a show so others will think well of them. Jesus calls it being "honored by men" (Matthew 6:2). Jesus said that when you give to the poor, don't let your left hand know what your right hand is doing. This is what is known as "oriental hyperbole." It is an extreme statement in order to make a point. Give in secret, just because it honors God. He will be your reward. A perspective which a good friend would teach and I have followed for years is, "to give, to get to give more." The Lord is my supply. He is my source and the one who honors me in my giving. Jesus said, "That your alms may be in secret; and your Father who sees in secret will repay you" (Matthew 6:4).

Examine your heart today. Give the Holy Spirit control of your finances, giving and trusting your heavenly Father to be your reward.

## April 6 –FAST SECRETLY BEFORE YOUR HEAVENLY FATHER

Matthew 6:17-18 – When you fast, anoint your head and wash your face so that your fasting will not be noticed by men, but by your Father who is in secret; and your Father who sees what is done in secret will reward you.

Fasting is a practice found in many religions. When I was in Pakistan some years ago, I experienced Muslims fasting during Ramadan, one of the most important religious times among Muslims. Fasting would take place from sunrise to sundown. Christians could not eat in front of Muslims during their fasting time. At night, those practicing fasting during the day would gorge themselves at night. This went on for a whole month.

The fasting that Jesus was speaking about was not for the purpose of trying to impress God or man, but to *humble* oneself before God. In the discipline of fasting, one is helped to focus on areas that can be easily neglected. For example, sexual appetites are being brought under control. Eating and sexual activity are both connected to needs of the flesh. They are not sinful practices in the contexts of God's Laws, but are appetites of the flesh. Paul connects prayer and abstinence when he says to the married, "Stop depriving one another, except by agreement for a time that you may devote yourselves to prayer, and come together again lest Satan tempt you because of your lack of self-control" (1 Corinthians 7:5).

Fasting is good, sexual relations within marriage are good, and both are related to self-discipline. The sexual relationship is the most intimate relationship and is confined to the marriage covenant. Fasting is part of an intimate relationship with God our Father. It is never to be flaunted before men, but done secretly before God. Fasting is an act of humility and carries the purpose of humbling oneself before God. The biblical exhortation is to discipline the flesh and learn self-control.

The practice of fasting is a discipline of kingdom-minded people. Jesus said, "*When* you fast," not *if* you fast. Act as if you're not fasting by preparing yourself to eat so men do not know that you are fasting. Your Father in heaven will notice and He promises His reward for your humility before Him.

If people do notice your fast, it is neither a sin nor a cancellation of God's promise of reward. The issue belongs to the heart. In other words, your motivation for fasting is the crucial factor. Ask the Holy Spirit to strengthen you in a fasting lifestyle. All we do before God should be the work of the Spirit in us, and not our own religious drive.

## April 7 – STORE UP FOR YOURSELVES TREASURES IN HEAVEN

Matthew 6:19-21 – Do not lay up for yourselves treasures upon earth, where moth and rust destroy, and where thieves break in and steal. But lay up for yourselves treasures in heaven, where neither moth nor rust destroys, and where thieves do not break in or steal; for where your treasure is, there will your heart be also.

The Holy Spirit has come to connect us to heaven. Most of the time, the human goal is survival, to hopefully achieve amassing as much money as possible for security in this life. Multitudes around the world are oppressed and not able to realize that human desire. On the other hand, there are those in this life that have amassed great fortune and have no issues with security as it relates to substance. The Holy Spirit wants to help turn our attention toward a greater treasure than the wealth of this world. Whether one is poor or wealthy, the true treasure is in the storehouse of heaven. The fundamental issue is choosing from where one derives their security.

The development of relationship with the Holy Spirit causes us to grow in our confidence in God's Word and all His promises. I am grateful for how my heavenly Father has blessed me. I realize though, that in the same way my possessions have come they can also all disappear. It is an absolute of God's Word that temporal things will vanish. The Scripture declares, "But by His word the present heavens and earth are being reserved for fire" (2 Peter 3:7).

One of the great treasures in life is found in relationship with family and friends. Many have acquaintances, but fewer people have real friendships. Lasting relationship comes from the work of the Holy Spirit who restores us to the Godhead through the redemptive work of Christ. Jesus, the Christ, is the "Pearl of great price" spoken of in Matthew 13:46. He is the true treasure! Let us seek the Lord for His grace to let go of anything that we might be holding on to as a wealth other than the Lord. It is fine to have possessions. In fact the Word of God promises material blessings in this life. It is not okay for those possessions to possess us in any way that runs interference with our relationship with the *true treasure,* the Lord Jesus Christ. The Holy Spirit is present to help us "fix our eyes on Jesus, the author and perfecter of our faith" (Hebrews 12:2).

Ask the Holy Spirit to give you grace to store up treasures in heaven and to be freed from bondage to the possessions of this life "for where your treasure is, there your heart will be also" (Matthew 6:21). Father, I ask you to give me a heart after your will and a right viewpoint about possessions.

## April 8 – LIGHT ENTERS INTO THE BODY THROUGH YOUR EYES

Matthew 6:22 – The eye is the lamp of the body; so then if your eye is clear, your whole body will be full of light.

According to a well-known saying, "the eye is the window of the soul". When I speak with a person, I look them in the eyes. By doing this, it seems I make a better connection with them. As I listen to what they are saying, I am better able to respond when I communicate back with them. If the issues of honesty are involved, by looking a person in the eyes you have a better chance of discerning truth from untruth. In the counseling ministry, eye-to-eye contact is vital to imparting truths that can help set people free. In the deliverance ministry, eye-to-eye contact is vital to casting out demonic entities.

The physical eye, of course, is connected to the brain and affects the emotions and the will. Jesus goes on to say, "If your eye is bad, your whole body will be full of darkness" (Matthew 6:23a). How can the eye be bad in the moral sense? When you put together the mind, emotions and will, you essentially have what the Bible speaks of as the "heart," the innermost region of a person. The physical eye is controlled by what is found in the heart. When the heart chooses to take in darkness it causes the eye to become bad.  When the heart is pure, it chooses to take in light and rejects the darkness.

Jesus goes on to say that, "If then the light that is in you is darkness, how great is that darkness" (Matthew 6:23b). What is Jesus saying? The Bible declares that some will call good evil and evil good. "Woe to those who call evil good, and good evil; who substitute darkness for light and light for darkness" (Isaiah 5:20). There are those who know what is right and true, but still promote darkness in what they say. Many religious leaders in Jesus' day knew what the scriptures taught, but still added to the scriptures and put heavy burdens on the people. It is in the "mixture" of religion that light becomes a greater darkness.

Day by day, surrender your eyes to the Lord. Job said, "I have made a covenant with my eyes" (Job 31:1). Ask the Holy Spirit to protect your eyes and thus your soul from darkness and to fill you with light.

# April 9 –CHOOSE WHOM YOU WILL SERVE, GOD OR WEALTH

Matthew 6:24 – No one can serve two masters; for either he will hate the one and love the other, or he will be devoted to one and despise the other. You cannot serve God and wealth.

A two-headed creature is always a freak. Jesus is not saying that you cannot be rich and serve God. He is saying you cannot "serve" both God and wealth. It is one thing to have possessions and use them for God's glory, and quite another to allow possessions to have you. Hold loosely to all you own. It is easy to become emotionally tied to one's possessions, such as a house, a car, toys, etc. A worthwhile evaluation is to determine what it is that you serve. I serve my family, many in the family of God, and friends. But none are my masters, only God is that. I enjoy my hobby, my house, and the car I drive, but none of those things control me. I am not saying that it would be easy, but if required, they all must go in order to serve the Lord's larger purpose.

In Luke 6:46 Jesus asked this question of His disciples, "Why call Me 'Lord, Lord' and do not what I say?" An employer has the right to expect certain actions from an employee in order to accomplish the task. Our Lord and master Jesus Christ also has certain expectations of our lives. If we call Him Lord and sing about His Lordship, worship Him as the all-worthy one, He can expect us to do all that He has commanded. Serving another is a choice of our free will. Each day we are presented with the opportunity of choosing who and what we will serve.

Jesus was given the opportunity to choose also. In Matthew 4, we find the story recorded of Jesus being led into temptation. The evil one gave Him opportunity to choose what had been given into Satan's control. Jesus knew by the Word of God, that all these things had been promised to Him in due time. He chose to resist the offer of the enemy for immediate gratification and rather chose to wait for His heavenly Father to give all things to Him.

Today, would you choose to surrender all things to the control of Jesus? Would you wait on God for His timing rather than taking things into your own hands? Let Him be the master by serving His timing and His provisions for His glory. Holy Spirit, I give to you the reigns of my life. Take perfect control!

## April 10 –THE CURE FOR ANXIETY

Matthew 6:25 – For this reason I say to you, do not be worried about your life.

The instructions of Jesus from verse 25 to 32 are to help focus the believers on their relationship with our heavenly Father. They help the believers to be assured that God cares more for them than all of His creation for which He provides. In verse 30, Jesus clarifies that our trust of God is a "faith issue." All worry is associated with a lack of faith. The Holy Spirit was given to bring us into the "faith of Jesus." If anyone had a right or opportunity to be worried, it was Paul. "Three times I was beaten with rods, once I was stoned, three times I was shipwrecked, a night and a day I have spent in the deep" (2 Corinthians 11:25). Paul the apostle proclaims to the Galatians his own declaration of faith and rest in the work of Christ. In Galatians 2:20, Paul identified his resting place as being crucified with Christ. He further understood that the life he now lived was a life lived by "the faith of the Son of God."

Paul knew what it meant to die to his self-life and to live unto Christ. Through the power of the Holy Spirit, Paul was not anxious about anything. He learned to be content in all things according to Philippians 4:11. Whatever his state, he learned contentment. Paul came to know Jesus as his Sabbath Rest. In other words, he knew Jesus as his resting place. Worry and anxiety bowed to the Lord Jesus Christ. The Holy Spirit baptized us into Christ and into His body. He buried us with Jesus in baptism. He raised us up and has seated us in heavenly places with Christ. Why worry? Why be anxious? Our Father knows what we need.

Today, make a fresh commitment to "Trust in the Lord with all your heart and do not lean on your own understanding. In all your ways acknowledge Him, and He will make your paths straight" (Proverbs 3:5-6).

# April 11 – BE A SEEKER OF HIS KINGDOM AND HIS RIGHTEOUSNESS BEFORE ALL ELSE

Matthew 6:33 – But seek first His kingdom and His righteousness, and all things will be added to you.

The focus of the New Testament is the kingdom of God and its accompanying righteousness. John the Baptist said, "Repent for the kingdom of God is at hand" (Matthew 3:2). This also was the opening proclamation of Jesus' ministry as recorded in Matthew 4:7. Throughout the ministry of Jesus, He teaches of the coming Holy Spirit, "Now on the last day, the great day of the feast, Jesus stood and cried out, saying, 'If any man is thirsty, let him come to Me and drink. He who believes in Me, as the Scripture said, from his innermost being shall flow rivers of living water.' But this He spoke of the Spirit, whom those who believed in Him were to receive; for the Spirit was not yet given, because Jesus was not yet glorified" (John 7:37-40). In John chapters 14-16, the focus of Jesus' conversation with His disciples was about the Holy Spirit and His coming work.

Paul declares that, "the kingdom of God is in the Holy Spirit" (Romans 14:17). He also emphasizes that "righteousness, peace, and joy," is the product of the kingdom's manifestation. Jesus tells us to "Seek first the kingdom of God." Is the kingdom of God and His righteousness our first priority? In John 7 He says, "If any thirst." Seeking God for His will and purpose is an evidence of thirst. Thirst is a physical symptom that manifests when one begins to feel dehydrated. The nation of Israel was "spiritually dehydrated" when Jesus arrived. The Gentiles had no place to drink, being separated from God and His Covenants of promise. Jesus brought to the earth "spiritual bread and spiritual drink." He prophesied of the coming Holy Spirit in John 7:37, declaring that He would bring the river of "living water" which would flow out of the inner being of those who believe.

Do not look for the river to come from the outside, but understand that the Holy Spirit comes into the believer and will release a river from within. It will be a river of "righteousness, peace and joy" which will satisfy the thirsty soul. Drink deeply of the river today.

# April 12 –DON'T WORRY ABOUT TOMORROW. TODAY'S PROBLEMS ARE MORE THAN ENOUGH TO BE CONCERNED WITH.

Matthew 6:34 – So do not worry about tomorrow; for tomorrow will care for itself. Each day has enough trouble of its own.

Stress has always been a great emotional and physical health problem. Worry is at the heart of stress and is the opposite of rest. Worry and stress come from trying to control our circumstances. They prevent us from finding a place of rest for our mind and our body. Jesus says, "So do not worry about tomorrow." The emphasis is mine. After Jesus teaches on the cure for anxiety in Matthew 6, He concludes with this statement found in verse 34. The word so means; based on what I have taught you "don't worry"! I can't help but think of the old hymn, "I Surrender All." It is in the act of surrender that we open the door for the Holy Spirit to enter our situations and give us God's perspective. Jesus is at the right hand of God the Father and is seated, meaning He is at rest. He is not pacing heaven, trying to solve the troubles of today and of tomorrow.

A friend of mine would always say "one step in front of the other." What a concept and what an attitude! Stability in physical walking comes through balance and coordination. It is also true in the spiritual realm. If your thoughts are all over the place, so will be your spiritual walk. The Holy Spirit wants to establish us in the promises of His Word. He wants to strengthen us to receive the Word and then to apply the Word of God in our daily life. This is harder than it sounds, but with the Holy Spirit's help, we can apply the Word of God and enter into His rest. I will not worry about today's problems, and for certain I will not worry about tomorrow's. Some people practice mind over matter and positive thinking in this regard. That might help, but I am not speaking of my works, but His power through His Word and His Spirit.

Trust Him today by turning every worry you have over to Him. Speak it to Him and say, "Holy Spirit I give this worry over to you." I receive from You the rest of Christ. Show me what to do, for You have said, "The steadfast of mind, You will keep in perfect peace, because he trusts in You. Trust in the Lord forever, for in God the Lord we have an everlasting Rock" (Isaiah 26:3). I choose to trust fully in You my Lord.

## April 13 – IN THE WAY YOU JUDGE, YOU WILL BE JUDGED

Matthew 7:1-2 – Do not judge, so that you will not be judged. For in the same way you judge, you will be judged; and by your standard of measure it will be measured to you.

This is a powerful statement made by the Lord Jesus Christ. He can make such a statement and set such a rule because He is the Lord! He was anointed by His heavenly Father to declare the will of Heaven on Earth. He prepared the way for the Holy Spirit to be poured out by removing our sins through the work of the cross and making it possible for Heaven's obedience to be established on earth. For our sakes, Jesus took the judgment of God upon Himself. He alone has been given the right to judge. As I look upon another, I must understand Christ has carried their sins. Unless an individual has been born again, through the work of the Holy Spirit, they are left to their human nature to try and improve. Their only hope is through His cleansing blood. If the offending person is a Christian, then we should share with them the offence toward us and give them an opportunity to repent and ask forgiveness (Matthew 18:15).

It is through a standard of measurement we judge the value of a particular item. For example, 1 oz. of gold is worth a certain amount of money. At one time, we used the gold standard to determine the value of paper money. We all have standards which we use for measuring other people's views and conduct. Jesus is saying that whatever you use to measure another's conduct or actions will be used to measure your conduct or actions. The believer has Jesus as the standard. Consider what the apostle John tells us, "For God did not send the Son into the world to judge the world, but that the world might be saved through Him" (John 3:17). He is my standard for judgment. Ultimately, the world will be judged, but the cross came first. Today, my life is lived in the light of the cross of Christ. I will not judge, but I must pray for the offender's salvation.

Ask the Holy Spirit to help you to always make Jesus the standard. Surrender your judgments to God and ask Him to help you share His love through the power of His love. This is made possible by His forgiveness and the gift of His indwelling Spirit.

## April 14 – REMOVE THE LOG FROM YOUR EYE SO YOU CAN SEE CLEARLY

Matthew 7:5 – You hypocrite, first take the log out of your own eye, and then you will see clearly to take the speck out of your brother's eye.

It is easy to look on another person and to evaluate all that is wrong with them. It is very difficult to look inside one's self and rightly evaluate our own condition. Hypocrisy is a powerful attitude in religious circles and I dare say some hypocrisy is demonic at its core. The religious hypocrites of Jesus' day had as their father, not Abraham, but the devil (see John 8:44). Those religious leaders had a huge log in their eyes. In fact, Jesus called them blind (see Matthew 23:16-26). Jesus sent the Holy Spirit to remove the log from our eye. He does this by enabling us to be "crucified with Christ." Only death can cure the self-centered hypocrisy that lives in all of us. "Nevertheless I live." I live, because the same Spirit that raised Jesus from the dead dwells in me (see Romans 8:11). Now, that being said, "The life that I now live, I live by the faith of the Son of God" (Galatians 2:20). It is only by Jesus' faith that I can live free from judging others and His faith operates in me by the power of His Holy Spirit.

Paul said, "Wretched man that I am! Who will set me free from the body of this death?" (Romans 7:24). He goes on to answer his own question by giving thanks. "Thanks be to God through Jesus Christ our Lord!" (Romans 7:25). Yes, the Holy Spirit of God gives the life of Christ to us and enables us to do what was impossible in our own ability and strength. He helps us to remove the log in our own eye and graces us to help others remove the speck in their eye. That speck is really a log to God, but was a speck to us because of the log which blinded our eye. How wonderful it is to have one's sight recovered and to look on another without judgment and condemnation, but to see through the eyes of Jesus a new person redeemed by Christ's precious blood.

Today, let the Holy Spirit do surgery and remove all the obstacles that cause you to be hindered in your sight. Ask God to help you see others as Christ does.

## April 15 – GUARD WHAT IS HOLY

Matthew 7:6 – Do not give what is holy to dogs, and do not throw your pearls before swine, or they will trample them under their feet, and turn and tear you to pieces.

The Jewish people called the Gentiles dogs. We know that there came a time when the Gentiles were accepted and qualified for salvation. Jesus is using the term "dogs" referring to any that reject God's provision and treat it as a dog might treat a precious possession belonging to his master. What God the Father has given to us is compared to a "pearl." A swine would not care anything of the pearl's value. He would just bury it in the mud and slop. Likewise, the swine might turn on you and do you great damage.

Jesus was preparing kingdom-minded people for the reality of the tribulations that lay ahead for those trusting Christ. In our witnessing, we need to use wisdom and not flaunt what Christ has done for us. The conduct of our lives is our real witness to the unsaved. Vocal volume and many words will not bring the lost to Christ. It is our steady and faithful lifestyle that will ultimately convince people of the kingdom of God and create a desire to follow Christ.

Many Christians suffer persecution because they do not follow the counsel which Jesus gives to us in this verse. The Holy Spirit is our guide in witnessing. We cannot hope to be effective without His power and leading. We must learn to hold our counsel as well as share it as the precious Holy Spirit leads. Paul's witness on Mars Hill gives us valuable lessons regarding receptivity. "Some began to sneer, but others said, we shall hear you again concerning this" (Acts 17:32-34). A third group received the Word of God freely and became disciples of the Lord Jesus Christ.

Be wise as a serpent and harmless as a dove. Ask the Holy Spirit to be your guide, to give you power to proclaim the gospel, and live a consistent Christian witness before all.

## April 16 – DO UNTO OTHERS AS YOU WOULD HAVE THEM DO UNTO YOU

Matthew 7:12 – In everything, therefore, treat people the same way you want them to treat you, for this is the Law and the Prophets.

In the classic sense, this verse is known as the "Golden Rule." For many people, Christian and non-Christian, the Golden Rule sums up Jesus' ministry. Jesus took from the Law and the Prophets and expressed all the Law and all the Prophets in this simple statement found in Matthew 7:12. If we are not treating someone the way we would like to be treated, the Holy Spirit is not empowering us. The Holy Spirit will never violate this word of Christ. The verse gives us cause for regular repentance. For married folks, the application of this verse would heal many a marriage. For church leaders, the application would bring peace to many a "Deacon Meeting." For pastors, the application would bring peace between church bodies. For those in secular work the application of this verse would bring peace at the office.

What a brilliant Savior and Lord we serve! O, the wisdom of heaven. "By His doing you are in Christ Jesus, who became to us wisdom from God, and righteousness and sanctification and redemption" (1 Corinthians 1:30). You and I have the potential to live by this Golden Rule. The wisdom of heaven is dwelling in each believer through the Holy Spirit. "I can do all things through Him who strengthens me" (Philippians 4:13). Many apply the Philippians passage to difficult situations in their life, but it is a great passage to be applied for the changing of our attitudes and allowing for the development of the character of Christ within us.

Ask the Holy Spirit to help you consider how to view other people. Invite Him to give to you the right attitude about others. Commit yourself daily to trust the Holy Spirit in helping you treat others as you want to be treated.

# April 17 – ENTER THROUGH THE NARROW GATE

Matthew 7:13—Enter through the narrow gate: for the gate is wide and the way is broad that leads to destruction, and there are many that enter through it.

Jesus is teaching an eternal truth that is important for us to grasp. The serpent gave Eve a broad choice in tempting her to eat of the tree. "God knows that in the day you eat from it, your eyes will be opened, and you will be like God, knowing good and evil" (Genesis 3:5). It is clear from Scripture that God always had it in His heart to elevate man, and open his understanding. God's ways are narrow and time-tested. He proves us, before giving to us greater responsibility. He wants to protect His sons and daughters from the pitfalls which will stop us from experiencing His very best. This is what Paul meant when he said, "No temptation has overtaken you, but such as is common to man; and God is faithful, who will not allow you to be tempted beyond what you are able, but with the temptation will provide the way of escape" (1 Corinthians 10:13). The way of escape for Eve was Adam who had received the Word of God. Instead of turning to her husband, she ate the fruit. Adam's way of escape was to turn to God, but instead he followed his wife's choice. They opened the broad way which humans follow. Jesus teaches we must "enter through the narrow gate." He is that gate!  He chooses the cross, rather than an easy way out. He established the narrow gate for all of mankind from that point on.

America has become a "pluralistic" society. This means we have swung open the gate to all of the false religions of the world. The original intent of America's founding fathers was a "Christian Society," made up of all the different Christian denominations. Everyone could express their Christian faith as their conscience dictated. The founding fathers knew that only the Christian faith would provide an atmosphere for other religions to survive. America, for many years, honored the narrow gate of the gospel of Christ. In more recent times, the narrow has been rejected and replaced with the broad, leading us down a road of destruction. Only by allowing the Holy Spirit to lead us back to the narrow gate, which is Christ, will our nation and its institutions survive.

Will it be relativism, whatever feels good and right to you, or will it be God's Laws, which are narrow by worldly standards, but lead to life and that abundantly? The Holy Spirit is present to empower us to choose life.

Father, today I choose life. Life in Christ by obeying Your word through the power of the Holy Spirit.

## April 18 – EVERY GOOD TREE BEARS GOOD FRUIT

Matthew 7:16 – You will know them by their fruits.

The context of Jesus' teaching is "be aware of false prophets, who come in sheep's clothing." They look and sound good on the outside, but inwardly are "ravenous wolves." We are to be fruit-checkers. If a person claims to be an authority on some subject, it is important to examine what has been produced in their life. Words are cheap, but godly fruit comes with a price tag. Any prophetic voice that has not been through the fire is suspect. Anyone who claims to be an apostle and has not known rejection is not being truthful. Growth, most of the time, is frustrating and painful. Paul instructs, "Know those who labor among you" (1 Thessalonians 5:12). In the context of Matthew 7:15-23, Jesus uses the understanding that a tree can be either good or bad. The proof is in the fruit it produces.

Jesus likens Himself to a vine in John 15. He makes it clear that this vine is fruit bearing. The Holy Spirit has made us a part of that vine as branches which are to bear fruit. If the branch bears good fruit it is pruned so it might bear more good fruit. If the fruit is bad or the branch is fruitless, it is removed. If the branch is no longer receiving the life of the tree it shrivels up and dies. Jesus declares, "apart from Me you can do nothing" (John 15:5). Our life is derived from Him. He is the vine and we are the branches. The Holy Spirit made the connection and the Holy Spirit supplies the life that flows from the vine to the branches. It is the Holy Spirit who anoints us to be fruitful.

I want the fruit of my life to be known as "good." I want that fruit to be a product of the vine, the Lord Jesus Christ. Ask the

Holy Spirit to make you fruitful for Jesus' sake and in Jesus' name.

## April 19 – MANY WILL SAY TO ME ON THAT DAY, LORD, LORD

Matthew 7:21 – Not everyone who says to me Lord, Lord, will enter the kingdom of heaven, but he who does the will of My Father who is in heaven *will enter.*

Many associate the kingdom of God with Israel. Some actually teach that Jesus failed to establish the kingdom on earth because of Israel's rejection of Jesus as their Messiah. This is a wrong understanding of God's kingdom. The kingdom is in the Holy Spirit. Many in Jesus' day called Him Lord, but never submitted to him as Lord. It is not simply in the words, but in the actions. In Matthew 7:21, Jesus is speaking about the future judgment day. In that day, there will be an accounting for things said and done. On that day, Jesus says there will be those who will declare what they have done in His name, but Jesus will tell them to be gone because He never knew them. He calls them "workers of iniquity" (Matthew 7:23 KJV). The word iniquity means "lawless" as translated in the NASB. This means they did a lot of things in Jesus' name, but not by His authority.

Today, much is done in the name of the Lord, but not all is done as a directive from Him. In my own life, I have both done things that He directed through the Holy Spirit and I have done those things that turned out to be by my own directive in His name. When He revealed to me my error, I quickly repented. It is so important to wait on the Holy Spirit, allowing Him to direct and lead us. Only what the Spirit does will last and be accepted by the Lord Jesus Christ. Often, our human pride causes us to think, "I am doing this for Jesus." Maybe we are, but if He did not direct us, it is lawless at best. It is good to question our motives; it is good to receive approval from godly authority and let the Lord confirm our decisions as we wait upon Him for direction. As the old adage says, "haste makes waste." The Lord is never in a hurry.

Invite the Holy Spirit to be in control of all your plans. Know that as you wait upon the Lord, He will bring it to pass. "Wait for the Lord, and keep His way, and He will exalt you to inherit the land; when the wicked are cut off, you will see it" (Psalm 37:34).

## April 20 – UPON WHAT FOUNDATION ARE YOU BUILDING?

Matthew 7:24 – Therefore everyone who hears these words of Mine and acts on them, may be compared to a wise man who built his house on the rock.

A rock represents a solid foundation, which does not move easily. Jesus teaches truths that are the foundation of the kingdom He came to establish in the earth. Note, Jesus says that the one who "hears and acts" upon His words is wise. There are many of God's people who hear the Word of God regularly, but do not act on the Word consistently. What good is a solid foundation if we do not build upon it? The truths contained in the Sermon on the Mount are the Foundation on which the Holy Spirit builds us into Christ and His kingdom. The Holy Spirit soon was to be given to all those putting their trust in the Lord Jesus Christ. He brings to the believer power to transform his life into a Christ-like life. The foundation laid by Jesus on the Mount becomes the expected foundation of practice for each one trusting in the Lord. Power to live out the life which Jesus is teaching in this magnificent sermon is realized through a daily fellowship with the Holy Spirit and the word of God He reveals to us.

"So faith comes from hearing and hearing by the word of God" (Romans 10:17). Hearing God's Word produces one level of faith which includes an expectation. Another type of hearing is when the Lord makes a Scripture alive to us personally. Both types of hearing God's Word require the Holy Spirit's leading. He creates an expectation in our spirit and soul. Faith begins to develop, first in our spirit man, and then in our thinking. As one hears a personal word from the Lord, faith demands an action, not just a mental assent. In order to obey the Sermon on the Mount, it requires faith, which produces power to live a kingdom life and testify to others what it is like to live under the government of King Jesus.

In summary, hear and act on the Words of our Lord. Ask the Holy Spirit, in Jesus' name, to help you walk in the faith of expectation and the faith of acting on the words of Christ.

# April 21 – HOW ARE YOU BUILDING, ON SAND OR ON A ROCK?

Matthew 7:24 Therefore everyone who hears these words of Mine and acts on them, may be compared to a wise man who built his house on the rock.

Building is an ethical issue. God is a builder, from the time He spun off universes to building a church that the gates of hell will not prevail against! If we find ourselves going through life without purpose or productivity, the Bible considers it to be unethical. The Book of Proverbs speaks of two kinds of men, those that are building on solid ground and those that are carelessly drifting along, whose lives are headed for destruction. Jesus teaches it is in the hearing and acting on His words that one receives wisdom. Too many of God's people go week after week hearing God's Word, but not applying what was taught. We must chose to act upon what is biblically taught. By not acting upon God's Word one is being unethical. In effect, one is building on sand and this will prove to be unwise and devastating. One example is found in Christian marriages that are in trouble today. Many go for counseling, but they do not act upon the word given to them. Thus, nothing changes and many times the marriage relationship becomes worse.

The Holy Spirit is waiting for believers to act upon the Word of God. As we act upon the word given, He, the Holy Spirit, goes into action to help us understand and apply God's Word. The net result becomes wisdom to build a life which becomes more and more Christ centered. In our lessons, beginning in Matthew 5, we read of Jesus speaking of those who will be blessed through their action. We learn of being salt and light in the world. We learn of a righteousness that exceeded that of the religious leaders. We also learn in Matthew 5 of the correct relationships that begin in the heart as well as the outward actions that follow. We learn how our forgiving others releases God to forgive us. We also have learned the correct response concerning money, anxiety, and seeking first His kingdom and His righteousness, with the promise that everything else will be added to us. Finally, we learned that the way we judge others is in turn the same way we will be judged. Furthermore, we should ask and expect to receive the promise of the Father, the Holy Spirit. The Spirit is bringing forth a good tree that produces good fruit.

Let the Sermon on the Mount become a well-known portion of Scripture. Allow the Holy Spirit to build into your life these principles in an ever-deepening way. These chapters reveal the Laws of the kingdom of God which guide the new man born of God's Holy Spirit. In Jesus' name, pray daily for the Father to give to you His plans for building and ask the Holy Spirit to empower you in the application.

## April 22- HE TAUGHT AS ONE HAVING AUTHORITY

Matthew 7:28 – When Jesus finished these words, the crowds were amazed at His teaching; for He was teaching them as one having authority and not as their scribes.

One of the most amazing aspects of Jesus' ministry was the authority from which He taught. People's amazement is recorded a number of times in the gospels. What good is teaching if it does not have weight behind it? The Holy Spirit is the one who gives weight to the teachings and works of the Lord Jesus Christ.

There are many in the body of Christ who can teach the Bible, but lack the anointing of the Holy Spirit to teach with authority. Consequently, those teachings are delivered as words and opinions. This is what the people in Jesus' time were accustomed, words that did not carry Heaven's authority. It helps us to understand what Paul meant when he said, "My message and my preaching were not in persuasive words of wisdom, but in demonstration of the Spirit and of power, that your faith should not rest on the wisdom of men, but on the power of God" (1 Corinthians 2:4). Authority is associated with power. The words of Jesus and the words of Paul were both filled with power because the Holy Spirit anointed their words.

The same Holy Spirit is at work in the Lord's church today. He is speaking too many outside the body of Christ, inviting them to become a part of God's family. Many ministers of the gospel do not see converts to the faith because they are not speaking by the power of God found in the Holy Spirit. Many depend on their intellect rather than waiting on the Lord for His guidance. Many simply preach other men's messages rather than waiting on the Lord for His Word to be revealed to them. When the Word is preached with power, some are converted. Through the power of God, many find salvation and some receive healing. Others experience judgment because of their rejection of God's provisions. All of this is the power of God manifested by His Holy Spirit. There are times when God's power is manifested in "signs and wonders" – things happening outside of the rational which can only be explained by the power of God. He delights to act in power on behalf of an individual or group of people hearing His Word.

The Holy Spirit wants to cause your words to be those of authority as you represent the Lord and His purposes. Ask the Holy Spirit for revelation and understanding given by Him, and see if your words do not have a divine effect on others.

## April 23 – THROUGH FRUSTRATION AND PAIN WE GROW AND BECOME STRONG IN FAITH

James 1:2 – Consider it all joy, my brethren, when you encounter various trials, knowing that the testing of your faith produces endurance, and let endurance have *its* perfect result, so that you may be perfect and complete, lacking nothing.

This Scripture is hard for many to receive because it appears to be a negative statement. It is not our human desire to encounter different kinds of trials, but James says to "count it all joy"! We are to count "trials" as joy, because if we endure them, they will produce maturity in us. The word "perfect" here means "mature," so James instructs us "to let endurance have *its* perfect result." The translators put the word "its" in italics for emphasis. It takes endurance to go through problems. Many times, we want to just give up. The Holy Spirit is always with us as He supplies the grace and the vision for us to see and endure our trials until the end. Then, and only then, will we see the fruit of our enduring trials as we hang in there.

"If any of you lacks wisdom, let him ask of God, who gives to all generously and without reproach, and it will be given to him" (James 1:5). What a great promise to each believer. When we are in the midst of a trial, it is wisdom that we need the most. The Holy Spirit is God's agent to give us the "wisdom of God." His promise is that we will receive a generous portion from Him, and we do not have to be ashamed to ask for it. Verse 6 says that the asking must be in faith without any doubting. Of course, when one is in the midst of a trial, doubt is lurking and ready to defeat us. It is a battle to continue in faith. That is why James uses the word "endure." Asking God is the beginning of faith, but not the end. Jesus said to "ask" in Matthew 6. The literal translation is to "ask and keep on asking." Thus, we need to endure, to keep on asking and expecting God's help. He will give you wisdom to know what to do. The result will be growth.

Identify whatever trial you may be presently having and ask God to give you wisdom through His Holy Spirit to endure those trials. Keep asking until the victory appears and you will rejoice in the growth you will experience in your life.

## April 24 – LIFE FADES LIKE THE GRASS AND FLOWERS OF THE FIELD

James 1:9-10 – The brother of humble circumstances is to glory in his high position; and the rich man *is to glory* in his humiliation, because like flowering grass he will pass away.

Here we read of the wisdom of God. The Lord always sees both sides of the coin. On the one hand, the person who does not possess a lot of this world's goods should recognize in Christ that he has been highly exalted. He is the son of a king and everything his Father would choose for him to have is his for the asking. On the other hand, the one who has been blessed with this world's goods should walk in humility. He only has what he has by God's goodness. Life is a fleeting journey that will end in death for both the rich and the poor. Possessions and pursuits will all fade away like the grass. The Holy Spirit wants us to focus on those things that will remain, which principally have eternal substance attached to them. The question for each believer remains, "Is this God's will?" The transforming power of Holy Spirit in a believer's life is to help us live for God's pleasure and not our own. This is good proof of a more complete restoration to God's plan and purposes.

If I am poor, I am not to dwell on my poverty, but rather embrace my wealth which is found in Christ Jesus. If I am poor because of laziness or misuse of funds, I need to repent and ask for the Holy Spirit to help me. But if I am poor because of my plight in life, I am to rejoice, as James states, "in my high position" as a son of God, "blessed with all spiritual blessings in the heavenly places in Christ" (Ephesians 1:3). If I am rich, then I am to make the riches secondary. My rejoicing is to be in the saving grace of God. I am to rejoice that the riches did not stop me from humbling myself before almighty God and confessing my absolute poverty and my hopeless condition without God's saving work. The Scriptures are so incredible when made alive by their author, the Holy Spirit. He helps us to apply their eternal truths in this temporal life.

Whatever your situation may be, take the appropriate position. By the power of the Holy Spirit, claim your portion in the Lord Jesus for your daily need. Remember your high state in Christ. Glory in your absolute poverty without Him and give thanks in the midst of plenty. Always remember, He saved you in spite of your temporal position.

## April 25 – PERSEVERANCE UNDER PRESSURE WILL BRING WITH IT A GREAT REWARD

James 1:12 – Blessed is the man who perseveres under trial; for once he has been approved, he will receive the crown of life which *the Lord* has promised to those who love Him.

To persevere is always admirable. Just keep thinking "I can do it!" I remember in High School when I ran my first cross country race thinking to myself, "I don't know if I can make it to the finish line." I began to set goals to help me make it from one point to another. Finally, the finish line was in sight and it became my final goal. I persevered and overcame to receive the prize. James has added another dynamic to "perseverance" that is "under trial." If I had been sick and running, that would have qualified for "under trial". Many are running the race of this life and are under trials. I think of members of the "persecuted church" throughout the world, trying to live as a Christian in some of the most impossible situations. Many personal e-mails I receive are from people that are enduring some of the toughest situations. My heart especially goes out to parents that are carrying an extra load because of the illness of a child.

The Holy Spirit has come to guide us through the obstacles that interfere with our race toward the goal of His high calling. It is a race not in terms of speed, but rather the goal for the prize. The goal is the Throne of Grace and the Prize is the Lord Himself. James speaks of the "crown of life." He states that the Lord has promised the crown of life to all those that love Him. We receive His life when we are born again by the work of the Holy Spirit. As we enter into His life, we find that this natural life is full of trails determined to hinder our progress. You are blessed as you persevere through those trials. Although the life of Christ is presently in us by the power of the Holy Spirit, there is a promised day approaching when we will enter into the fullness of His life. We will be crowned with His Glory and enjoy His presence constantly. Receiving God's love and ministering it back to Him in doing His will assures us of the promise. Only in the power of the Holy Spirit can we successfully persevere under trial.

Today, cast all your cares upon Him, for He cares for you. Ask the Holy Spirit for strength to "persevere under trial." Keep drawing from the Comforter, who is an ever-present help in time of need.

# April 26 – ALL MEN ARE TEMPTED, BUT GOD IS NOT THE ORIGINATOR OF THE TEMPATION

James 1:13 – Let no man say when he is tempted, 'I am being tempted by God'; for God cannot be tempted by evil, and He Himself does not tempt anyone.

This is a very critical scriptural principle to understand. "God cannot be tempted by evil." I think of Job when I read this. In the Book of Job it tells us that Satan appeared before God. Satan pointed out Job to God and requested permission to tempt Job. Satan hoped to cause him to curse God. God gave Satan permission, but forbade him to take Job's life. Was God being tempted by evil? Was God tempting Job by giving Satan permission? I believe the answer is "no" on both counts.

First of all, God is Sovereign. He could have removed Satan from His presence if He had so desired. In the wisdom of God, He gave Satan permission to give Job trials that surpassed that which a human being should normally have had to endure. God knew His plan for Job and He allowed Satan to test Job.

Secondly, it was Satan who tempted Job. It was in his heart to tempt Job because he hated the "righteousness" that was in Job. God did not tempt Job directly. God only gave Satan permission to tempt Job. As James said, "He Himself does not tempt anyone." Temptation is a universal problem for all humans. It began in the Garden when Satan, in the form of a serpent, asked Eve "hath God said"?

All temptation is centered in one thing, "rejecting God's Word" over a suggestion. The suggestion is rooted in "lust," desiring what I want over what God wants for me. The weakness of the flesh is in "my want." Eve wanted to be like God, to be in control of her own destiny. The death of Christ was the only cure for dealing with the sin of mankind. The temptation offered by Satan was for Adam and Eve to receive immediate gratification. Jesus rejected the offer as a human and died an awful death for all of mankind. Once and for all, Satan was defeated and his power restricted by Christ.

He is still roaring like a lion, but has been defeated by the "Lion of Judah." Paul declares, "No temptation has overtaken you but such as is common to man; and God is faithful, who will not allow you to be tempted beyond what you are able, but with the temptation will provide the way of escape also, so that you will be able to endure it" (1 Corinthians 10:13).

The Holy Spirit will never leave us nor forsake us. He will provide wisdom and overcoming power if we will resist the tempter and trust in Christ's overcoming life. Job made a choice to trust God no matter what. Choose this day whom you will serve!

## April 27 – GOD IS THE GIVER OF EVERY GOOD AND PERFECT GIFT

James 1:16-17 – Do not be deceived, my beloved brethren. Every good thing given and every perfect gift is from above, coming down from the Father of lights, with whom there is no variation or shifting shadow.

The core of deception is rooted in keeping us from the intent of God the Father. He intends good for our lives and He wants to give us gifts, for this is His nature.

False religion is driven by so-called deities that demand obedience in some way that is tied to our flesh. The God of heaven enjoys obedience that comes from a willing heart, motivated by the love which God the Father has lavished upon His creation. Life itself came from Him. As I look out on the beauty of large oak trees, a small lake filled with fish and other living creatures, I am reminded of His love for me. When I look up into the heavens and see the multitude of stars that no man can number, I am taken back by the fact that my Creator knows who I am and loved me enough to become like me in human form.  He chose to die on a lonely tree that I might be restored to Him. Even in death He reigned and took from the evil one the keys of death and hell (Revelation 1:8). In His resurrection; He gave gifts to mankind (Ephesians 4:8). The greatest of His gifts was His own Holy Spirit to indwell me and minister the Father's love to me. Of course, I will serve and obey Him! How could I do any less, seeing all He has done for me?

Today, stop and give thanks that every good gift and every perfect gift is from above, coming down from the Father of lights and they belong to you. Especially, thank Him for the Holy Spirit whom He freely gave to us through the great sacrifice of His Son, Jesus Christ.

## April 28 – I HAVE BEEN BROUGHT FORTH BY THE WORD OF TRUTH

James 1:18 – In the exercise of His will He brought us forth by the word of truth, so that we would be a kind of first fruits among His creatures.

God exercises His will, motivated by His nature of love. The will of God is always rooted in truth and righteousness. There is no deception or hidden motive in what our Lord does. God has fully revealed His motives in His Word, the Bible. If that was not enough, He revealed Himself by sending Jesus, His only begotten Son. Both would have been sufficient, but He also chose to send His Holy Spirit to indwell the believer and reproduce what He created in Christ Jesus. The first century Christians became the "first fruits" of this new creation He is forming in the earth. His motivation and His purpose were to join heaven and earth in one accord through the life of His Son. The mandated work of the Holy Spirit is to accomplish this purpose of the Father. If you have received, by faith, the work of Christ and the Blessed Holy Spirit, you too are part of the exercise of His will by "the word of truth."

All truth is eternal. Truth can only come from an eternal God. It may be revealed truth concerning the natural creation as science explores the heavens and the earth. Moment by moment, man is discovering hidden truths of this marvelous creation. It might be the revelation of the "word of truth" found in the pages of Scripture. The early apostles came to understand the truths the Holy Spirit was revealing to them out of the Old Testament. They also received new truths because of what Christ accomplished in His death, burial and resurrection. The Reformers received fresh understanding to restore the church back to her original purpose. Today, God is still revealing truth to His people. None have completely discovered the depths of God's Word. I never cease to be amazed, how after knowing Christ and studying the Word of God for many years, He is still taking me into deeper understanding of His Truth. I am so finite and He is so infinite! As I hunger for more truth, He is present to help me apply what He has already shown me. He is also pleased to pull back the curtain a little more and show me more of His mysteries hidden in His love and grace.

Are you hungry for more understanding of His word of truth? The Holy Spirit stands ready to accommodate us. All we need to do is apply what He has already revealed and ask for more from the Holy Spirit. You will be surprised how much He will open your spirit and affect your mind with His powerful word of truth.

## April 29 – BE QUICK TO HEAR, SLOW TO SPEAK, AND SLOW TO ANGER

James 1:19 – *This* you know, my beloved brethren. But everyone must be quick to hear, slow to speak, and slow to anger; for the anger of man does not achieve the righteousness of God.

Did they know? James seemed to think they did. He lists three things that he felt they knew. First, is to listen carefully. The word "quick" means "alive." In other words, be alive and pay attention. Secondly, be slow to speak. I learned a long time ago I should try to be the last one to speak in any discussion if I want my point to stick. So listen carefully and don't just say the first thing that comes to your mind. Thirdly, be slow to get angry. In communication, the opportunity for anger is lurking at the door. By keeping our cool, we keep the lines of communication open. Over the course of time, we are able to resolve volatile issues.

I have found that many of God's people do not know these principles, or at least they do not practice them. Many times, we are preparing our response rather than listening carefully to what another is saying. I cannot tell you how many times, in preaching or teaching, someone heard me say something very different than what the CD revealed I actually said. This is why I have found it important to solicit questions or comments after speaking to make sure others heard me clearly. If you are not sure what someone said or meant in a statement, it is healthy to ask the person to repeat themselves or clarify what they said or meant.

Paul instructs us to "be angry, yet do not sin" (Ephesians 4:26). James tells us to be "slow" to anger. Aren't you glad for these two Scriptures? Jesus became angry with the religious leaders of His day. Anger is an emotion that God put in us. Why? We are created in the image of God and throughout the Scripture we read of God's anger towards sin. Anger is an emotion that can produce the right results when used correctly, but can also be devastating when out of control and done hastily. God's anger, in most cases, was not about Him, but it was about what was happening to others as a result of sin.

Daily, commit to the Holy Spirit your hearing, your mouth, and your emotions. Lord, help me to hear more than the words spoken. Lord, help me to respond thoughtfully and allow my emotions to be kept under the control of Your Holy Spirit.

# April 30 – LIVE FEARFULLY DURING YOUR TIME HERE ON EARTH

1 Peter 1:17 – If you address as Father the One who impartially judges according to each one's work, conduct yourselves in fear during the time of your stay *on earth*.

This is a powerful statement and reveals why we always need the Helper, the Holy Spirit. It is a serious thing to call God "our Father." Receiving salvation, in and of itself, is an awesome thought. But it is even more awesome to realize that God has given us "power" to be His children. The implications are more than our finite minds can take in. He is no respecter of persons. To think that He made me alive in His Son through the power of His Holy Spirit causes me to take things very seriously. As a child of God, I have the personal responsibility to live and conduct myself in a manner that is fitting to the name I carry.

As my children were growing up, they had to give account to their mother and me. They had to answer directly to us about doing their chores, their school work, and their attitudes toward us and toward their siblings. They were our children, carrying our name, and we treated them the same without partiality. We wanted them to understand that there were consequences for yielding to the sin nature, for disobedience, and for neglecting their responsibilities. Our heavenly Father is the same toward us. The word fear as used here does not mean to be afraid in the way one might fear evil. The word is a beautiful word which carries the meaning of "reverence" and awesome respect. It is a respect that has the knowledge of one day standing before Him and giving Him an account.

The Holy Spirit wants to remind us that, as His children, we have all the blessings and benefits of heaven. We also have the responsibilities that are expected of a son and daughter of God. Our goal is not to "appease" God so we can make it into heaven. Jesus took care of that on the cross as He laid down His life for each of us. We have an increasing desire to "please" Father God, because we love Him for what He has done for us. We also fear Him as the God of all creation. This is a healthy attitude and one that will enable us to "conduct ourselves in the fear of God."

Today, ask the Holy Spirit to reveal any areas that are not submitted to your Father in heaven and to fill you with "godly fear" all the days of your life here on earth.

## May 1 – PUT ASIDE THE CORRUPTNESS OF YOUR HUMAN NATURE AND LONG FOR GOD'S PURE WORD

1 Peter 2:1-3 – Therefore, putting aside all malice and all deceit and hypocrisy and envy and all slander, like newborn babies, long for the pure milk of the word, so that by it you may grow in respect to salvation, if you have tasted the kindness of the Lord.

This Scripture reveals that the human nature with its corruptness does not just disappear when we are saved. Peter says to "put aside" these evil behaviors. The five areas that Peter named are summed up in the word "wickedness." Put aside all wickedness and become like newly born infants. What does a newborn want? Pure milk! As we begin our walk in

Christ, the Holy Spirit begins to create an appetite for the pure milk of God's Word. We must nurture that desire. This is our first step of cooperation with the Holy Spirit. We begin to think, "I need to read the Scriptures." We choose to put aside other things and make room for the reading of His Word so we may begin to learn God's will for our lives.

Peter relates this desire for God's pure word to growing in our salvation. True salvation ought to be accompanied by desires for God's presence; the learning of His Word and a life lived out in righteousness. This new desire for the Word of God is in contrast to the old desires of our flesh. I remember how I could hardly wait to get time to study God's Word. I had a hunger to know what it said and to be able to share with others what I had learned. I had a deep desire for others to experience what I had experienced through the Holy Spirit and God's pure Word. I had been saved from my old life and ways. I recognized my growth in respect to my salvation.

I began to recognize the kindness of God in saving me. I also sensed a growth in my knowledge of what it meant to be "a son of God." I began to experience the gifts of the Holy Spirit, and I knew that I was entering into His grace. Peter calls it "tasting the kindness of our Lord" (1 Peter 2:3). When we recognize this kindness, we cannot help choosing to put aside our human corruptness and longing for His pure Word.

Ask the Holy Spirit to renew your hunger for His Word. Begin by reading of His goodness in all that He has done in Christ Jesus for us. Lavish yourself in the love of God and begin to experience a renewed desire to know His Word. If you are living in the knowledge of His kindness already, worship Him for all He has done for you.

## May 2 – AS LIVING STONES YOU ARE BEING BUILT UP AS A SPIRITUAL HOUSE

1 Peter 2:5 – You also, as living stones, are being built up as a spiritual house for a holy priesthood, to offer up spiritual sacrifices acceptable to God through Jesus Christ.

We read in Peter about a work of the Holy Spirit. He is building a spiritual house for a holy priesthood. 1 Peter 2:4 speaks of Jesus as a living stone. Men rejected Him, but in God's eyes, He is "choice" and "precious." O that the Holy Spirit would help us see Jesus as the Father does. He is our Lord and Savior, our friend, but He is so much more. He is the stone that is perfect. He is the corner stone that is the foundation for the building which God is raising up. Remove Him and the building collapses. Jesus cannot be a small part of one's life. He cannot just be the God of Sunday morning. As the Scripture says, "in Him we live and move and exist" (Acts 17:28). He is called a stone, which represents something that does not move. In Him "there is no variation or shifting" (James 1:17).

Peter goes on to say; we too, are as "living stones." He created us in Christ to be solid. Paul expresses it like this. "Therefore my beloved brethren, be steadfast, immovable, always abounding in the work of the Lord, knowing that your toil is not in vain in the Lord" (1 Corinthians 15:58). The Holy Spirit is building a spiritual house, a house that is alive and called to be a house of intercession. This is what Peter means when he says, "being built up as a spiritual house for a holy priesthood." As priests of God, we offer "spiritual sacrifices acceptable to God through Jesus Christ." What kind of spiritual sacrifices is the Holy Spirit creating in us? Peter, in his first letter, helps to provide the answer. "But you are a chosen race, a royal priesthood, a holy nation, a people for God's own possession so that you may proclaim the excellencies of Him who has called you out of darkness into His marvelous light" (1 Peter 2:9-10).

WOW! What glory He has placed upon us. What privilege the Spirit of God has called us into. Think of it. You're part of the chosen race in the earth, part of the royal priesthood, and part of a nation that is like no other nation ever. A Christian belongs to a people that are God's own possession. That's us! Rejoice, O saint of God! Be strong and courageous, and shout the victory which is ours in Christ Jesus the Lord.

I thank you Holy Spirit for faithfully calling men and women to Christ Jesus. I thank you for placing me among the people of God. Please continue to build Your will and purpose in me. Strengthen me to be faithful. Help me to accomplish what the Father and the Son desire of me.

# May 3 – I WILL ONLY SPEAK OF WHAT CHRIST HAS ACCOMPLISHED THROUGH ME

Romans 15:18-19 – For I will not presume to speak of anything except what Christ has accomplished through me, resulting in the obedience of the Gentiles by word and deed, in the power of signs and wonders, in the power of the Spirit.

Some may think it is an egotistical statement by Paul to speak only of what Christ has done through him. One day, I received a letter from a sister in Christ, who felt she needed to write and tell me I was bragging of what Christ had done through me. Of course, I wrote her back, and thanked her for bringing this to my attention. I mentioned to her that I had taken her letter and shared it with other well-known pastors in our city. My purpose was to inquire of these pastors to find out if this might be true. They did not agree with her perspective and affirmed the reports of what the Lord had been doing.

It is easy to get caught up in drawing attention to self. One does need to be careful, and know one's motivation in testifying about what God has accomplished. Paul had totally surrendered his life to Christ. Those that knew Paul knew that he had learned to die daily to himself. It was factual that the Gentiles were turning to Christ in record numbers. The reason for these massive amounts of conversions was the combination of "words and deeds." There were numerous manifestations of "signs and wonders" which occurred through the power of the Holy Spirit. When God uses someone to bring about His purposes through one's speech, deeds, and supernatural means, one would be expected to share the great things God had done.

We too, should be asking the Lord to use us for His glory. Paul gives us a model of a life surrendered fully to Christ. He also models the combination of words and deeds. Today, many have lots of words, but no real proof of lasting results. Paul's ministry was based in "signs and wonders." The same Holy Spirit that was working mightily in Paul is with us today. He has not changed! The church has changed, but the Holy Spirit remains the same. We definitely live in a different time, twenty-one centuries later. What is not different is that signs and wonders are still happening.

Let us simply surrender to the Spirit of the Lord. Ask Him for divine appointments that you may speak and demonstrate His power in the life of others through your words and by deeds, even in signs and wonders.

## May 4 – BY THE LOVE OF THE SPIRIT, STRIVE TOGETHER WITH ME IN YOUR PRAYERS

Romans 15:30 – Now I urge you, brethren, by our Lord Jesus Christ and by the love of the Spirit, to strive together with me in your prayers to God for me.

Paul is writing to a church that he has not seen. He had longed to go to Rome, but the Spirit of God has had him focused on the Eastern Mediterranean. Many of Paul's friends, and fellow laborers were there in Rome with the Roman saints. Paul is strongly calling for them to join him in his labors by praying for him to be rescued from those that are disobedient in Judah. That was a nice way of speaking about the Jews who wanted to kill him. He asked for prayers concerning his outreach to Jerusalem. He also asked them to pray about giving money to the poor saints living there. He asked them to pray for his ability to come to them in joy, by the will of God and to find rest in their company.

His request to the Roman Christians was in the name of the Lord Jesus Christ and by the love of the Spirit. Jesus is reigning as Lord in this present time. The Spirit has come to administrate the love of God in the earth. The Spirit always has unity in love as the core of His purpose. It is the love of the Spirit that makes unity possible. Unity must have as its purpose the will of God in order to be accomplished. Today, we hear a lot of talk about unity. It is awesome to see pastors throughout a city joined together in prayer. It is tremendous to sing songs from a great variety of streams. It is always a joy to know that denominationalism is taking a back seat. Many different groups are being joined together in the unity of the Spirit to accomplish God's purposes in the earth. Paul is requesting prayer for himself from a large church in Rome. In fact, it was the only church in Rome. According to Paul's greetings in the sixteenth chapter of Romans, it appears the believers gathered in houses, but related as one church in the city.

The Lord is at work restoring His Church to the *simplicity* of those early days. He is continually at work through His Holy Spirit, raising up His servants all over the world who are laboring for the same cause. That cause is the advancing of His kingdom in the earth. Today, prayers are offered for poor saints, and the suffering church around the world. Large amounts of money are being raised in the same spirit in which Paul raised money for the poor saints in Jerusalem. We are living in *apostolic times,* as God the Father, by the Lord Jesus Christ and by the love of the Spirit prepare an end-time church to fulfill His purpose in the earth.

Ask the Holy Spirit to enlarge your vision for what the Lord is doing in these days. Ask Him to guide you in your prayers and to fill you with "the love of the Spirit" for all saints. Be generous toward the poor, especially those of the Household of God.

## May 5 – WALK BY THE SPIRIT

Galatians 5:16 – But I say, walk by the Spirit and you will not carry out the desire of the flesh.

Walking by the Spirit is a choice one makes on a daily basis. Once you begin to practice walking by the Spirit, it becomes something like breathing. You don't have to think about every decision or choice you make. Supernaturally, you just do it. It is supernatural in that you know it is the Holy Spirit who is leading your decisions and lifestyle.

The Spirit desires to make us *a lover of people* so we will instinctively respond in love. He wants to produce in us *peace* so that no matter what disturbances are happening around us, we are at peace. The Holy Spirit does not automatically produce these qualities in us. We choose to allow Him freedom to work and guide our lives for the glory of God. His nature is made up of the qualities Paul lists in Galatians 5 known as "the fruit of the Spirit."

First, we allow the Holy Spirit to deal with our issues. That includes our hurts, unforgiveness, perhaps childhood wounds, and whatever others might have done in the past to harm us. He wants to heal our heart. Secondly, He wants to establish us in the Word of God. It is the "washing of water with the word" (Ephesians 5:26), that renews one's mind. This begins to help us think correctly. Many years ago, an early mentor of mine would say "God is a do right God and we must therefore do right..." In essence, he was teaching me to be led by the Spirit because the Spirit of God always leads us to do the right thing. Thirdly, we must establish "Spirit-lead habit patterns." We choose to love another, we choose to be at peace and rest in God, and we choose to allow joy to be predominant in our lives. The Spirit of God will quicken our choices and empower us to live above the natural realm in His supernatural ability.

These three basic areas must be applied in our lives as we learn to be led by the Spirit. As we learn to allow the Spirit of God to lead us, the flesh begins to be brought under control. Paul expresses it like this: "You *will not* carry out the desires of the flesh" (emphasis is mine). Many saints struggle with "being led by the Spirit". Many still carry unforgiveness toward people who have inflicted past wounds. There are those who read the Word of God as a religious obligation, rather than for application purposes. Finally, many have not broken old habit patterns and are still being led by their carnal, fleshly nature rather than the new nature which the Holy Spirit gives at the time of new birth.

Ask the Holy Spirit to reveal any areas that are hindering you from being led by the Spirit. Forgive, forsake, and surrender to Him, as He reveals the objects which hinder your growth in the life of the Spirit.

## May 6 – THOSE WHO PRACTICE DEEDS OF THE FLESH WILL NOT ENTER

Galatians 5:21 – I forewarned you, that those who practice such things will not inherit the kingdom of God.

As we think about our relationship with the Holy Spirit, it should lead us to His nature. We know He is holy. We know He is spirit. Christ has given each believer His "holy" nature. In the early church, there were those who embraced forgiveness and eternal life, but who had not been fully converted. They did not understand that God, in the power of His Spirit, was raising up a new kind of man in the earth. Those born of the Spirit are now holy and not continuing to practice the base nature of the flesh.

The apostle John said, "No one who abides in Him sins; no one who sins has seen Him or knows Him" (1 John 3:6). This is a pretty difficult Scripture to understand in the light of the normal battling of the flesh. John is saying, if you abide in Him, you no longer practice the habit of sin. Your nature no longer is a "sinful nature" controlling you. We have received His nature that should be dominant in how we conduct ourselves. If we insist on making a habit of continuing to practice sin, it is evident we have not truly seen the Lord and certainly do not know Him.

Entering into the kingdom of God is not exclusively some future event, but it begins now, by entering into His life under His authority. This is evidenced by the fact that our life is to be lived under the control of the Spirit of our Lord and Savior Jesus Christ. Jesus only lived to do the will of the Father. He demonstrated a kingdom of God walk throughout His entire life, even by His death on the cross. Heaven becomes the end of the journey which ends at His Throne. It is there at the Throne "we will all appear" (2 Corinthians 5:10). There we will give Him an account of our life and the works done. Repentance and forgiveness bring us to the Throne. Kingdom work brings rewards from Him. When all is said and done, only Jesus stands worthy to receive all the praise, honor, and glory.

Ask the Holy Spirit to reveal to you any practices of the flesh that are hindering you from entering fully into His kingdom. Repent, and forsake any such practices. Ask the Lord to fill you with His Holy Spirit to help you in yielding to His Kingly rule.

## May 7 – PUT TO DEATH THE FLESH WITH ALL OF ITS PASSIONS AND DESIRES

Galatians 5:24 – Now those who belong to Christ Jesus have crucified the flesh with its passions and desires.

Jesus laid the foundation for the truth that Paul is giving to the believers at Galatia. "Jesus said to His disciples, 'If anyone wishes to come after Me, let him deny himself, and take up his cross, and follow Me' " (Matthew 16:24-25). Part of entering into life with Christ is the putting off of the flesh which is rooted in the old nature, also called the old man. Oh, the absolute genius of our God! God becomes human in the Son. Christ lives the sinless life; He dies in our place as our substitute. God the Holy Spirit raises Him from the dead, enthrones Him as a resurrected man seated at the right hand of God the Father. The Spirit of God is poured out in the earth to bring forth a new creation. We choose to put the old nature to death and we choose to receive the new man. We live life through the power of God's Holy Spirit. What power has been given to man! What eternal joy is ours to possess! What victory over death and hell!

Once again, the Scriptures put the onus on our choosing to "crucify the flesh". The ability to crucify one's flesh is utterly impossible! You can hammer the nail into one hand, but someone else must hammer a nail into the other. That is why the Lord has set us into a community of believers. It takes another to finish the job of crucifixion. Sometimes it takes more than one, a few to hold us down while others drive in the nails.

Beloved, this is a serious matter and not to be taken lightly. In a marriage, often our partner has the hammer to help finish the job of crucifixion. Many run to another hoping to escape, but it does no good because our flesh still needs to be crucified. This is a part of Christianity that none of us like, but it is so necessary if we are to attain what God has for us in this life.

As the Holy Spirit was with Christ in His time of death, so will He be with us. God promises, "I will never desert you, nor will I ever forsake you, so that we confidently say, The Lord is my helper, I will not be afraid. What shall man do to me" (Hebrews 13:5-6)? "I will never" literally means, "I will never, no never, leave you." David declares, "Even though I walk through the valley of the shadow of death, I will fear no evil, for You are with me" (Psalm 23:4).

Let us be bold in the Lord and face our cross even as Christ faced His for us. Power will be released from His death on the cross and in His resurrection. Power will be released as we step into the new realms of His kingdom. By His power, we can guide others into the glorious freedom found in Christ Jesus our Lord!

# May 8 – WORSHIP IN THE SPIRIT
# PUTTING NO CONFIDENCE IN THE FLESH

Philippians 3:3 – For we are the *true* circumcision, who worship in the Spirit of God, and glory in Christ Jesus, and put no confidence in the flesh.

One of the theological battles today is whether the "kingdom of God" is in a natural people or in the Spirit. I have never understood why this is such a challenging area to understand. Paul is absolutely clear in this passage of scripture. The true circumcision are not those who have had the foreskin cut off, claiming to be the "the children of Abraham." Rather, the true circumcision is those who worship in the Spirit. Jesus also made this abundantly clear when speaking to the woman at the well. She was confused about who the true worshippers were and where they worshipped. Jesus said, "Woman, believe Me, an hour is coming when neither in this mountain nor in Jerusalem will you worship the Father. But an hour is coming, and now is, when the true worshippers will worship the Father in spirit and truth; for such people the Father seeks to be His worshippers (John 4:21 and 24).

A contemporary song says "take me back to the heart of worship." The heart of worship is not connected to a mountain in the earth, a natural city, or a natural people. The true worshipers are all those born of the Holy Spirit. This includes Jews (Acts 2), Samaritans (Acts 8) and Gentiles (Acts 10). In Him you were also circumcised with a circumcision made without hands, in removal of the body of the flesh by circumcision of Christ" (Colossians 2:11). The Jews thought that the foundation was in "the law of circumcision," but Jesus and Paul state clearly, it is a circumcision not made with hands, but of the Spirit, who creates a new heart. The heart of worship springs from what the Father did for us in Christ through the power of the Holy Spirit.

Our flesh is weak. No matter how hard we try, we cannot meet God's demands. On the Day of Pentecost, when the Holy Spirit was given, a new day began. A new breed was born in the earth on that day. A new nation came into being on that day. The power of religious bondage was broken forever. A new priesthood was formed. A new voice was heard in the heavens, the voice of redeemed saints worshipping the Father in spirit and in truth. It threatened all those who had confidence in the flesh. It was a whole new level of confidence, Spirit-led and Spirit-filled confidence. Emmanuel is with us. Yes, He is with us in the Spirit.

Ask the Holy Spirit to show you where your confidence is rooted. If it is not in the Spirit of God, then repent of trusting anything else and surrender to the Holy Spirit as the One you have fully trusted, placing confidence in His presence.

## May 9 – THE FRUIT OF REVELATION

John 14:26 – The helper, the Holy Spirit, whom the Father will send in My name, He will teach you all things, and bring to your remembrance all that I said to you.

The fruit of revelation came with the teachings of Jesus. All those that heard Jesus' teachings were amazed because He did not teach in the way they had become accustomed. He taught "with authority" to which Jesus was not just repeating what the writers of the Old Testament had written. He brought revelation to the Scriptures. He revealed their true meaning and fulfillment found in Him. This became revelation to many of those who heard Him. Not only did Jesus explain the Scriptures accurately, He demonstrated them through signs and wonders.

The Holy Spirit is the great teacher of truth. He does not concern Himself with theoretical views, but absolutes that will transform our lives. For the believer, He is the source of all reality. Jesus is teaching His disciples about the Father sending the Helper. The Helper would teach them "all things." The Holy Spirit is our helper too. Truth comes from the Spirit of Truth who lives in us. We study and listen to messages by Bible teachers, but seeing clearly is rooted in the Spirit of God giving us revelation power. The Holy Spirit's purpose is to transform our thinking. When we learn the teachings concerning past revelation, it helps to establish us. For example, the "just shall live by faith" or the "priesthood of every believer" are truths that were revealed to past generations. When we hear and receive from the Holy Spirit on a personal level, it can have a great impact and bring dramatic change into our lives. That change not only changes us, but will also affect others.

George Whitefield, one of the great revivalists during the first great awakening is an example of what I am saying. God gave him a simple revelation, "preaching could be done outdoors." It seems simple to us, but in the liturgical church of the mid-1,700's it was not only unusual, but thought by many to be heretical. He was mocked and persecuted.

This simple revelation produced dramatic fruit. By age 24, Whitefield had preached to over 40,000 people in outdoor settings. He persuaded Wesley to do the same. Whitefield made six trips to America and once preached to 23,000 people in Philadelphia. There were estimates that during his life, he preached to half the population of the colonies, from Georgia to New England.

Father, in the name of Jesus, I ask for the Helper to teach me all things that You would have me to know. Give me simple revelations that would have dramatic fruit in my life and in the lives of others I touch.

## May 10 – GOD'S WILL IS FOR US TO LIVE ABOVE REPROACH

1 Thessalonians 4:3 – For this is the will of God, your sanctification; that is, that you abstain from sexual immorality.

Paul sent Timothy to Thessalonica to strengthen and encourage the Thessalonians in their faith. Paul was concerned that they would be hindered from following Christ because of the afflictions they were suffering. The opposition was coming through their own countrymen from the very beginning of their service for Christ. Paul was concerned that they would grow weary and give opportunity for Satan to hinder their growth. In their culture, as with ours, there was much immorality. Satan uses affliction and difficulties to discourage us and draw us back into fleshly desires. Fleshly gratifications only last a short time. Paul wanted them to understand the true purpose of affliction. God uses affliction to help complete what is lacking in our faith.

Each time a believer chooses to trust God in the times of affliction by going through the difficulties and their faith becomes stronger and stronger. Paul is contrasting two opposite sides of the struggle. First, God's will is our "sanctification." This addresses our separation to His kingdom and to His kingdom purpose. It begins in the spirit, but is always tested in the flesh. God is seeking to raise us up as a people of sanctification and honor. This is what living above reproach really means. If we are ridiculed for a righteous lifestyle, it brings honor and praise to God. If we choose to walk in the flesh, we become a reproach to God's kingdom purpose.

The Father sent the Holy Spirit in Jesus' name to be our Helper. We must draw from His almighty power to be sustained when afflicted. He is the one who supplies all our needs according to His riches in glory by Christ Jesus. This is not just material needs that so many are claiming, but our need for His holiness, His character, and His strength when we feel like giving up. Resist the broad road of just living for the flesh and the feel-good moment. The life separated to God is the life filled with fruitfulness and fulfillment.

Lord Jesus, I know that You gave Your all for me. You lived above reproach and totally honored Your Father. Help me, by the power of Your Holy Spirit whom You have sent, to live above reproach and honor the Father by faith in Your precious blood.


## May 11 – YOU WILL TESTIFY OF ME

John 15:26 – When the Helper comes, whom I will send to you from the Father, *that is* the Spirit of truth who proceeds from the Father, He will testify about Me, and you *will* testify also.

We must always remind ourselves of Jesus' words, "when the Helper comes." As He was pointing His disciples to the soon future event of the coming of the Holy Spirit, He was establishing the thought that they would never be alone. Jesus is clear in this passage that both "the Helper" and His disciples would testify of Him. The Helper is here with us as He was with them. Nothing has changed in the purpose of God. The Spirit testifies of the Lord Jesus Christ by filling us with boldness to open our mouths and declare the Lord's presence to save and deliver. He testifies with mighty acts of power, but He chooses to work through weak beings. It is in weakness that the grace of our Lord is revealed. Consider the Lord's word to His servant Paul, "My grace is sufficient for you, for power is perfected in weakness" (2 Corinthians 12:9).

The Holy Spirit always bears witness to the truth, for He is the "Spirit of truth"! Jesus tells us the Spirit of truth "proceeds from the Father." He is the "Spirit of the Father and the Spirit of the Son." The Holy Spirit in us is how the Father and the Son have taken up residence in our being. They are with us in the Holy Spirit. This too, is how we are with them and why Paul could say, "He raised us up with Him, and seated us with Him in the heavenly places in Christ Jesus" (Ephesians 2:6). The Father already sees us seated with Christ. For Him, it is a done deal. For us it should embolden us to testify of what the Lord has accomplished.

Our testimony is not theoretical, but is a reality because of this presence of the Helper. Believers believe in the Holy Spirit as stated in the Apostles Creed, "I believe in the Holy Ghost." It is more than believing He is the "Third Person of the Trinity." We are called into a vital relationship with the Spirit Himself. Our relationship with the Holy Spirit is revealed through a joint cooperation of His testimony and our testimony. He is not on the outside, but on the inside of every believer. He is there to bear witness to the Son through us. He desires, on a daily basis, a working relationship with each believer. Out of that relationship He reveals to an unbelieving world the power of Jesus' victory at the cross and an overcoming life because of the resurrection.

Ask the Holy Spirit to reveal Himself more and more to you as the Helper. Ask Him to reveal truth. Ask Him how He desires you to cooperate with Him in testifying of the risen Christ.

## May 12 – THAT YOU MIGHT NOT STUMBLE

John 16:1 – These things I have spoken to you so that you may be kept from stumbling.

It should be no surprise that the "world" hates true believers. The system of the world is against all that God has established. The three major systems of the world that resist God's plan and purposes are Governments, which are driven by ego and pride to control people, Economics, which is driven by greed and separates classes of people, and Religion, which seeks to oppress the masses through fear and domination. God the Father has His plan, called "The Kingdom of God." The Kingdom of God is ruled by a benevolent Father through His Son who is full of grace and truth and the Holy Spirit from whom flows righteousness, peace, and joy.

What a contrast between God's kingdom and the world's systems dominated by the kingdom of darkness under Satan's control. Jesus defeated those systems through His overcoming life. He sent His Holy Spirit to overcome those systems through "Spirit-filled and Spirit-led believers." The world will persecute us as they did the Lord and the early church. Jesus warned His disciples concerning the times in which they lived. His word of truth rings true in our day as well. Those disciples, filled with the Holy Spirit, squared off against the powers of hell manifested through the systems of men and overcame even unto death.

Many of God's people stumble when affliction and persecution comes, because they have not read or have not believed the words of Jesus. Our Lord wants to keep us from stumbling, but we must accept His word and be filled with His Holy Spirit in order to stand. Paul expressed it this way, "Therefore, take up the full armor of God, so that you will be able to resist in the evil day, and having done everything, to stand firm" (Ephesians 6:13-14). We live in an evil day, but the enemy's time is short. His complete defeat is near. Jesus judged him in His victory on the cross and overcame Satan in the power of His resurrection. His church is commissioned with the assignment of cleaning up the mess. As His servants, we are to declare to the world the freedom Christ has made possible from the kingdom of darkness. The Holy Spirit makes available to every believer overcoming power to live above the system of this world.

Believe the words of Jesus as given to His first disciples. Be prepared to be persecuted for His Name's sake. Be filled with His Holy Spirit and stand firm, resisting in the evil day. Lord, grant me grace to stand and not stumble. Fill me with Your Holy Spirit every day. Use me to demonstrate Your overcoming life in the power of Your Holy Spirit and lead others to Your victory.

# May 13 – I WILL NEVER LEAVE YOU, NOR FORSAKE YOU

Psalm 51:11 – Do not cast me away from Your presence and do not take Your Holy Spirit from me.

Psalm 51 is one of the most hopeful and encouraging passages of Scripture.
David, out of his own sin and brokenness, reveals what a truly repentant heart looks like. Beginning in verse 5, David identifies the root of our human problem. "Behold, I was brought forth in iniquity; and in sin my mother conceived me."

Many times, people are convicted over a sin, but do not identify the root of the issue as David has done. Our basic nature is one of lawlessness, which is the meaning of "iniquity." The reason the Law of God, which is perfect, could not save us is in the "weakness of our flesh" (Romans 8:3).

David confessed to God that his conception was rooted in sin. His appeal to God was the full recognition of his absolute depraved condition. One cannot express more sincere humility than the position David took in this Psalm. David appealed to God in verse 11, asking "not to be cast away from God's presence." He knows the only real thing that matters is a life lived in the presence of God. David also understood that this life is a life lived in the Spirit: "Do not take your Holy Spirit from me." David knows that he is in danger of losing that presence and favor of God because of his sin. This is why David was a man after God's own heart (1 Samuel 13:14). He recognized his absolute lost condition without God and his absolute dependence upon God.

When one comes to Christ, one needs to take the same posture as David in recognizing their true condition. A true confession of our need of Christ must contain these two components: recognition of my utter depravity and my desperate need for God's Holy Spirit. A shallow confession of faith will lead to a life full of challenges and frustration, because it is not wholly dependent upon God's Holy Spirit. The Holy Spirit led Christ to the cross. He is also leading us to our own personal cross of self-sacrifice and surrender to the Father's will.

Today, ask the Lord to reveal your true depraved condition and to give you a desire for an absolute dependence upon His Holy Spirit. Ask for the grace to freely take up your cross and follow Him.

## May 14 – I WILL BE SUSTAINED BY A WILLING SPIRIT

Psalm 51:12 – Restore to me the joy of Your salvation, and sustain me with a willing spirit.

As we consider the life of David and his revelation concerning his depravity and his desperate need for God's Holy Spirit, we also observe that he confesses he had lost his joy and a willing spirit. Very few people live in joy. There is a difference between being happy and being joyful. Happiness depends on things going well in life. Joy is an inward feeling that is there whether all is well or not. Our salvation in Christ is the fountain of our joy. I had a fellow employee ask me this question one day as I entered the shop, "What gives you the right to be happy all the time?" He did not know the difference between "joy" and "happiness." It gave me opportunity to tell him of the source of my joy that he saw as happiness.

I love how David ties together his request for restoration of the "joy of God's salvation" and "a willing spirit." David recognized that true salvation comes from the willingness of his inner man. A willing spirit is the foundation of true submission to the will of God. Many times people say they are willing to serve God, no matter what, in the emotion of the moment. To serve God takes *"a willing spirit"*! It is the health of the spirit of a person that will sustain. A willing spirit comes from God Himself.

Over many years of ministry, I have found that the root of people's struggles can be located in *"a broken spirit,"* The hurts of life and the hurts caused by others can break an individual's spirit to cause them to give up trying. God's Holy Spirit wants to heal the broken spirit, but it begins in taking personal responsibility. First, acknowledging one's own sin against God. Second, one must release others who have hurt them. The Holy Spirit will then begin the process of healing the "broken spirit" and creating a "willing spirit," which will become the key to sustaining the individual. The Holy Spirit will restore the joy of God's salvation and sinners will be converted as a result (Psalm 51:13).

Thank You, Lord, for what You did for David. For the joy of Your salvation, which is my portion as well. Heal my brokenness and sustain me with a willing spirit. Let me see sinners converted as a result of Your mighty work in me.

## May 15 – I WILL TEACH TRANSGRESSORS YOUR WAYS

Psalm 51:13 – I will teach transgressors Your ways and sinners will be converted to You.

A result of our salvation should be to "teach transgressors God's ways." Once we deal with our own issue of iniquity (lawlessness) and our sin nature by receiving God's work to save us through His Son, the Lord Jesus Christ, we should turn our attention to others. An evidence of true conversion is a concern for others that are as lost as we once were.

David had asked for a "willing spirit." Peter tells us that "The Lord is not slow about His promise, as some count slowness, but is patient toward you, not wishing for any to perish, but for all to come to repentance" (2 Peter 3:9). When David recognized his depravity and confessed his sin, he desired to be an instrument to help others that were in the same condition. A "willing spirit" is one that aligns itself with the will of God. The Holy Spirit has come to "reveal the Father's will." From that revelation, we are to align our self with God's will and pray for the Holy Spirit to lead us to do the will of God. It is clear, God's will was to heal David and re-establish Him in God's Divine Purpose. David, in turn, began to focus on other broken lives around him.

Is our relationship with God all about our need being met or do we also have that component of "a willing spirit" to do God's will? Another way of expressing this concept would be to ask God to "give us a willingness to do His bidding." God has called us to be His representative to others. First by wholeness in our own life, and then to declare God's desire to save and restore others to God's salvation.

My testimony is of my own "depravity" and God's "love" toward me. He has answered my prayer which is after that of David's: "Create in me a clean heart, O God, and renew a steadfast spirit within me" (Psalm 51:10).

Lord, please help me to be willing to do Your will by sharing with others how You forgave my sins and clothed me with Your great salvation so rich and so free. Give me grace to lead others to Your wonderful love and presence.

## May 16 – I WILL GIVE GOD A BROKEN AND CONTRITE HEART

Psalm 51:17 – The sacrifices of God are a broken spirit; A broken and a contrite heart, O God, You will not despise.

Brokenness is the true sacrifice which God desires. It is not a sacrifice in Old Testament terms of animals or grains. In New Testament terms, it is not about good deeds. Jesus offered Himself as "the sacrifice." Jesus became broken for all of us. In His brokenness, I can recognize my own brokenness and need for His saving grace. On the cross, Jesus cried out to His Father and said, "Into Your hands I commit My spirit" (Luke 23:46). Some believe that Jesus died more quickly than usually experienced on a cross as a result of a broken heart. He was broken for us, broken over our sins. Jesus is the only sacrifice that fully pleases the Father.

In Psalm 51, David came to understanding that the sacrifice God is waiting to receive a broken and contrite spirit. Our hearts should be broken over our own sin, and then the sins of others. God is looking to find broken and contrite hearts to work through. Religion is full of self-serving attitudes and fleshly attempts trying to *appease God*. Many run after religion, trying to get their needs met by God and also hoping that God will accept them. True faith in the living God is rooted in this one thing, *"brokenness"*! Brokenness will produce *humility* and a heart desiring to serve.

David concludes this verse with the confident cry, "O God, You will not despise." God will never turn away from the broken spirit or a contrite heart. Even as David, the king, had to come to this place in his life, so also God's people must learn of brokenness, hopefully not in the same way David had to. Many in the Lord's church are *filled with self-approval* and *self-serving attitudes* making them vulnerable to the enemy. Brokenness begins with the individual, develops in the congregation, and becomes the spirit of the church throughout a city, which in turn will cause sinners to be converted!

Pray with me for the Spirit of God to deal with our individual heart condition. Pray for your local church community and for the church of your locality. Pray that we will bring to God a "broken and contrite heart." Claim the salvation of sinners and their conversion to God's glorious kingdom.

## May 17 – ORDER ON ORDER AND LINE ON LINE

Isaiah 28:10 – For He says, "Order on order, order on order, Line on line, line on line, A little here, a little there."

What is Isaiah speaking about through the Spirit of the living God? I was taught early in my Christian walk that this meant God gives us a little here and a little there. That thought may be true in regard to how God deals with His children, but it is not what the Prophet had in mind. He is describing how the Lord saw the Israelites as a mocking people. In response, the Prophet is mocking them in what he has to say from the Lord.

How do we receive the Word of the Lord? Many of God's people today, as Israel of old, regard lightly God's Word to them. It is easy to reject a sermon when the minister begins to deal with one's heart condition or one's attitudes. Today, many want the minister of the gospel to make them feel good about themselves. There are those who feel safe because they are sitting comfortably in a church with a pastor who is feeding them *pabulum*. Israel, in Isaiah's day, was comfortable in their religion and their compromise of God's true purposes through them.

God began to speak to His people through the Assyrians who threatened the Israelites' safe abode. The Assyrians represented a pending judgment to the people of God. They spoke a language that was foreign to the Hebrews. God was warning Israel to repent and turn back to Him. They refused to listen to the Spirit of God through the Prophet. They continued to mock the Prophet's word. Calamity came upon them.

Today, as in Isaiah's day, the Lord is looking for His people to open their hearts to Him. In this passage, God used foreigners that did not speak the Hebrew language to be the instrument of His judgment. What is the Lord using in our lives? Could it be the threat of radical Islam? What about the possibility of economic collapse? Could it be poor leadership in the State and Federal government?

Ask the Spirit of God to increase your respect and honor of God's Word. Ask Him to protect you from mocking the Word of the Lord in your life, and open your heart to hear and receive His corrections. Ask Him for power in the Holy Spirit to live godly in an ungodly culture. Pray for revival!

## May 18 – REST TO THE WEARY

Isaiah 28:11-12 – Indeed, He will speak to this people through stammering lips and a foreign tongue, He who said to them, "Here is rest, give rest to the weary and here is repose," but they would not listen.

Yesterday, we saw how God chose to speak through the Assyrians as their conquering army was poised to swoop in and take Israel captive. God's people mocked the word of the Prophet and rejected the protection that Jehovah was offering His people.

It is interesting how the Scriptures can have more than one meaning, and prophecies can have a couple of applications. The apostle Paul, in 1 Corinthians 14:20-21, chose to use Isaiah 28:11 to explain the purpose of the "gift of tongues." Paul says, "Do not be children in your thinking; yet in evil be infants, but in your thinking be mature" (1 Corinthians 14:20). In Isaiah's passage, he reveals that Israel was not being mature. They acted like children as they mocked the Prophet. The Corinthians were misusing the "gift of tongues." They acted immature in the operation of the gifts of the Spirit. In 1 Corinthians 14:22

Paul teaches, that tongues are for a sign, not to those who believe, but to unbelievers.

In Isaiah 28:10-12, the stammering lips and a foreign tongue was a "sign" to Israel. When God poured out His Spirit as recorded in Acts 2, once again "tongues" was a sign to Israel. This time, it was evidence the kingdom of God had come with the out-pouring of the Holy Spirit, and the accompanying sign of tongues. Paul is reminding the Corinthians "tongues" was God's means of getting His people's attention. Isaiah said, "This is the rest whereby I will cause the weary to rest, this is the refreshing, but they would not hear." The "rest" was found in receiving God's warning through the sign of pending judgment. In Acts 2, the rest is found in receiving the Spirit who brings the Good News of the kingdom of God through the Apostles' preaching.

The rest and refreshing for the people of God is found in an open heart poised to receive God's word by making the needed corrections and moving in the direction of God's will. The Spirit of God has come with gifts that will refresh God's children as they receive them. Many resist the Spirit's gifts because they seem strange or because their hearts are fixed on other things.

Today, let us choose to be mature in our thinking. Open your heart to what God has for you. He may choose to speak to you through His written Word or through another individual. Holy Spirit, lead us to be aware of when You are speaking, though it sounds like a stammering lip, help us to hear and obey.

## May 19 – RECEIVE MY REST

Isaiah 28:12— "Here is rest, give rest to the weary and here is repose," but they would not listen.

The "rest" of God comes through obedience to His will. The Assyrian army was a growing threat to Israel's safety and peace. What Israel had known under God's protection was on the verge of disappearing. Once again, Israel, which had known the deliverance of Jehovah's great power, was about to be taken into bondage and slavery by a people who spoke a different language. This people also had a different world view than that of Israel. Israel confessed faith in Jehovah and His redemptive power, but lived like the heathen nations around them. As we have seen in previous devotions, they mocked the word of the Lord and the Lord's messenger.

The height of Israel's rebellion and arrogance came during the times of Jesus. The religious leaders mocked Jesus and rejected the deliverance Jehovah was offering through His Son. As in the past when they killed the prophets, they planned the murder of Jesus, and later the murder of God's apostles. In Peter's first sermon, he warned Israel when he testified and kept on exhorting them, saying, "Be saved from this perverse generation" (Acts 2:40-41)!

There are three words that are important to consider as we speak about the rest God has provided for His people. The first word is to *reflect.* God sends His word and allows circumstances in order to get our attention. Many times obstacles are allowed by God to draw us toward Him. In those times, we need discernment. The second word to consider is the word *received*. The Lord sends His word and it is important to take a posture of receiving His word. I like the use of the word *embrace* because it speaks of getting close. It is possible to agree with God's word in terms of doctrine, but not embrace His word as relevant to my circumstance. Our third word to consider is the word *respond*. Responding is obedience to God's word. James expressed it this way, "Prove yourselves doers of the word and not merely hearers who delude themselves" (James 1:22).

Ask the Father, in Jesus' name, for the help of the Holy Spirit to discern words spoken to you and the circumstances that surround your life. Ask Him to give to you grace to embrace the word of God and apply it appropriately. Finally, set your heart to obey God's word and all of its implications to your situation.

## May 20 – SEEK EARNESTLY THE BEST GIFTS

1 Corinthians 12:8 – To one is given the word of wisdom through the Spirit

Natural wisdom is the ability to apply possessed knowledge and experience. The "word of wisdom" is not natural or human wisdom, but supernatural wisdom from God. This Wisdom cannot be developed because it is already perfect. The word of wisdom is the supernatural revelation by the Spirit for divine plans and purpose concerning things, people, places, and events. The "word of wisdom" should not be confused with deep spiritual insight in God's Word. The latter comes from study and revelation. The gift of the "word of wisdom" comes directly from the Spirit of God.

In a sense, the word of wisdom is the revelation of the purpose of God concerning things in the now and in the future. This wisdom is given to direct us in our decisions and provide safety from deception. Some Scriptural examples of the use of the word of wisdom will show how indispensable this gift is to a finite people.

In the Old Testament there are many examples of a word of wisdom given to those walking in a relationship with the Lord. The wisdom that comes from above always carried a redemptive purpose. Consider Genesis 6:13-22. God's knowledge of future peril was communicated in a supernatural way to Noah. Noah was given the wisdom necessary to build the Ark and accomplish God's will of saving the human race from the soon coming flood. King Solomon provides another example in I Kings 3:16. Solomon received supernatural wisdom to shepherd God's people. The issue of the two women claiming to be the mother of the same baby is a great example of this wisdom given by God (1 Kings 3:16-22).

Paul tells us, "By His doing you are in Christ Jesus, who became to us wisdom from God." Today, all wisdom is found in the Lord Jesus Christ. Paul understood more fully than most about wisdom. "We proclaim Him, admonishing every man and teaching every man with all wisdom" (Colossians 1:28). The gospel of Christ is the wisdom of God unto salvation for every individual.

Be bold and ask the Holy Spirit for the wisdom of heaven. Every day, ask for wisdom and expect the Lord to release your portion as needed. The Father, through the Holy Spirit, is waiting for us to ask and receive of the wisdom that comes from above.

# May 21 – SEEK EARNESTLY GOD'S WISDOM

1 Corinthians 1:31 – Let him who boasts, boast in the Lord.

Today, I want us to look further into this subject of wisdom. Throughout the Scriptures, wisdom is highlighted as a gift given by God. In Matthew 2:13, we read of a word of wisdom given to Joseph through a dream which instructed Joseph to take Mary and the babe to Egypt. Compare this with Matthew 2:20 when the angel instructed Joseph to return to Israel. In Acts 13:2, the command by the Spirit to separate Barnabas and Saul was a word of wisdom as to the timing of God's will to take the Gospel to the Gentiles. It had a bearing upon their walk and experience. In Acts 15:5-27, a word of wisdom is given through James as to what commands should be placed on the converted Gentiles. In Acts 26, Paul is defending himself before King Agrippa and Festus. Festus thought Paul to be insane. Paul testifies of the wisdom from the Lord given to him at his conversion which directed his life in the message he carried as the Apostle to the Gentiles.

The above Scriptures are but a few examples of this wonderful gift the Spirit of God has made available to the Church of the Lord Jesus Christ. In 1 Corinthians 1:31, Paul warns us not to boast in ourselves, but in the Lord. In wisdom, he is quoting from the prophet Jeremiah. "Thus says the Lord, Let not a wise man boast of his wisdom, and let not the mighty man boast of his might, let not a rich man boast of his riches; but let him who boasts boast of this, that he understands and knows Me, that I am the Lord who exercises loving-kindness, justice and righteousness on the earth; for I delight in these things, declares the Lord (Jeremiah 9:23-24).

I believe Jeremiah gives to us the sum total of the subject of wisdom. Paul establishes the need for us to pursue wisdom in our personal and corporate life. Today, receive God's wonderful grace of wisdom. If you can identify times this grace has been released in your life, rejoice and thank the Lord continuously. Rejoice in the Lord, and again I say rejoice!

Today, ask the Holy Spirit to give you this gift as needed. Open up yourself to receive a deposit of supernatural wisdom from God by asking for the gift of wisdom, especially when you are at the end of your own sufficiency. If you are anything like me, that would be quite often.

## May 22 – SEEK EARNESTLY GOD'S KNOWLEDGE

1 Corinthians 12:8 – To another the word of knowledge, according to the same Spirit.

The word of knowledge is a supernatural revelation given to believers by the Holy Spirit of certain facts in the Mind of God. God keeps ever before Him in the storehouse of His Mind all the facts of heaven and earth. He knows every person, place, and thing in existence. He has them ever before Him. That is a real knowledge base! The word of knowledge is a revelation to an individual by the Holy Spirit of some detail that would help them to know what to do or say. It is supernatural "knowledge" such as the existence, condition, or whereabouts of some person or object. It might be the place, location or occasion of some event. It is a gift of revelation, revealed to one's spirit and mind. It is usually not vocal, but given as a thought, a picture, or some other type of impression.

The word of knowledge is not natural knowledge, but supernatural information. A few examples of the use of this gift in Scripture will help to make this clearer to us. In today's lesson, we will consider a few Old Testament examples. In tomorrow's lesson, we will look at a few from the New Testament.

In I Samuel 3:10-21, a word of knowledge was given to the child Samuel, who was to become the Prophet of Israel. God spoke to the child and said, "Behold, I am about to do a new thing in Israel" (1 Samuel 3:11). Even a child can hear the word of knowledge the Lord wants to give. In II Kings 6:8-12, the word of knowledge is used to warn a king of the enemy's plan. A man of God sent a word to the king warning him where his enemy was about to attack. In 1 Kings 19:14-18, the word of knowledge was given to enlighten and encourage Elijah, a discouraged servant of the Lord. In II Kings 5:20-27 a word of knowledge was given to expose a hypocrite.

As one can see, the word of knowledge is not new to the New Testament. God has been giving this supernatural grace throughout His dealings with His people. The word of knowledge has been made available to any of God's servants through the Lord Jesus Christ.

If you have not already done so, begin to ask the Father, in Jesus' name for the "word of knowledge" to be activated in your life. Yield your mind to the Holy Spirit, inviting Him to be free to give you words that only He has to give. Lord, please help me to speak for You, as Your servants did throughout the Old and New Testaments.

## May 23 – THE WORD OF KNOWELEDGE HELPS TO CONVINCE SINNERS

John 4:18 – You have had five husbands and the one whom you now have is not your husband.

The woman at the well is an excellent example of how powerful this New Testament gift of knowledge can be. As Jesus speaks with the Samaritan woman, He tells her life history with men. As we continue to read on in John 4:19 – 29, we learn how the whole city came to hear Jesus as a result of this one word of knowledge spoken to the women. That word helped to convince a sinner of her need of the Savior; she in turn was used to reach others by pointing them to Christ.

Acts 9:10-11 speaks of how the word of knowledge came through a vision and pointed out to Ananias a man in need. That man happened to be Saul of Tarsus, who later became the Apostle to the Gentiles. Notice how this word came in a vision to Ananias. He responded, "Here I am Lord".

Peter received a word of knowledge about corruption in the church (Acts 5:3). The result was fatal for a man and his wife because they purposed in their heart to lie to the Holy Spirit. Today, it seems like many get away with lies and deception, but let me assure you, when this gift of knowledge begins to operate in the Lord's Church at this level, judgment will also follow as it did in the days of the early apostles.

Please do not confuse this gift of knowledge with learning. The word of knowledge is a special supernatural revelation of facts given by the Holy Spirit. The examples are too numerous for all of them to be included. The "foretelling" of events to come is an operation of this blessed gift. To treat this gift as a vocal gift by suggesting that it is about preaching and teaching that came through studies, is to rob it entirely of its supernatural and miraculous character.

Holy Spirit, I am limited in what I know. I invite You to use me as often as it is pleasing to You through the gift of knowledge. Reveal to me what I need to know to encourage a child of God or help one to come to know the Savior. If You will, use me to point out sin, that the one in bondage may be set free to experience Your love.

## May 24 – THE GIFT OF FAITH CAN BE YOURS

1 Corinthians 12:9 – To another is given faith by the same Spirit.

Let us remember that *through faith* we are saved (Ephesians 2:8). We call this "saving faith." The first work of the Spirit in our life is to lead us to faith in Christ. Faith that believes the Word of God which declares what the Lord has done for us through His death on the cross. This is faith that began to work in us before salvation actually takes place. Paul calls it "The faith of the Son of God" (Galatians 2:20).

Faith is named in the fruit of the Spirit as seen in Galatians 5:22. This kind of faith can only be developed by the Spirit as we learn to walk in the Spirit. Fruit can only be grown, not made. This fruit of faith speaks of God creating us to be a faithful people. We begin in faith that saves us. Then we learn to walk in faith, learning to trust the Holy Spirit on a daily basis. At times, we may experience the gift of faith which the Holy Spirit gives at His will for special times of need.

The gift of faith **is** distinct from saving faith and the fruit of faith. The gift of faith is in the family of the power gifts. When one operates in this gift, they believe God in such a way that God honors their word as His own. He miraculously brings to pass those things spoken in faith. It is a supernatural endowment by the Spirit whereby what is uttered or desired by a person shall eventually come to pass. This faith utterance covers blessing, cursing, destruction, and is different from the gift of the working of miracles and the gifts of healing in that often its operation is not immediately or even generally observed.

The operation of Miracles is more of an act, as when the Red Sea was rolled back by Moses, while the operation of the gift of faith is more of a process. The Gift of Faith begins with a sudden surge or boost of faith given by the Holy Spirit, when needed, as seen in Joshua 10:12-13, Acts 9:40, and Acts 13:11. Peter is a great example of this operation of faith. He entreated the Lord to bid him to come as the Lord was walking on the water and approaching the disciples. The other disciples in the boat thought Peter had lost it for sure, but when he came back in the boat with Jesus, Peter was their hero of "faith." You just have to know, each one of them wished they had done what Peter did!

Holy Spirit, there are times when only the "gift of faith" can bring us through to Your intended purpose. Make me a willing vessel to allow You to give me that gift to help me do Your will when my natural ability fails me.

## May 25 – HEALING THE OPPRESSED AND HURTING

1 Corinthians 12:9 – To another is given gifts of healing

One of the most powerful verses of scripture states, "You know of Jesus of Nazareth, how God anointed Him with the Holy Spirit and with power, and how He went about doing good and healing all who were oppressed by the devil, for God was with Him" (Acts 10:38). Our Lord sets the standard for ministry. Jesus takes of His anointing and gives a portion to each believer.

One of the gifts of power is "healing." Of the gifts of power, healing is the most widely distributed. The gifts of healing are for the supernatural healing of disease and infirmities without natural means of any sort. I must emphasize the entirely supernatural character of the "gifts of healing." These gifts of healing must not be confused or mixed with medical science in any fashion. Healing through these gifts is brought about by the power of God in the name of Jesus Christ through the Holy Spirit who resides in believers. Please notice, Paul's plural use of the word "gifts" as it relates to healing. One possible reason is there are so many different kinds of sickness and diseases which afflict the human race. Not all sickness is physical. Consider other needs such as emotional suffering, a wounded heart, sexual brokenness, and deliverance from all kinds of demonic inflicted bondage

The Lord still has compassion on the sick today; He still delivers from the power of the enemy. He is still healing people in the old fashioned way revealed in His Word. His way is a safe way, a painless way, and is free. It is a holy way because it is His Way. It is helpful to understand the working and purpose of these gifts of healing by considering their operation as revealed in the Scriptures. If you remove from the scriptures all the references to healing, you would not have much of the Bible left.

Consider three reasons helpful in seeking God for the gifts of healing to be operating in and through our life in Christ. I suggest looking these scriptures up and asking the Holy Spirit to give you a greater understanding of God's will to heal.

Healing is used of the Spirit to help convince men of the Son-ship of the Lord Jesus Christ (John 10:36-38). Healing authorizes the Gospel message as preached by God's servants (Act 4:29-30; 5:12; 8:6-17). Healing establishes the Resurrection of the Lord Jesus Christ (Acts 3:15-16).

Father, fill me today with the compassion of our Lord Jesus Christ for those that need Your healing power. Release gifts of healing through me to minister Your love to those needing to be touched by Your Holy Spirit.


## May 26 – THANK YOU FATHER, FOR YOUR MANY HEALING GIFTS

1 Corinthians 12:9 To another is given gifts of healing.

Healing is the only gift spoken of in the plural. The term "gifts" is used because there are many manifestations of the Spirit regarding healing. It is undoubtedly a gift that contains gifts. "There are varieties of gifts, but the same Spirit" (I Corinthians 12:5). There are differences of manifestations and operations of the gifts of God. Separate from the working of miracles is the miracle of healing. My definition of the "gifts of healing" is "the supernatural healing of diseases and infirmities without the aid of natural means."

Healing is a command of Jesus to His disciples. "As you go, preach, saying, the kingdom of heaven is at hand. Heal the sick, raise the dead, cleanse the lepers, and cast out demons. Freely you received, freely give" (Matthew 10:7-8). Jesus Bore Our Sins and Sickness according to Isaiah 53:3-5. Matthew 8:16-17 and 1 Peter 2:24 both reveal this to be the correct interpretation of the Isaiah passages. Jesus associated sin and sickness in Mark 2:1-12 when He told the paralytic, "Son, your sins are forgiven" (Mark 2:5). It has been said that 90% of Jesus' ministry was involved in the healing of the sick.

There are so many more Scriptures which give evidence of God's desire and will to heal. He has made us participants in this great part of His Son's ministry by providing these "gifts of healing." The gifts are distributed in His body by the Holy Spirit. What an important topic and ministry from our Lord. He wants to anoint His sons and daughters with an increased expectation and release of His presence through His gifts. We will take a couple more days in our devotions to consider further scriptures instructing us about the subject of healing.

I have had the privilege of praying for multitudes of people around the world to receive healing. It has been one of my greatest delights to have watched the Holy Spirit release His gifts with mighty power over all kinds of sickness and disease. I praise His Holy Name for what He has accomplished in the lives of so many through this wonderful gift!

Ask the Holy Spirit for deepening insights in the scriptures relating to healing. Ask Him to prepare your heart and to give you divine appointments for ministering to those who He would touch with His healing power.

# May 27 – JEHOVAH ESTABLISHED HIS COVENANT OF HEALING LONG AGO

Exodus 15:26 – If you will give earnest heed to the voice of the Lord your God, and do what is right in His sight, and give ear to His commandments, and keep all His statutes, I will put none of the diseases on you which I have brought on the Egyptians; for I, the Lord, am your healer.

Jehovah God established His Healing Covenant with His Covenant people after turning the bitter waters sweet. He said, "For I, the Lord, am your healer." Throughout the Old and New Testament, *healing* was part of the covenant which the Lord provided for His people. In the New Testament, we see healing extended to unbelievers as a gift to draw them to God's mercy and grace.

Many Scriptures speak to this tremendous truth of God's grace of healing. Consider some of those healed in the Old Testament. Abimelech was healed when Abraham prayed (Genesis 20). God healed Israel while in the wilderness (Psalm 107:20). Naaman was healed when he followed Elisha's instructions (2 Kings 5). Jeroboam, Hezekiah, and David all experienced God's healing power (Psalm 103:1-5).

In the Gospel of Luke, we find twenty-four cases of healing recorded. We read of Jesus healing the sick and sending His disciples to do the same (Luke 10:8-9). In verse 9, Jesus directly connects healing to the message of the kingdom of God. He healed some and the result was apparent later (Luke 17:14). He healed others and they recovered instantly (Matthew 8:13). He healed all manner of sickness and disease: lunacy, palsy, epilepsy, fever, paralysis, blindness, lameness, deafness, withered limbs and, He raised the dead as with Lazarus (John 11:38-44). He healed those that were far away (John 4:46-54). He healed chronic cases, such as the woman with the issue of blood for 12 years (Luke 8:43); the man lame for 38 years (Luke 5:5-9) and, the woman bent over for 18 years (Luke 13:18).

God still heals today. He uses willing people who will just simply believe God's Word and obey as the Holy Spirit prompts them to pray for those in need. Today, rooms of healing are being raised up all over the world. God's people come together in a building or house to take time to pray for the sick. Not only are many healed, but many are coming to know Christ as a result of God's divine touch.

Ask the Father in Jesus' name for the "gifts of healing" to operate in your life. There are so many people that need to be healed. There are many that need to be touched by the power of God. It has been said that "healing is the dinner bell to salvation."

## May 28 -THE CHURCH IS CALLED TO HEAL THE SICK

Mark 16:18 – . . . they will lay hands on the sick, and they will recover

In the early church, the gifts of healing were displayed many years after the resurrection of Christ. Paul had power to heal through special miracles. "God was performing extraordinary miracles by the hands of Paul, so that handkerchiefs or aprons were carried from his body to the sick, and diseases left them and the evil spirits went out" (Acts 19:11-12). It is recorded that Paul prayed for Publius' father and then "laid his hands on him and healed him" (Acts 28:8).

Twenty-six years after the resurrection of Jesus, ordinary believers were still operating in the gifts of healing. Paul speaks of healing gifts in the plural in I Corinthians 12:9. In Galatians, Paul asked a question concerning the Spirit and miracles. "So then, does he who provides you with the Spirit, and work miracles among you, do it by the works of the Law or by hearing with faith" (Galatians 3:5)? James, many years after the earthly ministry of Jesus, gave direction for the Elders to pray for the sick, with a promise of healing and forgiveness (James 5:l4-16).

The Scriptures are filled with many divers operations of the gift of healing. I have listed a number of references which speak about this wonderful gift. Take time to study the Scriptures for yourself. Ask the Father to reveal His will to you concerning healing. Trust Him in faith that the Holy Spirit would give gifts of healing to you. Ask Him to use you to bring healing to those in need. Father, supply my life with Your gifts of healing as You would direct. There are many in need of God's healing power. There is a great need for God's people to allow the Holy Spirit to minister His gifts through their life.

Here are a few examples of the diversity of the healing gifts: Touch of a hand – Matthew 9:21; Sending the Word – Psalm 107:20; Peter's shadow – Acts 5:15; Aprons and garments – Acts 19:12; Anointing with oil. – James 5:14; Laying on of hands – Mark 16:18; Prayer in Jesus' Name – Acts 3:6; The Word of Knowledge – Acts 9:11.18 and 14:8.10; Through the means of special directions to the sick one: Mark 7:31-37 – Fingers in his ears and touching the  tongue; Mark 8:22-26 – Saliva placed on the blind man's eyes; Acts 20:9-10 – Paul embracing a dead man who revived; Action taken by the sick one to show faith. In John 5:1-9 is the example of the man at the pool of Bethesda picking up his bed and walking. Another time in Matthew 9:1-7, Jesus told the man to "pick up his bed and go home." And he got up and went home. It was in Jesus' healing ministry that, "the crowds were awestruck, and glorified God, who had given such authority to men" (Matthew 9:8).

God has always been the healer of His people. He heals today as well. Won't you receive His healing grace in your life and allow Him to use you to bring His healing power to others? Remember what Jesus said about those who believe on Him, "They will lay hands on the sick, and they will recover" (Mark 16:18).


## May 29 – OUR GOD IS A GOD OF MIRACLES

Mark 16:17 – These signs will accompany those who have believed.

What a wonderful promise our Lord has given us. The word miracle denotes a non-natural, beyond natural, supernatural order of things. A miracle is a work contrary to nature, the accomplishments of which we are unaccustomed to experiencing. The gift of the working of miracles operates by the energy or dynamic force of the Spirit of God. It is a sovereign act of the Spirit of God, irrespective of laws or systems that we understand.

Some of the operations of this gift are found both in the Old and New Testament. They are seen when God delivered His people from bondage, Exodus 14:16. God provided for those in need while in the wilderness, Exodus 17:5-6. In the New Testament, miracles confirm the preached Word, Acts 8:6. Miracles deliver people at times of unavoidable situations of danger, Acts 19:11-12. Miracles display God's power and magnificence, Psalm 150:2. Miracles show forth His excellent greatness!

Miracles are explosions of God's almighty signs and wonders. Miracles are an expression of the divine, walking among men. Miracles are tokens of His invisible power. Miracles fall into the realm of recreation, not just mere healing. There are miraculous occasions we find mentioned in the Scriptures and recorded in history. Some examples are the deliverance ministry, when evil spirits come out of people. There are occasions when new limbs are given, blind eyes are opened, deaf ears are unstopped, a new organ given, and unexplainable events taking place. The most powerful miracle is the resurrection of the dead.

God's people, who have been saved by the power of God, need to give time to meditating on the "miraculous." The miraculous should be a part of our walk with Christ, in the Power of the Holy Spirit. A lifestyle of the miraculous should not be foreign or strange. As a believer in the Lord, we should come to expect the Holy Spirit to break into our natural world and perform "signs and wonders." Those that want to argue against the miraculous will be those that seldom see God's miraculous hand. I choose to live a life of expectation resulting in many experiences of God's intervention into my natural world with supernatural occurrences.

Won't you join me in expectation of God's promises to those who believe? Ask the Holy Spirit to perform mighty signs and wonders through you on behalf of those in need of the power of God. Father, raise my expectation of Your mighty power working with me and through me on a daily basis for Your glory.

# May – 30 EACH OF GOD'S NEW TESTAMENT PEOPLE CAN PROPHESY

1 Corinthians 14:31 – You can all prophesy one by one, so that all may learn and all may be exhorted.

The subject of prophecy is at the heart of Paul's teaching in 1 Corinthians 14. Earlier, Paul told these believers, "You know that when you were pagans, you were led astray to the mute idols" (1 Corinthians 12:2). Paul goes on to share about those who speak by the Spirit of God. God the Father always intended His people to be a voice for Him. Moses said, "I would that all God's people were Prophets" (Numbers 11:29). Revelation 19:10 states that "The testimony of Jesus is the spirit of prophecy."

Let's review what Paul teaches concerning prophecy. In 1 Corinthians 14:1, Paul commands us to "Pursue love, yet desire earnestly spiritual gifts, but especially that you may prophesy." In verse 3 he writes, "But one who prophesies speaks to men for edification, and exhortation, and consolation." He goes on in verse 4, "One who prophesies edifies the church." In verse 5, Paul shares a deep desire, "Now I wish that you all speak in tongues, but even more that you would prophesy; and greater is the one who prophesies than the one who speaks in tongues, unless he interprets, so that the church may receive edifying."

Remember, Paul is dealing with these gifts in the corporate gathering of the church. The instruction applies to the church as a whole being edified not just ministering to one person. Paul writes in verse 6, "What will it profit you unless I speak to you either by way of revelation or of knowledge or of prophecy or of teaching?" These are four clear spoken ways of building up the body of Christ! In verses 7 through 33, Paul illustrates his point using musical instruments, the natural way of speaking, and the call to war. Paul states, "I thank God, I speak in tongues more than you all; however, in the church I desire to speak five words with my mind so that I may instruct others also, rather than ten thousand words in tongues" (1 Corinthians 14:19). In verses 31-33 Paul teaches us that "you can all prophesy one by one, so that all may learn and all may be exhorted; and the spirits of the prophets are subject to the prophets; for God is not the God of confusion but of peace, as in all the churches of the saints."

Paul is not dealing with the private use of tongues in these passages. He is concerned for the church when she gathers together. There, the focus must be "edification of one another." In the corporate gathering, there is no place for being self-focused or drawing attention to oneself. The concern is always to be toward building up others in Christ.

Pray with me for the Holy Spirit to make us an instrument for Him to speak through Him to others. Lord, cause me to both hear You clearly and to speak clearly Your word to others that they may be edified. Release the "gift of prophecy" in my life as You please. I am listening Lord, use me.

## May 31- DISCERN THE SPIRITS

1 John 4:1 – Beloved, do not believe every spirit, but test the spirits to see whether they are from God, because many false prophets have gone out into the world.

The gift of discerning of spirits gives a supernatural insight into the secret realm of the spiritual world. Through this gift, one receives information that could not be known apart from the gift. By discernment, we may know the true source and nature of any supernatural manifestation. One is able to know whether it is divine, satanic or just human. It should be noted, this is not discernment, but "discerning of spirits." One might naturally discern a situation, but this gift is for the purpose of the discerning of in the spirit world.

There are three kinds of spirits to be considered in our devotional. First is the Divine, God's Holy Spirit promised to every believer by the Father. The divine also includes angels. Angels are known for manifesting and bringing messages from God to humans. Second is that the demonic is associated with the kingdom of darkness. Last is the human spirit. Both joy and pain can flow out of the human spirit. The gift of discernment is given to distinguish the source of activity. Is it coming from the divine, from the satanic or the human spirit? The use of the gift today is the same as seen in the Scriptures. Consider with me some applications of discernment found in God's Word.

The gift is used in delivering the afflicted, oppressed, and tormented from the enemy's clutches. Many infirmities, cruelties, and suicides are attributable to evil spirits. The natural world has difficulty conceiving of the spiritual world. Lives can still be driven and wrecked by cruel, tormenting spirits (Mark 5:1-15; Luke 9:38-43; Acts 5:16; Matthew 12:22; and Luke 13:11-16). Obviously, not all impediments are the work of evil spirits, but as Matthew 4:24 reveals, many that Jesus healed were tormented by evil spirits. Another application was to discover a servant of the devil. Paul, by the gift of discernment, discovered the true heart of the magician (Acts 13:6-10). This was not a case of deliverance, but judgment. Another time was to aid in discovering the plans of the adversary. After many days, Paul discerned the evil spirit and cast it out of the young woman. Thus, a wicked master was deprived of his gains and a woman was delivered (Acts 16:16). This gift is used to expose error (1Timothy 4:1-2; 2 Peter 2:1; 1 John 4:1).

The gift of discernment can help in knowing if an angel is interacting with you (Luke 1:12 & 22). "Do not neglect to show hospitality to strangers, for some have entertained angels without knowing it." (Hebrews 13:2).

Let us earnestly seek this gift that we may recognize when we come against a spirit of the enemy, the spirit of error, or even a wrongly motivated human spirit. Let us also be discerning of true ministers of God, whether human or angelic. Pray that the Holy Spirit will activate this vital gift in you and use you mightily for His kingdom's sake.

## June 1 – UNDERSTANDING THE GIFT OF TONGUES IN OUR DEVOTIONAL LIFE

1 Corinthians 14:14-15 – If I pray in a tongue, my spirit prays, but my mind is unfruitful. What is *the outcome* then? I will pray with the spirit and I will pray with the mind also; I will sing with the spirit and I will sing with the mind also.

An unknown tongue is a supernatural utterance initiated by the Holy Spirit. It is a language that has not been learned by the speaker nor understood by the mind of the speaker. It has nothing whatsoever to do with linguistic ability, but is a manifestation of the Spirit of God employing human speech organs. Some may ask, what is the use or purpose of speaking with tongues?

In the Acts of the Apostles, the gift of tongues is seen as a "sign gift." It was a sign to the Jews that the kingdom of God had come as revealed by the Prophets (Acts 2). It was also a sign to the Jews that the Gentiles were accepted and made part of the kingdom (Acts 10). Tongues were also a sign to the twelve disciples Paul found at Ephesus. When Paul prayed for them to receive the Holy Spirit, they spoke in tongues and prophesied.

In 1 Corinthians 14 Paul makes a distinction between the gift of tongues in bringing a message in the assembly and tongues as a devotional help in prayer and worship. Paul speaks of tongues as a sign to the unbeliever or the ungifted person (1 Cor. 14:22). Earlier in the chapter, he spoke of tongues as a help in prayer and worship (1 Cor. 14:14-15).

Paul says that the one who speaks in tongues does not speak to men, but to God. In his spirit he speaks mysteries, in other words, things unknown to the speaker or listener (1 Corinthians 14:2). As in the apostolic days, so it is today. Many of God's people have received this gift. Tongues are most useful in assisting our prayer life and worship of the Lord. Sometimes they may be used to bring a message with the gift of interpretation, but more often, the gift is personal and useful in prayer and worship.

Paul teaches that "One who speaks in tongues does not speak to men, but God (1 Corinthians 14:2). While Peter preached the Gospel to the Gentiles, they received the Holy Spirit and spoke in tongues. "All the circumcised believers who came with Peter were amazed, because the gift of the Holy Spirit had been poured out on the Gentiles also. "For they were hearing them speaking in tongues and exalting God" (Acts 10:45-46). There are no terms in natural speech appropriate to express the Greatness and Excellence of God. Those who have had the joy of seeing others filled with the Holy Spirit and speaking in tongues can recall how most, lovingly adored Jesus.

Paul asks the rhetorical question, "All do not speak with tongues, do they?" He also indicates throughout 1Corinthians

14 that all could. Ask the Holy Spirit to empower you to speak with His help in your prayer and worship of our great king. Pray, Lord, I yield my voice to You. Use me to speak of Your greatness and Your glory.

# June 2 – THE GIFT OF INTERPRETATION OF TONGUES

1 Corinthians 12:10 – To another is given the interpretation of tongues.

Seven of the Gifts of the Spirit are common to both Testaments, but two gifts, the gift of tongues and the gift of interpretation of tongues have come into operation since the Day of Pentecost. The gift of interpretation of tongues is the only gift dependent upon another. It could have no meaning without the gift of tongues.

Interpretation of Tongues is the supernatural showing forth by the Spirit of God the meaning of an utterance in tongues. It is not an operation of the mind of an individual, but of the Mind of the Spirit of God.   The interpreter never understands the tongue being interpreted. The interpretation is just as much a miracle as the original utterance in tongues. The purpose of the gift is to render the gift of tongues intelligible to others, so that the church may be edified (I Corinthians 14:5, 27).

Note, it is "the gift is interpretation of tongues," not the translation of tongues.  A "translation" is a rendering from one language to another in equivalent words. An interpretation is a declaration of the meaning (1 Corinthians 14:11). The Greek word means to explain thoroughly. Many varieties of expression might be used and many details added without altering the sense of the words.  This explains why sometimes the message in tongues is much briefer than the interpretation. The speaker is not translating, but interpreting.  The Holy Spirit is explaining the meaning in a miracle of utterance called the "gift of interpretation."

There are two reasons, I suggest, why this gift is not experienced as much as other gifts. First, as Paul explains in the fourteenth chapter of First Corinthians, the gift is given to bring understanding to the church when the gift of tongues is exercised to declare the gospel in the known language of an unbeliever coming into the assembly. Paul encourages in the church gathering the use of the gift of prophecy where no interpretation is needed. In the early days of the Pentecostal movement in the twentieth century, tongues and interpretation were common. Today, the gift of prophecy is emphasized for the corporate gathering. Tongues are encouraged for one's prayer life, bringing balance to these gifts and a great alignment to Paul's teachings.

You may or may not ever operate in this gift of the Spirit. Yet today, ask the Lord for a great sensitivity to the Spirit's presence and His desire to use you to help another understand more perfectly God's mind and His will for them.

## June 3 – GOD JUDGES HIS PEOPLE WHEN THEY FORGET HIM

Judges 3:10 – The Spirit of the Lord came upon him, and he judged Israel.

The first Judge in Israel was Othniel, the younger brother of Caleb. God raised up Othniel after Israel had cried out to the Lord for deliverance from their enemies. Israel had a habit of falling into idolatry and becoming the slaves of others. Idolatry always leads to "servitude"! God had mercy on His people and sent them a deliverer. Othniel prevailed over the enemies of God's people and the land had rest for forty years.

Whenever we find ourselves in bondage to others or things, it is important to examine our hearts to see if we have made people or things a god to us. A dear sister in the Lord received deliverance from the Lord as she recognized she had made her husband a god. She depended on him for everything and found herself with a bad attitude when he did not meet her expectations. She had stopped seeking the Lord for herself and hearing the Spirit of Lord speaking to her. As she repented and released him to his rightful place as her husband and not a god, she experienced God's rest and peace filling her soul once again.

Idolatry can take on many forms. For Israel, it came in the form of sexual sins. The nations around Israel worshipped the creature more than the Creator (Romans 1:25). It takes a warfare attitude to defeat the enemy and overcome the sin of idolatry. Othniel led the people of God into war against their enemies and God gave him great victory. First we must identify the "sin of idolatry." Then we must rout it out of our lives. We do this by confessing the sin of idolatry, repenting of any idolatrous activity, renouncing it as wrong and against God. Finally, ask that the blood of Jesus cleans you from all unrighteousness (1 John 1:5-10). Once this is done, rest will return and a renewed fellowship with the Spirit of God.

Society around the world is filled with the sin of idolatry. It is almost impossible not to be touched by it in some form or fashion. Ask the Lord to show you any idolatry in your life. With a willing heart, repent and let go of every form of idolatry the Spirit of God reveals to you.

Father, I recognize that the sin of idolatry has always plagued Your people, please show to me any form of this sin in my life. I ask You for the overcoming victory of Jesus to reign in my life.

## June 4 – NOW THE SONS OF ISRAEL AGAIN DID EVIL IN THE SIGHT OF THE LORD

Judges 3:15 – When the sons of Israel cried to the Lord, the Lord raised up a deliverer for them, Ehud the son of Gera.

We must always be vigilant when it comes to sin. The enemy is always waiting to lure us away from our relationship with the Lord.  Israel had known the peace of God for forty years and then they reverted to idolatry. The Lord strengthened Eglon the king of Moab against Israel, because they had done evil in the sight of the Lord.

The Lord will strengthen the enemy against us in order to bring us to repentance. Jesus covers this point in Matthew 18:31-35 when he tells the story of how a king dealt with an unforgiving servant who failed to forgive one that owed him a little compared to what he owed the king. The king throws him in jail until he paid his debt to the king. Jesus then says "My heavenly

Father will also do the same to you, if each of you does not forgive his brother from your heart."

In God's great love, He will discipline His children to get their attention and draw them back to serving His kingdom of righteousness. Ehud went straight to the king of Moab. Ehud told him that he had a message from God. For the king it was a message of death as Ehud plunged a knife into Eglon's abdominal area. We must be intentional and ruthless when dealing with the enemies of God's people. In New Testament terms, disobedience to God's word is an enemy. Carnality is an enemy. An unforgiving heart is an enemy to God's purposes.

Regardless of the sin, it will separate us from God's intended relationship with us. Ehud knew what it would take to restore the people of God and he accepted the responsibility to go after Moab and put an end to the tempter's power. God accomplished this for us in Christ. Our deliverance has been purchased, but we must implement what Christ has done. It is our responsibility to rebuke the enemy of our souls. We are to remind him of his utter defeat by the Lord Jesus Christ. We can stop his aggressions against us by using the weapons the Lord has supplied. The sword of the Spirit is our weapon. "The weapons of our warfare are not of the flesh, but divinely powerful for the destruction of fortresses" (2 Corinthians 10:4). Today, be resolute in your determination to overcome sin and binding the enemy by putting to death the lusts of the flesh through the overcoming life of Christ that resides in you.

Father, in Jesus' name, I put on the armor of God so I can stand against all the trickery of the enemy. Help me, in the power of the Holy Spirit, to be resolute in my resistance against sin, the world and the devil. Father, I ask You to empower me to restore others to You.

## June 5 – DEBORAH AND BARAK DELIVER ISRAEL FROM THE CANAANITES

Judges 5:31 – Thus let all Your enemies perish, O Lord; But let those who love Him be like the rising of the sun in its might.

This verse is taken from the song of Deborah which covers the whole fifth chapter. It is her song of victory after defeating the Canaanites. The enemy had created problems for the work force in Israel. The highways were deserted and travelers went by roundabout ways. Society was in turmoil without security for tomorrow. When God's people are serving the Lord and His purpose there are "pleasantries." But when God's people choose to serve the gods of this world, the pleasantries cease.

At the time of this writing, our nation has forsaken the Spirit of the living God and we are hurting in many areas, just as Israel was at that time. The nations of the world that serve false gods of secular humanism have taken control. Many in the church seek after worldly ways to expand the church, but God's Spirit is frustrating their efforts.

Deborah, a prophetess and a judge over Israel, received a word from the Lord that He was about to deliver the Canaanites into Israel's hands. She gave that word to Barak who was told to take an army against Jabin's army and that Israel would conquer the enemies of God. God's Spirit is looking for those who will hear and obey God's word today. The world is in crisis and only the people of God can bring the deliverance that is needed. It will take those consecrated to the Lord's will. Judges 5:2 sums up our thought in today's devotion, "That the leaders led in Israel and the people volunteered."

God is looking for those called to lead. He is seeking a people that will volunteer. It is time for the people of God to arise and take down the enemies of the Lord. The Spirit of the Lord is looking for the Deborah's and the Barak's of today. Read over Deborah's song in Judges Chapter five and see if the Lord has things to say to you.

Oh Lord, my prayer is that all Your enemies will perish and that those who love You will be like the rising of the sun in its might. Father, strengthen me to be an example in my life of how to overcome the enemies of God. Cause me to be a volunteer wherever Your Holy Spirit leads me to serve in order to accomplish Your purposes in this season.

# June 6 – I AM THE LORD YOUR GOD; YOU SHALL NOT FEAR

Judges 6:7 – Now it came about, when the sons of Israel cried to the Lord on account of Midian, that the Lord sent a prophet to the sons of Israel.

The prophet prophesied deliverance to the children of Israel. Gideon is the man that the Spirit of the Lord chose to deliver Israel. He did not look like a deliverer or sound like one either. When the angel of the Lord addressed Gideon, He said to him, "The Lord is with you, O valiant warrior" (Judges 6:12). Gideon had "why" questions for the angel. Why has all this happened to us? Where are the miracles which our fathers told us about?

Again, we see when God's people cried out to the Lord, the Lord responded. The Spirit of God raises up prophets to proclaim what is in God's heart. In the New Testament, all of God's people are called to be prophetic. Some are called into the office of Prophet. He also anoints those called to lead into the battles that face us. Leaders are developed to lead God's people to fulfill God's purpose. Both leaders and people work together in defeating God's enemies and to establish righteousness in the land.

A leader is first called, but then must be forged. The story of Gideon is the story of how the Spirit of God called a farmer and formed him into a leader. Gideon became a judge of God's people. The character of leadership is something that all of us should press unto. As a believer, one is automatically called to be a leader. It might be at work or school or in the neighborhood. God has called for His people to learn to lead in society. It is time for the people of God to arise and volunteer to take back territory the enemy has stolen.

As Gideon was visited by the angel of the Lord, he asked hard questions. He sought to prove what he was hearing. God wants us to prove Him. A key to being developed by the Spirit of God is to wait upon Him and test all that we hear so we can obey with true faith. The expression of true faith is found in obedience. Obedience must first be expressed by obeying God's written word. Obedience requires studying and praying concerning the word of God preached by His servants. Obedience is expressed by becoming sensitive to the Holy

Spirit's promptings in one's life. This kind of obedience demonstrates a true faith toward God.

In the normal flow of life, the Spirit of the Lord will speak to us and call us to a place of influence in our sphere. When He does, ask the questions that are in your heart. Prove Him fully and then simply obey as Gideon did. Our God wants to show Himself mighty through His willing servants.

Father, speak to me and cause me to be an influence for righteousness in my sphere of influence. Help me to obey as Gideon obeyed and to prove you mighty through my life.

## June 7 – TELL OF THE GREAT THINGS THE LORD HAS DONE

Judges 6:34 – So the Spirit of the Lord came upon Gideon; and he blew a trumpet.

After the angel of God had called Gideon, He gave him instructions to tear down the altar of Baal using his father's bull. He was further instructed to take a second bull, seven years old and offer it as a sacrifice using the wood from Baal's altar. Gideon did as he was instructed. Of course, this caused a great anger among the men of the city and they sought to kill Gideon. The Spirit of the Lord came upon Gideon and Gideon blew a trumpet to summon the men of Israel to battle.

Jesus was anointed with God's Holy Spirit and power to destroy the works of the devil (Acts 10:38). Jesus, in turn, when raised from the dead and ascended to the Father's right hand poured out the Holy Spirit on all those who believed in Him. We, like Gideon of old, are called to "blow the trumpet" of God's Word. We are to proclaim that "Jesus is Lord" and that the "promise of the Father" has come, the Mighty Holy Spirit. We are to proclaim the "command to repent" for the Day of the Lord has come. This repentance includes turning from a lifestyle of self to living for the Lord Jesus Christ. The trumpet sound is going out in the entire world calling for the nations to surrender to Jesus, God's eternal king. As believers, we are to declare justice and righteousness throughout the land.

In Gideon's day, false religion had taken control of society. God raised up a deliverer in the man Gideon. Today, false religion dominates society throughout the world, but a Savior/Redeemer is among us. Jesus has torn down the altars of false gods and is reigning as God's Anointed King. He is summoning a people, filled with His Holy Spirit, to be bold like Gideon and stand against the gods of our times. The Lord is looking for the Gideon's who might have some fear, who will test the Lord's Word, but ultimately will obey and subdue the enemy in their life and the lives of others. As the people of God, we must stand together against unrighteousness in the nation. It is our responsibility to help lead our nation back to God's will and His purpose.

Gideon presented a fleece and put it before the Lord because of what he had heard. What has the Lord been saying to you? If you have not heard His Spirit speaking to you, take time in his presence and in His Word. Then, as He speaks, prove the Word in the way He directs you. Fear not, the Lord declares, for I am with you!

## June 8 – FEW OR MANY TO ENSURE VICTORY

Judges 7:2 – The Lord said to Gideon, The people are too many for Me to give Midian into their hands, for Israel would become boastful, saying, 'My own power has delivered me.'

What a powerful story of how God delivered His people from the control of Midian. God gave Midian into the hands of His people. The Spirit of God identified one of the largest issues we contend with, "pride." It is so human for us to take the credit when we are successful, rather than giving God the glory due His holy name. As revealed here in the story of Gideon, God's wisdom is given to cause His people to be faced with impossible situations by creating a scenario where only God can be glorified.

We should not trust in our own ability or our circumstances in order to have a testimony of success, but in the power of God. Because of Jesus' death, burial and resurrection, the Holy Spirit has come to indwell each believer. It is by His indwelling presence that we are assured of good success. Our victory, as with Gideon's small army, is rooted in God's great power.

God told Gideon to "release those that were afraid and trembling." 22,000 men returned home, which left 10,000. God said, "The people are still too many". God tested the 10,000 by bringing them to the water. There, Gideon separated those who drank by lapping the water with their tongue from those who drank by getting down on their knees. Only 300 lapped the water. Those on their knees were not being diligent to watch for the enemy. Those that lapped were able to look around and watch for the enemy as they quenched their thirst.

The Holy Spirit is the one who supplies power through His gifts. The first gift mentioned in 1 Corinthians 12 is the gift of wisdom. God is looking for willing and diligent people to allow Him to work His mighty power through. It is not an issue of "multitudes," but a willing and watchful people. 32,000 people were too many for God to have success against Midian, but 300 were perfect for the battle because they were vessels through whom God could manifest His glory.

In what ways are you watching and being diligent on behalf of God's kingdom? Have you come to the water simply to get your thirst satisfied or have you come to drink to be refreshed for the battle?

Pray with me, "Holy Spirit; create in me the spirit of Gideon's 300 warriors. Cause me to be ready to do Your bidding through watchfulness and diligence. Use me, Lord, to extend Your kingdom reign in the midst of Your enemies."

## June 9 – CONFUSING THE ENEMY IN THE MIDST OF BATTLE

Judges 7:22 – When they blew 300 trumpets, the Lord set the sword of one against another even throughout the whole army, and the army fled.

The seventh chapter of Judges is a wonderful example of the wisdom of the Holy Spirit as He directs Gideon and his 300 fellow Israelites fighting against Midian. The wisdom of God is certainly greater than the multitude of counselors that try to understand simply by means of their natural reasoning. God's people must move by faith. "Without faith it is impossible to please Him, for he who comes to God must believe that He is and that He is a rewarder of those who seek Him" (Hebrews 11:6).

The Lord had Gideon send home thousands of his countrymen because there were too many for God to use. The scripture says that Midian's army was like the "sand of the sea." The natural man would have said "the more the better", but the Spirit of God said, "I only need 300 to defeat the enemy."

Israel failed to enter the land under Moses leadership when the Lord said, "Now." They took things into their own hands by sending spies into the land of the Canaanites. The Lord simply said "Go in and take the land that I have given you." He did not instruct them to send the twelve spies. He allowed them to do it their way, but later had to judge that generation for their "unbelief," produced by not initially obeying the Lord's command.

Faith is not driven by the rational, but by the Spirit of God. In the New Testament, the Lord confused the enemy's plans by sending His only begotten Son with the purpose of Christ Jesus going to the cross and dying for the sins of unregenerate man. "God's wisdom, which none of the rulers of this age have understood; for if they had understood it they would not have crucified the Lord of glory" (1 Corinthians 2:8). In the Father's wisdom, He raised Christ from the dead and seated Him at His own right hand, a man, raised to rule. In His wisdom, those that receive Christ as Lord and God also now have authority over the kingdom of darkness in their personal life. God's people, united, can now triumph over the enemy and send confusion into the enemy's camp. The Lord's people can do this again and again by simply obeying the leadership of the Holy Spirit.

Make it your determination not to reject the Lord's plans, as foolish as they might sound to your rational mind. Confirm His leadings by the Word of God and walk closely with others that trust the leadership of the Holy Spirit. Pray always that your spirit may be sensitive to His directions.

# June 10 – BE CAREFUL WHAT YOU VOW TO THE LORD

Judges 11:35 – I have given my word to the Lord, and I cannot take it back.

This is a very solemn portion of Scripture that contains the story of Jephthah's tragic vow. He vowed to the Lord to sacrifice the first thing that came out of the doors of his house if the Lord gave him victory over the sons of Ammon. He did triumph over the sons of Ammon, for the Scripture says "The Lord gave them into his hand" (Judges 11:32).

Making a vow to the Lord is a serious matter. In today's vernacular, we might call it a promise. In the emotion of the moment, perhaps because of a stirring message or a crisis situation one may promise the Lord things that have not fully been thought through. A rash promise is a sure way to bring grief into one's life. The Lord takes our words very seriously.

The story of Jephthah is difficult for many of us to relate to. How could the Lord allow this? How could this man follow through with his rash vow?  How could his daughter be so submissive to her father?   There probably is no answer that will satisfy the rationale of the human mind. It is an answer that must be heard in one's spirit.

The Spirit of the Lord must bring revelation to us over such deep questions. The Scripture is clear about the priority the Lord puts on "keeping one's word." Even the Lord has "magnified His Word according to His name" (Psalm 138:2). Your word is the most valuable possession you have. It establishes who you really are. If one cannot trust a person's word, there is no real basis of trust.

Thank God for the cross of Christ that dealt with all our sins. Only Christ could truly fulfill God's Word and make it possible for us to become keepers of our word. Through daily intimacy with the Holy Spirit and time spent in God's Word we learn how to regulate our words and be kept from rash promises.

"Let the words of my mouth and the meditation of my heart be acceptable in Your sight, O Lord, my rock and my Redeemer" (Psalm 19:14).

Lord, I ask You, as the Scriptures say "Set a guard, O Lord, over my mouth; Keep watch over the door of my lips" (Ps 141:3). I am weak, but Your Holy Spirit strengthens me and will keep my heart from evil.

## June 11 – BEING STIRRED TO FULFILL GOD'S PURPOSE

Judges 13:25 – The Spirit of the Lord began to stir him.

In Judges, chapter thirteen through chapter sixteen, we find the life story of Samson. Samson's life began in a supernatural way. His mom was barren. The angel of the Lord visited her and told her that she would bare a son who would deliver Israel from the hand of the Philistines. The angel of the Lord appeared a second time to both Monoah and his wife declaring again that the child would be a Nazirite from birth.

Samson grew up and the Lord blessed him. The Spirit of the Lord began to stir in Samson. When the Spirit of God begins to stir an individual it means that God is directing that one to fulfill the Lord's purpose. Samson's purpose in God was to deliver Israel from the enslavement imposed by the Philistines.

The twelve disciples were men that the Spirit of the Lord began to stir. They did not understand what was happening in their lives, but they followed Jesus and learned to obey Him. Throughout the book of Acts many were stirred to action by the Spirit of God. They not only received the Lord's forgiveness and His promise of eternal life, but they were stirred to give up their lives for a much higher calling and purpose. They had only known their own natural rationale, but when the Spirit of God came upon them, they began to know God's will and purpose.

Down through history we have numerous stories of those stirred by the Spirit of God to an uncompromising life of surrender to fulfilling an assignment given to them. We are presently living in historic times as the Spirit of the Lord is stirring the next generation of mighty men and women of God. I say historic because of the number of youth that the Lord is calling.

The same Holy Spirit is anointing today a generation of young people. They are operating in unusual amounts of power. They are appointed and anointed to carry out His purpose in the earth. They are being called from every nation to the kingdom of God. They look like average people, but they have the Spirit of the Lord resting upon them. The Spirit is doing great feats in order to accomplish the Lord's bidding in the nations.

I have spoken of the young people, but it includes older ones as well that are young in the Spirit. The Spirit of God is joining the older generation with the younger to form a mighty nation that will be victorious in fulfilling the Lord's desires. Samson, like many of us, had his failings, but the Lord has promised a "victorious church."

Father, I pray that Your Spirit would stir me and thrust me forth into the battle. I pray for the power of Your Holy Spirit to rest upon me to fulfill every assignment You have appointed me to fulfill.

## June 12 – LEARNING TO HEAR THE SPIRIT OF GOD

Matthew 16:15-17 – But who do you say that I am?  Simon Peter answered "You are the Christ, the Son of the living God." And Jesus said to him, "Blessed are you, Simon Barjona, because flesh and blood did not reveal this to you, but My Father who is in heaven."

Peter was listening and the Spirit of God *revealed* to him this powerful truth that the other men had missed. Our natural mind is great for natural things, but is dull when it comes to spiritual understandings. Another way of expressing what Jesus told Peter is, Peter you did not learn this in Sabbath School, but from my Father. In Jesus' day, even the teachers of God's Law had missed that He was the long awaited Messiah. Only by the Spirit of God can one know eternal truth. The Lord is eager to speak if we are eager to listen.

Based on Peter's confession, Jesus begins to share the greater purpose of God with His disciples. He must go to Jerusalem, suffer many things, and be killed. Peter, who had heard clearly from the Father, now pulls Jesus aside, and rebukes him, saying, "God forbid it, Lord! This shall never happen to You" (Matthew 16:22). It is hard to imagine Peter saying "no and Lord" in the same sentence. Satan is always standing ready to deceive us, in order to prevent God's truth from establishing our ways.

Jesus then rebuked Satan who had inspired Peter to resist the will of God and run interference with God's eternal purpose in Christ. It is amazing that in such a short time, one moment Peter was in tune with God's will and soon after, speaks for Satan. This illustrates how easy it is to let our rational mind take over, and let the enemy lead. What Peter said made perfect sense to him, but it was foolishness to God's purpose.

In the next five devotions, we will discover five hindrances to our hearing the Spirit of the Lord. Ask the Father to help you hear His Spirit better. Ask Him to remove every hindrance. Ask to be protected from Satan and his subtle attempts to distract you from the will of God our Father.

Father, my prayer is that the Holy Spirit will have complete control in my life. Deliver me from all double-mindedness. Please keep me from ever saying *no* to You, my Lord.

## June 13 – THE HINDRANCE OF ANGER AND UNFORGIVENESS

Ephesians 4:26-27 – Be angry, and yet do not sin; do not let the sun go down on your anger, and do not give the devil an opportunity.

Anger either is a result of unforgiveness or leads to unforgiveness. It is one of the greatest hindrances to a believer being able to hear clearly from the Spirit of God. Paul makes room for the human emotion of anger. God gets angry. Jesus expressed anger at the unbelieving religious leaders He encountered. He never gave way to His own emotions, but expressed His Father's view of those hardened leaders.

Paul says, "Don't let the sun go down on your anger." I call this "keeping short accounts." Sin creeps in and settles in one's heart if not dealt with quickly. Anger at another is one of the most common ways for this to happen.

Jesus addresses the issues of unforgiveness in Matthew 18:23-35. He shares the story of a king forgiving one of his servants a large debt he owed. That same servant did not forgive a fellow servant who owed him only a fraction of what he was forgiven. The wicked servant had his fellow servant thrown in jail until he paid the whole debt. When the king heard what had happened, he summoned that wicked servant. The king sentenced him to jail as the wicked servant had done to his fellow servant.

In Verse 35 it states, "My heavenly Father will also do the same to you, if each of you does not forgive his brother from your heart" (Matthew 18:35). Anger and unforgiveness gives the enemy access to our mind and heart. When the enemy begins to affect our emotions, we become dull of hearing the Spirit of God and we find ourselves being directed by our feelings and natural reasoning rather than by the Holy Spirit. We become our own authority in the affairs of our lives and the Holy Spirit loses His rightful place of control and guidance. The enemy has put many of God's people into prison because of anger and unforgiveness that remains in their hearts.

The Lord wants to speak to us and lead us in the way of righteousness. Let Him reveal to you any anger and unforgiveness. Ask the Holy Spirit to help you each day to keep short accounts with others. Do not let the sun go down on any anger you may have.


## June 14 – BE QUICK TO HEAR, SLOW TO SPEAK, AND SLOW TO ANGER

James 1:19-20 – This you know my beloved brethren. But everyone must be quick to hear, slow to speak, and slow to anger; for the anger of man does not achieve the righteousness of God.

In James' letter, he writes of the testing of our faith, a need of wisdom and humility to be demonstrated. He writes of the blessing for the one who perseveres under trial. He deals with the subject of temptation and deception. He establishes God's character in his statement, "All good and perfect gifts come from God, the Father of lights" (James 1:17). God brought us forth by the word of truth and James declares, "This you know." James reminds us, "We must be quick to hear, slow to speak, and slow to anger."

An evidence of maturity in the life of a believer is the ability to carefully listen to another as they share their perspective. Unfortunately, few are careful listeners. Most are caught up with their own views, rather than carefully listening to another's perspective. The Holy Spirit will give us the ability to be a good listener if we allow Him to take control of our emotions.

The same is true about speaking. How many times has a word quickly left your mouth that you immediately wanted to pull back? Words are powerful. Note what Solomon tells us by the Spirit of God: "Death and life are in the power of the tongue" (Proverbs 18:21). The Holy Spirit desires to take control of our tongues and causes us to speak only words of life to others. By the power of God's Spirit, the tongue can become a source of encouragement. "One who prophesies speaks to men for edification, exhortation, and consolation" (1 Corinthians 14:3).

One who speaks quickly and does not listen to the other person sets themselves up for *anger*. Anger is a natural part of our human makeup. Anger alone is not a sin. It becomes sin when it gets out of control and evil things happen. Things such as broken relationships, words that become difficult to forgive, rage that can lead to murder.

James focuses the believer in chapter 1:19. To paraphrase James, You know the things I have been sharing. So be a good listener, be slow to speak and don't let anger get out of control. Beloved, the anger of man never produces the righteousness of God.

Father, I want to produce the righteousness that You have provided in the Lord Jesus Christ. I ask for the power of the Holy Spirit to control my tongue. Please cause me to be a quick listener and a slow speaker. Please protect me from unrighteous anger and demonstrate to others the patience which You have toward me.

# June 15 – THE PERFECT LAW OF LIBERTY

James 1:25 – One who looks intently at the perfect law, the law of liberty, and abides by it, not having become a forgetful hearer but an effectual doer, this man will be blessed in what he does.

This is an interesting Scripture. James connects liberty with listening. Our relationship with the Holy Spirit should be more about His speaking to us than our speaking to Him. He has a great deal to say to us in helping to bring our life into the liberty Christ has provided for every believer.

"Anyone who is a hearer of the word and not a doer forgets what kind of person he was" (James 1:23-24). An aspect of our liberty is located in remembering what kind of person I had been. As I read God's Word, I am always reminded of the true lost condition I was in. Many believers hear the Word, but stop and camp on who they were in their fallen nature. The liberty James is addressing comes not only from hearing, but also by doing God's Word. The "perfect law of liberty" is located in what Christ has done for us and our response by receiving what He has done.

"It was for freedom that Christ set you free; therefore keep standing firm and do not be subject again to a yoke of slavery" (Galatians 5:1). What a tremendous declaration of God's purpose in Christ. Our *freedom*! Consider a few things He has accomplished: our freedom to obey the Holy Spirit as He reveals God's Truth to our hearts, our freedom to love others, especially those not so lovely, and our freedom to retain God's Word, and by His power allow the Word to change us into His likeness and image *perfect* in me.

Outside of Christ, this liberty does not exist. The only law we need, is the "law of Christ." Paul gives us clarity as to what that law is, "Bear ye one another's burdens, and so fulfill the law of Christ" (Galatians 6:2 KJV). It is that simple, beloved, learning to bear the burdens of others. This is what the Lord had in mind when He said to His disciples, "A new commandment I give to you, that you love one another, even as I have loved you, so love one another" (John 13:34).

Father, I thank You for the *perfect law of liberty*. My great desire is for the Holy Spirit to daily empower me to look into "the perfect law" and fulfill its liberty by hearing and doing all You have commanded me to do.

## June 16 – HELP ME TO BRIDLE MY TONGUE

James 1:26 – If anyone thinks himself to be religious, and yet does not bridle his tongue, but deceives his own heart, this man's religion is worthless.

I believe this to be one of the most powerful scriptures in the Bible. It goes right to the heart of "religious" matters. Religion is filled with words, but the real evidence of true religion is how those words are used. Around the world, religious words are spoken to kill and destroy people or put them into bondage to systems. This is true of every religion of the world.

The problem actually began in the Garden at the "tree of the knowledge of good and evil." It was there that the Serpent initiated the religions of the world when he asked Eve, "Hath God said." Religion, at its core, is a rejection of God's commands to obey His Word. It is man trying to get to God on man's terms rather than God's established Word. Everything changed in that moment, when Adam and Eve submitted to the Serpent rather than the Word of God.

Words were used to affect the enemy's plan. Instead of Adam and Eve *listening* to God's Word and *obeying* it, Eve chose to listen to the Serpent and Adam chose to listen to Eve. When God came in the cool of the day calling for Adam, He found both Adam and Eve hiding and then blaming. Adam blamed God for the woman God had given to him. Eve blamed the Serpent who beguiled her. Before God, the Serpent had nothing to say. From that moment on, mankind has tried to get back to God, but on man's terms. It is called "religious systems." The only way back to God is through the law of sacrifice, the innocent dying for the guilty. God sent His own Son to pay for man's redemption.

The Son said to the Father, "not My will, but Yours be done" (Luke 22:42). In order to receive God's provision of salvation through Christ, we must confess with our mouth "Jesus *as* Lord, and believe in our heart that God raised Him from the dead" (Romans 10:9). As James implies, deception comes from saying too much. Bridle your tongue, listen to God's Word and obey it, then experience more of God's view of religion: His glorious liberty purchased for all those who will trust in Him.

Father, forgive me for speaking more than listening to Your Word. Protect my heart from deception by helping me to bridle my tongue. Holy Spirit, make me an instrument of Your grace, always living in truth and demonstrating pure religion.

## June 17 – PURE RELIGION CONSIDERS ORPHANS, WIDOWS AND PURITY

James 1:27 – Pure and undefiled religion in the sight of *our* God and Father is this: to visit orphans and widows in their distress, *and* to keep oneself unstained by the world.

Our great desire should be to have our minds changed from the world's viewpoints to embracing God's perspective. Paul exhorted the church, "Put on the new self who is being renewed to a true knowledge according to the image of the One who created him" (Colossians 3:10). The "new self" is Christ in us. Again, Paul says to the Philippians, "Have this mind in you that was also in Christ Jesus" (Philippians 2:5). Christ's mind was one of humility, to do only what the Father willed.

The Lord Jesus Christ was not moved by the religion which had been hijacked by Jewish religious leaders. His was a pure religion, "unstained" by the world's systems. One of His first sermons made this clear when He said, "The Spirit of the Lord is upon Me, because He anointed Me to preach the gospel to the poor. He has sent Me to proclaim release to the captives, and recovery of sight to the blind, to set free those who are, oppressed, to proclaim the favorable year of the Lord" (Luke 4:18-19).

The same Holy Spirit that was in Jesus wants to rest on and be in us to fulfill what Christ came to do. Jesus made it possible for us to participate with Him in the great purposes of God. Pure religion is not legalism, not dogmas, but ministering the life of

Christ, in the power of the Holy Spirit to all those who will receive.

Before ascending to His Father, Jesus instructed His disciples, "Stay in Jerusalem until you are clothed with power from on high" (Luke 24:49). Jesus knew that only in the power of the Holy Spirit could His disciples accomplish what He was sending them to do. So it is in our lives as well. We must have the power of the Holy Spirit if we are to accomplish the Father's purpose in the earth. Only the Father's "pure religion" can defeat the enemy's religious systems.

Father, I choose to give myself to pure religion. Holy Spirit, I yield to You to be on me and to be in me for the purpose of fulfilling the anointing that rested on Christ in His human ministry. I choose to put on the "new self" and to be "renewed to the true knowledge according to the image of Christ."

## June 18 – THE SIN OF PARTIALITY

James 2:1 – My brethren, do not hold your faith in our glorious Lord Jesus Christ with an attitude of personal favoritism.

Unfortunately, much of Christianity, as expressed in denominationalism and independence, moved from a particular understanding of a restored truth the Lord was communicating to an *attitude* of separatism and favoritism by God. Many in the Lord's church view their expression of faith and doctrinal understanding to be closer to the truth than anyone else's. This is at the root of denominations and is secular in nature, rather than godly.

In the First Century church it was understood through the apostle's teachings that only one church existed. The church found its expression in each city, such as Corinth or Rome. When the apostles spoke of "churches," they were speaking of a region which contained more than one city. The early believers had their understanding rooted in the teachings of the apostles. "They were continually devoting themselves to the apostles' teaching" (Acts 2:42). Over the centuries, teachers of Scripture fell away from the teachings of the apostles. Men began to adhere to false doctrine and move the church in a new direction contrary to the apostle's teachings. The church became divided and wrong attitudes were developed against other believers.

In James 2:1, the apostle is dealing with the attitude of partiality in the early church that set the rich against those who were not rich in worldly possessions. James implies, when we have an attitude of partiality, we dishonor the Lord's purposes. His purpose is for us to see one another as brothers and sisters in the Lord. This means, rich or poor, bond or free as well as our particular expressions of faith in Christ. The Lord has been reviving His church for centuries and bringing it back to the foundations which the apostles taught: "One Lord, one faith and one baptism" (Ephesians 4:5). The entire book of Ephesians supports what I am saying in our devotion today.

Ask our Father in heaven if there is any partiality in your heart. Ask the Holy Spirit to reveal any kind of bias against others in the body of Christ. Pray that He would open your heart to receive greater revelation of the apostles' teachings and a willingness to set aside any teaching of men that God's Word does not support.

## June 19 – DON'T BE BIASED IN YOUR RELATIONSHIPS

1 Timothy 5:21 – I solemnly charge you in the presence of God and of Christ Jesus and of *His* chosen angels, to maintain these *principles* without bias, doing nothing in a *spirit* of partiality.

The subject of partiality is an important topic in God's Word. Paul uses very strong language to encourage Timothy to not fall into the trap of bias as it relates to the principles in which he is to instruct God's people. All the believers are to be treated equally in regard to instruction and discipline.

It is easy to have favorites and to give some individuals special treatment. We are to remember that the Lord is no respecter of persons. Whether a person is rich or poor, a leader, or simply a member of the fellowship, we must not show favoritism. Peter learned about bias the hard way when Paul called him out in a mixed room of Jewish and Gentile believers (Galatians 2:11-14).

Peter was comfortably having fellowship with Gentile believers. Being a Jew, he had been raised with terrible bias against the gentiles. The Jews viewed the Gentiles as dogs. Peter had come a long way since his dream concerning God's acceptance of the Gentiles in Acts 10. He preached the gospel to Cornelius and his household, a Gentile in search of truth (Acts 10).

Peter still had some degree of bias in his heart. When some Jewish believers who were part of James' team arrived from Jerusalem, Peter broke off fellowship with the Gentile believers and moved toward the Jewish believers. Paul saw this take place and rebuked Peter publicly for his bias.

Bias and partiality have always have been a large problem in the church. There has been bias against the Jews, believing that it was the Jews that murdered Christ. The Scriptures declare that we are all guilty before God. There has been bias toward various parts of the church. This was especially true between the Western Church and the Eastern Church. It was true between the Roman Catholic Church and Protestant churches. It was true among various Protestant churches known as denominations. It is still true today among many believers in regard to other believers.

God sees us through Christ. All bias has been crucified with Christ. This is the basis for God's view of being impartial toward all peoples. When the gentiles received the Holy Spirit, Peter recognized God's view and says, "I most certainly understand now that God is not one to show partiality" (Acts 10:34).

Father, create in me Your heart of impartiality. Help me to see others the way You do, through Christ and His atoning death and resurrection.


## June 20 – FORGIVENESS

Proverbs 4:23 – Watch over your heart with all diligence, for from it flows the springs of life.

The Scriptures teach us that "God is love" (1 John 4:16). Three words for us to consider that relate to the heart of God are covenant, relationship and forgiveness. God's nature is rooted in covenant. Webster defines "covenant" as "a binding and solemn agreement to do or keep from doing a specified thing" (Webster's New World Dictionary, Third College Edition.) "My covenant I will not violate, nor will I alter the utterance of My lips" (Psalm 89:34). When God forgives, He does so because of His covenant promise. His promises are certain. The Psalmist declares, "As far as the east is from the west, so far has He removed our transgressions from us" (Psalm 103:12).

The Holy Trinity is the greatest picture of relationship we can find. There is no contradiction with the Father, the Son, and the Holy Spirit. God created Adam and Eve because He wanted a relationship with mankind. Even after they sinned and the human race was tossed into darkness, God, out of His loving-kindness made it possible for man to be restored to Himself. This is how we know the love of God. God the Father gave His best for us, His Only Begotten Son.

The forgiveness of our sins takes place through the Son. Forgiveness flows from God's covenant nature. Forgiveness speaks of God's great desire for relationship with mankind. Through His desire for relationship with mankind He draws close to His creation, man. Covenant and relationship lay the foundations for forgiveness.

Many Christians have a difficult time forgiving others because they have not connected God's covenant nature with His desire for relationship. His covenant nature relates to His commitment to His creation man. He committed Himself to humanity and has never turned from that commitment. This requires His forgiveness again and again.

The Lord does not forgive us just because He wants to rescue us from hell and take us to heaven. That would be a very narrow understanding of His purposes. It also reveals how self-focused one might be. He forgives because that is His nature. He forgives because He wants to nurture and increase the relationship He began in the Garden and has restored us to Himself through the Lord Jesus Christ. He has given to us His Nature by giving us His Holy Spirit. The Holy Spirit gives us the power to forgive. "Let this mind (attitude) be in yourselves which was also in Christ Jesus" (Philippians 2:5).

Father, thank You for Your forgiveness, Your covenant love, and Your desire for relationship with Your creation man. I pray that Your covenant nature will grow in me. Help me to forgive others, even as I am forgiven.

## June 21 – FORGIVENESS IS A HEART ISSUE, NOT A HEAD ISSUE

Matthew 18:35 – My heavenly Father will also do the same to you, if each of you does not forgive his brother from your heart.

Forgiveness keeps one out of prison. In the spiritual realm, the tormentors are demonic entities that bind up lives from living freely, as God intended. Unforgiveness is one of the strongest "control mechanisms" the enemy has in his arsenal. The seeds of unforgiveness will produce roots that begin to go deep into one's heart. These become known as *roots of bitterness*.

Acts 8:19-24 tells the story of a man, Simon, who had bitterness in his heart, yet he wanted the power of God, but with a wrong motive. "Give this authority to me as well, so that everyone on whom I lay my hands may receive the Holy Spirit." But Peter said to him, "May your silver perish with you, because you thought you could obtain the gift of God with money! You have no part or portion in this matter, for your heart is not right before God. Therefore repent of this wickedness of yours, and pray the Lord that if possible, the intention of your heart may be forgiven you. For I see that you are in the gall of bitterness and in the bondage of iniquity." But Simon answered and said, "Pray to the Lord for me yourselves, so that nothing of what you have said may come upon me."

Before Peter and John had arrived, Simon had repented; he had been baptized and continued in the faith because of the miracles he saw Philip performing. Like Simon, we can desire the authority, but fail to deal with our heart condition. God's power and a troubled heart are a dangerous combination.

There are times in my life when I have had to ask others, including my wife and my children, to forgive me for a word or a wrong action. This was necessary for my heart and for theirs. Conversely, there have been times when I have been deeply hurt by another. I had to choose, but to forgive them from my heart so I would not be brought into bondage to their action or words toward me.

Forgiveness is the releasing of another person from the debt they owe. This means not holding any remnants of the past in your heart. This is what the Father has done for us through His Son, the Lord Jesus Christ. He is able to freely deal with the nations and their peoples because "He so loved the world" (John 3:16).

Father, I pray for Your heart of forgiveness to be given to me. Help me to forgive others in the same manner that You have forgiven me. I choose to walk in the glorious liberty and freedom that Jesus has made possible for all believers. Keep my heart free from any unforgiveness and open for Your great love to fill me.

## June 22 – THE GOAL OF RESTORATION

Acts 3:21 – Whom heaven must receive until the period of restoration of all things about which God spoke by the mouth of His holy prophets from ancient time.

The Father's aim is the "restoration of all things." In the Garden, the Lord looked down the annals of time and said, "The seed of the woman would bruise the head of the serpent" (Genesis 3:15). God was laying the foundation for the "restoration" of His intended purpose to restore mankind. Repentance is the beginning point of this process.

Forgiveness is the result of repentance. Repentance essentially means to see things from a higher perspective (God's vantage point). It requires us to change our minds and behavior accordingly. Peter's strong message in Acts 3 was, "Therefore repent and return, so that your sins may be wiped away, in order that times of refreshing may come from the presence of the Lord" (Acts 3:19).

True restoration takes time to allow God's truth to filter past layers of guilt and shame, to bring about deep down change at the root level. It takes time to rebuild equity and trust. It takes time because the heart of man is *deceitful*. "The heart is deceitful above all things, and desperately wicked; who can know it? I, the Lord, search the heart, I test the mind, even to give every man according to his ways, according to the fruit of his doings" (Jeremiah 17:9-10). Jesus knew the heart and thoughts of men. "Jesus knowing their thoughts said, "Why are you thinking evil in your hearts?" (Matthew 9:4).

Forgiveness and trust are not one in the same thing. Believers can be confused over these two areas. Forgiveness is when your heart is free to love a person that hurt you, to have the mind of Christ towards them. Trust is built upon proven character. Paul instructs us with a word of wisdom. "Conduct yourselves with wisdom toward outsiders, making the most of the opportunity. Let your speech always be with grace, seasoned, as it were, with salt, so that you may know how you should respond to each person" (Colossians 4:5-6). One who walks in this word has a clean heart.

Father, I pray that restoration would become an important goal for me. I pray for wisdom in my inner actions and relationship with others. Give me speech that is filled with grace and seasoned with salt. Help me to know how to respond to each individual with whom I connect.

## June 23 – THE GRACE OF GIVING

2 Corinthians 9:8 – God is able to make all grace abound to you, so that always having all sufficiency in everything, you may have abundance for every good deed.

In chapter nine of second Corinthians, Paul addresses being prepared to give financially to poor saints. He reminds us that God is our source. He is able, through grace, to supply our needs. Jesus speaks a great deal about finances in His teachings. Finances are very closely related to the heart of man. Three times in the Sermon on the Mount (the Beatitudes), Jesus addresses issues of the heart as it relates to money and wealth. For example, in Matthew 5:2-4, Jesus teaches not to make our giving to the poor public, to be seen of men.

Three words that need close examination and meditation are covenant, motivations, and generosity. In our next few devotionals we will consider all three words. We will ask the

Holy Spirit to establish us in covenant giving, right heart motivations, and generosity.

The giving of the tithe is a covenantal subject and not a legalistic one. The law of first mention comes into play with the subject of tithing. This law means that the central concepts are contained in seed form when a subject is introduced in the scriptures. Tithing is introduced to us in Genesis 14:20, "Abraham gave a tenth of all." This is confirmed in Hebrews 7:4, speaking of Abraham's tithing to Melchizedek. Hebrews 7:5 says, Levi, who was directed to receive tithes under the Law, tithed to Melchizedek while still in the loins of Abraham. In others words, Levi had not yet been conceived. Abraham freely gave a tenth of all to the King and Priest Melchizedek who was called "The king of peace" (Hebrews 7:2). Melchizedek brought Abraham the bread and the wine or "the covenant meal."

The Lord ties the giving of money together with covenant and relationship. Jesus freely gave of His body and blood to bring us to God. We freely give back of the "sweat of our brow" or the work of our hands to support God's work in the earth. Paul confirms this when he says, "If we sowed spiritual things in you, is it too much if we reap material things from you" (1 Corinthians 9:11)? This is his theme throughout this ninth chapter.

God is our Covenant God and we are His covenant people if we have been born of God's Holy Spirit. Covenant is our basis of relationship and all we do, including the giving of our finances. Always keep in mind that "God is able to make all grace abound toward you."

Father, I thank You for Your covenant love and Your abundance of grace. Establish Your covenant nature more deeply in me. Cause me to give with the same heart that You freely give to us.

## June 24 – KEEP YOUR HEART WITH ALL DILIGENCE

Matthew 5:21 – Where your treasure is, there your heart will be also.

Throughout Jesus' earthly ministry, He established this principle of the heart. He was raising the bar for His covenant people Israel far beyond what they had ever learned from their religious leaders. Their religious leaders perverted the Law of Moses, and put heavy burdens on the people. Jesus came to free us from heavy burdens and give us His heart through the power of His Holy Spirit. A heart to obey God's law, but with liberation power that causes the motives to be pure and not self-seeking.

Our heart is a tricky area to handle. In the natural man, the heart is deceptive and impossible to know (Jeremiah 17:9). In Christ, we are to receive the heart of God. Our heart is tied to our emotions so it can change quickly. We can choose to harden our heart against a person or situation, as many do. We can choose to allow our heart to be softened and touched by God's compassion, reaching out to people when in the natural we would not do so.

The disciples were discussing the problem that they had no bread. Jesus, aware of this, said to them, "Why do you discuss the fact that you have no bread? Do you not yet see nor understand? Do you have a hardened heart" (Mark 8:17-18)? Earlier in Mark 7:21-22 Jesus told His disciples, "that from within, out of the heart of men, proceed the evil thoughts, fornications, thefts, murders, adulteries, deeds of coveting and wickedness, as well as deceit, sensuality, envy, slander, pride and foolishness."

In Christ, our hearts are being transformed. "But we all, with unveiled face, beholding as in a mirror the glory of the Lord, are being transformed into the same image from glory to glory, just as from the Lord, the Spirit" (2 Corinthians 3:18). "So, as those who have been chosen of God, holy and beloved, put on a heart of compassion, kindness, humility, gentleness and patience; bearing with one another, forgiving each other" (Colossians 3:12-13).

As you can see, we are being transformed. The work is complete in Christ, but being worked out in us. Our part is very important. Through the Holy Spirit we must access the heart of Christ so His heart can be operating in and through us. "Take care, brethren, that there not be in any one of you an evil, unbelieving heart that falls away from the living God. But encourage one another day after day, as long as it is still called "Today," so that none of you will be hardened by the deceitfulness of sin. For we have become partakers of Christ, if we hold fast the beginning of our assurance firm until the end, while it is said, "Today if you hear His voice, do not harden your hearts, as when they provoked Me" (Hebrews 3:12-15).

Father, I want to hear Your voice. I receive the heart of Christ through the power of Your Holy Spirit.

## June 25 – FATHER, GIVE TO ME YOUR HEART OF GENEROSITY

2 Corinthians 8:3 – For I testify that according to their ability, and beyond their ability, they gave of their own accord.

Paul is speaking about poor saints living in Macedonia who could have made excuses not to give to other needy saints. In their heart was the desire to give of what they could. Giving is related to our ability. The amount is not the issue; a heart of generosity is what the Lord desires. In 2 Corinthians 9, Paul speaks in terms of sowing and generosity. He underscores that God gives the most and quotes David who said of the Lord, "He scattered abroad, He gave to the poor, His righteousness endures forever" (Psalm 112:9).

As I have walked with the Lord, I have experienced God's faithfulness of supply. At first, it was hard to give because I had not received a heart of generosity. As I began to first sow to God what was rightfully His, the Tithe, a giving heart began to grow in me. Notice that I said "grow." Learning to give liberally is a matter of growth and maturity. Today, I do not calculate how much money I will be left with to meet my needs. I just give! In my giving, I do consider my responsibility to others where I have legal and moral commitments such as mortgage payments, utility bills, helping my own family, and so on. Generosity does not keep me from paying my tithes, for my heart bears witness to the scriptures about tithing. I both pay tithes and give to the needs of others because of my covenant relationship with God.

Paul helps us when he states, "My God will supply all your needs according to His riches in glory in Christ Jesus" (Philippians 4:19). We give because He gave. We give because He is our source. We give because we are the children of God. We give generously because our Father God has been generous toward us. Generosity testifies of a growing state of maturity in Christ Jesus.

Based upon the Palmist's statement, "He Scattered Abroad, He Gave To The Poor, His Righteousness Endures Forever" (2 Corinthians 9:9), Paul lays a foundation of faith for the Corinthian believers when he says, "Now He who supplies seed to the sower and bread for food will supply and multiply your seed for sowing and increase the harvest of your righteousness; you will be enriched in everything for all liberality, which through us is producing thanksgivings to God" (2 Corinthians 9:10).

Father, I pray for a heart of generosity. I thank You that all my needs have been supplied in Christ the Lord. Help me to receive Your supply of resources so not only my needs are met, but I may freely give to others in their need.

## June 26 – SEARCH THE SCRIPTURES

John 5:39 – You search the Scriptures because you think that in them you have eternal life.

Life is not found in the scriptures, but in Christ, "the living word" of God. Jesus tells the religious leaders that the scriptures "testify" about Him. The Scriptures are the testimony of our great God and king. They record His will. In the Old Testament, an innocent animal was sacrificed in order for the covenant to be exercised. In the New Testament, Jesus Himself gave up His life. Jesus freely offered His body as an acceptable sacrifice to God. His life was seen as acceptable to God because He was the perfect human sacrifice. He gave Himself totally to His Father's will, fulfilling all that the scriptures testified to. As John 5:40 instructs us, Jesus is the only one that can give eternal life.

Searching the Scriptures is a vital discipline for any believer. How else can we know God's thoughts? Paul instructed

Timothy, "Study to show yourself approved unto God, a workman that needeth not to be ashamed, rightly dividing the word of truth" (2 Timothy 2:15 KJV). A more modern translation such as the NASB states "present yourself" rather than "study." The studying of the Scriptures is an important way of presenting one's self to God. We must be diligent about learning God's Word beyond Sunday school lessons or church sermons. It is wonderful learning how God met with others, but even better experiencing God meeting with us. The scriptures lay a foundation of faith so we might experience God in our daily lives.

The religious leaders of Jesus' day took pride in their knowledge of Scriptures, but refused to yield to the One to which the Scriptures testified. Many today take pride in their knowledge of God's Word, but refuse to allow the Holy Spirit access and control of all they think and do. The Holy Spirit is God's source for the life of Christ. We must search the Scriptures to learn of God's will for our lives in how we should respond to the Godhead, how to respond to family, how to respond to other believers, and how to respond to the world. All are necessary understandings. But we must press into Christ through fellowship with the Holy Spirit. It is He that is an ever-present help in time of need.

Father, place in my heart a love for Your Word. Strengthen me to "present myself to You by studying Your Holy Word. I come to You that I might have life and that abundantly. You and You alone are my source for life.

## June 27- THE WORD OF GOD IS MY COUNSELING MANUAL

John 14:16 – I will ask the Father, and He will give you another Helper, that He may be with you forever; that is the Spirit of truth.

The Holy Spirit is the One given by the Father and the Son to help us apply the Word of God. The word "Helper" could be translated Counselor. We should not need a human counselor because we have both the Holy Spirit and the "Counselor's Manual," the Bible, to instruct us. As we read and apply the eternal principles recorded in the Word of God, the Holy Spirit is present to help us by giving counsel. It is the Holy Spirit that breathes life on the Word and causes us to have understanding. Sometimes that understanding comes through others. Counsel can come through life experience. Other times, counsel can be given by a trained individual, such as a pastor or a licensed counselor. Our main source of counsel should be God's Word and our relationship with God's Holy Spirit.

One of the most powerful Scriptures is found in 2 Timothy 3:15. Paul instructs Timothy by reminding him that from a child he had known the sacred writings, which are able to give wisdom that leads to salvation through faith in Christ.

First, we must know the writings of Scripture. Then wisdom comes as a result of knowing God's Word. It is that wisdom which leads to salvation, not only eternal life, but wisdom that delivers and helps make us free in this life, by helping to transform our thinking. Biblical thinking helps to produce peace and joy found in the Holy Spirit. Many are bound up in their relationships with others. This freedom enables us to relate properly to others. Many are in bondage economically. The wisdom that the Scriptures give us about handling money will cause one to be stable financially. These and many other life-relating topics are covered by the 2 Timothy 3:15 verse.

I have found it helpful to make up lists of biblical principles that I study and memorize to apply in my life. The book of Proverbs is one of the great portions of scripture that instruct us in every type of situation life can produce. For years, I would read a Proverb a day. I would meditate and memorize verses that stood out as I was reading a particular chapter. Try it for a month and see how much wisdom you will gain and how many bad experiences you avoid.

Father, thank You for the counseling book You have given me. I recognize that I need Your Holy Spirit to help me understand the Scriptures. I ask in faith for the Holy Spirit to help me apply Your eternal principles of truth in my daily life.

# June 28 – LEARNING TO WAIT ON THE LORD

Isaiah 40:31 – Those who wait for the Lord will gain new strength; they will mount up with wings like eagles, they will run and not get tired, they will walk and not become weary.

Waiting can be one of the most difficult areas of life. I admit that I am not a good waiter. I want to know now. I want to get the job done. I want to resolve the problem sooner than later. Learning to dial down and just simply wait on the Lord will produce great benefits. As we learn to wait on the Lord we will become sensitive to His timing. As we wait upon the Lord, we will receive greater knowledge to accomplish the task before us. As we wait upon the Lord, less of our energy is required and more of His life is received.

Waiting does not mean just standing around with nothing to do. Life in Christ is a dynamic relationship. A life of prayer, studying God's Word, and sharing one's faith is a full time activity. Waiting means to be watching for opportunities to serve Christ and His purposes. I am asking the Lord to help me learn to wait on Him throughout the day. The other day I needed a little fuel for a project. I went to two nearby stations, neither sold diesel. I then went to one a little farther away. As I was pumping the fuel, a man came up to me. He was cordial and I knew he needed money. He told me of his need and showed me a severe physical problem. I knew it was a God moment. I prayed for him and then gave him a little money. I am waiting on the Lord for revival, but here was an opportunity to share God's love and perhaps be used to start a revival in this man's life.

Isaiah says that waiting will produce strength. I see many people that look older than their age. Their strength has faded. God's people who wait upon Him seem to age much better. Isaiah also declares that those who wait on the Lord will soar like an eagle. The eagle allows the currents to move it along. It is not stressed over food or nesting. It keeps its eyes open, looking for the prize. When we allow the current of the breath of God to carry us, there is a rest we experience. Stress is set aside and new energy is given to us. It is the energy of the Holy Spirit.

Isaiah further encourages us when he says, they will run and not be weary, they shall walk and not faint. When I ran cross country in my high school days, I experienced what was known as "the second wind." After the first mile, a new energy would begin to fill your body. You established a stride and breathing becomes easier. As one learns to run and walk in God, the same results take place. Rather than hard labor you enter into a stride, a place of resting in His strength. Finally, Isaiah asks the Lord to teach him to wait. Waiting is not automatic. We must learn how to wait on the Lord. Waiting is found in one's intimacy with the Father. In other words, it is time spent in His presence.

Father, teach me to wait upon You. I choose to spend time in Your presence. I ask for Your strength to fill my life in order to do Your will throughout my days.

## June 29 – PREPARING FOR THE LORD'S PROMISES

Acts 1:8 – You will receive power when the Holy Spirit has come upon you; and you shall be My witnesses both in Jerusalem, and in all Judea and Samaria, and even to the remotest part of the earth.

By this time, the eleven disciples had walked with Jesus for over three years. I say eleven, because Judas, after betraying Jesus took his own life. Many others followed Jesus as well. 1 Corinthians 15:6 tells us that over 500 brethren saw Him at one time after His resurrection. Acts 1:15 records that one hundred twenty disciples waited in Jerusalem for the promise of the Father of which Jesus had spoken.

Days after the resurrection it is recorded, "These all with one mind were continually devoting themselves to prayer" (Acts 1:14). These disciples were seeking to obey Jesus' command to "wait" by preparing for the promise of the coming Holy Spirit. It is evident that they did not know what to expect, but they prepared the best they could to receive what the Lord had promised.

After the resurrection, when the disciples encountered the risen Lord, they did not recognize Him (Luke 24:31-32). The years in which they had walked and lived with Jesus were an encounter with the Lord in the flesh. Now, they were experiencing Him in the Spirit, and they did not really know Him (2 Corinthians 5:16). We have not known Christ after the flesh. We have only known Him by the Spirit. Although we, as they, were born of the flesh, it becomes quite a challenge to learn to respond to the Holy Spirit as He leads us in becoming a "new creation" person in Christ (2 Corinthians 5:17).

It is important for us to prepare for the Lord's presence. Many just assume He is present around us. I believe that He is present in our daily lives, but He wants to show Himself to us in ways we have not known and cannot imagine in our rational mind. These disciples "devoted themselves to prayer." They devoted themselves to searching the Scriptures about what was happening. They sought to set some things in order in preparation for the coming Holy Spirit. Notice, the scriptures state that, "they were of one mind," as previously mentioned.

Father, help me to prepare myself for what You want to accomplish in and through me. I ask for You to help me prepare my heart and lifestyle for what You are planning. Give me an ear to hear what the Spirit is saying today to the church. Father, I pray for Your people to be of one mind in their willingness to allow the Holy Spirit to accomplish the Father's will.

## June 30 – THE ORDER OF GOD'S KINGDOM

Mark 9:35-36 – If any wants to be first, he shall be last of all and servant of all.

In Jesus' statement to His disciples, and to us now, He establishes the order of God's kingdom. This is in direct contrast to the systems of the world. In the world, the order is to do whatever you must to succeed and get to the top. This is an attitude which is directly related to the problem of sin and evil. Men, ever since the fall, have striven for authority, control, and domination. These are major struggles in the human experience.

The solution is found in Christ. Headship begins with a benevolent Heavenly Father who so loved the world that He gave His only begotten Son. This amazing favor flows from God's Throne to earth. True authority originates with God. God sends to all humanity His "Obedient Son." Because of Christ's obedience to the Father's authority, the kingdom of God is established in the earth. The authority of God is reigning in a Man. The Lord Jesus Christ first endured the cross as God's perfect sacrifice for sin. He broke Satan's power over humanity and made it possible once again, to be restored to God. God established Christ, the Man, as Sovereign over mankind. When we choose Christ and obey His command to repent and be baptized, we exchange one type of authority, the kingdom of darkness, for another, the kingdom of God.

The Father promised the Son Their Holy Spirit would be given to everyone who would trust in Christ. Through the "Power of Their life-giving Spirit," we receive of the kingdom of God and are given authority in the earth. An authority over Satan's kingdom, an authority in our sphere of influence, an authority over sickness and disease and most importantly, an authority over the self-nature that is rooted in sin.

In the Holy Spirit, we have authority to receive the "new creation man." In the earth, God's people are reigning with Christ. The Lord's Church is to be led by those surrendered to the Life of the Holy Spirit as "gifted" (grace-filled leaders) who are watching out for the souls of God's people. They are to be servant-minded individuals who see themselves as last of all and servant of all.

Father, I thank You for the order of Your kingdom. Fill me with the Holy Spirit and create in me the heart of a servant. Help me choose a daily posture of humility and servanthood.   I choose to walk under Your authority that begins at Your Throne. I pray for Your new creation man to be fully manifested in my life.

## July 1 – THE GOSPEL

1 Corinthians 15:1 – Now I make known unto you, brethren, the gospel which I preached unto you, which also you received, in which also you stand, by which also you are saved.

The Corinthians had received the gospel by the revelation of the apostle Paul. In his letter, he wants to make sure that they have understood the message he had preached. By the time Paul is writing to these believers, many had brought confusing words to them about the gospel. Paul states, "Now I make known unto you." The gospel needs clarification because of all the various individual views that are represented. In today's contemporary church, there is still confusion regarding the gospel.

The word gospel means to announce good news. The question we must ask is, "what good news?" Paul helps us know what good news he is speaking about, "For to this end Christ died and lived again, that He might be Lord both of the dead and of the living" (Romans 14:9). Again Paul states, "For He must reign until He has put all His enemies under His feet" (1 Corinthians 15:25). We see that the good news is that Christ died and lives again. The rest of the good news is laid in the fact He is presently reigning as God's appointed king. The early church represented Christ as "Lord." In that day, the Romans declared Caesar as Lord, but the Christians declared, "Jesus is Lord!"

God's purpose in the gospel is for Christ to reign over all of God's creation. "The aim of the gospel is to declare and enthrone Jesus as King" (Charles Simpson, What Is the Gospel? page 2). This is exactly what the angels declared to the Shepherds at the birth of Jesus in Luke 2:10-11 "a Savior, who is Christ the Lord."

For many years, in parts of the church, the emphasis has been on salvation, based on Romans 10:9-10. Verse 13 must also be included, *"For whosoever will call on the name of the Lord will be saved,"* (emphasis mine). It is clear throughout the New Testament that the desired end is not simply salvation, but to make Jesus Lord.

John the Baptist and Jesus both declared, "Repent, for the kingdom of heaven is at hand" (Matthew 3:2; 4:17). Paul ended his ministry in his own rented house; "solemnly testifying about the kingdom of God" (Acts 28:23). The enemy has sought to stop the message of the "good news," through martyrdom and by distorting the message. He has failed! The good news of the gospel is being revived around the world. Today, multitudes are declaring that "Jesus is Lord!"

Have you embraced the full gospel of the kingdom of God? If not, why not receive Jesus, not only as your Savior, but your king? Begin to speak the full message of the gospel, the good news that Jesus is Lord.

## July 2 – RULING OVER SELF

Ephesians 4:22-24 – In reference to your former manner of life, you lay aside the old self, which is being corrupted in accordance with the lusts of deceit, and that you be renewed in the spirit of your mind, and put on the new self, which in the likeness of God has been created in righteousness and holiness of the truth.

Jesus is Lord! The heavenly Father intends that the Lord Jesus Christ find His reign manifested in the lives of those He has redeemed through His blood and the work of the cross. Jesus' Lordship is not abstract, but very specific as it relates to every believer. Jesus said, "He who does not take his cross and follow after Me is not worthy of Me" (Matthew 10:38). The strong implication is that we must die to self as He did and enter into His life through the power of His resurrection.

Paul is clear, in Ephesians 4:22-24, that we have a part in this new life that Christ has provided. We must "lay aside the old self." The old self is corrupted because of "lust" that is rooted in "deceit." Lust is a phrase which describes the emotions of the soul, the natural tendency towards things evil. Such "lusts" are not necessarily base and immoral, they may be refined in character, but are evil if inconsistent with the will of God. (Vine's Expository Dictionary of Biblical Words, Copyright ©, 1985 Thomas Nelson Publishers).

"Therefore, do not let sin reign in your mortal body so that you obey its lusts, and do not go on presenting the members of your body to sin as instruments of unrighteousness; but present yourselves to God as those alive from the dead, and your members as instruments of righteousness to God" (Romans 6:12-13). Sin is rooted in lust. Paul says, "Do not let sin reign in your mortal body." The issue is who and what will reign in our life. The will of God is that Christ would rule in us, not sin which once had dominion. Sin is still in our members, but the body of sin has been destroyed through the victory of the Lord. "Knowing this, that our old self was crucified with Him, in order that our body of sin might be done away with, so that we would no longer be slaves to sin; for he who has died is freed from sin" (Romans 6:6-7).

By the power of the Holy Spirit the believer can live free from sin by daily choosing not to let sin "reign in your mortal body," choosing rather to let Christ reign through the power of the Spirit. Our salvation is to bring us to His reigning daily in our lives. His reign begins in the individual, from there to the family, and on into the community. The message of the gospel is for all men everywhere to repent. "Therefore, having overlooked the times of ignorance, God is now declaring to men that all people everywhere should repent, because He has fixed a day in which He will judge the world in righteousness" (Acts 17:30-31).

Father, I give myself to the rule of Christ. I ask for the power of the Holy Spirit to govern in my life, that sin would no longer rule in me. I choose Your dear Son and His nature today.

## July 3 – BAPTIZED INTO PEOPLE

1 Corinthians 12:13 – For by one Spirit we were all baptized into one body.

For every time the Bible speaks of Jesus as "Savior," it speaks twenty-nine times as "Lord." With much of the preaching we hear today through television and other forms of media, it sounds like God is only "blessing" us, as we define blessing emotionally. I thank God for the music, ministry, times of healing, and encouragement. All are a part of the celebration of our joy. Underneath all of the celebration and blessing is a move of the Holy Spirit to fulfill the ministry that He was sent to perform. The Holy Spirit is the one who *baptizes* us into the body of Christ and is raising up God's redeemed community in the earth.

Baptism in water confirms identity with Christ's death and resurrection as well as our covenantal relationship with God.

Paul said, "You were baptized into death" and "You were buried in baptism." That cut you off from the Adamic society as a controlling influence in your life. We have also been cut free from the demonic realm as an influence over us. As we rose out of the water, it was God's intent to "baptize us with the Holy Spirit." We were given a new life principle, that is, to walk in newness of life.

Another dimension we were given in baptism is that we were baptized into people. That dimension is missing in contemporary church life. "For by one Spirit, we were all baptized into one body." Paul goes on to say, "We have been made to drink into one Spirit." To be baptized in water and in the Spirit is only two thirds of God's intent. The other third is that I am baptized into people. Acts 2 tells us that over 3,000 brethren were added to the Lord's church that day. With women and children, perhaps it was closer to twelve thousand. Immediately, they began to hang out together, going from house to house with gladness and singleness of heart, breaking bread. "The Lord was adding to *their number* day by day those who were being saved" (Acts 2:47, emphasis mine).

The beauty of what God is doing in the earth is when people are brought together in the unity of God's government. We are not brought together in some kind of indefinable mass. We are brought together in a definable, governmental structure under God that is clearly delineated in the Word of Truth as the churches of God in the earth, with their elders, with their leaders, and with their authorities.

Father, I affirm my faith that You, according to Your Word, bring all things into one in Christ (Colossians 1:28-29). Further, I affirm You are building me together with others, "into a dwelling of God in the Spirit" (Ephesians 2:22). Teach me to be yielded to Your governmental structure which is ordained by the Holy Spirit who is living in me.

## July 4 – GOD'S VIEW OF INDEPENDENCE

Galatians 5:1 – It was for freedom that Christ set us free; therefore keep standing firm and do not be subject again to a yoke of slavery.

Freedom and independence are very closely related. The independence that the Lord has purchased for all mankind through the Lord Jesus Christ and His death on the cross is an independence from Satan's control. Before the Lord went to the cross to bear the penalty of our sins and overcome the power of the kingdom of darkness, all humanity was enslaved to Satan's kingdom. That slavery prevented anyone from being truly free and independent.

God views freedom through His Son, the Lord Jesus Christ. Our God views the world He created through the lenses of Christ's atoning work. It was two thousand years ago that freedom was established for mankind. The Lord does not see seven billion people in the world, but two men. Adam, who through his disobedience, thrust humanity into bondage and the Last Adam, through whom freedom was purchased. We are either related to Adam, our original parent, drawing from his natural life, or we are related to the Last Adam, drawing from His life in the Spirit.

In Galatians, Paul is addressing freedom from religious bondage under the Law. The Law was necessary because of bondage to our sin condition. But the Law could not free us from that condition of sin. Only the Lord Jesus could do that by becoming the sacrifice for sin. His sacrifice was acceptable to God the Father. Now the Father receives all those who come to Him through faith in the sacrifice of His only begotten Son.

Freedom and independence have been secured in the world through the gospel of the kingdom of God. The nations that receive God's king, by receiving the message of the kingdom of God, are nations that have enjoyed true freedom and independence given by God. When a nation that has received the gospel draws back, they lose the liberty that the Lord has provided for them and it allows the kingdom of darkness to have increased effect on that nation.

Father, I thank you for the freedom You have provided in Christ. By faith, I receive all You have done for me. By the power of Your Holy Spirit, help me to keep standing firm and not be subject again to a yoke of slavery. Use my freedom to share with others that they too may be free from sin and stand firm in the victory of Christ. I pray for all people to come to know the freedom You have made possible. I pray for the nations to be discipled as You have commanded. I especially pray for my country to surrender to Your appointed king, Jesus the Christ.

## July 5 – HONOR AUTHORITY

1 Peter 2:13-14 – Submit yourselves for the Lord's sake to every human institution, whether to a king as the one in authority, or to governors as sent by him for the punishment of evil doers and the praise of those who do right.

The Lord set us free from the dominion of sin and Satan's kingdom. Our "independence," does not mean we are free to do anything we want or to be independent of God ordained authority. Jesus redeemed us to the Father's divine order. The government of God ,must start with you and me. It must start with our personal submission to authority. It must start with our understanding that the government of God is imperative in our lives. When we were born again, we were born into government. We were born into a kingdom; we were born into the realm of King Jesus and His delegated authorities. To fully recognize King Jesus, we must also recognize His delegated authorities.

We need to grasp that the government of God in the earth is the realm of our highest joy (The Government of God by Ern Baxter, page 15). True joy is not found in one's "independence" but in submission to God's government under Jesus in the Holy Spirit. God the Father governs our lives through His settled Word, through our personal relationship with the Holy Spirit, through submission to His delegated spiritual leaders, and the authority structures in the earth as stated by Peter in our verses for today.

Many of God's people try to walk independent of the authority that others carry. True joy comes when we submit to the laws of the land (see Romans 13:1-7), when we learn how to submit to one another in the Lord (see Ephesians 5:21), and when we receive God's true leadership (see Hebrews 13:17). Paul establishes that "Righteousness, peace, and joy is in the Holy Spirit" (Romans 14:17). For many, independence means "I am in complete control of my life." Each one must take responsibility for their choices in life and then deal with the outcome of those choices. For the kingdom of the God-minded person, submission to God's appointed authorities brings true and lasting peace and joy established in righteousness.

Father, I confess that my life belongs to You. Your King, the Lord Jesus Christ purchased my salvation and set me in Your kingdom. I choose to submit to Your will and to the order of Your kingdom in the earth. Holy Spirit, guide me and establish me in Your government.

## July 6 – THE COMING KINGDOM

Matthew 6:10 – Your kingdom come, Your will be done, on earth as it is in heaven.

For the believer in Christ, there should be no question about the ultimate fulfillment of God's government. E. Stanly Jones said, "Every man is built for the Kingdom. Even the most hardened sinner, and intransigent violator of God's law is constitutionally structured to relate to God's Kingdom," (What on Earth Is the Kingdom of God? by W.A. Young, Jr., page 115). Because we were created in the image of God, there is no rest outside of His Kingdom or Government. Saint Augustine said, "You made us for Yourself, and our hearts find no peace until they rest in You."

In Matthew 6:10, Jesus was helping His disciples to understand the centrality of His message of the kingdom of God. "Your kingdom come" is not a request for some future event, but it is what the Father had begun in Christ during His earthly life. The disciples were seeing the kingdom of God beginning to be established in the Earth as they experienced life with Jesus. God's will was realized in the cross as the Lord freely gave His life for lost humanity. The Day of Pentecost brought the fulfillment of what the Prophets had been looking for, God living in the person of a human being on earth. It was what Nebuchadnezzar saw in his forgotten dream which Daniel revealed, described, and interpreted. He saw a stone cut out of the mountain. A stone which grew until it became large and smashed the feet of the image. This was a prophetic picture of God's kingdom being established in the earth and overcoming all other kingdoms on earth (Daniel 2:44-45).

The kingdom of God came in the person of the Lord Jesus Christ. The kingdom of God grew as believers received the Holy Spirit. The kingdom of God continues to grow in the earth as believers surrender to God's will and to His kingdom purposes. The nations are hearing the message today. God's kingdom is growing in the earth. Repent and submit to the king. If you do, the blessing of heaven will come. If you refuse, God's judgment will overcome your plans.

The emerging of the kingdom of God and the will of God being done in the earth is the future for all humanity. God's kingdom will not be overcome by any other kingdom, as has been the experience of the nations throughout history. Will you permit the Holy Spirit to rule in your life today and walk in His favor?

Father, I choose to live under Your kingdom purposes. I thank You for Your grace that has led me to surrender to Your appointed King, the Lord Jesus Christ. Please use me to declare Your governmental rule in the earth.

## July 7 – HIS LORDSHIP, THE CENTER OF OUR AUTHORITY

Matthew 16:18 – I also say to you that you are Peter, and upon this rock I will build My church.

Jesus came to build His church. He did not come to start a church, but to build a church. Building requires a sure footing on which a foundation can be laid. Once the foundation is laid, then the building can begin. As Jesus is talking with His disciples in Matthew 16, He asks them what the general consensus is among the people about His identity. He then got more specific with them and asked, "Who do *you* say that I am?" Peter boldly states, "You are the Christ, the Son of the living God." Upon Peter's statement, Jesus goes on to tell His disciples that "upon this rock I will build My church." What rock? The eternal truth that Peter had stated!

The name Christ means, "The Anointed One" or "Messiah." He is not only "God's Anointed One," but the living Son of God. The Christian faith is rooted in this eternal truth. If any one does not believe this, they are not Christian. Jesus gave up His human life on the cross, in order to build a "new building" from His resurrected life. His whole spirit, soul, and body were raised from the dead on the third day by the power of the Holy Spirit.

"You are no longer strangers and aliens, but follow-citizens with the saints, and are of God's household, having been built on the foundation of the apostles and prophets, Christ Jesus Himself being the corner *stone*, in whom the whole building, being fitted together, is growing into a holy temple in the Lord in whom you also are being built together into a dwelling of God in the Spirit" (Ephesians 2:19-22).

Jesus the Rock, Jesus the Builder, Jesus who laid the foundation in both His Apostles and Prophets is building by using people as the stones of His church building. "Coming to Him as to a living stone which has been rejected by men, but is choice and precious in the sight of God, you also, as living stones, are being built up as a spiritual house for a holy priesthood, to offer up spiritual sacrifices acceptable to God through Jesus Christ" (1 Peter 2:4-6). The Church is not mortar or brick. The Church is not an ecclesiastical system. The Church is a people made alive by the Holy Spirit. The Church is not "static," but "dynamic" in its spiritual core. In other words, The Church is alive on earth. Another metaphor which Jesus used in John 15 is that we are branches which are attached to Him, a fruit-bearing Vine. Today, celebrate your life in Christ as a living stone and a fruit-bearing branch for His glory!

Father, I thank You for raising me up from the dead in Christ. Thank You for the breath of Your Holy Spirit who causes me to be a living stone in the building You are building in the earth by Your Son Jesus, the Christ. Cause me to be a dynamic force for Your glory in my sphere of influence.

## July 8 – HE WAS RECEIVED UP INTO HEAVEN

Mark 16:19 – When the Lord Jesus had spoken to them, He was received up into heaven and sat down at the right hand of God. And they went out and preached everywhere.

Jesus prepared His disciples for three and a half years. He gave them some final instructions and then was "received up into heaven" to be seated next to His Father. Please notice that

Jesus was "received." As believers, we have been received as well. "If I go and prepare a place for you, I will come again and receive you to Myself, that where I am, there you may be also" (John 14:3). Both Jesus and His Father had worked (John 5:17). Now it was time for the disciples to go to work. Our work must come out of what the Father and the Son have done. It comes from their resting position, seated in heaven.

The "Work" is finished, but as His disciples, we are cleaning up the mess in the lives of those for whom Jesus died and rose again. We are His "workers"! The starting point for our work is to be His witnesses. "You will testify also, because you have been with Me from the beginning" (John 15:27). It started with the apostles testifying of the Lord's finished work for Israel. Paul took the message to the Gentiles as a result of the revelation that God had extended salvation to all peoples in the earth. We have received the "witness" of the apostles if we have put our faith in God's finished work in Christ Jesus, the Lord. We not only have received salvation, but are on assignment to declare to others that, Christ is alive and He reigns over the nations.

Receiving the Lord implies a sense of responsibility. His salvation is free in the sense that God purchased us with the shed blood of His Son. Jesus freely gave His life for the sins of the world. In receiving God's salvation, we are submitting ourselves to His authority over our lives. He is now our King! His mandate to the apostles and now applies to us, "Go" into the entire world. "All authority has been given to Me in heaven and on earth. Go, therefore, and make disciples of all the nations, baptizing them in the name of the Father and the Son and the Holy Spirit, teaching them to observe all that I commanded you; and lo, I am with you always, even to the end of the age" (Matthew 28:18-20). The Gospel of Mark says they "preached everywhere" (Mark 16:19).

Father, I thank You for my salvation in Christ Jesus. Help me to be faithful in my responsibility to share with others what You have accomplished through Your Son. Thank You for the authority I have received because of Your finished work. I commit myself to finish the work You have called me to accomplish. I rest in Your power and not my own strength!

# July 9 – I WAS APPOINTED A PREACHER

2 Timothy 1:11-12 – I was appointed a preacher and an apostle and a teacher.

Paul is instructing a young minister named Timothy. Previously Paul had taught Timothy to not be ashamed of his testimony of Christ or of Paul who was totally dedicated to Christ through his sufferings. Paul states, "Who has saved us and called us with a holy calling, not according to our works, but according to His own purpose and grace which was granted us in Christ Jesus from all eternity" (2 Timothy 1:9).

We are included in the "us" to which Paul is referring. Jesus saved you and me. Jesus called you and me with a holy calling. That means we have been separated to God's eternal purposes and His grace. Relax, for only in Christ Jesus can we accomplish what God wants done. Paul realizes he was "appointed." Timothy was being reminded by Paul that he too had been appointed. The Scriptures remind us as well of our appointment. Paul and Timothy took responsibility for their appointment. We too must take responsibility for His assignment in our lives. This is done through the power of the Holy Spirit.

Paul further tells Timothy, "By the appearing of our Savior Christ Jesus, who abolished death and brought life and immortality to light through the gospel" (2 Timothy 1:10). Every revelation we receive from God comes as a result of what Jesus did through His earthly ministry. Faith tells us that death has been abolished. Faith tells us that life and immortality have been granted. Faith operates because of the light which came through the gospel. Paul, in verse 11 says, "I have been made a preacher and an apostle and a teacher." Paul is describing that he was called in three specific areas of the gospel. First, he was called to proclaim the good news (Romans 10:14). Secondly, as an apostle, Paul is a builder. "According to the grace of God which was given to me, like a wise master builder I laid foundation, and another is building on it. But each man must be careful how he builds on it" (1 Corinthians 3:10-11). Finally, Paul is called as a teacher. "For this I was appointed . . . as a teacher of the Gentiles in faith and truth (1Timothy 2:7).

We, as Paul, need to know what God has called us to in the body of Christ. We all have a responsibility to proclaim the good news. We are to be a consistent witness to others daily. We are all called to build our lives upon the Lord Jesus Christ. We are then to help others build strong Christian lives. Finally, we need to know God's Word and be available to instruct others in the admonition of the Scriptures.

Father, I ask for divine appointments to share with others Your eternal truths.

## July 10 – I AM NOT ASHAMED

2 Timothy 1:12 – For this reason I also suffer these things, but I am not ashamed; for I know whom I have believed and I am convinced that He is able to guard what I have entrusted to Him until that day.

Paul, more than most, knew the sufferings of Christ. Jesus had brought Paul from being one of the chief persecutors of His church, to one of the most persecuted for the gospel's sake. Paul, who had been known as Saul, encountered the "Living Christ" on his way to put the Disciples of Christ in jail at Damascus (Acts 9:1-9). On the Damascus road, his life was suddenly interrupted by the King of the entire creation. The Lord Jesus Christ had only one question for Saul, "Why are you persecuting Me?" (Acts 9:4).

Acts 9:15 tells us, Jesus sent Ananias to Saul to give him instructions saying, "He is a chosen instrument of Mine, to bear My name before the Gentiles and kings and the sons of Israel; for I will show him how much he must suffer for My name's sake." Saul, whose name was changed to Paul, was appointed by Jesus to suffer for His name's sake. Suffering is part of the normal Christian experience. We are called to make up what was lacking in the sufferings of Christ. "Now I rejoice in my sufferings for your sake, and in my flesh I do my share on behalf of His body, which is the church, in filling up what is lacking in Christ's afflictions" (Colossians 1:24). Paul identifies with the sufferings of Christ to the point that he sees his sufferings as part of being a member of Christ's body.

When we suffer affliction for Christ's sake, we are partakers with Him in suffering. In eternity, our suffering will become part of His glory that is to be revealed. Paul said, "I rejoice in my sufferings." Do we have an attitude of "rejoicing" when we suffer for Jesus? It is hard to imagine the sufferings that some believers have experienced for Christ's sake. In contemporary Christianity there is still a great deal of suffering. Those believers that live under communism have suffered a great deal. Those in Islamic lands have unimaginable hardships because they are identified with Christ. I think of committed Christians seeking a University Education who are persecuted by the proponents of Secular Humanism.

"For I consider that the sufferings of this present time are not worthy to be compared with the glory that is to be revealed to us" (Romans 8:18). "Just as the sufferings of Christ are ours in abundance, so also our comfort is abundant through Christ" (2 Corinthians 1:5). When we go through sufferings, let us be reminded of all those who have suffered before us. I choose to trust in Christ when suffering, knowing it does not compare to the "glory" God has planned for us.

Thank You Father, for "abundant comfort" that You have promised through Christ, when we experience "abundant sufferings." My hope is steadfast in You and all Your promises. I am not ashamed of all You have done on my behalf.

## July 11 – RETAIN THE STANDARD OF SOUND WORDS

2 Timothy 1:13 – Retain the standard of sound words which you have heard of me, in faith and love which are in Christ Jesus.

Words are about as important as anything can be. Words form the basis of communication, understanding, and being able to successfully move forward toward a goal. There are many kinds of words spoken among people. There are foolish words, silly words, and meaningless words. There are sound words, educated words, and eternal words. "Death and life are in the power of the tongue" (Proverbs 18:21). It is a worthwhile activity to go through the Book of Proverbs and study all that Solomon writes concerning words.

Paul encourages Timothy, a spokesperson for Paul and called of God, to "*retain the standard of sound words*" (emphasis mine). When under pressure, it is easy to speak from our emotions rather than sound, well-thought-through words. Timothy was under pressure as Paul's deputy to the church at Ephesus. Timothy felt pressure because he was young and correcting older individuals (1 Timothy 4:12). He felt pressure because many were "teaching strange doctrines, myths, and endless genealogies" (1Timothy 1:3-4).

There has never been a day like the one in which we live. It is a day of many words from so many people. There are words coming from books, magazines, cable TV, satellites, videos, and talk radio. Consider the diversity of the Internet, such as YouTube, Facebook, Tweeter and the like. As we read, watch, and listen, we must take Paul's counsel to Timothy seriously, "retain the standard of sound words." This standard, of which Paul speaks, is a standard that begins with the "Word of God." All truth is eternal! Jesus declares, "Heaven and earth will pass away, but My words will not pass away" (Matthew 24:35). What Jesus spoke in Matthew 24 came to pass in 70 AD in the destruction of the Temple and Jerusalem. Throughout His ministry, He gave God's people, Israel, "sound words." Through the inspiration of the Holy Spirit, the apostles gave to mankind the writings of the New Testament.

Western civilization has much of its foundation laid in the writings of the Scripture. The educational system of America was originally grounded in the words of the Bible. Noah Webster, the Father of American Christian education, wrote the first American dictionary and established a system of rules to govern spelling, grammar, and reading. This master linguist understood the power of words, their definitions, and the need for precise word usage in communication to maintain independence. Webster used the Bible as the foundation for his definitions.

Father, I ask that You help me retain the standard of sound words. Give me an increased love for the Word of God. Holy Spirit, direct my thinking and my words to line up with the eternal truths revealed in Scripture. I ask to be used to help others in their thinking and their speaking as well.

## July 12 – GUARD THE TREASURE

2 Timothy 1:14 – Guard, through the Holy Spirit who dwells in us, the treasure which has been entrusted to you.

I have not been able to move on from this instructive word of Paul to Timothy. I have been asking myself before the Lord, "How well do I guard the treasure?" The treasure is Jesus Christ and the life He has given to each believer. That life came through the power of the Holy Spirit. This life can only be kept through His power as well. Paul says to "guard" through the Holy Spirit. Daily I need to be asking the Holy Spirit for His help to protect what the Lord has given to me by His grace.

Life is filled with little foxes that "spoil the vines." "Catch the foxes for us, the little foxes that are ruining the vineyards, while our vineyards are in blossom" (Song of Solomon 2:15). Foxes quietly sneak into the vineyard and ravage the vines while the owner is asleep. The enemy tries to sneak into the vineyard of our lives in order to spoil what the Lord has been growing. It is important to be diligent in guarding the treasure of His life that lives inside of us. We do this by guarding our life through the Holy Spirit. We are the Lord's vineyard and He is looking for the fruit of the vine which Jesus calls "the new wine."

I believe the little foxes to be "the cares of the world." It is a subtitle because the cares of the world are tied closely with the daily needs to sustain living in this natural life. We all have basic needs which the Lord promises to supply. "Do not worry then, saying, 'What will we eat?' or 'What will we drink?' or 'What will we wear for clothing?' For the Gentiles eagerly seek all these things; for your heavenly Father knows that you need all these things. But seek first His kingdom and His righteousness, and all these things will be added to you" (Matthew 6:31-33).

Part of the task of guarding is to not worry. We are to trust our heavenly Father for all. Another part of guarding is to "seek first God's Kingdom." It is important to evaluate our life by looking at our priorities. Does the kingdom of God take first place in everything? Where you find it is not, stop and repent and surrender that area to the Lord. Then immediately ask for the Holy Spirit's power to help you. Look up the word "guard" in a concordance and see how often believers are instructed "to guard" particular areas of their lives.

Father, I ask You to raise the level of my awareness of guarding the treasure You have entrusted to me. Show me the "little foxes" so I can drive them off and protect the vines that You are growing to produce the fruit of new wine. I trust in the help of Your Holy Spirit who "dwells in me.

## July 13 – THE LOVE OF THE FATHER

1 John 3:1 – See how great a love the father has bestowed on us, that we would be called the children of God, and such we are.

**For the next few devotions we will consider eight expressions of the Father's Love.**

**In the Garden** – God's love is revealed through the boundaries He set for His creation. Adam was given assignments by the Lord. If he stayed within the boundaries the Lord gave, Adam would increase in the favor of God. He was given responsibility for the care of the entire Garden. He was to protect the Garden from any harm, and he was assigned the naming of all the animals. Eve's call was as a helpmeet to Adam's work. Proverbs 31 gives us God's view of the virtuous women. Adam and Eve only had one area forbidden by the Lord. Don't eat of the tree in the middle of the Garden (Genesis 2:17). Knowledge comes from God through intimacy with Him. Adam and Eve forsook that principle and lost the presence of the Lord's favor. In God's love He made a promise of redemption through the seed of the woman.

**On the Mountain** – God's love is revealed through Moral Law. Moral law is the foundation for freedom, health, and prosperity which the Father wants for His children. Found recorded in Exodus 20:1-7 are 10 Commandments, four upward and six outward, The Law was not done away, but fulfilled, "Do not think that I came to abolish the Law or the Prophets; I did not come to abolish but to fulfill. For truly I say to you, until heaven and earth pass away, not the smallest letter or stroke shall pass from the Law until all is accomplished. Whoever then annuls one of the least of these commandments, and teaches others to do the same, shall be called least in the kingdom of heaven; but whoever keeps and teaches them, he shall be called great in the kingdom of heaven. (Matt 5:17-19). Jesus summed up the Law when He said, "You Shall Love The Lord Your God With All Your Heart, And With All Your Soul, And With All Your Mind. This is the great and foremost commandment. The second is like it, 'You Shall Love Your Neighbor As Yourself.' On these two commandments hang the whole Law and the Prophets" (Matt 22:37-40).

God's love is then revealed as He sets boundaries around our lives. These boundaries are to protect us from the schemes of the enemy and to prepare us for God's purpose and His determined destiny for every believer. His Moral law is the expression of His love for society. Through moral law, God's people can grow in freedom, remain healthy, and develop financially for their own welfare and to bless others through God's favor.

Father, I thank You for both "boundaries' and "Moral Law" to protect and guide me. I receive Your freedom, health, and prosperity in my life.


## July 14 – THE LOVE OF THE FATHER, continued

**God's love is manifested through the prophets** as they give revelation of the plans which God wants His people to know. "Surely the Lord God does nothing unless He reveals His secret counsel to His servants the prophets" (Amos 3:7). "For I know the plans that I have for you, declares the Lord, plans for welfare and not for calamity to give you a future and a hope. Then you will call upon Me and come and pray to Me, and I will listen to you. You will seek Me and find Me when you search for Me with all your heart. I will be found by you, declares the Lord, and I will restore your fortunes and will gather you from all the nations and from all the places where I have driven you, declares the Lord, and I will bring you back to the place from where I sent you into exile" (Jeremiah 29:11-14).

God desires that His people have such a relationship with Him, so that He can reveal His will to them. He wants them to voice God's will so that others will know. "God is no respecter of persons" (Acts 10:34). He reveals His desire that all of His people would "prophesy" in 1 Corinthians 14:31 when Paul says "For you can all prophesy one by one." Paul goes on to reveal that prophecy has purpose; that it is "for learning and the exhorting" of God's people. Prophecy is not the natural man trying to figure out God's will, but the Spirit of God making known His will to the spirit of a person. What one believes the Spirit of God has revealed to them is subject to others hearing God as well. No spirit of prophecy is "private," but is to be confirmed by what others are hearing God say. "The spirits of the prophets are subject to the prophets; for God is not a God of confusion but peace as in all the churches of saints" (1 Corinthians 14:32-33).

God's love is revealed in the Son. God so loved the world that He gave His very best – He wants our very best as well. Our best is not our efforts, but His Son revealed in us by the power of the Holy Spirit. His love is revealed in the "Gift of His Holy Spirit." The Spirit only produces Christ's life, not our opinions or wants.

In the Spirit, God gave a helper: "I will ask the Father, and He will give you another Helper, that He may be with you forever" (John 14:16). Through the Spirit He does not leave us as orphans (John 14:18)

Father, I thank You for the spirit of prophecy. I pray for You to stir up the prophetic gift in my life. You want me to convey Your will and Your love. I choose to give You my very best, my utmost for Your highest. I am dependent for all I have from the Helper which You have given.

## July 15 – GOD'S LOVE REVEALED IN GOVERNMENT

Hebrews 13:17 – Obey your leaders and submit to them, for they keep watch over your souls as those who will give account.

The Government of God is His divine order. It is an expression of His Love for His people in the watching out for their souls. Many think of obeying another person as a form of bondage, but the scriptures speak of obedience as true liberty. Obviously, when we are submitted to leaders there is the possibility of abuse. God's command of our obedience to His leaders is in the context of leadership being submitted to Christ.

Earlier in Hebrews 13:7 the writer says "Remember those who led you, who spoke the word of God to you; and considering the result of their conduct, imitate their faith." Leadership is called to a high degree of modeling the attitude and conduct of Christ Jesus. We are called to look at the lives of our leaders and consider the results of their faith.

When Paul calls the people of God to a life of prayer, he first directs their attention to praying for all men and begins with "kings and all who are in authority" (1Timothy 2:2a). Government and authority are close to the heart of God. Paul further states the purpose of remembering these in prayer, "so that we may lead a tranquil and quiet life in all godliness and dignity" (1Timothy 2:2b).

"Submit yourselves for the Lord's sake to every human institution, whether to a king as the one in authority, or to governors as sent by him for the punishment of evildoers and the praise of those who do right" (1 Peter 2:13-14). Peter affirms this to be the will of God for all those who name the Name of Jesus. The Christian is to be known as the most law-abiding citizen in the society.

Peter ends his thoughts on honoring authority by saying, Honor all people, love the brotherhood, fear God, honor the king (1 Peter 2:18). The Lord has called His sons and daughters to be the example of submitted, law abiding people as a testimony of the "divine order" of His Kingdom in the earth.

Father, I ask for the grace of the Holy Spirit in my life to obey Your word in all things. Help me in this area of Divine Order. Grace me to be a good citizen in the society, to be an example of godliness in all I do.

# July 16 – GOD'S LOVE REVEALED IN HIS PROMISES

2 Corinthians 1:20 – For as many as are the promises of God, in Him they are yes; therefore also through Him is our Amen to the glory of God through us.

What a great statement Paul makes through the inspiration of the Holy Spirit. The promises of God are yes and Amen through us. Not a no and not a maybe, but yes. One of the first words a child learns is the word no. For safety reasons, a parent is constantly saying no to their young children. Father God has also given in His Word warnings for the protection of His children. In our passage, Paul focuses our attention on God's promises.

Reward is a vital part of training a young child. They must learn that there are consequences for misbehavior, but at the same time, they need to be rewarded for their obedience. God's promises are rewards for responding in faith to His Word. The promises are connected to God's Covenant nature. Jesus fulfilled all the requirements on our behalf. He satisfied God's wrath toward sin and made it possible for us to respond to God in faith and receives promises through Christ. Jesus is the "Amen" to all the promises of God. He glorified the Father and became the way for each believer to also bring glory to God.

The Holy Spirit is God's power in the believer to receive the promises of God. He creates the Amen in the believer's heart. Each believer needs to know in their inner man that God wants to fulfill His promises in their life.

Father, I ask for the power of the Holy Spirit to be able to trust You for all Your promises made possible through the Lord Jesus Christ. I thank You that Jesus is the Amen to Your glory. By Your grace I am secure in His finished work.

# July 17 – GOD'S LOVE REVEALED IN OUR DESTINY

Revelation 22:12 – Behold I am coming quickly, and My reward is with Me, to render to every man according to what he has done.

Our rest is in what the Father has done through Christ in providing salvation. We can rest in what He has promised for our future. The future is guaranteed for those who receive God's love. Multitudes spend huge amounts of time worrying, even fearful of their future. The subject of death is not usually the hot topic at family get-togethers or the focus of parties. For the believer, though, it is an exciting area to think about because our eternal future is centered on the other side of the grave.

The river Jordan is seen as a type of the grave in Scripture. Israel was baptized into Moses as they crossed over from Egypt to Canaan or the "Promised Land. "All were baptized into Moses in the cloud and in the sea" (1 Corinthians 10:2). Baptism speaks of the grave. In Baptism we die to the old man by joining Christ in death, but rise up in the new man as we participate in Christ's resurrection (Romans 6:1-7). You could say that our hope in the future is manifested in the now.

As believers, we have peace and He has given us rest; we walk in power by the Holy Spirit. God's love is a present reality. It is an eternal absolute. The believer has entered into an eternal position through Christ by the indwelling Holy Spirit. Our past is forgiven and forever cleansed. Our present is a daily walk in the eternal rest of God if we will receive what He has provided us. Our future is sealed by the promise of God through Christ's resurrection. What a mighty God we serve!

Father, I thank You that my future is guaranteed in Christ. I receive Your love today. Help me  Holy Spirit, in the weakness of my flesh, to trust You in all things. Empower me day by day to pass Your saving love on to others so that they too might know that their future is guaranteed in Your love.

# July 18 – CALLED TO WALK OUT THE PROCESS

2 Corinthians 5:7-8 – We walk by faith, not by sight — we are of good courage, I say, and prefer rather to be absent from the body and to be at home with the Lord.

We are called to walk out the process between the cross and the throne, experiencing His love and sharing His love with others, beginning with the family of God and taking His love to the lost. In 2 Corinthians 5, Paul teaches about the new creation man. That walk is a walk of faith. It is faith because we are not led by our natural senses, but by the Holy Spirit who lives in the believer. He is preparing us for eternity and living at home with the Lord.

Paul speaks of his desire to leave this present world and be with the Lord (2 Corinthians 5:2). Love motivated him as he lived in his earthly body. His life was dedicated to the Gospel and reaching the lost. Paul had a clear understanding of his purpose as a result of the cross. He longed for the Throne of God, but not in an unhealthy way. He did not just mope around awaiting his death, but served the Lord's purpose until the day he was separated from his earthly body to receive the body prepared for him by the Lord Jesus Christ.

Love and faith motivated the apostle as it did all of the Lord's apostles. Love and faith is to be our motivator as well, as we walk out the process the Lord has led us to possess. This process of love and faith includes our families, other believers, and the lost people we encounter along the way.

Father, I ask for the power of the Holy Spirit to infuse my life with love and faith in the process of my walk before You and others. Thank You for Your presence that is continually with me to give me good success.

# July 19 – RECOGNIZE NO ONE ACCORDING TO THE FLESH

2 Corinthians 5:16 – Therefore from now on we recognize no one according to the flesh.

If we look at people in the flesh, it will be an exceedingly difficult task to be a person of reconciliation. Reconciliation is a work of the Holy Spirit and He keeps His eyes on the new creation in Christ and not the old which comes from Adam.

Paul informs the Corinthian believers that God committed to each of us the "word of reconciliation" (2 Corinthians 5:18). Reconciliation is an "apostolic function. If an individual has been given an apostolic gift, reconciliation must be manifested in their life and ministry. It is reconciliation that causes the church to be "apostolic" in its core being. Any church that does not manifest the ministry of reconciliation cannot be considered fundamentally solid.

The key to carrying the ministry of reconciliation is found in the principle of our verse for today. Paul is emphatic when he says, "from now on we recognize no one according to the flesh." We must see through the eyes of the Spirit of God. His filter is the cross where the blood of Christ was shed for the sins of the world. In my flesh, I am filled with judgments. Some may be accurate, but judgments nevertheless. In the Spirit, I am to receive the judgments of Christ which are viewed through the work of the cross.

There will be an end time judgment for all those who have rejected God's offer of reconciliation. But until that day when Christ returns, our judgments are to be viewed through the cross and God's grace. If we judge after the flesh, our judgments will condemn us because of the weakness of our own fleshly failures. If we judge through the cross, then we commit all true judgment to God who will judge the heart of all men.

Father, I ask for grace to not see anyone after the flesh, but through the eyes of the Holy Spirit. Fill my heart with Your love and a desire to see all men and women brought to the cross and new life in Christ. Help me to walk in the "word of reconciliation."

# July 20 – JUDGMENT BELONGS TO GOD

John 3:19 – This is the judgment, that the Light has come into the world, and men loved the darkness rather than the Light, for their deeds were evil.

Jesus draws a line in the sand as He begins His three and half year earthly ministry. The subject of judgment revolves around "light." Then Jesus again spoke to them, saying, "I am the Light of the world; he who follows Me will not walk in the darkness, but will have the Light of life" (John 8:12). Since the advent of Christ, light has been in the world. There is no more excuse for men to walk in darkness. Not only is light in the world, it has been increasing in intensity ever since the Holy Spirit was poured out on the Day of Pentecost.

Judgment follows the light. Presently, mankind is called to repentance and to turn from darkness to the light. When individuals harden their hearts against the light of God, there is only a pending judgment that waits. The reason Jesus could say, "I did not come to judge the world" (John 3:17), is because the rejection of the Son of God brings the judgment of God. Jesus came to save. You could say His campaign was not negative, but positive although filled with clear defining lines. As one chooses the light, salvation will result. When one rejects the light, there remains only a fearful looking ahead to judgment.

Believers become carriers of the light. "You are the light of the world. A city set on a hill cannot be hidden; nor does anyone light a lamp and put it under a basket, but on the lampstand, and it gives light to all who are in the house. Let your light shine before men in such a way that they may see your good works, and glorify your Father who is in heaven" (Matthew 5:14-16). God's plan was that the light in His Son would be lit in the believer through the Holy Spirit. It is through the believers throughout the earth, that light in now filling the planet. Many believe that darkness is increasing, but the truth is that light is spreading through the Gospel of the Kingdom of God.

Father, I thank You for the light of Christ which is in me. Thank You for delivering me from judgment and calling me to be a light bearer in the world today.

# July 21 – HONOR TO THE SON

John 5:22-23 – For not even the Father judges anyone, but He has given all judgment to the Son, so that all will honor the Son even as they honor the Father. He who does not honor the Son does not honor the Father who sent Him.

What a wonderful picture Jesus draws concerning the relationship between the Father and the Son. Relationship is a great deal about honor. The Father's heart was to elevate His Son in the eyes of mankind. The Son, in His earthly ministry always gave the honor to the Father. One of the reasons our judgments are not valid many times is because they are self-serving rather than honoring another.

We live in a world filled with opinions that are rooted in emotionalism. In times past, a man's word was his honor. A written contract was not necessary, a spoken promise with a handshake was sufficient. The honor of an individual was related to one's upbringing. The family background was an important foundation to the honor given an individual. I personally have experienced great favor in my life because of the good reputation my parents had established among their friends, neighbors, and in the community.

The delight of a parent is to have children that can be trusted. It is wonderful to watch one's children grow up when they have developed a reputation of trust in the community. Our heavenly Father so trusted His Son that He gave into His hands "all judgment." As I view earthly affairs anywhere in the world through modern day instant news, I find my hope and rest is in knowing that the Lord Jesus reigns on high and that all judgment is in His hands. He judges the nations; He raises up and puts down leaders after His own counsel. The Father has trusted all things into the hands of His Son. The Son trusts His disciples to carry out His bidding in the earth through the power of the Holy Spirit.

Father, I pray for Your grace to rest on me to be a trustworthy child of God. I pray for the Holy Spirit's help in honoring the Son even as the Son has honored the Father.

# July 22 – FROM DEATH INTO LIFE

John 5:24 – Truly, truly, I say to you, he who hears My word, and believes Him who sent Me, has eternal life, and does not come into judgment, but has passed out of death into life.

We learned yesterday that all judgment has been given to the Son. John 5:24 is an example of that judgment that Jesus possesses. Jesus emphatically decrees the one who hears His Word and believes what they heard has eternal life. He decrees that they do not come into judgment, but pass out of death into life. What an interesting way Jesus has of saying they are saved from eternal damnation.

Jesus creates the law of grace and judges the one who hears His word; the one who believes the Father sent Jesus "has eternal life." Eternal life in Christ is a state of being. I was lost, but now I am found. Daily I thank the Lord, "I have eternal life," not going to have it, but indeed I now have it because Jesus has judged it to be so.

The believer "has passed out of death into life." Our daily walk is to be founded in hearing and believing God. Daily, the believer grows in their relationship with their Lord by drawing from the eternal life in them.  It is learning the process of discipleship. The believer learns how to walk in their salvation by not choosing death, but life in the everyday situations they encounter.

Conversion is the process of rejecting the old ways of thinking and responding through the life supplied by the Holy Spirit. The old ways came from our experiences while we lived in the death state, lost in our sins. Because we have passed out of that state of death, we are now to draw from His life in us by the Holy Spirit. Think life and not death. Draw from the eternal life that is in you, not the old life and habits from which you have passed.

Father, I have heard the word of Jesus. And I believe you sent Him for me. I receive the eternal life that the Son has given to me. Holy Spirit, I ask to be quickened day by day in the life of the Father and the Son through Your abiding presence.

# July 23 – AUTHORITY TO EXECUTE JUDGMENT

John 5:27 – He gave Him authority to execute judgment, because He is the Son of Man.

The Father planned from the beginning of creation for His creation man to rule with Him. Jesus is called the Son of Man because He came in human form through the virgin birth. When he was anointed with the Holy Spirit as He came up out of the water from His baptism, the Father gave Him authority to execute judgment. He operated in His authority in a number of ways.

The people were astonished at His teachings because He taught differently than the religious leaders. He taught with authority (Matthew 7:29). The people also observed that His teachings were followed by supernatural evidence. "They were all amazed, so that they debated among themselves, saying, 'What is this? A new teaching with authority! He commands even the unclean spirits, and they obey Him'" (Mark 1:27). He always seemed to have the correct answer for His accusers. At the end of His ministry before enduring the cross, He judged the evil religious leaders as He stood in the Temple, which was the place of the Government of God (Matthew 23:13-39).

It was a "man" that did all these things. He is God, but in human form. In His ascension He is seated at the right hand of God. The right side is the place of judgment. He reigns as God's man, David's greater son upon the eternal throne of heaven. What a mighty God we serve!

It is important for believers to think upon these things. Jesus' disciples were reminded everyday as they walked with Him and watched the work of the Holy Spirit minister through Jesus' life. They too experienced His authority to judge. They watched Him cast out demons and heal the sick. Then, they experienced His power to judge the kingdom of darkness as they were sent out to heal the sick and given of His authority over demons (Luke 9 and 10).

Today, the Son of God continues to pour out His Holy Spirit upon those who have received His kingdom authority in their lives. The same Holy Spirit is working through believers to administer God's judgments in the earth. Judgment on the kingdom of darkness, judgment on false teaching, misuse of authority, and judgment in the nations, as the Lord arranges things for His own eternal purposes.

Father, I thank You for judging my sin on the cross through Your Son. Thank You for giving ~~to~~ me power to rule over sin and darkness. I thank You for the authority to execute the spoken word of God in order to see Your kingdom purposes established.

## July 24 – GOD SETS APART THE GODLY

Psalm 4:3 – Know the Lord has set apart the godly man for Himself

The Palmist asked two questions in verse 2: "O sons of men, how long will My honor become a reproach? How long will you love what is worthless and aim at deception?" These are questions that could be asked of people today. Those who represent the God of righteousness are seen as a reproach by a secular culture that has rejected the principles of right for worthless and deceptive norms.

We live in a time of "virtual reality shows," that in truth, are unreality at its highest. Culture is filled with a love for fantasy and a disdain for truth. The greater issue is how individuals lie to themselves. It is difficult to face the truth, but only truth can bring freedom and destroy deceptive thinking. True repentance comes when one faces the truth or reality of where their life is really at.

The great lie is that we don't need God. It was the lie the serpent deceived Eve with in the garden. It remains an effective lie for multitudes. The goal of Secular Humanism has been to totally remove God from culture. The "I'm okay, you're okay" is *not* okay philosophy. Secularism is a lie. The American society has become a bigger loser because she has believed the lies of the secularists. Of course, this manifests in the lives of millions of individuals.

It is difficult to face reality at times. It is hard to hear truth when spoken about areas of one's own life that ~~is~~ are bound by a lie. Paul, when trying to help the Galatians asked them this question; "So have I become your enemy by telling you the truth?"(Galatians 4:16). Later, Paul spoke this word to the Galatians, "Be not deceived. God is not mocked; for whatever man sows, that he shall also reap" (Galatians 6:7). As a good friend of mine once said, "Pay day can be delayed, but not forever denied."

At present, nations, churches, and families face a crisis of not requiring much accountability. Bailouts, subsidies, and entitlements are a way of life. The truth is this, it cannot be sustained. Reality will set in and great loss will follow.

The Lord has set apart the godly for Himself. There is a cry going out from the godly. It is a cry for repentance, the changing of the mind, a cry for reality, the turning from fantasy. It begins with each individual taking stock of their affairs. To be set apart by the Lord requires a yielding to the Spirit of God. It is the Holy Spirit alone that produces righteousness. Ask for His power to think clearly, face reality, and be established in godliness.

Father, I ask to be empowered, to throw away what is worthless and embrace what You deem valuable. Use me to help others to be set apart for Your glory by dealing and facing reality.

## July 25 – WHAT FOUNDATION HAVE YOU BUILT UPON?

Matthew 7:24 – Everyone who hears these words of Mine and acts on them may be compared to a wise man who built his house on the rock.

True grace is an absolute revelation of the total work of Christ through the cross. By faith, I receive His work on my behalf. By allowing the Holy Spirit to manifest Christ's life through me it reveals that I am a wise person. The Holy Spirit only builds upon the words of Jesus. Jesus warns us against the flesh and the devil in His messages. Both the flesh and the devil want to hinder the life of the true conqueror, Jesus, from being manifested through believers. Believers are members of His body, joined together and representing Jesus' will in offering to an unregenerate world, "reconciliation" through the death/resurrection process accomplished by the Holy Spirit.

What wonderful grace we have been given. My efforts are worthless; my rest is in His finished work. Yet, my awesome responsibility is to allow the Holy Spirit complete control of my spirit, soul, and body for the glory of God. My awesome responsibility is to share with others this marvelous grace with the hope that they too will receive the love of the Father, and be transformed by His power becoming part of filling the earth and heaven with the "one new man," even Christ. One day we will see the King, but the question today should be; is the King being seen in me?

In our passage for today, Jesus is addressing the Jewish covenant people. Their lives had been shaky for centuries as they built contrary to Moses instructions. Now Jesus had appeared to give them a new foundation "full of grace and truth" (John 1:14). He came to fulfill the law and thus provide a better foundation than that of Moses. Jesus came to build His house, built upon His words. The building process is both hearing His words and acting on His words. This cannot be done in our own efforts, but only through the power of the Holy Spirit which the Lord sent after the cross and His resurrection.

Father, I ask You to help me evaluate how I am building. I pray for You to work in my heart to only build on the foundation Christ has given: His words and acting on those words daily.

## July 26 – LORD, LORD

Matthew 7:21 – Not everyone who says to me Lord, Lord, will enter the kingdom of heaven, but he who does the will of My Father who is in heaven will enter.

For some, this is a difficult passage to understand. Many activities are done in the name of the Lord. Few are direct initiations of His will. I have known over the years many that accepted the Bible's testimony of Jesus as Lord, but their lifestyle did not demonstrate that they had received Him as Lord. Saying that Jesus is Lord and doing things in His name, even supernatural activities, does not qualify one for the kingdom of heaven, only doing the Father's will brings qualification. And His will is rooted in Jesus Christ.

The Father sent Jesus to be the one and only sacrifice for sin. The first issue of the kingdom of God is rooted in repentance regarding our views and actions. Changing my mind and exchanging it for His perfect view. I am undone, He is fully complete. I am wrong and He is right. I have nothing left to defend. When I stand before Him, I have nothing to say, only listen and obey.

As Jesus teaches on the Mount, He has all of Israel in mind. They had chosen a broad way, as the Law of God had been distorted by their religious leaders. Jesus came as the fulfillment of the Law. He also had appeared as the "stumbling block that the builders rejected" (Psalm 118:22). The Father had made Him the "head of the corner."

The practice of lawlessness is rooted in pride, false religion, self-effort, and anything else that does not come from the moral law of God. God's law was established in the garden when He said "do not eat from the tree of the knowledge of good and evil" (Genesis 2:17). The narrow way had been set. Only what God permits! There is no other way to life, but through Jesus, the Christ. This makes the world crazy. Jesus is the offense. Anything but this, please.

Let the cross of Jesus be your filter. Measure everything up against the old rugged cross. The Holy Spirit is committed to honor the cross. Satan and his kingdom are committed to making it an offense. Lord, Lord only resonates with the cross. Anything else is a deception.

Father, I choose to cling to the old rugged cross. I choose Jesus, the narrow way to life. The One who is the complete fulfillment of Your heart's desire. Holy Spirit, lead me daily through the narrow gate.

# July 27 – MAKE SURE YOUR FOUNDATION IS SOLID

Matthew 7:24 – Therefore everyone who hears these words of Mine and acts on them, may be compared to a wise man who built his house on the rock.

Jehovah God gave to Israel through Moses and the prophets, the material to build a sound foundation. Solid, because the words that formed the Law and the words the Prophets spoke perfectly of Christ who was created in the image of God and of man. Jesus is that man and He is the foundation of the new creation. The Holy Spirit is God's instrument in the earth to bring forth God's will through His new creation man born of God's Spirit. First Christ, then all those who believe on Him.

A solid foundation begins by "hearing" the words of Jesus. Hearing is not simply hearing with one's ears, but applying what has been heard. The key is in "acting" on Christ's words. Jesus is the foundation, but the believer does the building with the help of the Holy Spirit. Jesus says the one who acts on His words is "wise." We begin with a solid foundation then build wisely through obedience to the words of our Lord.

The Scriptures, in many places, guarantee that what we are building will be tested. The testing will be by rain, floods, and winds that will slam against our building. Each of these natural conditions is representative of events that bring destruction. Jesus uses these as examples for spiritual conditions that will arise against the building. If the building was not built wisely, it will not stand.

The truth which Jesus is teaching applies not only to individuals, but to nations as well. It is important that we examine our hearts and examine what we have built in our lives. Is it built upon the Lord Jesus Christ and His words? Are we dependent on the Holy Spirit to empower us in the building process? When we read the Scriptures it is important to ask the question, "How am I applying this truth in my life?"

Father, I ask for understanding concerning the building of my life in Christ. I ask for the Holy Spirit to show me any part that is not up to Your divine code. I pray that I might be a wise builder that brings glory to You as the tests come and as others observe what has been built.

## July 28 – THE CHALLENGE OF OBEDIENCE

Mathew 21:28 – But what do you think?

Mathew 21:28-32 records the parable of the two sons. Jesus asked the chief priests the question, "What do you think?" after they had tried to trap Him with their question about the authority of John's baptism, whether it was from heaven or from man (see Matthew 21:23-27).

Jesus uses the parable to reveal the heart of these religious leaders. The first son was asked by his father to go work in the vineyard, but he answered "I will not." Eventually he did go. The father came to the second son and instructed him to go work in the vineyard, and he answered, "I will sir." This son did not go. Jesus then asked, "Which of the two did the will of his father?" They answered "the first."

Jesus responds to their answer with an amazing response. "Truly I say to you that the tax collectors and prostitutes will get into the kingdom of God before you." They gave the correct answer, but their lives demonstrated the attitude of the second son's rebellion.

Jesus then answers their first question about the authority of John's baptism. "For John came to you in the way of righteousness and you did not believe him, but the tax collectors and prostitutes did believe him; and you, seeing this, did not even feel remorse afterward so as to believe him" (Matthew 21:32).

Belief is always the issue and belief is demonstrated in action. Some believe that James and Paul had two different views about faith. I believe they were dealing with two different issues. James was combating a superficial faith that had no wholesome effect in the life of the professed believer. Paul, on the other hand, was combating legalism—the belief that one may earn saving merit before God by his good deeds" (Expositor's Bible Commentary).

Father, I trust You for a belief system that evidences wholesome faith. Faith that is evidenced by my obedience to Your word as I allow the Holy Spirit to lead me.

## July 29 – PROTECTING YOUR VINEYARD

1 Kings 21:3 – But Naboth said to Ahab, "The Lord forbid me that I should give you the inheritance of my fathers."

The story of Naboth and Ahab is a powerful example of how the Lord respects the inheritance of our fathers. Ahab wanted Naboth's vineyard for selfish reasons. Ahab moved from desire to coveting the vineyard. For Naboth it was more than the money or even the offer of a better vineyard. It was about his inheritance which he had received from his fathers. It was about the generations. It was about identity. It was, for Naboth, an integral issue.

Ahab did not understand "integrity." Ahab's evil wife certainly did not understand. She only knew the lust in her heart. She plotted to have Naboth killed so evil Ahab could have his heart's desire. "The thief comes only to steal and to kill and destroy . . ." (John 10:10). Satan is a thief and his objective is to steel our inheritance from Father God. John 10:10 concludes by saying, "I came that they might have life, and have it abundantly."

The enemy tried to rob the vineyard of God, but failed through the power of the cross and in the resurrection of Jesus Christ (see Matthew 21:33-46). As the parable declares, "He will bring those wretches to a wretched end, and will rent out the vineyard to other vine-growers who will pay him the proceeds at the *proper* seasons" (Matthew 21:41).

The parable of the landowner is an illustration of Israel and Christ's church made up of Jew and Gentile. The Lord protected His vineyard when He judged those who were in charge (*the religious leaders of Jesus' day*). He has installed new vine-growers through the new birth. The Baptism of the Spirit is the all-inclusive work of the Holy Spirit in the life of the believer. The Spirit causes the believer to be a fruitful branch on the "*Vine*" who is Christ (see John 15). The Spirit makes us a worker in the Lord's vineyard and calls us to give Him increased fruit.

Our inheritance is in the Lord. We must, through the power of the Holy Spirit, protect the portion of the vineyard He has assigned to us. It is our inheritance. Do not let an Ahab or a Jezebel rob you. We have authority over Satan's kingdom as it affects our life and inheritance. Resist the devil and he will flee.

Father, I pray for an infilling of the Holy Spirit to be a successful worker in Your vineyard. I pray for increase that I might give to You, knowing it all belongs to You.

## July 30 – EXCHANGING FATHERS

2 Thessalonians 2:16-17 – Now may our Lord Jesus Christ Himself and God our Father, who has loved us and given us eternal comfort and good hope by grace, comfort and strengthen your hearts in every good work and word.

The main purpose for Jesus' living among His creation was to reveal the Father. Jesus is the express image of the Father in human form. The disciples really did not truly understand, even after three and a half years of walking with Jesus. This was demonstrated by Phillip's comment in John 14, "Show us the Father and it will be enough." Jesus responded to Phillip by saying, "Have I been so long with you that you do not yet understand that when you have seen Me, you have seen the Father."

Fathering is at the heart of restoration in the human race. Adam is the father of all on a human level. In his sin of disobedience, he lost the human standing before God. We have inherited his nature of self. Self is manifested in "selfishness." Jesus came in human form, but did not have Adam's nature of self, thus He did not have a sin nature. Jesus came with the nature of His heavenly Father (see Philippians chapter 2). It is a nature of "selflessness." He gave up all His glory for every human being. "For God so loved the world, that He gave His only begotten Son, that whoever believes in Him shall not perish, but have eternal life" (John 3:16).

When the Holy Spirit's power "gave the right to become children of God" (John 1:12), we exchanged fathers. In baptism we die to Adam and are raised up in Christ a "new creation" (see Romans 6 and 2 Corinthians 5). God is now our Father. As His new creation we become part of His whole new work in Christ. Consider what Peter writes, "But you are a chosen race, a royal priesthood, a holy nation, a people for *God's* own possession, so that you may proclaim the excellencies of Him who called you out of darkness into His marvelous light; for you once were not a people, but now you have received mercy" (1 Peter 2:9-10).

Father, I thank You that I can call You Father. I thank You for the redemptive work of Christ Your Son. I thank You for the power of the Holy Spirit who is working mightily in me.

## July 31 – REJOICE IN THE LORD ALWAYS

Philippians 4:4 – Rejoice in the Lord always; again I will say, rejoice!

We can rejoice always because of all the Lord has done for His children. He has given to the children of God His divine nature (see 2 Peter 1:3). Maturing in Christ is yielding to the Holy Spirit's help in developing the nature of God in the believer. It is *not* trying to become a better person. We can never attain to God's righteousness by our own effort. Only by the power of the Holy Spirit can we grow up into Christ.

As Paul writes to the Philippians he goes on to instruct, "Let your gentle spirit be known to all men. The Lord is near" (Philippians 4:5). Father God is gentle. The Lord Jesus is gentle. The Spirit of God is gentle. The gentleness of God has been placed in the believer's spirit in the new birth. The Holy Spirit will help us exercise that gentleness in a world that attacks and can make us reactionary. Paul says "The Lord is near." I believe that Scripture can be understood in two ways.

First, the Lord is near in His coming for His own. In the first century, the Lord did come, not in the promised Second Coming, but in the promise of judgment on that generation (see Matthew 24:34). Second, He is near to be our helper. "Therefore let us draw near with confidence to the throne of grace, so that we may receive mercy and find grace to help in time of need" (Hebrews 4:16). David writes, "God is our refuge and strength, a very present help in trouble" (Psalm 46:1). We can see God is the same in the Old or New Covenant.

Paul goes on to say, "Be anxious for nothing, but in everything by prayer and supplication with thanksgiving let your requests be made known to God" (Philippians 4:6). The reel proof of trust in God is the absence of anxiety. Anxiety is controlled by a life given to prayer and supplication connected to gratitude. Not just coming to the Lord when we are in trouble, but a lifestyle of communication with our heavenly Father.

The peace of God surpasses all our comprehension. The peace of God is what guards our hearts and our minds (see Philippians 4:7). That peace is rooted in Christ Jesus. Gentleness, absence of anxiety, peace of God, and a heart and mind that is protected comes to those who "rejoice in the Lord always."

Father, I rejoice in You. Help me to learn how to rejoice always. No matter what is happening around me, I ask for the Holy Spirit to release gentleness and peace to my heart and mind in Jesus' name.

## August 1 – CREATED IN THE IMAGE OF GOD

Genesis 1:26 – Then God said, "Let us make man in Our image, according to Our likeness.

This verse of Scripture is packed with a lot of information. It reveals the eternal purpose of the one and only true God. He purposed that mankind be created in His image. Two questions arise: "What is the image of God?" "Who is the *Us* to whom God is *referring*?" Throughout the scriptures, the Eternal One is revealed as Triune in His being. In this passage, the Hebrew word "Elohim" is used, which is the "plural" form of God's name.

The first question in some catechisms is, "What is the chief end of man?" "Man's chief end is to glorify God and to enjoy Him forever." We will experience God in such fashion—we will glorify Him and enjoy Him—only in proportion as we know Him. The knowledge of God is more essential for the Christian, and indeed for the entire world, than the knowledge of anything else. Jesus prays, "This is eternal life, that they may know You, the only true God, and Jesus Christ whom You have sent" (John17:3). Paul sums up the goal of his life when he declares, "That I may know Him" (Philippians 3:10).

God's image is triune in terms of nature. He revealed Himself to His creation man as Father, Son, and Holy Spirit. He created man triune as well: spirit, soul and body. When communicating to the church in Thessalonica, Paul said "Now may the God of peace Himself sanctify you entirely; and may your spirit and soul and body be preserved complete, without blame at the coming of our Lord Jesus Christ" (1Thessalonians 5:23). Only the Word of God can bring adequate understanding to this great mystery. "For the word of God is living and active and sharper than any two-edged sword, and piercing as far as the division of soul and spirit, both joints and marrow, and is able to judge the thoughts and intentions of the heart" (Hebrews 4:12). Just as God is One, the human is one. It is the Scriptures that reveal God's makeup to us and it is the Scriptures that reveal how we have been created in His image and likeness. Through the study of the Scriptures, we learn all that God has chosen to reveal to us concerning Him. Through the study of Scriptures, we also learn what we need to know about God's plan for His creation man and may apply it to our personal lives. The great promise of God was that His Spirit would dwell with those who trust Him forever (John 14:16-17).

Father, I thank You for creating man in Your image and Your likeness. Father thank You for "eternal life" by knowing You and Jesus Christ whom You sent. Father, I thank You for sending Your Holy Spirit to dwell in all those who put their trust in You.

## August 2 – TRIUNE MAN IS SEEN IN THE PERSON OF CHRIST

Psalm 16:10 – You will not abandon my soul to Sheol, nor will You allow Your Holy One to undergo decay.

The Psalmist David writes prophetically concerning Christ in Psalm 16. In Jesus' sufferings and death we can clearly see the triune nature of man. When hanging on the cross, Jesus cried out to His Father saying, "Father into Your hands I commit My spirit" (Luke 23:46). Just as Jesus is about to draw His last breath, He commits His spirit to God. Next, David's prophetic words come to pass as His body is removed from the cross and laid in the tomb and Jesus' soul descends into hell. The Hebrew word for hell is Sheol. There were two parts to Sheol, upper and lower. Both parts were described in Jesus' story of the rich man and Lazarus (Luke 16:19-31).

As Jesus' soul descended into Sheol, He first preached the gospel to those who died during the Flood. He then took the keys of death and hell from Satan. Lastly, as Jesus arose, overcoming death and hell, He brought with Him all the dead that waited in upper Sheol, waiting for His Day. His whole spirit, soul, and body were united on the third day. When He revealed Himself to His apostles after His resurrection, they were afraid, thinking it was a spirit that had come into the room. Listen to what Jesus says to them, "See My hands and My feet, that it is I Myself; touch Me and see, for a spirit does not have flesh and bones as you see I have" (Luke 24:39).

Jesus was fully raised from the dead. His disciples could see and touch Him. Notice He pointed out His flesh and bones, but did not mention the blood. His blood was in heaven witnessing to our redemption and our pardon (Revelation 5:9-10). For the natural man, "the life is in the blood and God offers it on an altar for atonement for the soul" (Leviticus 17:11). Jesus no longer needed to depend upon blood coursing through His veins for life. His life was now fully sustained by the resurrection power of the Holy Spirit. One day, we too, will know His full resurrection power as our bodies, along with all the saints, are raised from the dead. If we are alive when He comes back for His own, then we will be changed immediately (1 Corinthians 15:50-58).

Rejoice saints! You will live on with Him throughout eternity with your spirit, soul, and body. By the Holy Spirit we know His resurrected life even now, while awaiting that blessed day and His glorious return.

Father, as Jesus committed His spirit into Your hands on the cross, I too surrender and invite You to have complete control of my inner man. Because Jesus suffered in His soul and descended into hell on my behalf, I freely give You control of my soul. As Jesus' body was raised from the dead, I am looking forward to the day of resurrection when death will have no more control over mankind.

## August 3 – THREE-FOLD PURPOSE OF GOD'S WILL

Hebrews 11:40 – God had provided something better for us, so that apart from us they would not be made perfect.

What an amazing statement the writer of Hebrews makes as he sums up this chapter! This chapter is known as "The honor roll of the faithful." None of those listed in the honor roll of the faithful experienced the full purpose of God. His full purpose could only be experienced in Christ through the power of the Holy Spirit. The faithful of the Old Testament were those waiting in upper Sheol for the Son of God to come and release them to the promise of perfection. The "better" spoken of in this verse is the Lord Jesus Christ, who we receive through the Spirit.

The Spirit of God spoke of Christ throughout the Old Testament. The Spirit created the Holy One in the womb of Mary. The Holy Spirit revealed the Father through the earthly ministry of our Lord. The Holy Spirit empowered Jesus to suffer and die for our sins. It was the Holy Spirit who raised Jesus from the grave. Along with Jesus, many Old Testament saints arose from the dead and testified to many in Jerusalem (Matthew 27:52-53).

Salvation is complete in the Lord Jesus Christ. He has provided deliverance for our spirit, soul, and body. "The Son of Man has come to seek and to save that which was lost" (Luke 19:10). "How will we escape if we neglect so great a salvation? After it was at first spoken through the Lord, it was confirmed to us by those who heard, God also testifying with them, both by signs and wonders and by various gifts of the Holy Spirit according to His own will" (Hebrews 2:3-4).

The triune God who revealed Himself to man as Father, Son, and Holy Spirit made it possible for every person to enter into His life and become part of the divine community in perfect unity with His threefold nature. In the beginning, man was perfect. Sin destroyed the unity in our nature. The work of salvation is to heal the brokenness of our life and restore us in Christ to God's original plan.

Father, I thank You for Your salvation, so rich and so free. I thank You for making it possible for my spirit, soul, and body to be healed and restored through Your Son and my Lord. Holy Spirit, continue the process in my life that leads me to Your perfect will.

## August 4 – THREEFOLD SALVATION FOR HIS TRIUNE CREATION

2 Corinthians 1:10 – God delivered us from so great a *peril of death*, and will deliver *us*, He on whom we have set our hope. And He will yet deliver us.

As Paul writes to the church in Corinth, he is describing the comfort he knows even in times of affliction. The kind of affliction he is speaking of was "beyond his strength" (2 Corinthians 1:8). Paul says, "We had the sentence of death within ourselves so that we would not trust in ourselves, but in God who raises the dead" (2 Corinthians 1:9). In verse 10, Paul reveals the threefold order of God's salvation. First, God delivered us from "so great a death." The great death is what the Scriptures call the "second death" (Revelation 20:6). We were dead in our "trespasses and sins" (Ephesians 2:1). Through the blood of Christ, our sins have been forgiven and washed away, according to the riches of His grace which He lavished on us (Ephesians 1:7-8). Salvation begins in our spirit and is renewed and made alive in Christ daily.

Second, "God will deliver us." Paul is speaking of the salvation we experience through our trust in God. We need His help on a daily basis. Sin is always there looming to trip us up in our daily walk. Afflictions in this life can discourage us from going forward with the Lord and His eternal purpose. The work of salvation was finished in the cross of Christ. Daily, the Holy Spirit is our helper to apply and walk out this salvation in personal victory. Our soul is challenged daily in our intellect and our emotions. Through our will, we can choose to trust God or we can choose not to. What God has begun in our spirit: faith in God, true worship, His love, peace and joy, He intends for us to experience daily in our soul.

Finally, we will experience the final part of our salvation at the Lord's return. "This perishable must put on the imperishable, and this mortal must put on immortality" (1 Corinthians 15:53). In the now, we can experience healing for our bodies. When God heals the physical, He is releasing eternal life in the now. There is coming a day when these bodies will be changed into the likeness of His glorious body. "Behold, I tell you a mystery; we will not all sleep, but we all will be changed, in a moment, in the twinkling of an eye, at the last trumpet; for the trumpet will sound, and the dead will be raised imperishable, and we will be changed" (1 Corinthians 15:51-52).

Father, I thank You for the provision of full salvation in my spirit, soul, and body. I trust You for Your life to be released daily to my being. My hope is in the promise of Your resurrected power, that one day I will be raised from the dead. Until that day, I trust You to keep me healthy and strong to serve Your eternal purpose on earth.

## August 5 – SALVATION BEGINS IN OUR SPIRIT

John 3:3 – Truly, truly, I say to you, unless one is born again he cannot see the kingdom of God.

This is one of the most familiar Scriptures. During his 1976 presidential campaign President Carter made it a popular saying when he declared that he was born again and served as a Baptist Sunday school teacher. The phrase originated with Jesus when he was speaking to Nicodemus, a Jewish teacher. Nicodemus understood that Jesus must be from God. Because of the signs Jesus was performing such as healing and miracles. Nicodemus was trying to figure Jesus out through his intellect. Jesus gave to Nicodemus a new paradigm to consider. Even though Nicodemus saw the signs, he had not truly seen the kingdom of God.

The kingdom of God in not an intellectual experience, it is a "spiritual birth." Many today are still trying to get to God through their intellect, but that is impossible to do. "God is spirit, and those who worship Him must worship Him in spirit and truth" (John 4:24). As Jesus ministers to the woman at the well, He introduces her to this new paradigm of thinking. She thought that worship had to do with the location of worship. Jesus tells her that a new day is coming when the "true worshipers will worship in the spirit."

The kingdom of God is in the Spirit. "The Spirit Himself testifies with our spirit that we are children of God, and if children, heirs also, heirs of God and fellow heirs with Christ, if indeed we suffer with *Him* so that we may also be glorified with *Him*" (Romans 8:16-17). What powerful understanding Paul brings to the church in these passages. Salvation begins at the point of "His Spirit testifying to our spirit." I remember in the eleventh grade at a Youth for Christ gathering, I said to God, "Tonight I want eternity settled when I leave this place." As I left the building, His Spirit testified to my spirit that I had eternal life. From that moment until now, I have never doubted my salvation in Christ. I have grown in the knowledge of my inheritance given to me from God. I know that I have an eternal inheritance with Christ.

I have known many blessings as a child of God, but I have also experienced sufferings with Him. Suffering begins in denying self, submitting to the death of self and receiving His resurrected life daily as well as in the eternity to come. Nurture your spirit man with the Word of God, with prayer, and with the fellowship of like-minded people.

Father, I thank You for drawing me to Yourself and causing me to be born again. Help my spirit to grow and become strong in Christ. Teach me how to deny my fleshly appetites and hear Your Holy Spirit better.

## August 6 – DEVELOPING MY INNER MAN

Romans 7:22 – I joyfully concur with the law of God in the inner man.

When the Scriptures speak of the "inner man," they are referring to the human spirit which has been regenerated by the power of the Holy Spirit. Before the new birth, our human spirit was dead in its knowledge and relationship to God. It is simply our natural life which had its beginning in Adam. He lost his standing before God when he chose sin and death over obedience and life (Genesis 2-3).

When one is "born again," their human spirit is regenerated by the Holy Spirit. "But when the kindness of God our Savior and His love for mankind appeared, He saved us, not on the basis of deeds in righteousness, but according to His mercy by the washing of regeneration and renewing by the Holy Spirit, whom He poured out upon us richly through Jesus Christ our Savior, so that being justified by His grace we would be made heirs according to the hope of eternal life" (Titus 3:4-7). We know by the Scriptures and through life experience that the soul of man is not born again of the Spirit. The soul is changed as one allows their spirit to take control and help change the thoughts of the mind. That is why Paul says, "Let this mind be in you, which was also in Christ Jesus" (Philippians 2:5 KJV).

The inner man must be renewed "day by day." The human spirit does not have life of its own, but its life comes by the "renewing of the Holy Spirit. Eternal life is resident in the believer because the Holy Spirit indwells the believer's life, being joined with the believer's spirit, or inner man or heart. All three terms are used interchangeably. "Therefore we do not lose heart, but though our outer man is decaying, yet our inner man is being renewed day by day" (2 Corinthians 4:16-17).

Paul, communicating with the church of Ephesus, tells them how he is praying. "That He would grant you, according to the riches of His glory, to be strengthened with power through His Spirit in the inner man, so that Christ may dwell in your hearts through faith; and that you, being rooted and grounded in love, may be able to comprehend with all the saints what is the breadth and length and height and depth, and to know the love of Christ which surpasses knowledge, that you may be filled up with all the fullness of God. Now to Him who is able to do far more abundantly beyond all that we ask or think, according to the power that works within us, to Him be the glory in the church and in Christ Jesus to all generations forever and ever. Amen" (Ephesians 3:16-21).

Father, I claim the prayer of Paul for my life. I am asking to be strengthened with power through Your Holy Spirit in my inner man, receiving the riches of Your grace. Renew my inner man daily that I might be faithful and do Your will throughout all my days on earth.

## August 7 – EXERCISING THE SENSES OF MY SPIRIT

Romans 8:5 – Those who are according to the flesh set their minds on the things of the flesh, but those who are according to the Spirit, the things of the Spirit.

Paul describes two categories of people, those of the flesh and those of the Spirit. The believers are to set their minds on the things that concern the Spirit of God. Today, we will consider five specific areas the Spirit of the Lord wants to develop in our spirit. Each of the five is a characteristic of God's nature. Faith, love, peace, joy, and true worship are in us because of the new birth. Each one provides a basis for everything else the Holy Spirit accomplishes in our life.

Faith is an attribute of God's heart, not simply a mind-set. Jesus said, "Have faith in God" (Mark 11:22). A close look at this verse reveals that the original language should be translated "have the faith of God." This kind of faith is given to the believer through the Holy Spirit. God's faith is made alive through the new birth and resides in our spirit. Faith has a "substance" to it called hope. "Faith is the substance of things hoped for, the evidence of things not seen" (Hebrews 11:1 KJV). The hope spoken of in this verse means a "sure expectation."

There are many types of love known to man. The most important is "the love of God". His love is placed in our spirit in the "new birth." As we set our mind on the love of God, it changes how we relate to people. God's will is that His love dominates our thoughts and practices.

Peace is what the Lord made possible in the work of salvation. "Therefore, having been justified by faith, we have peace with God through our Lord Jesus Christ" (Romans 5:1). It is the peace of God that keeps our hearts and minds from being distracted and confused.

Joy comes out of peace. Many experience happiness, but not joy. Happiness changes with the circumstances, but Spirit-filled joy is a result of walking in God's love and peace. I find very few people that exercise godly joy. One reason is that their minds are not fixed on the love of God, but their own selfish needs.

True worship flows from faith built on hope, love, peace, and joy. We worship God to celebrate all He has done for us. At times, we offer "the sacrifice of praise" (Hebrews 13:15). We sacrifice our selfish desires and the works of our flesh on His altar. The evidence of our worship is seen in "doing good and sharing, with such sacrifices God is well pleased" (Hebrews 13:16).

Father, thank You for giving to me Your nature. Let these senses grow and develop in my spirit. I ask for the Holy Spirit to empower my thinking and my actions through the senses of my spirit.

## August 8 – LEARN TO EXERCISE THE SENSES OF YOUR SOUL IN GODLINESS

James 1:21 – Putting aside all filthiness and *all* that remains of wickedness, in humility receive the word implanted, which is able to save your souls.

In his letter to the church, James helps us understand that salvation is not a matter of simply believing, but that we must participate in salvation's application to our soul in our daily walk. It is impossible to save one's self through human effort. Through Christ, in the power of the Holy Spirit, one can apply salvation's provision daily.

There are areas of the soul which I call "the senses of the soul" that need to be washed, cleansed, and surrendered to Christ each day. The soul is to become dependent on the work of God's grace that took place in our spirit man when we were "born again." It is by grace through faith our life is lived in the Spirit (see Ephesians 2:8). The five senses that were once fully controlled through the natural man and influenced by the world are: reason, imagination, affection, memory, and conscience.

First is our reasoning. "Immediately Jesus, aware in His spirit that they were reasoning that way within themselves, said to them, why are you reasoning about these things in your hearts?" (Mark 2:8). Jesus knew in His spirit man how the religious leaders were thinking about the healing of a crippled man through Jesus' words, "Son, your sins are forgiven" (Mark 2:5). They determined in their minds that Jesus was "blaspheming" because only God can forgive sins. The Holy Spirit wants to lead us to "reason" by God's word and not from our natural thinking. Their reasoning was rooted in their evil hearts which affected how they viewed the ministry of Jesus.

Second, is our "imagination." "The weapons of our warfare are not carnal, but mighty through God to the pulling down of strong holds; casting down imaginations and every high thing that exalts itself against the knowledge of God, and bringing into captivity every thought to the obedience of Christ" (2 Corinthians 10:4-6 KJV). The King James uses the word "imagination" while other translations use the word "speculations." Jesus wants to help bring this strong area of our soul under the control of His word by the power of the Holy Spirit. It is in the realm of our imaginations or speculations that the enemy of our souls works to cause us to doubt God and trust our own natural thoughts. The further one studies the realm of reasoning and imagination of the mind, one becomes aware of the direct relationship these two areas have on each other. Tomorrow, we will examine the remaining three senses of our soul.

Father, I ask for the work of Your Holy Spirit to be activated in my reasoning and my imaginations so that You may have control in both of these major areas of my soul. I pray that my thoughts would be made captive to Christ.

## August 9 – SENSES OF THE SOUL, continued

1 Corinthians 2:16 – We have the mind of Christ.

Yesterday we saw that the Lord wants to transform our reasoning and our imaginations and bring them under the control of the Holy Spirit. Today, we will consider three more areas of the soul. The third sense is our affections. Paul addresses this subject when he teaches, "If ye then be raised with Christ, seek those things which are above, where Christ sits on the right hand of God. Set your affection on things above, not on things on the earth. For ye are dead and your life is hid with Christ in God" (Colossians 3:1-3 KJV). The things of the Spirit can only function through the cross of Christ. You cannot set your affections on things above without walking in the risen life of Christ. Once our affections were attached to this world, but now they are to be joined to the Lord.

The fourth sense is memory. Jesus told His disciples in the upper room, "The Helper, the Holy Spirit, whom the Father will send in My name, He will teach you all things, and bring to your remembrance all that I said to you" (John 14:26). Paul made known the gospel to the Corinthians. They received the gospel and he tells them, "in which also you stand, by which also you are saved, if you hold fast (*keep in memory)* the word I preached unto you, unless you have believed in vain" (1 Corinthians 15:2). Over the years I have met some who at one point believed, but did not keep in mind what they received and their faith turned out to be vain. David instructs us when he says, "How can a young man keep his way pure? By keeping it according to Your word. With all my heart I have sought You; Do not let me wander from Your commandments. Your word I have treasured in my heart, that I may not sin against You (Psalm 119:9-11). David treasured God's word by committing it to memory and applying it in his daily walk.

The last sense we will consider is conscience. The writer of Hebrews prays that, "The blood of Christ, who through the eternal Spirit offered Himself without blemish to God, cleanse your conscience from dead works to serve the living God (Hebrews 9:14). Peter says, "Keep a good conscience so that in the thing in which you are slandered, those who revile your good behavior in Christ will be put to shame (1 Peter 3:16-17). It is vitally important to know in our hearts that we are right with God, regardless of what others may say. Paul said to Timothy, "The goal of our instruction is love from a pure heart and a good conscience and a sincere faith (1Timothy 1:5-6).

Father, I commit my soul to You. I pray for the Holy Spirit to control my reasoning, imagination, affections, memory and conscience. I pray that each of these senses of my soul would be yielded to the work of Your grace in my inner man.

# August 10 – REIGNING IN LIFE

Romans 5:17 – For if by the transgression of the one, death reigned through the one, much more those who receive the abundance of grace and of the gift of righteousness will reign in life through the One, Jesus Christ.

The reign in life is present, not simply future. The Scriptures are clear that we died when we were buried with Christ. We rose from the dead when we were raised up in His resurrection. "When we were dead in our transgressions, God made us alive together with Christ (by grace you have been saved) (Ephesians 2:5).

We are aware that our body has five senses. They are extremely helpful in navigating in this natural world. The problem is that because the senses are connected to the natural world, they feed the appetites of the flesh. The entire book of James deals with this reality. Consider James' statement, "Each one is tempted when he is carried away and enticed by his own lust" (James 1:13). Temptation enters through the eye and ear gates. John speaks to this when he says, "All that is in the world, the lust of the flesh, and the lust of the eyes, and the boastful pride of life" (1 John 2:16).

Our daily challenge is to bring the natural man into submission to the spiritual man. It is the will of God that we reign in this life with Christ. Ruling our soul and our body is the key to ruling in other areas. Paul taught, "By grace you have been saved" (Ephesians 2:5). The theme of God's grace is seen throughout the entire New Testament. For some, grace is only speaking of God's gift of eternal life. It is true, "I am a sinner, saved by grace," but there is so much more. Paul teaches, "So that, as sin reigned in death, even so grace would reign through righteousness to eternal life through Jesus Christ our Lord" (Romans 5:21). The reign through righteousness to eternal life is in the now, not just the future. Paul declares how grace operates, "I die daily" (1 Corinthians 15:31). Paul goes on to say that his battle is not rooted in "human motives." "Become sober-minded as you ought, and stop sinning; for some have not the knowledge of God" (1 Corinthians 15:34).

The attitude of grace is, I have died with Christ, and I am buried with Christ.

The attitude of grace is, I too may walk in newness of life.
The attitude of grace is, I have become united with Him in the likeness of His death.
The attitude of grace is, certainly, I shall also be in the likeness of His resurrection.

Take time to study thoroughly Romans 6 to grasp Paul's view of grace and reigning in life through Christ.

Father, I thank You for Your amazing grace applied to my life. I surrender my body to You, along with my soul and spirit. I claim the prayer of the apostle Paul in 1 Thessalonians 5:23, that You would sanctify me entirely; that my spirit and soul and body be preserved complete, without blame at the coming of our Lord Jesus Christ.


## August 11 – JUSTIFIED

Romans 5:1 – Therefore, having been justified by faith, we have peace with God through our Lord Jesus Christ.

In Romans 4, Paul lays the foundation of justification by faith from the life of Abraham as recorded in the Old Testament. He tells us that Abraham's faith was "credited to him for righteousness" (Romans 4:22). Not for his sake only, but for our sake also (Vs. 23). So Paul begins Romans 5 with "Therefore" having referred to Abraham in chapter 4. Abraham walked in peace with God, knowing that God was faithful. We too have peace with God as we have trusted the Lord Jesus in faith. It is faith that leads to "justification." Justification takes place in our spirit man. The Lord sees us just as if we have never sinned. He sees us through the cross of Christ.

The first phase of our salvation takes place in our spirit. We have spoken of this previously. Our spirit has been regenerated, or born again. The work of justification brings us into a right standing with God. Our position before Him is not only forgiven, but accepted in every way because of the work of Christ. The penalty of sin has been paid in full by the Lord Jesus. We were baptized into the body of Christ by the Holy Spirit when we were born again. I am not speaking about water baptism, but the Spirit's work of immersing us into the body. "For by one Spirit we were all baptized into one body, whether

Jews or Greeks, whether slaves or free, and we were all made to drink of one Spirit" (1 Corinthians 12:13).

The blood of Christ gives testimony in our spirit to the Father that we are justified, having authority to stand before the Throne of Grace, knowing that we are sons and daughters of the living God. God faith works in our spirit. We have a sure expectation of God's promises. We have God's love ruling in our spirit and a reverential fear of God. True worship flows from the new birth of our regenerated man. In our spirit, we become God-conscious, whereas before the new birth took place in us, we were self-conscious.

The Tabernacle of the Old Testament provides a symbol of God's triune man. The holy of holies speaks of the spirit of man which is the dwelling place of Christ. God's covenant is sealed by Christ's blood. Jesus offered His blood for the forgiveness of our sins. Jesus applies His blood to our spirit as the High Priest would apply the blood of the sacrificial lamb to the Ark of the Covenant and the Mercy Seat each year on behalf of God's covenant people.

Father, I thank You for what You have done in Christ for me. Thank You for the blood of Christ which has been applied to my spirit man. Thank You for all of the provisions You have made for my spirit and my right standing in Your presence.

## August 12 – SANCTIFIED

John 17:17 – Sanctify them in the truth; Your word is truth.

The word sanctification means "to be set apart. The Word of God testifies that those who have put their faith in Christ have been set apart for God's eternal purposes. In Jesus' high priestly prayer, He is requesting His Father to "sanctify the disciples in the truth." Jesus said of Himself, "I am the way, and the truth, and the life; no one comes to the Father but through me" (John 14:6). We too are called to be His disciples. If one is a disciple of the Lord Jesus, that one is sanctified through Christ. The Scriptures declare that we are set apart to the Father. Jesus, the truth, has set us apart for His kingdom. The Holy Spirit has been given to empower us in our sanctification.

Justification deals with our position in Christ before the Father. Sanctification deals with our daily walk in surrendering our life to the Father's will. Sanctification is the process of our daily salvation. Paul instructs us, "So then, my beloved, just as you have always obeyed, not as in my presence only, but now much more in my absence, work out your salvation with fear and trembling (Philippians 2:12-13). In justification we trust the work of Christ for our redemption. In sanctification, we have a part in the work. Sanctification is a life of obedience to the Father, through Christ, in the power of the Holy Spirit.

"If you continue in My word, then are you truly disciples of Mine" (John 8:31). This is a qualifying statement by Jesus. There are many which say, "I believe in Jesus." The question becomes, what do you believe? In the gospel, belief is not a mental assent, but rather a life surrendered to the King of kings. It is a life sanctified for the Master's purpose. A disciple of the Lord Jesus Christ bears witness of faith by the life they live. Jesus' word to Saul on the road to Damascus tells him of the Lord's call on his life toward the Gentiles which was "To open their eyes so that they may turn from darkness to light and from the dominion of Satan to God, that they may receive forgiveness of sins and an inheritance among those who have been sanctified by faith in Me" (Acts 26:18).

The disciple of Christ is justified, sanctified and one day will be glorified when Christ returns for His own. What a salvation He has given us! In our next devotion, we will look at glorification, the future dimension of our three-fold salvation.

Father, I am grateful for all You have done for me in Christ. I ask for the Holy Spirit to help me live out my salvation daily for Your glory. I receive Your sanctifying power to obey and separate myself to Your eternal purposes in and through my life.

## August 13 – GLORIFICATION

1 Corinthians 15:42-43 – So also is the resurrection of the dead. It is sown a perishable body, it is raised an imperishable body; it is sown in dishonor, it is raised in glory.

Glorification is the final result of salvation for God's triune creation man. In our spirit, we are in right standing before God. In our soul, we are sanctified or set apart to God. Our bodies will be glorified at His appearing when the dead in Christ will rise. Paul describes the resurrection in 1 Corinthians 15. He makes several comparisons to the natural creation. He begins with questions concerning the resurrection. "How are the dead raised? And with what kind of body do they come?" (1 Corinthians 15:35). Paul compares the resurrection to a seed that first must be buried in the ground. When it comes to life, the body that is produced does not look like the seed that was planted. Each seed is given a body of its own. Paul describes the many types of flesh that have bodies. He describes heavenly bodies and earthly bodies. He speaks of the differences in the heavenly bodies and their glory such as the sun, the moon, and the stars. The stars themselves differ in their glory.

Paul says, "So also is the resurrection of the dead. It is sown a perishable body, it is raised an imperishable body; it is sown in dishonor, it is raised in glory; it is sown in weakness, it is raised in power; it is sown a natural body, it is raised a spiritual body. If there is a natural body, there is also a spiritual body" (1 Corinthians 15:42-45).

The Lord's coming and the resurrection of the dead has been the glorious hope of the church throughout the ages. Just as God raised Christ from the dead and joined His spirit, soul, and body in resurrected life, He will do the same for every believer. "Flesh and blood cannot inherit the kingdom of God; nor does the perishable inherit the imperishable. Behold I tell you a mystery; we will not all sleep, but we will all be changed, in a moment, in the twinkling of an eye, at the last trumpet; for the trumpet will sound, and the dead will be raised imperishable, and we will be changed. For this perishable must put on the imperishable, and this mortal will have put on immortality, then will come about the saying that is written, Death is swallowed up in victory" (1 Corinthians 15:50-54).

What could I ever hope to add to Paul's inspired words? Today, simply bask in the promise of our glorified bodies. Rejoice in the blessed hope of the church. Hope toward the day that we will all be as He is, glorified, fulfilling all the Father has willed.

Father, this is the day that You have made and I will rejoice and be glad in it. Thank You for Your complete salvation. Holy Spirit, help me to walk in the resurrection life and power of the Lord Jesus Christ until the day I am joined with Him and see Jesus face to face.

## August 14 – THE SOUL INCLUDES MIND, EMOTIONS, AND WILL

Mark 12:30 – You shall love the Lord your God with all your heart, and with all your soul, and with all your mind, and with all your strength.

In Mark 12:30, Jesus covers four areas in which we are to love the Lord our God. The heart would speak to the emotions. The soul would speak to our whole being. The mind would cover our intellect and strength would cover our will. In the next few devotions we will address the mind, emotions and will as critical areas of the soul which the Holy Spirit desirers to dominate for the kingdom of God.

When we speak of the mind, we are speaking of the intellect. From one's childhood, mindsets are established in one's thinking and reasoning. All begin with the natural man whose thinking and reasoning is affected by family up-bringing, education, and life experience. For many, by the time they come to the Lord, their mindsets are well established and changing of one's mind becomes a great challenge. This is why it is so important to give one's self to the study of God's eternal word. The word of God "washes" our mind and removes the abuse that has taken place over the years. Paul instructs the church, "A natural man does not accept the things of the Spirit of God, for they are foolishness to him; and he cannot understand them, because they are spiritually appraised" (1 Corinthians 2:14-15). God's purpose in the new birth is not exclusively to get us to heaven, but to give us the capacity to discern or appraise spiritually. Paul goes on to say in the 16th verse, "We have the mind of Christ." Daily, we can give up the natural mind of man and activate the mind of Christ. His mind is in us by the work of the Holy Spirit. All the potential of Christ's mind is in our spirit. Through God's word and through

God's dealings in our life, we learn to surrender our natural mind and receive His.

Years ago my spiritual father taught me to pray, "Help me to see things from Your point of view. Help me to see from heaven's perspective." One day the Lord challenged me by asking, "Do you believe I am answering your prayer"? I said, "Yes I do." He then instructed me to receive the things He was showing me and not to argue or think they were merely my thoughts. He said to me, "Examine everything carefully; hold fast to that which is good; abstain from every form of evil" (1 Thessalonians 5:21-22).

The "spiritual man" receives from the Spirit of God. Our mind, that is, our intellect, is to be dominated by Christ. Paul, the apostle was one of the most educated men of his day, but he had to surrender his education to Christ and as he said, "Whatever things were gain to me, those things I have counted as loss for the sake of Christ. More than that, I count all things to be loss in view of the surpassing value of knowing Christ Jesus my Lord, for whom I have suffered the loss of all things, and count them but rubbish so that I may gain Christ" (Phil 3:7-9). Is it our highest goal to gain Christ?

Father, today I commit my heart, my soul, my mind, and my strength to you. Give me heaven's point of view in all that I do and fill me with Your love through the Holy Spirit's power.

## August 15 – THE HEART IS THE SEED BED OF THE EMOTIONS

Jeremiah 11:20 – But, O Lord of hosts, that judges righteously, who tries the feelings and the heart.

In the KJV, the word for feelings is "reins" and means the innermost feelings The Jeremiah passage is dealing with judgment. The prophet is crying out to the Lord, who is the only one that looks at a matter righteously. It is God alone that can see the intent of the heart, the motives of an individual, the very "seed bed" of what drives a person. The word "emotions" is not used in the Scriptures. As we read the Scriptures, we become aware that when we read about feelings and the heart it is referring to one's emotions.

"You shall not oppress a stranger, since you yourselves know the feelings of a stranger, for you also were strangers in the land of Egypt (Exodus 23:9). The King James Version translates the word feelings as "heart." When we speak of having "empathy" for another person, it is because we can relate to what they are going through. The Lord is gracious to make room for this area of our soul. The Lord Himself is moved in His emotions, feelings, and heart. When Abraham interceded for Sodom and Gomorrah on behalf of his nephew Lot, the Lord was moved in His emotions (Genesis 18). Moses, as he interceded on behalf of rebellious Israel, moved God's heart to repentance, that He would not destroy the children of Israel.

The greatest picture of the Lord's heart and emotions is seen in the life of Jesus. Many times in the Gospels it is recorded that He was "moved with compassion." God's healing; His deliverance, His forgiveness, and His redemption come from the "seed bed of His emotions" toward mankind. Man, because of the evil in his heart, questions the motives of God saying, "If God is love, why does He permit evil and tragedy in the world?" In their hearts, they are blind to the "kindness" of God. "Or do you think lightly of the riches of His kindness and tolerance and patience, not knowing that the kindness of God leads you to repentance?" (Romans 2:4-5).

The subject of human emotions is large. In our next devotion, we will look deeper into this major area of our soul life. As we put on the mind of Christ and think like Jesus, our emotions will be freed to be filled with compassion and kindness while maintaining a strong knowledge and wisdom of God's word and how to apply it.

Father, I confess that my human emotions take over at times and I am not led by Your Holy Spirit, but by my own feelings. I surrender my emotions to You. I ask that my feelings would be more controlled by the Holy Spirit. Help me to bring together my mind and my emotions in a better way and be more fully led by Your Word and Your Spirit.

# August 16 – EXAMINING OUR HEARTS

Jeremiah 17:9-10 – The heart is more deceitful than all else and is desperately sick; who can understand it? I, the Lord, search the heart, I test the mind, even to give to each man according to his ways, according to the results of his deeds.

The Word of God spoken through Jeremiah His prophet is a beginning point for our understanding of the heart. There are many verses before Jeremiah's statement we could examine, but these Scriptures go to the depth of the human problem and God's dealings with mankind.

David, as a young man, treasured God's word in his heart. "Your word I have treasured in my heart, that I may not sin against You (Psalm 119:11). David understood his need to get the Word of God into the deepest area of his life, his heart. Many are aware of what God's word declares, but have not treasured the word by memorizing and meditating on the Word.

Solomon exhorts us in Proverbs 3 concerning the heart. "My son, do not forget my teaching, but let your heart keep my commandments; For length of days and years of life and peace they will add to you. Do not let kindness and truth leave you; bind them around your neck, write them on the tablet of your heart. So you will find favor and good repute in the sight of God and man. Trust in the Lord with all your heart and do not lean on your own understanding. In all your ways acknowledge Him, and He will make your paths straight." How could I ever say it better? This is the Holy Spirit speaking through Solomon.

Consider verse 3: "do not let kindness and truth leave you." I call these the "twin sisters." Both heart and mind are tied together. One can be so into the mind they are unkind in the application of truth. On the other hand, one can be so kind, they are kinder than God. God's kindness never violates His eternal truths. The human danger is to be led by our emotions and not by the eternal truth of God's Word. For some, they become legalistic in the application of God's word and death is produced rather than life. God is always redemptive in His purpose. We too, need to be redemptive in our dealings with people.

The disciples of Jesus were arguing among themselves to which of them might be the greatest. "But Jesus, knowing what they were thinking in their hearts, took a child and stood him by His side, and said to them, 'Whoever receives this child in My name receives Me, and whoever receives Me receives Him who sent Me; for the one who is least among all of you, this is the one who is great'" (Luke 9:46-48). There are so many New Testament Scriptures about the heart, this is one of my favorites. It captures the problem and the solution of our heart condition. Today, meditate on Jesus' words to His disciples and see what the Lord reveals to you.

Father, help me to let go of any high mindedness that is in my heart and receive in Your name, a heart of humility toward others.

## August 17 – DO NOT LOSE HEART

Galatians 6:9-10 – Let us not lose heart in doing good, for in due time we will reap if we do not grow weary.

One of the most often encountered problems in the lives of God's people is the loss of hope. Many times, I hear people say, "I have tried, but it does not seem to help." Discouragement tries to find its way into the heart. When it does, it opens the door for unbelief. Unbelief is not just an attitude of the mind, but is a stronghold of the heart.

The writer of Hebrews establishes principles that will help to keep the believer strong in their heart when he says, "Let us draw near with a sincere heart in full assurance of faith, having our hearts sprinkled clean from an evil conscience and our bodies washed with pure water. Let us hold fast the confession of our hope without wavering, for He who promised is faithful; and let us consider how to stimulate one another to love and good deeds, not forsaking our own assembling together, as is the habit of some, but encouraging one another; and all the more as you see the day drawing near" (Hebrews 10:22-25).

To keep our hearts from discouragement, we must be in regular fellowship with the Lord. "Draw near with a sincere heart." Next, as we draw near to the Lord, come with a "full assurance of faith." Come to the Lord with His word fresh in your heart and mind. Allow the blood of Jesus to cleanse you constantly, making sure your "conscious is clean." Remind yourself of your baptism when you died with Christ. We must "hold fast" our confession that originally brought us to hope. The challenges of the Christian walk can cause some to "waver." If one does waver in their faith, the enemy gets an upper hand.

"For consider Him who has endured such hostility by sinners against Himself, so that you will not grow weary and lose heart" (Hebrews 12:3). The key to strong faith and not losing heart is staying focused on the Lord Jesus Christ. When we remind ourselves of what Christ endured in His human life, we are strengthened and able to press forward in our own walk. I find that when I reach the point of giving up, I am about to encounter a breakthrough. When my back is up against the wall, I know that the Lord is ready to help.

Father, I ask You to help keep my heart from discouragement by drawing close to me as I regularly fellowship with You. I come to You with a sincere heart. I come with full assurance of faith. Help me to be disciplined in Your Word that it will be fresh in my heart and mind. Thank You for the blood of Jesus that cleanses me constantly and gives me a clean conscious. My confession is Your victory in Christ.

## August 18 – NOT AS I WILL, BUT AS YOU WILL

Matthew 26:39 – My Father, if it is possible, let this cup pass from Me, yet not as I will, but as You will.

This passage is the clearest picture mankind has of absolute surrender to the will of God. This is the turning point leading away from Adam's rebellion, insisting on his will and not God's. Christ, whom Paul calls "the Last Adam," fully fulfills God's redemptive purpose for humanity. A man, Jesus, chose to lay aside His will for the will of God. Once and for all He made it possible for the one who puts their faith in His redemptive work, to be able to do the same as He did. Our minds, emotions, and will have been liberated to fully surrender to God the Father.

Peter stood strong before the religious leaders that wanted to kill the disciples. Peter chose the will of God even in the face of death. One of the Pharisees named Gamaliel gave sound counsel to the group of religious leaders saying, "Men of Israel, take care what you propose to do with these men. I say to you, stay away from these men and let them alone, for if this plan or action is of men, it will be overthrown; but if it is of God, you will not be able to overthrow them; or else you may even be found fighting against God" (Acts 5:33-39).

Because of what Jesus accomplished for mankind, setting our will against God's will becomes a much more serious matter. Gamaliel's counsel is good counsel for us as well. We never want to find ourselves setting our will against His. When we do, we are fighting against God. Later, the disciples found themselves in need of help in caring for the needs of the people. They made a determination to appoint seven men full of the Holy Spirit to serve the people and their needs. They willed to do the will of God and to devote themselves to prayer and to the ministry of the word (Acts 6:4-6).

Paul declared, "I am ready not only to be bound, but even to die at Jerusalem for the name of the Lord Jesus." And since he would not be persuaded, we fell silent, remarking, "The will of the Lord be done!" (Acts 21:13-14). Here is another example of choosing God's will over one's own will and the will of friends. The elders of Ephesus tried to persuade Paul not to go to Jerusalem, but Paul felt that He had heard from God. They came to the conclusion that they should become silent concerning the matter, and acknowledged that God's will be accomplished.

"Come now, you who say, 'Today or tomorrow we will go to such and such a city, and spend a year there and engage in business and make a profit.' Yet you do not know what your life will be like tomorrow. You are just a vapor that appears for a little while and then vanishes away. Instead, you ought to say, 'If the Lord wills, we will live and also do this or that'" (James 4:13-16).

Father, teach me and empower me each day to say, "If the Lord wills."

# August 19 – WHEN YOUR STRENGTH
# IS LIMITED

Proverbs 24:10 – If you are slack in the day of distress, your strength is limited.

Today, I want to tie together the area of strength and the will of man. Solomon is saying that when adversity comes, if you give up, you do not have much strength. I find in working with many people over the years that the "will" of an individual is in direct proportion to their strength. A good example is in the counseling arena. Many times, I find people come for counseling hoping that the counselor will provide the answer to their problems. They misunderstand the purpose of the counselor which is to help the counselee to understand the root of the problem and the principles that could help them change their circumstances.

When the counselee can hear the counselor and make the necessary application of principles to their situation, there is hope for change and healing. For many, "their strength is limited." In other words, they do not have the strength to apply the counsel given. Their will is not strong toward resolving their issues. They want others to take responsibility or they want the counselor to side with their emotions and views. Many are weak in terms of their "will" to change and do their part in resolving their problems. Doing the will of God takes an inward strength and determination. Many times, the will of an individual is so set it overrides God's will and purpose for their life. At times, individuals simply choose against common sense.

Our intellect and our emotions are driven by our will. As we strengthen ourselves in God's word and develop intimacy with Father God through His Son by the power of the Holy Spirit, our will to do His Will is strengthened. In order to be a kingdom man or woman, a relationship with the Holy Spirit is critical in the formation of a strong and healthy will.

Consider what Paul testified concerning his own afflictions, "For we do not want you to be unaware, brethren, of our affliction which came to us in Asia, that we were burdened excessively, beyond our strength, so that we despaired even of life; indeed, we had the sentence of death within ourselves so that we would not trust in ourselves, but in God who raises the dead; who delivered us from so great a peril of death, and will deliver us, He on whom we have set our hope. And He will yet deliver us, you also joining in helping us through your prayers, so that thanks may be given by many persons on our behalf for the favor bestowed on us through the prayers of many" (2 Corinthians 1:8-11). Paul was first and foremost committed to the will of God. He surrendered his will to God's will. He found strength in the difficulties he faced because his will was given over to God. Our will and our strength are tied together. If you feel weak in the midst of affliction and difficulty, examine your will. Is it self-will, focused on what you want? If so, change your mind and commit your will to God's will and pleasure?

Father, give me Your insight to my will. I ask for the strength of Your Holy Spirit to help me surrender fully to Your purpose in and through my life.

## August 20 – DELIVERANCE FROM PENALTY OF SIN

John 5:24 – Truly, truly, I say to you, he who hears My word, and believes Him who sent Me, has eternal life, and does not come into judgment, but has passed out of death into life.

What a powerful promise Jesus gave to those listening to His teaching. The disciples came to realize that only Jesus had the words of eternal life. "Simon Peter answered Him, 'Lord, to whom shall we go? You have words of eternal life. We have believed and have come to know that You are the Holy One of God.' Jesus answered them, 'Did I Myself not choose you, the twelve, and yet one of you is a devil?'" It is God's will that all would come to repentance (John 6:68). Judas' heart was set against receiving the "words of eternal life." His will was fully committed to his self-interests. Jesus carried the words of eternal life even for someone like Judas, but Judas would not hear.

In Christ, as a result of the cross, the penalty of sin has been addressed. Paul taught the Roman church that, "the wages of sin is death, but the free gift of God is eternal life in Christ Jesus our Lord" (Romans 6:23). The biggest choice in this life is to choose between eternal "death" and eternal life." *Christ paid the penalty for sin, once and for all.* We now must choose to trust and follow Him or continue on the path that leads to death and separation from God. "Therefore, brethren, since we have confidence to enter the holy place by the blood of Jesus, by a new and living way which He inaugurated for us through the veil, that is, His flesh" (Hebrews 10:19-21). It took the blood of Jesus to deliver us from the penalty of sin, which is death and separation from the Eternal One. "If we walk in the Light as He Himself is in the Light, we have fellowship with one another, and the blood of Jesus His Son cleanses us from all sin" (1 John 1:7).

God the Father has provided deliverance from sin's penalty. Jesus freely offered His blood for the redemption price. The Holy Spirit applies the blood of Jesus to a repentant soul, giving us a right standing before God in our spirit. No longer will the penalty of sin affect us. "I saw the dead, the great and the small, standing before the throne, and the books were opened; and another book was opened, which is the book of life; and the dead were judged from the things which were written in the books, according to their deeds" (Revelation 20:11-12).

If you are a believer in the redemptive work of God through Christ, rejoice that your name is written in the Book of Life. The penalty of sin was paid on your behalf. There is no second death in your future. The penalty for sin was paid, which is the starting point for an overcoming life through the Lord Jesus Christ.

## August 21 – DELIVERED FROM THE POWER OF SIN

Acts 1:8 – You will receive power when the Holy Spirit has come upon you; and you shall be My witnesses.

The power which the Lord is promising comes from heaven's authority. That authority was given to proclaim the good news of the gospel of the kingdom. It is an authority to live a life above sin. It is an authority to set captives free from Satan's control. In Acts 1:7, the KJV uses the word "power" from the Greek word, exousia, which means "authority". In Acts 1:8, the Greek word for power is "dunamis," where we get our English word "dynamite." The Lord is giving His disciples delegated authority which comes from His Father.

Many have the idea that the benefits of receiving the Holy Spirit are limited to being born again and going to heaven. Jesus makes it clear that receiving the Spirit is so much more. The Spirit of God brings "authority" and "power" to live a life of victory over Satan's control through sin and darkness. As we walk in the light, as Christ is in the light, we walk in delegated authority to live out His life presently and release that life to others. The Lord has delivered us from the "authority" of Satan, his kingdom of darkness, and the power of the enemy through sin.

As we have seen previously, we were set free from the "penalty" of sin. That freedom began in our spirit when it was regenerated by the renewing of the Holy Spirit. See Titus 3:4. Today we are learning that the Holy Spirit empowers us to be free from the "power of sin" in our daily walk. Sin takes root in the areas of our intellect or human reasoning, imagination, memory, affection, and conscience. It is a daily battle to bring our reasoning into alignment with God's word. Paul instructs us to cast down imaginations that exalt against the knowledge of God (2 Corinthians 10:4-5). Hurts and wounds of the past are stored in our memories. Unclean images can also be stored in the memory of our mind. Have we set our affections on earthly realms or things above, as Paul admonishes in Colossians 3:2? If we do not deal with sin daily, it is possible for our conscience to become seared and fail to work on behalf of godliness. See Hebrews 9:14; 10:22.

Today, receive the power of the Holy Spirit to live a life free from the power of sin. Let us choose to walk in the authority the Lord has given to every believer. In our daily walk, let us choose His kingdom rule over our soul, mind, emotions, and will.

Father, I choose to be an over-comer in my daily walk. I receive the authority and power that You have made available through Christ Jesus the Lord. Thank You for power to overcome the enemy, to allow the Holy Spirit to rule in my life, and to minister Your victory to others day by day.

# August 22 – DELIVERED FROM THE PRESENCE OF SIN, OUR FINAL VICTORY

2 Peter 3:7 – By His word the present heavens and earth are being reserved for fire, kept for the Day of Judgment and destruction of ungodly men.

Judgment is a difficult subject to talk about because people want to think they will be ok in eternity. Notice that Peter says, "The present heaven and earth are being reserved for fire." It is important for the believer to stay focused on the promises of God regarding our future. The new creation of God, created in Christ, is not reserved for judgment, because Christ Himself bore the wrath of God on our behalf. Judgment is reserved for "ungodly men."

A day is coming for the believer when our salvation will be complete. We have considered, in the last couple of days, freedom from the penalty of sin and the power of sin. Today, we consider the final stage of deliverance, "sin's very presence." Peter encourages believers by reminding us that God is not slow concerning His promise in the way some think of slowness. Our God lives in eternity, not a time-space world. Using Peter's reasoning recorded in 2 Peter 3:8-9, it has only been 3 days since the cross and the resurrection of our Lord. "But do not let this one fact escape your notice, beloved, that with the Lord one day is like a thousand years, and a thousand years like one day. The Lord is not slow about His promise, as some count slowness, but is patient toward you, not wishing for any to perish but for all to come to repentance."

There is a New Heaven and Earth coming. "But the day of the Lord will come like a thief, in which the heavens will pass away with a roar, and the elements will be destroyed with intense heat, and the earth and its works will be burned up" (2 Peter 3:10). This is a powerful exhortation not to trust in this world's goods. Peter goes on to reason, "Since all these things are to be destroyed in this way, what sort of people ought you to be in holy conduct and godliness, looking for and hastening the coming of the day of God, because of which the heavens will be destroyed by burning, and the elements will melt with intense heat! But according to His promise we are looking for new heavens and a new earth, in which righteousness dwells" (2 Peter 3:11-13).

Peter, in his explanation of our future hope, keeps it simple. Today, there are so many viewpoints about the end and what things will look like. Many people are confused and many are filled with questions about the end of the world. Why not lay aside all the reasoning's of men and just believe the apostles and their revelation of the end? This is a vast subject so we will continue with Peter's thoughts in tomorrow's devotional.

Father, today help me to see the present world with a correct viewpoint. Focus my eyes on the world to come where sin's presence has been completely removed.

## August 23 – BE DILIGENT FOUND IN PEACE, SPOTLESS, AND BLAMELESS

2 Peter 3:14 – Therefore, beloved, since you look for these things, be diligent to be found by Him in peace, spotless, and, blameless.

Because we are looking for the promise of future things, Peter says "be diligent." Diligence is one of the greatest qualities of the Christian life. Peter qualifies diligence "to be found by Him in peace, spotless, and blameless." This covers a lot of Christian living.

Peace speaks of "His Rest." For the Christian, watching the news should be a different experience than what the world experiences. The world knows "anxiety," but the believer knows "His promises," Our life should be a reputation of being "spotless" from the world. I am burdened for many in the church today that do not keep themselves spotless from the world. Many believers converse and conduct themselves like the world. They participate with great enthusiasm in worldly practices. Except for attending church services, it is hard to tell them apart from the world. The world accuses the church, meaning Christians, of hypocrisy. The world knows what kind of life we should be living and many times the Christian is not found "blameless." Peter says, "Regard the patience of our Lord as salvation." Peter gives testimony that Paul said the same things. He also says that "the untaught and unstable distort the Scriptures to their own destruction" (2 Peter 3:14-16).

Peter's exhortation for the believer is to "be on your guard so that you are not carried away by the error of unprincipled men and fall from your own steadfastness, but grow in grace and knowledge of our Lord and Savior Jesus Christ" (verses 17-18). Do not accept everything you hear. Today, there are some who speak and write not having the right motives, not led by principles which lead God's people into "steadfastness." Our great need is to "grow in grace and the knowledge of our Lord." The Lord Jesus is our standard. His Apostles are our example of Christ's life and give us the foundations of our faith. It is Christ alone that fills all in all.

Peter finishes his instructions to the church by saying, "To Him be the glory, both now and to the day of eternity. Amen" (verse 18). As we devote ourselves to the Lord Jesus Christ, let it always be about His glory. He wants the glory now and He will have the glory throughout eternity. Let us be a people that take the glory with us into eternity and not wait for eternity to give to Him what He alone deserves.

Father, thank You for expressing Your heart through Your servant Peter. Give me grace to receive all that Peter teaches in 2 Peter 3. Help me today, and throughout my earthly life to live for Your glory and honor. My hope is fixed on eternity and the day You have prepared for all who trust in You.

## August 24 – BAPTIZED – SPIRIT, SOUL, AND BODY

Hebrews 6:1 – Leaving the elementary teaching about the Christ, let us press on to maturity.

The word "baptized" comes from the Greek *baptismo*, meaning to dip. The writer of Hebrews includes the doctrine of baptisms (plural) in his list of things that are the elementary teaching about Christ. There are many baptisms we find listed in the New Testament. There are baptisms in water, Spirit, fire, the cross, and sufferings. There are three to consider here in regards to our three fold-salvation for spirit, and soul, and body.

The first baptism is for our spirit man. Paul teaches, when we were redeemed, we were baptized into the body of Christ by the Holy Spirit. As the blood of Jesus covers us, we are immersed in the blood and are justified, becoming members of His body. "Much more being justified by His blood, we shall be saved from wrath through Him" (Romans 5:9). This baptism applies to our spirit man and is a spiritual baptism. "For by one Spirit are we all baptized into one body, whether we be Jews or Gentiles, whether we be bond or free; and have all been made to drink into one Spirit" (1 Corinthians 12:13).

The second baptism is "water" baptism. It is God's ministers that baptize us into water. Peter writes, "it is not the putting away of the filth of the flesh, but the answer of a good conscience toward God" (1 Peter 3:21). In Romans 6, Paul speaks of this baptism as the place we join Christ in death and are united in His resurrection.  Paul powerfully outlines what we have gained in Christ when he writes, "In Him all the fullness of Deity dwells in bodily form, and in Him you have been made complete, and He is the head over all rule and authority, and in Him you were also circumcised with a circumcision made without hands, in the removal of the body of the flesh by the circumcision of Christ; having been buried with Him in baptism, in which you were also raised up with Him through faith in the working of God, who raised Him from the dead" (Colossians 2:12). This is a large sentence, but necessary to keep the thought fully intact.

The third baptism is to be baptized with the Holy Spirit. John the Baptist pointed to Jesus as the one who would baptize us with the Holy Spirit, "John answered, saying unto them all, 'I indeed baptize you with water; but one mightier than I cometh, the latchet of whose shoes I am not worthy to unloose: He shall baptize you with the Holy Spirit  and with fire'" (Luke 3:16). As one receives the Spirit, power is available to live a life for Christ on a daily basis. The Bible calls this daily walk "sanctification" which means to be "set apart."

Father, I accept Baptism, not as a religious act, but for what You intended as described by Paul. I invite the Holy Spirit to circumcise my heart and remove the body of the flesh. I pray to walk in the Spirit daily, being led in the power of resurrection life received through Christ the Lord.

# August 25 – THREE WITNESSES THAT TESTIFY IN THE EARTH

1 John 5:7-8 – There are three that testify, the Spirit and the water and the blood; and the three are in agreement.

The Holy Spirit came to earth after the Son ascended to the right hand of the Father. Consider this, a man is ruling from heaven at the Father's right hand. The Spirit of God has come to earth to bring forth a new creation out of mankind who has been bound by Satan's control. He is here to create all men in the image of Christ. The process which the Holy Spirit leads us into is "the water," where we are to experience death with Christ and His resurrection power. It is a death to the flesh and the receiving of His life. The cleansing of Christ's blood from our sins is applied as the Holy Spirit quickens our spirit and the new birth takes place.

As one receives the New Covenant in the blood of Christ, one is accepting the conditions of the covenant, which is giving up our life in exchange for His. This means I must die to self. Our death to self transpires in the waters of baptism. It is in the waters of baptism that death transpires. Coming out of the water, resurrection life takes place. The Spirit testifies we belong to God through Christ. The blood testifies, we are clean and accepted by God. It testifies that Christ' blood was shed for our sins, destroying all enmity between God and man. Faith in His blood establishes peace with God. The water testifies of our death to our flesh and to our new life in Christ.

Let me be clear, I am not saying that regeneration happens because of the act of going into the water, but it is important to understand the water is more than a religious action. Paul's teaching is quite clear concerning baptism. "How shall we who died to sin still live in it? Or do you not know that all of us who have been baptized into Christ Jesus have been baptized into His death? Therefore we have been buried with Him through baptism into death, so that as Christ was raised from the dead through the glory of the Father, so we too might walk in newness of life" (Romans 6:2-4). The water is a very important witness on earth to the reality of our salvation.

The Spirit bears witness to our spirit that we are sons and daughters of God. The water testifies to the world, we died to this life and now belong to another age. And the blood witnesses of our cleansing that we are now partakers of His life. Let us go forward with great hope and expectation of God's eternal purpose that He has chosen for us in Christ.

Father, I receive the witness of the three You have given the Spirit, the water, and the blood. I thank You for the relationship with You that the Holy Spirit has brought into my life. I praise You for the water which testifies that I am no longer my own. I belong to Christ who cleanses me with His precious blood and witnesses that God is absolutely delighted in me.

## August 26 – THE BLOOD TESTIMONY TO GOD

John 10:25-29 – You do not believe; the works that I do in My Father's name, these testify of Me.  But you do not believe because you are not of My sheep.  My sheep hear My voice, and I know them, and they follow Me;  and I give eternal life to them, and they will never perish, and no one will snatch them out of My hand.

There are three works of Jesus that testify of His redemptive work in each believer and take place in our spirit, soul, and body. These works testify of the complete salvation our Lord has provided for His redeemed people.

The beginning place of our salvation is in our human spirit. It is our spirit that is "born again." The blood of Jesus testifies to God the Father as His blood is applied to the life of the believer. "This cup which is poured out for you is the new covenant in My blood" (Luke 22:20). "For Christ did not enter a holy place made with hands, a mere copy of the true one, but into heaven itself, now to appear in the presence of God for us; nor was it that He would offer Himself often, as the high priest enters the holy place year by year with blood that is not his own. Otherwise, He would have needed to suffer often since the foundation of the world; but now once at the consummation of the ages He has been manifested to put away sin by the sacrifice of Himself" (Hebrews 9:24-27).

The Hebrew High Priest had to bring the blood of an innocent animal once a year into the holy of holies and offer it before God's mercy seat as a testimony from God's covenant people of their need of His mercy and forgiveness. When the Lord saw the blood of the sacrifice, He would have mercy and cover the sins of His covenant people. This yearly practice was a prophetic picture of the real sacrifice which took place when Jesus, our High Priest, offered His own blood as a testimony to His Father. Once and for all blood is before God testifying to the redemptive work of Christ.

As one, by faith, receives what Christ has done for them, the shed blood of Christ is applied to the individual's life and allows the Spirit of God to recreate the human spirit into the image of Christ. The believer becomes a new creation as a result of the blood's testimony to God the Father. A covenant testifies to both the one who created the covenant and the one who receives the covenant. The covenant we have in Christ is sealed with His own blood for all eternity.

Father, I thank You for sending Jesus to die in my place. Thank You Father, that the blood of Christ is the testimony of my redemption. I know I stand before You fully approved and fully complete because of Your Blood Covenant.

## August 27 – THE TESTIMONY TO THE BELIEVER

Romans 8:16-17 – The Spirit Himself testifies with our spirit that we are children of God, and if children, heirs also, heirs of God and fellow heirs with Christ, if indeed we suffer with Him so that we may also be glorified with Him.

When one is born again, the spirit of the person has witnesses of God's work of salvation in the life. Our souls are challenged because they are used to the witness of the world and not the witness of a regenerated human spirit. The Holy Spirit is given to "help" us enter into the full provision of a new creation life. "In Him, you also, after listening to the message of truth, the gospel of your salvation — having also believed, you were sealed in Him with the Holy Spirit of promise, who is given as a pledge of our inheritance, with a view to the redemption of God's own possession, to the praise of His glory" (Ephesians 1:13-14). The work of God is eternal, but we must learn how to receive His eternal work in our daily walk.

What a tremendous thing our Lord has done for each believer! He sealed us in the blood of Christ. He sealed us in the Holy Spirit who helps us day by day. We stand with a testimony before God and a testimony in our soul. As we have seen in previous devotionals, our soul is made up of our intellect, emotions, and will. These three areas of our soul can know the witness of the Holy Spirit. This is the true peace of which the Scriptures speak. There is peace in our intellect, knowing all that the Lord has done on our behalf. We have peace in our emotions. We do not need to be tossed by every wind of doctrine; we need to rely on the Holy Spirit and the Scriptures that witness to our salvation. "We are no longer to be children, tossed here and there by waves and carried about by every wind of doctrine, by the trickery of men, by craftiness in deceitful scheming" (Ephesians 4:14-15). Peace in our will is possible. We can walk in the strength of God and make right choices because of this witness in our soul. The Word of God gives us all the insight we need.

Our personal testimony to others comes out of the work of God in our soul life. The world is looking for reality, consistency, and stability. These areas are only possible in Christ, because He is the only one who was able to live out all of these completely. The believer can do the same, day by day, because of the Spirit's presence and His witness to our soul. Daily give the Holy Spirit the right to guide you and to bring the witness of heaven in all areas of your life. He is an ever-present help to us just as Jesus promised. He is our "Helper." Without the Holy Spirit, it is impossible to live the life of Christ.

Father, I am grateful for the full provision for my soul life. I thank You for the testimony of the Holy Spirit in my soul. I ask for an increase of my capacity to hear and embrace the Spirit's witness in me day by day.

## August 28 – OUR TESTIMONY TO THE WORLD

Acts 8:12 – When they believed Philip preaching the good news about the kingdom of God and the name of Jesus Christ, they were being baptized, men and women alike.

Acts 8:12 is a powerful Scripture that reports a number of things which are very important. First, "many believed" what

Philip was declaring. The good news of the kingdom is that the kingdom of God has come, but not in the way many Jews expected. There are many teachings within modern-day Christianity about future events. Not all of the events will happen the way they are being taught. The Lord has given us what He wants us to know about the future. The kingdom of God did not come as an earthly kingdom, as many Jews expected, but rather in the Spirit. Christ was raised from the dead by the Holy Spirit. The promise of God is that we will be raised from the dead by the same Spirit that raised up Christ. (See Romans 8:11). The Spirit brought transformation in human lives, both for Jew and Gentile. The Spirit of God has affected the nations throughout history. It is through the Holy Spirit that God's rule is known in the earth.

The kingdom that Philip and the apostles preached has a king presently ruling from a heavenly throne. God's covenant with king David was that his heir would rule on an everlasting throne. Jesus Christ is the son of David that is ruling just like God promised. This is why our message needs to contain both the good news of the kingdom and the name of Jesus Christ, "Savior Messiah." The good news to the world is that this King has overcome the powers of darkness that rule throughout the nations. This King's inheritance is the nations. "Ask of Me, and I will surely give the nations as Your inheritance, and the very ends of the earth as Your possession" (Psalm 2:8). The good news is that God's servant is reigning as both Lord and Christ (Acts 2:8).

The response of the men and women who believed was that they were baptized into Jesus' name. They identified with His kingdom as they were born again of the Spirit. In the waters of baptism, they testified to the world that they no longer belonged to this world's systems, but to Jesus Christ and His kingdom of righteousness.

The kingdom of God that Philip preached was a kingdom of power. Act 8:13 tells us the Simon, who was a sorcerer, also believed as he witnessed the miracles taking place through Philip. The world is filled with skeptics and many that participate with the realms of darkness. They are trying to discover reality, but only the kingdom of God contains the reality they need and that can satisfy. Our witness to the world is a vital part of our Christian life. Our testimony, that begins in the waters of baptism as we are baptized by God's ministers, should continue with a lifestyle born of the Spirit of God in righteousness and peace. We should expect signs and miracles to happen in and through our lives as we minister to others. Our testimony should not only be in what we believe, but in demonstration as well. The world is waiting for the testimony of Jesus lived out in power in the lives of His people.

Father, I embrace the King and His kingdom. Let my life be a testimony to the world that Jesus is both Lord and Christ.


## August 29 – RELATIONSHIP WITH GOD

John 1:12 – As many as received Him, to them He gave the right to become children of God, even to those who believe in His name.

In John 1:12, Jesus speaks of the most important right an individual can possess, "the right to become a child of God." The world thinks that we are all God's children. It is true, in biblical terms, that our genealogy can be traced back to Adam. The Bible speaks of Adam as "the son of God" (Luke 3:38). Adam lost his standing through sin. God established the law of a "blood sacrifice" in the Garden of Eden when He took the skins of an innocent animal and covered Adam and Eve's nakedness. Through what God did, we have the first prophetic picture of God's provision for fallen humankind through His Only Begotten Son. Paul calls Jesus the last Adam who has redeemed us back to God making it possible for each descendant of the first Adam to once again have a "right standing" with God the Father.  In our spirit, we have a sure standing as sons and daughters of the living God. Jesus' victory has secured our standing as children of God.

Paul writes of our relationship with God in his letter to the Romans, "All who are being led by the Spirit of God, these are sons of God" (Romans 8:14). The question each believer must ask throughout their life is, "Am I being led by the Spirit of God?" Sons do what the father directs. We live in a society where sons do their own pleasure and this even seems correct. Young people strive for independence. It seems like the goal in child development. Jesus came to do the will of His Father. Even as a child, He understood "being about His Father's affairs" (Luke 2:49). Later as an adult, Jesus taught, "I can do nothing on My own initiative. As I hear, I judge; and My judgment is just, because I do not seek My own will, but the will of Him who sent Me" (John 5:30).

Being led by the Spirit of the Father is what sons of God do. The Lord did not save us simply to transport us to heaven. The Father's plan is to have sons and daughters throughout the earth whose utmost desire is to do His will. The true witness of a son of God is someone who is seeking the Father to know His will in their life so that they may please Him in everything they do. When a person comes to know that their standing before God is absolutely sure, they must do God's will or simply be unfulfilled in their lives.

My personal experience has been to know absolute fulfillment by doing what the Lord has directed of me. Equally true, I have been miserable when disregarding God's will and pursuing my own interests. There is a contrast between a child and a son. I know I have the right to be God's child as Jesus taught in John 1:12. As I mature in my relationship with the Father, I now know I am a son of God because I must do His will as Jesus Himself came to realize.

Father, I thank You I have received Your Son Jesus and have been given the right to be a child of God. Strengthen my resolve to grow in sonship where my earnest desire is to do Your will at all times. Help me in my commitment to Your kingdom purpose.

## August 30 –GROWING IN CHRIST

Matthew 13:23 – The one sown on good soil is the man who hears the word and understands it; who indeed bears fruit and brings forth, some a hundredfold, some sixty, and some thirty.

Jesus taught many aspects of the kingdom of God through parables. Matthew 13:23 is an excerpt from the "parable of the sower." In this verse, Jesus is describing the effect of God's word on the person who is like good soil where seed has been sown. The soil represents a human soul. As we have seen previously, the soul is made up of our intellect, emotions, and will. Our soul is in a constant state of growth. No one can say they have arrived in terms of their total understanding of God's word. Our relationship with the Godhead is constantly developing and growing. Only in eternity will we find full development.

We begin our journey with the Lord like a newborn baby. "Be like newborn babies, long for the pure milk of the word, so that by it you may grow in respect to salvation" (1 Peter 2:2). The key to development and growth in the kingdom of God is a constant hungering for the Word of God. This longing should never disappear! The Holy Spirit gives us the desire to read, to study, and to search out the depths of God's truths. We should be moving from milk to the meaty food of Scriptures. The writer of Hebrews had to stop a theme he was developing in Hebrews 5, because he realized that his readers were not ready to go further. "Concerning Him, we have much to say, and it is hard to explain, since you have become dull of hearing" (Hebrews 5:11).

The Christian life is a life of development and growth. God's life in us is organic in nature. His life is measurable in our growth and development. That measurable growth can only come through longing for His word, regular times spent in fellowship with Him through prayer and supplication, and a relationship with other believers. All three of these areas are necessary in order to be healthy and growing. These three ingredients will affect growth in your mind, emotions, and will. Relationship with the Father and the Son through the Spirit will provoke much thinking and reshaping of our thought processes. This is also true as we interact with God's people. It will produce growth which helps us to mature as sons and daughters of God.

Growing and developing can be very painful at times. As this is true physically, it is equally true spiritually. This is why Peter declares that "the apostles were strengthening the souls of the disciples, encouraging them to continue in the faith, and saying, 'Through many tribulations we must enter the kingdom of God'" (Acts 14:22).

Father, I thank You for the seed which has been sown into the good soil of my life. I am depending on the Holy Spirit to continue to help me in my development and growth. Increase my love for Your word, for prayer, and the fellowship of Your people.

# August 31 – GROW UP IN ALL ASPECTS INTO HIM

Ephesians 4:15 – Speaking the truth in love, we are to grow up in all aspects into Him who is the head, even Christ.

Paul clearly articulates the will of God in this Scripture. The larger context of Paul's instruction begins with verse 11. There, Paul outlines five specific graces or gifts the Lord has given to His church for the purpose of producing growth in the saints of God. Apostles, prophets, evangelists, pastors, and teachers are gifts given to accomplish the Lord's purpose in the earth. In verse 12, Paul states their purpose, which is "the equipping of the saints for the work of service, to the building up of the body of Christ."

As an individual waits on God through study of His word and prayer, they receive much in terms of understanding and ability. In God's eternal purpose, He has established these ministries as a vital part of the "equipping" process. There is an anointing that is imparted through these gifts of God. "Equipping of the saints" has a core purpose of helping God's people achieve maximum potential in God's calling and service. Equipping includes many things such as structuring teachings, bringing correction, instilling vision, being an example to the saints, bringing understandings of God's purposes, and impartation of God's gifts, to name a few.

Our growth in Christ includes the "work of service." Jesus told His disciples, "even the Son of Man did not come to be served, but to serve, and to give His life a ransom for many" (Mark 10:45). Service is the cornerstone of the Christian life. Service is a heart attitude. It is not a "works mentality," but resides at the very core of the love of God. Jesus is our model for everything. He raises up leaders in His body that are to emulate Him. Unfortunately, some leaders take privilege to themselves and expect to be served. New Testament leaders understood they were to serve the body of Christ.

Service includes evangelism. Jesus said that "the Son of Man has come to seek and to save that which was lost" (Luke 19:10). The saints of God are called to serve the lost by sharing the good news of the kingdom of God. As saints of God, we are called to live a lifestyle that represents God's righteousness. The Holy Spirit supplies to each believer the power and grace necessary to serve the needs that come their way. The ministry gifts are intended to build up the body of Christ. As individuals, we should represent Jesus in the flesh. As a body of believers, the same is true. Christianity is not about a gathering that meets in a building, but a people who are equipped and given to the service of others. We are to portray the true nature of Christ in the earth.

Father, in Jesus' name equip me through the help of Your ministry gifts for the work of service. Increase in me a burden for the lost and an ability to bring others to a saving knowledge of Your Son. Strengthen me in my relationship with other believers that we might be built up together in Christ.

## September 1 – APOSTOLIC GROWTH

Ephesians 4:11 – He gave some as apostles.

In our next five devotionals, we will look at the Lord's purpose in these five ministry gifts for the growth and development of the body of Christ. These ministry gifts and their function are important to the maturation of individual believers. The first of the five is the "apostolic gift." The original apostles are known as "the apostles of the Lamb" (Revelation 21:14). Christ is building His church upon the foundation that the apostles and prophets laid, "Having been built on the foundation of the apostles and prophets, Christ Jesus Himself being the cornerstone" (Ephesians 2:20).

These men were given to Christ in His earthly ministry by the Father. "I have manifested Your name to the men whom You gave Me out of the world; they were Yours and You gave them to Me, and they have kept Your word" (John 17:6). There will never be more apostles known as the "apostles of the Lamb," since they were given to Jesus in His earthly ministry. It is important to understand that the "apostolic ministry" was meant to continue until the Lord returns. The apostolic ministry today reinforces what the apostles taught. They are used by the Holy Spirit to "equip the saints for the work of service and to build up the body of Christ: until we all attain the unity of the faith, and the knowledge of the Son of God, to a mature man, to the measure of the stature which belongs to the fullness of Christ" (Ephesians 4:13-14).

It is important to know what the Lord is presently doing in the earth. We started to hear teachings about these five ministry gifts around 1948. Since that time, each of the five gifts has been restored to the church and is still developing toward greater maturity. It is through the apostolic ministry that a great unity is manifesting in the Lord's church. It is unity around the message of the kingdom and not a particular church system. The church is unified throughout the world as we pray for the nations. There is increased city-wide unity as pastor's work together for the greater cause of Christ. The Lord is at work unifying the generations. There is much emphasis on fathering throughout the Lord's church today.

The church of Jesus is growing in numbers and in maturity. Individuals are growing in their commitment to the kingdom of God. The unity of the faith is happening. Increased knowledge of the Son of God is taking place. It is easy to be critical, but an honest examination of the church throughout the world reveals "apostolic times" are among us. Jesus is preparing His church for great things as He wraps up the ages and prepares to return for His bride.

Father, I present myself to You as a willing vessel. Help me attain to the unity of the faith. Increase my knowledge of the Son of God, causing me to become mature into the measure of the stature of Christ. Grow me up to be used by the Holy Spirit for Your pleasure.

## September 2 – PROPHETIC VISION

Ephesians 2:18-22 – Through Him we both have our access in one Spirit to the Father. So then you are no longer strangers and aliens, but you are fellow citizens with the saints, and are of God's household, having been built on the foundation of the apostles and prophets, Christ Jesus Himself being the cornerstone, in whom the whole building, being fitted together, is growing into a holy temple in the Lord, in whom you also are being built together into a dwelling of God in the Spirit.

As we give our attention to the five ministry gifts it is important to keep focused on Jesus. Each of the ministry gifts is a manifestation of the ministry of Jesus and does not stand alone on its own merits. Paul reminds us, *"through Him we have both access in one Spirit to the Father"* (emphasis mine). The Godhead determined for Jesus to build His church upon the apostolic and prophetic ministries. It is through apostolic teaching and prophetic vision God's will and purpose is communicated. John the apostle declares in the book of Revelation that he "fell at his feet to worship him. But he said to me, 'Do not do that; I am a fellow servant of yours and your brethren who hold the testimony of Jesus; worship God, for the testimony of Jesus is the spirit of prophecy'" (Revelation 19:10).

As with the apostolic gift, the prophetic gift is still needed. Today, the prophetic does not bring new revelation or anything "extra biblical," but helps to restore the Lord's church to His original intent. Throughout history, men have distorted the truth of God and have built their own systems. The writers of the New Testament warned God's people that this would happen. Consider what Peter said in his second letter, "False prophets arose among the people, just as there will also be false teachers among you, who will secretly introduce destructive heresies, even denying the Master who bought them, bringing swift destruction upon themselves" (2 Peter 2:1-2). The true prophetic voice points to Jesus. The true prophetic voice is anointed of the Lord to envision God's people in God's purpose for current times.

The writer of Hebrews tells us, "draw near with a sincere heart in full assurance of faith" (Hebrews 10:22). As we draw near to the Lord through the Holy Spirit and the study of His Word, our expected result should be "prophetic vision" for our life and service to Him. When listening to the preached word and as you pray for God's guidance in your life, expect to receive through the prophetic gift, what the Lord wants to reveal to you. Praise God for the apostolic and prophetic gift He has made available to His church.

When I listen to preaching and teaching, when I read articles and books, I am asking the Lord to reveal to me understanding for my life and what is being spoken and how it relates to culture and what the Lord is doing today. I am listening for His Spirit to give to me prophetic understanding about His church and the culture in which I live.

Father, thank you for the prophetic gift You have given to Your church. Thank You for prophets who hear Your voice and deliver to the church Your message for contemporary times. I ask for You to increase prophetic awareness in me that I might walk in a stronger relationship to "the testimony of Jesus."

## September 3 – THE GIFT OF THE EVANGELIST

2 Timothy 4:5 – Be sober in all things, endure hardship, do the work of an evangelist, fulfill your ministry.

The third ministry gift Paul mentions in Ephesians 4:11 is that of the "evangelist." Your fingers beautifully illustrate these five gifts which the Lord has placed in His church. The thumb speaks of the apostolic, as it touches all the other gifts. The prophetic is like the pointer finger, pointing the way. The evangelist, like the middle finger, reaches out the farthest. The ring finger illustrates the pastoral role and speaks of covenant relationship. The small finger speaks of the teacher. It is ideal for cleaning the wax out of your ears.

Paul addresses four areas of which he wants Timothy to be aware. He says be "sober in all things." The message of the gospel is serious. The souls of people are at stake. You can have fun witnessing, but understand you are speaking of the eternal destiny of a soul.

Paul says, "Endure hardship." Declaring the "gospel of the kingdom of God" will generate various kinds of hardships. Some examples are: financial, inconveniences, time and energy, persecution, mocking, rejection, and for some physical abuse, including death. Along with whatever hardships one might experience comes the joy of conversion. David declares, "Those who sow in tears shall reap with joyful shouting. He who goes to and fro weeping, carrying his bag of seed, shall indeed come again with a shout of joy, bringing his sheaves with him" (Psalm 126:5-6).

Paul tells Timothy, who carries pastoral responsibility, "Do the work of an evangelist." Timothy was not an evangelist, but was taught to think evangelistically. A man like Billy Graham is an Evangelist; his gift is obvious. We are all called to witness of the faith and win souls. Solomon wrote, "The fruit of the righteous is a tree of life, and he who is wise wins souls" (Proverbs 11:30). Whatever your gift may be in the body of Christ, do the work of an evangelist.

Finally, Paul says to Timothy, "Fulfill your ministry." One of the most fulfilling things in the life of a believer is to know your ministry of service. As I write these devotionals, I know, this task is a part of fulfilling my service to the body of Christ. No one person can do everything, but the Holy Spirit has assignments for each of us. Whatever assignments the Lord may have given to you, remember Paul's encouragement to Timothy. You can always ask a person if they have any prayer requests. It is a great lead into sharing the love of God with another.

Father, I thank You for the Gift of the Evangelist. As Paul instructed Timothy, help me to do the work of an evangelist. Open my heart and my eyes to see people as You do. Show me the lost and the perishing who need to hear of Your great love revealed in Christ Jesus our Lord.

## September 4 – OVERSEERS OF THE FLOCK

1 Peter 5:2 – Shepherd the flock of God among you, exercising oversight not under compulsion, but voluntarily, according to the *will* of God.

The English word for "pastor" is only found in the Ephesians 4:11. In the Greek it is found many times. A number of different Greek words are used in the New Testament with slightly different meanings. Words such as shepherd, overseer, elder, and bishop are found there. They all speak of pastoring the flock of God. Throughout history these words have been treated as separate ministries, but that is a wrong understanding and application. They all speak of the "care of

God's people." In our devotional, I will use the word shepherd because the word is used in our verse for today.

The shepherd is a "local" gift. The shepherd has an allotment of God's people for which he is responsible. The shepherd knows the people and their individual needs. The shepherd is to relate with other shepherds in the locality so that there is a healthy overall care for the body of Christ. Biblically speaking, shepherds are first recognized by the people for whom they are caring. An apostolic function is to recognize the shepherds and set them into their place before the people. This is clearly seen throughout Paul's writings.

The shepherd is to exercise oversight. Two important understandings are needed. First, the exercise of oversight is not to be an obligation or feeling, "I have to do this." It comes from knowing God's call. It is an attitude of "volunteerism." I do not "shepherd" for money, or guilt, or to be known or seen. The ministry gifts are to be utilized voluntarily Second, an overseer must be motivated by love. Jesus voluntarily laid down His life for the sheep giving us an example to emulate. The overseer is not to be controlling or consider they have a position of privilege. The shepherd is first a servant of God and a servant to God's people.

Shepherding must be according to the will of God. It is God who calls through the Holy Spirit at work in a person's life. I was called at age fourteen. I was planning a career in electronics, but as I walked across the Fellowship Hall of the church I attended, the Holy Spirit called me to serve the body of Christ. From that moment, I was ruined for anything else. I have done many things in my life, but I cannot escape being a shepherd. I feel no "compulsion," only an honor to serve my Lord and His people.

As God's people, it is important to understand the ministry gifts; this helps us pray for the shepherd/overseer. It is important for us to understand the grave responsibility that the shepherd carries. It is important so that we can work alongside the shepherd with their particular gifts. Finally, the Lord may call you to this ministry gift.

Father, I thank you for Your shepherds who represent Christ to the flock. I pray now for the shepherd that You have placed in my life. I pray that You would put a hedge of protection around him and his family. I pray that he would fulfill Your will through the calling that rests upon him.

## September 5 – GOD HAS PLACED SOME IN HIS CHURCH AS TEACHERS

2 Timothy 3:10-11 – Now you followed my teaching, conduct, purpose, faith, patience, love, perseverance, persecutions, and sufferings.

It is hard to know if the teaching gift is separate from the pastoral gift. Apostles, prophets, evangelists and pastors are clearly separate. The apostolic and pastoral ministries have teaching as a major component of their gift. The apostles laid the foundation of what was to be taught. I call this "structuring doctrine." The elders of the New Testament churches taught what the apostles set as proper doctrine. Teaching the things of the Spirit is definitely a gift given to the body of Christ. Biblical teaching is not rooted in academics in the sense of man's views. It is rooted in "revelation," or what God reveals.

Paul tells Timothy that any man who "aspires" to the office of overseer," among other things, must be able to teach (1Timothy 3: 1-7). As stated in our scripture for today, Timothy followed Paul's teaching. Paul's teaching was more than words. His teaching was also found in his conduct, purpose, faith, patience, love, perseverance, persecutions, and sufferings. Teaching should reflect a manner of living, not just information.

Teaching is a "fatherly function." Solomon gives instruction to his son when he says, "My son, do not forget my teaching" (Proverbs 3:1). We can assume that Solomon was taught by his father, King David. Not only do the scriptures speak of natural fathering, but spiritual fathering as well. "This command I entrust to you, Timothy, my son, in accordance with the prophecies previously made concerning you, that by them you fight the good fight" (1Timothy 1:18). Fathers teach their children. The real teachings come through the models that fathers and mothers set for their children. I believe that one of the weak points in church life is that the majority of teaching is simply informational rather than example.

Jesus' teaching was show and tell. "For truly I say to you that many prophets and righteous men desired to see what you see, and did not see it, and to hear what you hear, and did not hear it" (Matthew 13:17). Today, I believe we find that teaching is mostly about information. Biblically it is about modeling. A part of training is putting your hands to the work and practicing so you might develop the skill you are learning.

I worked in the television repair field for many years. My first boss wanted me to take classes at the local city college. It was helpful to be in the class, but my greatest knowledge base came in the field. I was fortunate enough to work with the shop's best technician. It was his modeling that laid the foundation for future success in the field of servicing. I found the same to be true in ministry development. I listened to a lot of teaching that was excellent and helpful, but it was in the doing, alongside mentors, that the real teaching took place.

Father, thank You for the teaching gift You have placed in the body of Christ. I pray to be taught as well as to teach others of Your wonderful ways and works. Help my life to model for others what You have taught me.

## September 6 – ATTAINING THE UNITY OF THE FAITH

Ephesians 4:13 – Until we all attain to the unity of the faith, and of the knowledge of the Son of God, to a mature man, to the measure of the stature which belongs to the fullness of Christ.

The fivefold ministry gifts were given to equip God's people until the church "attains" the unity of the faith. Paul's statement about attaining unity is as big a goal as one will find. It is hard to imagine the church in that kind of unity. Perhaps it is what we understand unity to be that is the problem. Unity is impossible in the natural. Biblical unity is the work of the Holy Spirit in the "hearts" of God's people, not simply in their heads. Today, I have unity with many in the Lord's church, not based on agreement about everything, but in agreement concerning God's kingdom purposes.

One reason unity has been difficult to achieve is that, around the second century, church fathers shifted the focus from the "kingdom of God" to the Church. The body of Christ began to be taught that where the Bishop is, there is the church. The apostles taught that the church is the people of God and bishops were "overseers" who provided care for God's people. The apostles further taught that the kingdom was in the Holy Spirit. He is the center of all that the Father and the Son are doing. This shift set the stage for "ecclesiastical structures" rather than the government of God that the apostles founded. The Reformation brought the church part of the way back to God's original purpose, but not all the way back. Out of the Reformation came many divisions over doctrine and the government of the church.

The twentieth century brought a fresh outpouring of the Holy Spirit reviving the Lord's church. Unity has been on the increase as the Lord changes the hearts of His men and women. There is more unity today than since the first century. The real shift began to happen around the 80's and 90's as the church began to focus on the kingdom of God and not on denominations. Unity prayer was at the foundation of this revival in the Lord's church. One of the first areas was united prayer for the nations and unreached people groups. Another important shift was united prayer in cities as pastors began to pray together to fulfill the "Great Commission." Marches for Jesus took place all over the world as God's people celebrated the kingdom of God and His Glorious King!

Unity begins in our family, our local church congregation, and our cooperation with what the Lord is doing in our locality. Search your heart today and see if there is any division toward others in the body of Christ. If there is, repent and give it over to the Lord. Ask the Father for grace to live in the unity of the Spirit and the bonds of peace with everyone. This does not mean compromise of your convictions. It does mean keeping our hearts right before God and others.

# September 7 – THE KNOWLEDGE OF THE SON OF GOD

Ephesians 4:13 – Until we attain the knowledge of the Son of God.

Knowing Jesus is not simply about an initial salvation experience. It is a matter of growing in relationship with Him until we are at one with His eternal purposes. The apostle Paul came as close as any in the knowledge of Christ. Paul said, "Whatever things were gain to me, I have counted as loss for the sake of Christ" (Philippians 3:8). Paul valued his relationship with Christ far above anything he knew in this life. Paul is the true example of dying and being buried with Christ. He is our example of what it means to live in Christ Jesus' resurrection power day by day.

The desire of Paul's heart was, "That I may know Him and the power of His resurrection and the fellowship of His sufferings, being conformed to His death; in order that I may attain to the resurrection of the dead" (Philippians 3:10-11). To know the sufferings of Christ, one must first partake in the power of His resurrection life. By faith, we receive Christ Jesus the Lord. This is the gate through which we enter into His life. Through "faith" in Him we are accepted by the Father. This is not the end, but the beginning of knowing Him. The Holy Spirit begins to lead us into the "fellowship of His sufferings." It is in the sufferings of Christ that we begin to truly experience the heart of God.

In verse 11, Paul speaks of purpose, "in order that I may attain to the resurrection of the dead." At first glance, it may seem like Paul is working to attain eternal life. We know by the study of Scriptures this is not the case. Paul is speaking about the "first resurrection" which every believer has entered into through baptism. "All of us who have been baptized into Christ Jesus have been baptized into His death. Therefore we have been buried with Him through baptism into death, so that as Christ was raised from the dead through the glory of the Father, so we too might walk in newness of life" (Romans 6:3-4). Paul was committed to walking in the power of Christ's resurrection. Walking in His resurrection life comes from knowing Him and the fellowship of His sufferings. Paul's life modeled this truth.

Father, I ask You to help me attain to the resurrection of Christ daily. I was dead in my trespasses and sins, but I rejoice that I am alive forever more in Christ Jesus. I want to know You more. I ask You to prepare me in my daily walk so I can live in Your Son's resurrection life.

## September 8 – ATTAINING TO A MATURE MAN

Ephesians 4: 13 – Until we all attain to a mature man, to the measure of the stature which belongs to the fullness of Christ.

As we continue to look deeper into these passages in Ephesians, we see that Paul is calling each believer to maturity in Christ. Christ Jesus is our model as a mature Son. The Lord did not save us simply to get us to heaven. Salvation is about a new man. It is about a man who is created in the image of God's Son.  God's intention was not that we would remain children, but to become mature people who are able to handle the Lord's business well.

The fivefold ministry has been given assignments by the Lord to help in the development of God's people. For example, the goal of an overseer is to develop those for whom he is responsible as mature individuals who are the image of Jesus in the earth. Jesus supplies the grace for these ministry offices to be able to accomplish their work. Jesus, through the Holy Spirit, also supplies grace for each believer so that they can grow up in the Lord.

When Paul says, "By grace you have been saved through faith; and that not of yourselves, it is the gift of God; not a result of works, so that no one may boast" (Ephesians 2:8), he laid the foundation for our entire Christian walk. Everything we do in Christ must come from grace through faith. We cannot do what God is requiring without a supply of grace. Many struggle in the Christian walk as they start out by grace and then try to go farther on their own. As we have seen in previous devotions, our "will" is involved, but the Holy Spirit supplies the grace. As He supplies grace, faith follows. Faith, beloved, is an operation of grace. Faith is not our effort, but His supply of grace.

Growing up in Christ is a continual process developed throughout our entire life. It is our salvation being worked out day by day. Each day we are to receive His grace and then exercise faith in obedience to His work in our lives. Doesn't that take off a lot of pressure, knowing you do not have to go it alone? Whatever is lacking in your maturity in the Lord, begin to ask for grace to be supplied in that area. Your flesh may resist, the Devil may fight you, and circumstances my create obstacles, but if you press into the Holy Spirit, He will give you the grace to overcome. Faith will rise and you will be victorious in Christ.

Father, help me to fulfill Your plan to grow up into Christ. I claim the maturity You have destined for me. I am willing to accept the trials that will be used by You to cause Christ to be formed in every area of my being. I gladly receive Your grace to do Your will throughout my life.

## September 9 – GROWING UP TO THE FULL STATUE OF CHRIST

Ephesians 4:13 – Growing to the measure of the stature which belongs to the fullness of Christ.

Ephesians 4:13 describes precisely God's intention for each believer. In every conceivable way, the Lord wants Christ to be revealed in us. The measure of the stature which belongs to the fullness of Christ is a statement that fills eternity.

The word "stature" is an interesting word which requires a little research. The word stature is derived from the Greek (helikia) meaning "an age." (Vines Expository Dictionary of New Testament Words). It came to mean a certain length of life, as when a person is said to be "of age."

Throughout the Scriptures, we find different ages revealed. Noah's flood was the end of one age and the beginning of another. God's call in Abraham's life was the beginning of an age and a new thing God was about to do in the earth. Abraham was the beginning of a nation and became known as "the father of us all" (Romans 4:11-12). The age of faith began with faithful Abraham. From Abraham, God created an entire nation. The nation Israel was named after Abraham's grandson Jacob, whom God renamed Israel, meaning "prince with God."

Israel came to full age with the emergence of the Christ, God's promised Messiah. Unfortunately, that generation did not walk in the faith of Abraham. "Jesus answered, 'If I glorify Myself, My glory is nothing; it is My Father who glorifies Me, of whom you say, 'He is our God'; and you have not come to know Him, but I know Him; and if I say that I do not know Him, I will be a liar like you, but I do know Him and keep His word. Your father Abraham rejoiced to see My day, and he saw it and was glad."

God's purpose in all the ages was to reveal His Son and to create a people in the image of Christ Jesus, the Lord. He purposed that all of Israel would come to know Him in faith and be recreated by the Holy Spirit as the sons and daughters of God. He intended through Israel's recreation in the Spirit that the Gentiles too, would be recreated by the Spirit and be joined with all of Israel as God's Covenant people in the earth. God's intent in this age is for Christ to be revealed to the nations though His people born of the Spirit.

A remnant of Jews believed and became the foundation of the "new creation". Believing Gentiles were added and "one new man" in the Spirit is filling the earth. "Abolishing in His flesh the enmity, which is the Law of commandments contained in ordinances, so that in Himself He might make the two into one new man, thus establishing peace, and might reconcile them both in one body to God through the cross, by it having put to death the enmity" (Ephesians 2:15-17). God's work was completed in Christ. He is the fullness of God. Now we are called to be formed into His likeness and grow up into His fullness, "to the measure of the stature which belongs to the fullness of Christ". This is the work of the Holy Spirit. Receive His work into every area of your life today.

## September 10 – RADICAL CHANGE IN THE WORLD

Daniel 2:28 – However, there is a God in heaven who reveals mysteries, and He has made known to king Nebuchadnezzar what will take place in the latter days.

September 11, 2001 is a day that will live in the hearts and minds of multitudes. Thousands were killed that day by terrorists driven by evil compulsion to change the world by eliminating those opposed to their theological persuasions. That day the world changed. No longer are we simply engaged with traditional struggles of corrupt philosophies and greed in the hearts of men, but a more sinister evil has manifested its ugly head. In 2011, as we watched planes crash into the Twin Towers and more than 3,000 people lost their lives, we saw the beginning of a battle that will last to the Coming of Our Lord.

Consider seven major changes that are taking place in the world.

> Geo-political – the overturning of dictatorships through-out the nations and ongoing conflict over geography.
> The Middle East – prominence of tribalism in relationship to the world community.
> Communist Nations that have embraced capitalism as a means of economic prosperity.
> Education – built on values now being controlled by relativism, humanism and false science.
> Economics – having left a gold standard in 1973 for a dependence upon a federal reserve system that borrows and prints money when desired.
> Sexual Orientation – once clear to be "male and female" now filled with all kinds of mixture.
> Climate Changes – being touted as man induced, not understanding God's control of the elements for his own purposes.

The Lord desires to give to His people a heavenly perspective. There are plenty of places one can go to learn the world's views. Just watch CNN, FOX, or worse. The battles we are engaged in do not originate in the natural, but come from the supernatural realm. If God's people are bound to their natural reasoning they will have no more understanding than the world does.

Daniel the prophet found himself caught in the geo-political struggles of His day, but he knew that the "God of heaven was the one in control. He knew that a relationship with his God was the key to understanding the world and his own people's success in their time of distress.

We must know in our heart of hearts that Daniel's God is our God and He alone is in control of world events. As we prepare to remember 9/11, let us also remember that God is taking back His earth through the Gospel of the kingdom. We, God's people, need to pray as Daniel of old prayed, trusting that God will reveal to us His plans for our day, and show us how to respond.

Father, I pray that I might have understanding in this changing world. I pray to receive Your wisdom and Your peace. I pray that I would learn to rest in Your word that is forever settled. Lead me each day by Your Holy Spirit dwelling within.

## September 11 – A DAY TO REMEMBER

Psalm 74:18-23 – Remember this, O Lord, that the enemy has reviled, and a foolish people has spurned Your name. Do not deliver the soul of Your turtledove to the wild beast; Do not forget the life of Your afflicted forever. Consider the covenant; For the dark places of the land are full of the habitations of violence. Let not the oppressed return dishonored; Let the afflicted and needy praise Your name. Arise, O God, and plead Your own cause; Remember how the foolish man reproaches You all day long. Do not forget the voice of Your adversaries, the uproar of those who rise against You which ascends continually.

As we remember September 11, 2001 and the heinous crime committed against humanity, know that God too remembers. Before evil manifested on earth, it manifested in heaven when Satan and his hosts set themselves against God and His kingdom purpose. The next few days we will devote ourselves to three men who understood the true warfare. This will serve to help in understanding the battle in which we are engaged.

Daniel 9 and 10 gives us insight into the warfare happening in the heavens. Daniel discovered God's timing for the completeness of judgment upon Israel in the book of Jeremiah. Daniel gave his attention to the Lord to seek Him by prayer and supplications with fasting, sackcloth, and ashes. I suggest reading the prayer of Daniel 9:3-19. In verse 20, Gabriel brings an answer to Daniel's prayer. In chapter ten, more insight is given to Daniel after he had been mourning and fasting for three entire weeks. This time, Gabriel told Daniel that "from the first day that you set your heart on understanding . . . your words were heard" (Daniel 10:12). In verse 13, Gabriel told Daniel, "the prince of the kingdom of Persia was withstanding me for twenty-one days; then Michael, one of the chief princes, came to help me, for I had been left there with the kings of Persia. In Verse 20, Gabriel informs Daniel, "he now will return to fight against the Prince of Persia and that the prince of Greece is about to come." In Verse 21, Gabriel revealed to Daniel that there is "no one who stands firmly with me against these forces except Michael your prince."

Today, we are still battling these princes of Persia and Greece. Persia is represented in the "false religion of Islam" and Greece with its "humanistic philosophies" that fill western culture and our educational system. The battle is not in the natural realm, as Daniel learned, but in the heavenly sphere. Today, Daniels are needed who will set their hearts on understanding and on humility before God. The two big fronts that God's people face are "false religion and humanistic philosophy." Their sources are not natural, but supernatural. The true warfare is the kingdom of darkness set against the kingdom of light. Our strength and courage comes from knowing our God has overcome, "He is head over all rule and authority" (Colossians 2:10).

Father, I ask You for understanding and courage to enter into my part of the battle. Strengthen me in faithfulness to pray with knowledge about the true warfare. I ask for the Holy Spirit to open up Your word to me so that I might know how to answer those who oppose Your truth. Lead me in prayer and supplications for myself, Your people, and the nation.

## September 12 – JESUS, OUR WARRIOR KING

Mark 1:23-24 – There was a man in the synagogue with an unclean spirit; and he cried out, saying, "What business do we have with each other, Jesus of Nazareth? Have you come to destroy us? I know who You are – the Holy One of God!"

What a powerful beginning of Jesus' ministry. The enemy's dominions could not hold their peace in the presence of their judge. When the Scripture says, "he cried out" it is speaking of the unclean spirit in the man using the man's voice to communicate. The man was not some mentally deranged individual. That kind of person would not have been allowed in the synagogue. He appeared normal, as many do, but he had an unclean spirit that controlled areas of his life.

The spirit in the man recognized Jesus as his destroyer. He asked Jesus, "Have You come to destroy us?" He spoke as a representative of other spirits in the man or spoke of the demonic realm in general. The spirits knew a day was coming when God would put an end to their existence. He knew that they would be destroyed by "the Holy One of God". As you continue in this passage you find Jesus did not accept the spirit's confession of His deity or His humanity, but rather "rebuked him, saying, 'be quiet, and come out of him'! Throwing him into convulsions, the unclean spirit cried out with a loud voice and came out of him" (Mark 1:25-26). The scene was messy, noisy, and a bit violent. This is not what most people want to happen in a church meeting. This kind of scene happened quite regularly in Jesus' ministry. When the kingdom of darkness and the kingdom of God collide, it is a violent encounter.

In Matthew chapter 12, we receive more understanding concerning these two kingdoms. Read the whole chapter for context. We find the religious leaders of Jesus' time telling the people that Jesus was casting out demons by the power of the prince of demons. Jesus countered their views with powerful responses, one of which was a parable. "Now when the unclean spirit goes out of a man, it passes through waterless places seeking rest, and does not find it. Then it says, 'I will return to my house from which I came'; and when it comes, it finds it unoccupied, swept, and put in order. Then it goes and takes along with it seven other spirits more wicked than itself, and they go in and live there; and the last state of that man becomes worse than the first. That is the way it will also be with this evil generation" (Matthew 12:43-45). Jesus is saying that generation was demonized. Later, in Mathew 23:13-39 Jesus gives eight scathing woes to the religious leaders. In Jesus' lament over Jerusalem, He cries out that "your house is being left to you desolate" (Matthew 23:38).

As the Gospel is preached in power, as supernatural manifestations of God's Holy Spirit increase, as we draw nearer to the Lord's coming, the kingdom of darkness will also manifest its evil, its violence, and its absolute resistance to God and His people. We are called to set individuals and nations free, those held captive to Satan's power.

Father, I pray for increased understanding of the unseen world. Help me to know how to pray and to be used to set those free who are held captive by the enemy's power. I pray for Your divine protection as we encounter the enemy and his dominions. May Your kingdom come and Your will be done.

## September 13 – PAUL'S INSTRUCTION CONCERNING OUR WARFARE

2 Corinthians 10:3-4 – Though we walk in the flesh, we do not war according to the flesh, for the weapons of our warfare are not of the flesh, but divinely powerful for the destruction of fortresses.

Paul was responding to his critics that accused him of walking in the flesh. He acknowledges that he is still walking in the flesh, but that he is not fighting this spiritual warfare by means of his flesh. Paul helps us understand, as believers, we are not using fleshly weapons in our battles. God has given us weapons to defeat the enemy which are "divinely powerful." Jesus promised that we "would receive power when the Holy Spirit has come upon you" (Acts 1:8).

Paul understood that the minds of people were in bondage to spiritual forces that exercised influence through the world and its systems. Paul calls this influence on the minds of people "fortresses." The enemy establishes ways of thinking, belief systems, and controls over humanity by his dominions known as "principalities and powers." Unbelief, false religion, and lust in the flesh are a few of the fortresses. Paul preached the good news of the kingdom of God to religiously bound people, primarily the Jews. He also preached to Gentiles bound by sexual and occult strongholds.

Paul knew the fortresses were established in people's thoughts. As he preached the gospel with power, he understood he was "destroying speculations and every lofty thing raised up against the knowledge of God, and taking every thought captive to the obedience of Christ" (2 Corinthians 10:5). Many believers think they are reasoning with others simply by logic and are trying to convince unbelievers to accept biblical truths by simply seeing the logic of their presentation. A well-presented message is important, but the battle in the reasoning of people's minds is spiritual. In the power of the Holy Spirit and by the authority of God's word, we too, like Paul, destroy fortresses set up in the minds of the unregenerate.  This makes it possible for them to receive God's grace of salvation through the Lord Jesus Christ.

Many believers who have been able to believe for their own salvation still need deliverance from the world's views. They are controlled by principalities and powers that are under Satan's domination. This is one reason why the study of the Word of God is so important. The word, by the power of the Holy Spirit, continues to wash our minds and set us free from the world's views to see and understand from God's perspective.

Father, in Jesus' name, I ask You to reveal anything in my reasoning which does not line up with Your Word. I pray that every fortress of the enemy would be destroyed in my thoughts and that the Holy Spirit would rule supreme in me so I might walk in faith, pleasing to You in every way.

## September 14 – PUT ON THE WHOLE ARMOR OF GOD

Ephesians 6:10-11 – Finally, be strong in the Lord and in the strength of His might. Put on the full armor of God.

Paul finishes his letter to the church at Ephesus by instructing them concerning spiritual warfare. Acts 18 – 20 records the founding of the Ephesian church and the spiritual warfare which the believers faced. Those struggles came from the Jewish religious community and the occult religion of Diana which filled Ephesus. These struggles produced riots against the believers who were being set free from Satan's power through the power of God.

Paul brings clear instruction to the established church at Ephesus saying, "Be strong in the Lord and in the strength of

His might." This was a clue that the battle was not over and their victory would not be in their own strength, but in the Lord's. The battle is not over for us either. In fact, it won't be over until the Lord comes. "Then shall that wicked be revealed, whom the Lord shall consume with the spirit of his mouth, and shall destroy with the brightness of his coming" (KJV).

Paul then instructs, "Put on the whole armor of God." The people were used to seeing the Roman soldiers, dressed in their full armor, so this provided a wonderful picture of the spiritual armor each believer is to put on. It is not automatic; one must "put on the full armor, so that you will be able to stand firm against the schemes of the devil" (Ephesians 6:11). Paul established the reason for this absolute necessity in the following verse. "Our struggle is not against flesh and blood, but against the rulers, against the powers, against the spiritual forces of wickedness in heavenly *places*" (Ephesians 6:12).

Ephesians 6:14-17 describes each piece of the armor we are to put on. First, gird your loins with truth. It is "truth" that holds all the armor in place. Next, put on the breastplate of righteousness. It is the righteousness of God that will protect our hearts. After this, put on the shoes of the gospel of peace. Only a walk of peace can protect us from the enemy's attacks of "anxiety and worry." In addition, take up the "shield of faith." It is the shield of faith that protects us from all the enemy will throw at us. The Roman soldiers linked their shields together creating a solid wall against what the enemy was throwing at them. We need each other beloved! As we walk in covenant relationship, the enemy is less likely to get through and defeat us. With a shield, which is defensive, one needs a sword, which is offensive. The Sword of the Spirit which has been provided to us is a two edged sword. It is "the Word of God."

Father, today I put on the whole armor of God. Thank You for Your protection in the battle against the schemes of the wicked one. Help me to stand strong in the power of Your might.

# September 15 – THE TABERNACLE OF GOD

1 Corinthians 6:19 Do you not know that your body is the temple of the Holy Spirit who is in you, whom you have from God, and that you are not your own?

The Old Testament gives us illustrations that are types and shadows of those things which were to come. The Tabernacle beautifully illustrates the triune make up of man. The Holy of Holies in the tabernacle is symbolic of the spirit of one who has been born again. The spirit in a person is the dwelling place of Christ through His eternal Spirit. God has met us in mercy as the atoning blood of Jesus is applied to our life. We have daily access to God by the Spirit.

The Holy Place, where the priests daily ministered to Lord, represents our soul and our daily service to God. The priests would bake fresh bread each day and offer it before the Lord. The priests would trim the candle wicks and supply fresh oil to fuel the candles. Each day, incense would be offered to the Lord as a praise offering. What a beautiful picture of our daily and priestly service to the Lord. Giving one's self to the word of God daily is very important in receiving fresh bread from God. That bread may take the form of instruction, encouragement, and perhaps new insights into the nature of God. "Man shall not live on bread alone, but on every word that proceeds out of the mouth of God" (Matthew 4:4).

Each day, we need to be filled with the Holy Spirit, keeping our vessels supplied with the fresh oil of God so we might be His lights in a darkened world. Jesus said, "You are the light of the world. A city set on a hill cannot be hidden" (Matthew 5:14-15). Paul admonishes us, "to know the love of Christ which surpasses knowledge, that you may be filled up to all the fullness of God" (Ephesians 3:19).

The altar of incense serves as a beautiful type of our daily worship unto our heavenly Father. "Through Him then, let us continually offer up a sacrifice of praise to God, that is, the fruit of lips that give thanks to His name" (Hebrews 13:15). Paul sums things up for us when he instructs God's people saying, "Do not get drunk with wine, for that is dissipation, but be filled with the Spirit, speaking to one another in psalms and hymns and spiritual songs, singing and making melody with your heart to the Lord; always giving thanks for all things in the name of our Lord Jesus Christ to God, even the Father; and be subject to one another in the fear of Christ" (Ephesians 5:18-19).

The Outer Court symbolizes our body and what the world sees. To the world we testify of the sacrifice of Christ and join Him in baptism as we testify to death with Him and the power of His resurrection. Paul states "We know that if our earthly tent which is our house is torn down, we have a building from God, a house not made with hands, eternal in the heavens" (2 Corinthians 5:1).

Father, I ask to be filled with Your Holy Spirit today. Feed me Your word, cause me to have sufficient oil and to have my candles trimmed. I stand before You as a priest of God, offering to You the sacrifices of praise.

## September 16 – BREAKING THE SHAME BARRIER

Hebrews 12:2 – Fixing our eyes on Jesus, the author and perfecter of faith, who for the joy set before Him endured the cross, despising the shame, and has sat down at the right hand of the throne of God.

A simple definition of shame is – a painful feeling of having lost respect of others and of oneself because of improper behavior, failure not to meet the expectation of another, and not living up to your own expectation of yourself.

Many Bible figures had to overcome shame. Abram felt shame not having a child for whom he could leave an inheritance. God changed Abram's name to Abraham, meaning "father of many." God not only gave him a child, He multiplied his seed so His posterity was like the sand of the sea. Jacob was shamed because he deceived his father into thinking that he was Esau, his older brother, from whom he stole the birthright. Later, God changed Jacob's name, which meant "deceiver" to Israel, meaning "Prince with God." Joseph was shamed by his brothers who sold him into slavery. In Egypt, God raised him up to serve Pharaoh and save the nation in a time of famine. Some others I could write about would be Moses – shamed from Egypt and shame that he was inarticulate. Saul felt shame because of his persecution of the church and Timothy because of his age. Then there is Peter, who denied his Lord three times.

People do shameful things because they live from a shame base in their life experience. They are acting out what they believe about themselves. Many see themselves as a failure, evil, rejected, ugly, unworthy of love, and a host of other things.

Jesus broke the shame barrier once and for all in life and death. He gave us power in our life to rule over shame. He has empowered us to receive His forgiveness and acceptance. He wants to equip us so we too might help others break off shame from their lives. The Lord's call for each of His children is to break shame's power and be free to serve in humility.

One of the strongest proponents of shame is religion. Religion can put the expectations of others upon an individual. In Christianity, one can come to church feeling shameful. When they hear and receive the gospel they experience the freedom Christ has for them. Shame lifts, but as they hang around the church, shame begins to creep back in as others put their expectations on the new believer. We should never shame someone into being a follower of Jesus. God certainly doesn't.

Father, I thank You for taking my shame upon Yourself. I thank You for the covering You have given to me in the Lord Jesus Christ who causes me to know I am loved and cared for by the power of the Holy Spirit. Help me to communicate that love to others as well.

## September 17 – EFFECTS OF SHAME IN A BELIEVERS LIFE

Romans 8:1-2 – Therefore there is now no condemnation for those who are in Christ Jesus. For the law of the Spirit of Life in Christ Jesus has set you free from the law of sin and of death.

I believe this to be one of the most powerful scriptures in the entire Bible. It is *now*, it is *in Christ Jesus*, and it is *the law of the Spirit*. Today, we will consider some of the results of shame in a person's life.

Shame produces a negative attitude. When one is under the bondage of shame, their tendency is to see life through a negative prism. They have only known negative feelings concerning themselves, so it becomes very difficult to see life any other way.

Shame causes a person to focus on themself rather than the needs of others. Shame is "self- consuming." On a natural level, it is our own self-esteem that permits us to view others in a healthy way. Shame makes it difficult to be concerned for another's circumstance.

Trust becomes an issue for the individual who feels shamed. Their defenses are up to prevent further embarrassment or hurt feelings. Shame is a killer of real friendships and intimacy. It is difficult to relate in a healthy way with others, if one cannot relate in a healthy way with themselves.

It is very difficult, if not impossible, for the shamed person to be sure of their salvation. Since trust is a root problem with the shamed individual, trusting the Lord and His promises is an ongoing challenge for the one struggling with shame issues. Faith is a constant battle. Rather than resting in the Lord, the shamed person is always in a state of unrest and anxiety. Without faith, it is impossible to please God. The shamed person can never fully become all that the Lord designed them to be. A spirit of doubt is a root spirit that can control a person who feels shamed.

Shame will keep us from being bold and courageous in our witness for Christ. The shamed person cannot handle rejection. Rejection will come from some as Christ is presented. Many are not interested in the gospel because it first brings conviction of sin. The shamed person turns "conviction" into a negative of condemnation rather than the means to salvation and freedom that is found in Christ.

Father, I ask You to reveal any shame in me. I pray for the power of the Holy Spirit to break that law of death. I ask You to fill me with the love of Christ, first for myself and then for others. Help me to reject shame and receive the full benefit of the law of the Spirit of Life in Christ Jesus.

# September 18 SHAME IS AN INHERENT PROBLEM

Genesis 3:7 – Then the eyes of both of them were opened, and they knew that they were naked.

Before Adam and Eve sinned and fell from the place of honor the Lord had given to them, they knew nothing of shame. When their eyes were opened they became self-conscious and aware of their uncovered condition. They instinctively felt separated from the love of God. They hid from each other and from God, trying to cover up their shame. It is shame that keeps us from our_destiny. The Greek word for shame means nakedness. We are born naked which speaks of our inherent condition.

It took God's intervention to begin a true process of recovery. Only when Jesus became sin for us could a true recovery of man's lost and shameful condition become possible. As we receive by faith His sub-stationary sacrifice, shame must go because we are now fully accepted in the completeness of Christ.

Jesus demonstrated the Father's commitment to removing shame when He ministered grace and broke shame in the life of an adulterous woman as recorded in John 8:1-11. Jesus turned the searchlight back on her accusers when He said, "He who is without sin among you, let him be the first to throw a stone at her" (John 8:7). I see Jesus' response as one of the greatest demonstrations of the love of God. Jesus found Himself alone with the woman. Her accusers had all left. Jesus asked her, "Did no one condemn you? She said, 'No one, Lord'. Jesus said, 'I do not condemn you either. Go. From now on sin no more'" (John 8:10-11).

Jesus broke the shame barrier by emptying Himself. In Philippians 2:5, Paul describes how Jesus totally emptied Himself so He could be shamed for each of us. Our shame was put on the Lord Jesus Christ. If we receive what the Lord has done on the cross, we are free to sin no more just like the woman in John 8.

Jesus overcame shame in both life and death. Jesus was born to die and to rise again. He went from swaddling clothes to grave clothes in order to break the shame barrier for all who would believe on Him. The writer of Hebrews instructs us when he says, "Fixing our eyes on Jesus, the author and perfecter of faith, who for the joy set before Him endured the cross, despising the shame, and has sat down at the right hand of the throne of God." Jesus broke through the shame barrier both in His life and in His death. We also can break shame through His life, which is in the power of the Holy Spirit.

Father, I thank You for a life free of condemnation. I rejoice because the Lord Jesus has broken the shame barrier once and for all. I celebrate the power of the Holy Spirit who enables me to break the shame barrier because of what Your Son has accomplished in the work of the cross.

## September 19 – HUMILITY BREAKS THE POWER OF SHAME

Philippians 2:5-11 – Have this attitude in yourselves which was also in Christ Jesus, who, although He existed in the form of God, did not regard equality with God a thing to be grasped, but emptied Himself, taking the form of a bond-servant, being made in the likeness of men. Being found in appearance as a man, He humbled Himself by becoming obedient to the point of death, even death on a cross. For this reason also, God highly exalted Him, and bestowed on Him the name which is above every name, so that at the name of Jesus every knee will bow, of those who are in heaven and on earth and under the earth, and that every tongue will confess that Jesus Christ is Lord, to the glory of God the Father.

The key to overcoming the flesh is humility. I'm not speaking of a feeling that I am not worthy. Many of God's people have an attitude of false humility which can generate self-righteousness, pride, and anger that is rooted in shame. Many say, "I'm just a sinner saved by grace!" Yes, you were a sinner. Don't stay there! You were saved by grace. Now be a son of God as He called you to be.

James writes, "Humble yourselves in the sight of God, and He will lift you up" (James 4:10). When the Lord lifts us up there is no sense of shame. Shame generates false humility while the grace of God generates a sense of true acceptance. True humility says, "I can do nothing of myself." If I receive anything, it comes from God! You lift your head and say, "Look what God has made me." This is biblical humility. Jesus said in John 5, "I can do nothing of myself, only what I see the Father doing." The Son did a lot, but He did not do things from His own initiation. The proper response when honored by another is to say, "Thank you for your recognition." Afterwards, deflect the glory and thank God for what He allowed you to do. "Lord, I thank You for working through me."

When we have a right attitude concerning humility and how God sees us in Christ, faith is generated and this enables us to do exploits for our God. He made us who we are through Jesus Christ. He empowers us to do His will. We acknowledge that we are simply yielded vessels, ready to be used by the Lord for His glory. That kind of attitude leaves no place for shame. Pride and self-will are both bound and we are free to live out what the Lord has made us to be.

Father, cause me to know the difference between false and true humility. Grant me grace to receive all You have done for me. Let the attitude that was in Christ reign in me, that I might be emptied of self and filled with Your holy presence.

## September 20 – SEVENFOLD EMPTYING PROCESS

Philippians 2:5-7 – Have this attitude in yourselves which was also in Christ Jesus, who, although He existed in the form of God, did not regard equality with God a thing to be grasped, but emptied Himself.

We must be emptied in order to be filled. Philippians 2 reveals seven areas of Christ Jesus' attitude about being emptied and allowing His Father to lift Him up through the exaltation of the resurrection. Through the resurrection, Christ is drawing men to Himself. "If I am lifted up from the earth, I will draw all men to Myself" (John 12:32). Jesus said this to indicate the kind of death by which He was to die, death on the cross. It is in dying, life is found.

➤ v. 7a – Don't exalt yourself

- ➤ v. 7b – Choose to be a servant
- ➤ v. 8 – Humble yourself through obedience, even to death of self
- ➤ v. 9 – Let God exalt and lift you up
- ➤ v. 9 – Let God give you a name that others honor
- ➤ v. 12 – Obey God in your private life
- ➤ v. 14 – Be content and don't murmur or argue

The Lord is bringing about a divine emptying process in our life. He has called us to fully enter into Christ's life and have His attitude in everything. The Lord Jesus Christ had one desire and that was to fully honor His Father, drawing all the attention to Him. What is our desire? Philippians 2 gives us the example that the Lord set for every believer. We are to follow His attitude. "I only want to be exalted in Christ and exalted by Christ." If you are exalted by anything else, it only draws attention back to you. The world is filled with self-exaltation and honors its own.

Paul leads us from humility to exaltation and an understanding that it is God at work in us for His good pleasure (Philippians 2:12). This process starts in us when we confess Jesus as Lord. From that day, we are to serve God's good pleasure. Christ's attitude in us will continue all of our life as we choose Jesus' Lordship in every choice we make.

Father, I choose for You to have Your good pleasure in me. My life is no longer my own, but it belongs to You. Establish in me the attitude of Christ, an attitude of humility and allowing Your Holy Spirit to be the One to exalt me for Your glory and praise.

## September 21 – MEEKNESS IS STRENGTH UNDER CONTROL

2 Corinthians 10:1 – I, Paul, myself urge you by the meekness and gentleness of Christ—I who am meek face to face with you, but bold toward you when absent!

We have discovered in previous devotions how the Lord is helping us "Work out our own salvation with fear and trembling." God is working in us for His good pleasure. He tells us, "Do all things without murmuring and disputing," because

He is working a divine emptying process in our lives to bring about biblical humility.

The Holy Spirit is not at work to make us weak and spineless, He is at work to reveal Christ in us through meekness and boldness. Society has emasculated manhood. God is not bringing us to weakness, but to be strong through gentleness!

Meekness is not weakness! Meekness is yielded strength under control. I think of the great stallion that has been broken and bridled. He still has the same strength and force, but he can be ridden and his power guided.

In meekness, Jesus was willing to empty Himself and do what the Father had appointed. Jesus chose to empty Himself and be guided only by the Holy Spirit throughout His entire human life. Jesus said, "Father, I will go through this shame and all the failure." He was willing to die, not in a hospital taking pain medicine, but on the cross in great suffering. It was cruel and humiliating. He took all the shame and all the humiliation for us. He was humiliated so we could succeed. I too must choose to empty myself and be filled with His meekness which will result in strength.

"Meekness is an inwrought grace of the soul, and the exercises of it are first and chiefly towards God. It is that temper of spirit in which we accept His dealings with us as good, and therefore without disputing or resisting; it is closely linked with the word humility. It is only the humble heart which is also the meek, and which, as such, does not fight against God and more or less struggle and contend with Him. This meekness, however, being first of all a meekness before God, is also such in the face of men, even of evil men, out of a sense that these, with the insults and injuries which they may inflict, are permitted and employed by Him for the chastening and purifying of His elect" (Notes on Galatians, by Hogg and Vine pp. 294 from Vine's Expository Dictionary of Biblical Words).

Why not say to the Lord, "Go ahead, Jesus, finish what you started in me." Whatever our age might be, simply yield to the Lord and allow His strength to work in you mightily. The Lord is meek, but He is strong. Paul learned to walk in the meekness and strength of Christ. It is possible to know both Christ's gentleness and His great strength as we yield to Him in the

Holy Spirit. Ask the Father today to give you both meekness and boldness as you live out your salvation.

## September 22 – THE LAW OF THE SPIRIT OF LIFE

Isaiah 11:1-2 – A shoot will spring from the stem of Jesse, and a branch from his roots will bear fruit. The Spirit of the Lord will rest upon Him, the spirit of wisdom and understanding, the spirit of counsel and strength, the spirit of knowledge and the fear of the Lord.

Jesse was King David's father. God promised David that the Messiah would come from his generational line. The promise of the Father was that the Spirit of the Lord would rest on David's promised son. Many of the common folks of Jesus' day recognized Him as the "Son of David" (Matthew 21:9).

Isaiah identifies six manifestations of the Spirit that would be seen operating in the life of David's greatest Son, the Lord Jesus Christ. The spirit of wisdom is mentioned first, followed by understanding, counsel, might, knowledge, and the fear of the Lord.

The spirit of wisdom is the discerning of consequences of wrong actions from an eternal perspective. Jesus knew the hearts of all men, which is to say, He knew their motives. He was able to respond in wisdom to all their trick questions and wrong motivations.

The spirit of understanding is the ability to bring into light why and how people behave as they do. It is the ability to identify wrong behavioral patterns and to establish healthy ones.

The spirit of counsel is the knowing of God's purpose and will in the life of an individual. It is to know how to reverse the effects of sin through understanding the counsel of God.

The spirit of might is the demonstration of God's power over the addictions sin produces. It is the power to bring deliverance and healing from sin's results.

The spirit of knowledge is having an eternal perspective that produces purpose and a fulfillment of divine destiny.

The spirit of the fear of the Lord is an awareness of God's presence and brings the healing of a seared conscience. The spirit of the fear of the Lord calls out hypocrisy and identifies a "seared conscience" (1Timothy 4:1-2). The fear of the Lord keeps one away from evil (Proverbs 16:6).

Father, I ask for these manifestations of Your presence to be operating in my life as it was in the life of Your Son, whom You call "the Son of David."

## September 23 – DEVELOPING A PLAN OF ACTION

Proverbs 28:13-14 – He who conceals his transgressions will not prosper, but he who confesses and forsakes them will find compassion.

When we are faced with situations in life which keep getting worse, it is time to stop and evaluate the problem and then develop a plan of action to turn things around. This is exactly what the Father did for mankind through the Lord Jesus Christ.

We must face our present condition head on. Many try to ignore the conditions that are creating havoc in their lives. Many of God's people have issues of depression, condemnation, and feelings of being bound with no way out of their circumstances. What is needed is a new way of thinking.

Here are some suggestions to help form a new way of thinking in developing a plan of action.

> ➢ Accept "The New Man" God has made you to be in Christ. It is not just a theological position, but in reality we have been made new in Christ by the work of the Holy Spirit.
> ➢ Apply biblical principles to your situation. Find out what the Bible has to say concerning your problem.
> ➢ Set goals. Part of developing a plan is the setting of goals. Make sure that your goals are realistic. Pray over

your goals and invite the Holy Spirit to empower you to attain what you have set.

➢ Let others participate with you as you try to attain the goals. Your spouse or a close friend needs to know what you're struggling with and what your goals are. It is a good idea to have a spiritual leader also involved.

➢ Make a clear determination to what you are to give your mind. Establish disciplines and be accountable daily, weekly, and monthly.

The plans of the diligent lead surely to advantage, but everyone who is hasty comes surely to poverty (Proverbs 21:5). What a helpful thought Solomon gives to us. Under the inspiration of the Holy Spirit, Solomon tells us that a plan gives us a distinct advantage. The old adage of "haste makes waste" is certainly true in the lives of many. If we have been hasty in the past, we can stop, evaluate our situation, make a plan and turn things around.

Father, I thank You for the plan You have for my life. I am sorry for any haste on my part in not waiting on You for clear direction. Help me to plan carefully, be accountable, and have a clear determination in my thoughts.

## September 24 – DETERMINATION

1 Corinthians 2:1 – I determined to know nothing among you except Jesus Christ and Him crucified.

One who is determined has their mind made up. They have decided or resolved to do a certain thing. They are resolute and unwavering in their decision. Paul's determination came from something beyond him. It came from the power of the cross of Christ through the Holy Spirit.

Watchman Nee wrote in his book, "The Latent Power of the Soul" that God put tremendous ability in man's soul beyond what we normally use. The problem is that "soul power" belongs to the old nature and not the new. Determination for the believer must be associated with the cross of Christ and not some natural reasoning from our old nature.

A sign the Holy Spirit is at work in us is in the destroying our confidence in the flesh (Philippians 3:3). In Philippians 3:4, Paul goes on to say that more than anybody, he could put his confidence in his flesh. He chose not to because he recognized he died with Christ and now his source of life came from the resurrection power of the Lord. If we try to cling to natural virtues while God desires to bring forth the life of His Son in us, we find ourselves fighting against God. The virtue of Christ is in the "Fruit of the Spirit" alone.

Our determination should be rooted in the freedom of Christ which brings true liberty in our life experience. The biblical order that leads to a determination to follow the Lord is found in repentance, forgiveness, conversion, and a life of trust in God.

Individuality, independence, and natural reasoning are all a part of self-preservation. True freedom comes when I let go of hurts, bitterness, resentment, and unforgiveness. This includes anything which relates to "self-preservation." Only the wisdom of God through the cross of Christ can supply the power for our human condition.

Now is a great time to embrace Christ's cross. For some, it may be the first time. For others, it could be a renewal of a commitment made years ago. Allow the Lord to conquer more of the natural man to include your plans, efforts, and reasoning. Ask Him to release a greater degree of His Life through the Holy Spirit in your planning, your work, and, your thought process. Be determined to know less of what you know and to know more of Jesus and Him crucified. Only through this kind of determination can we know the demonstration of His power and His life released through us.

Father, let the mind of Christ be in me. I want to embrace Christ more and more. Please conquer every area of the natural man. Cause me to become as determined as Paul became in knowing Christ and His cross each day of my life.

# September 25 – FREEDOM THAT BRINGS TRUE LIBERTY

Luke 22:32 – I have prayed for you, that your faith may not fail; and you, when once you have turned again, strengthen your brothers.

Peter thought he was ready to fully serve the Lord. After Jesus gave Peter His counsel, Peter replied "Lord, with You I am ready to go both to prison and to death!" From Peter's viewpoint, he had given his all to the Lord. Remember, it was Peter who had the confession, "You are the Christ, the Son of the living God" (Matthew 16:16). He was seen as a principal leader among the twelve. Peter thought the work in him was finished.

Jesus responds to Peter's commitment to go to prison and die for Jesus, telling Peter in verse 34, within the next 24 hours you're going to deny Me three times. I am sure that sent Peter into a tailspin. It is a good thing Jesus had prayed for Peter's faith not to fail. Peter was about to receive the greatest test of his life. Without the prayer of Jesus, there is no telling what would have happened to Peter.

True freedom is found in the Lord Jesus Christ as our High Priest. "For we do not have a high priest who cannot sympathize with our weaknesses, but One who has been tempted in all things as we are, yet without sin. Therefore let us draw near with confidence to the throne of grace, so that we may receive mercy and find grace to help in time of need" (Hebrews 4:15-16). As with Peter, our freedom begins in the knowledge that Jesus is praying for us so that our faith will not fail.

True freedom is found in conversion. I do not mean gaining information about Jesus and saying we believe in Him. True conversion is turning from depending on our natural life as our source to depending on the Holy Spirit as our source of life and knowledge. Peter was still trying to figure things out on his own. He thought he had surrendered all to Jesus, but he had not yet undergone the death process. Death to self is required in order to know true conversion. It is a process we learn and not a one-time experience we have. Note what Jesus said to Peter – "when once you have turned again" (verse 32). It is the *again part* that is difficult. Peter, like us, vacillated between his natural life and the new life the Spirit was generating in him.

After conversion we begin to turn our attention to others. An evidence of "self" being crucified is our willingness to give up our life to serve others in their need. Jesus knew Peter was not ready for the task he was destined to accomplish. The Lord pointed the way forward as He said "when you are converted" (KJV). Jesus has a purpose for each one of us, but there is a process we must go through. Many get hung up in the process. Some get burned out trying to "strengthen" others before they are fully converted themselves.

Father, I humble myself before You. Keep me from arrogance which causes me to think I can serve You out of my own strength. I am weak, but You are strong! Help me to live a lifestyle of conversion, walking in faith, being changed daily, and strengthening others in their journey.

## September 26 – REFINEMENT

Proverbs 17:3 – The refining pot is for silver and the furnace for gold, but the Lord tests hearts.

The natural man looks more for what he can get from a relationship than what he can give. Before sin dominated in the garden, Adam and Eve had their eyes on the glory of God and saw each other through the purity God had breathed into Adam's nostrils. Disobedience to God's word through listening to the voice of the tempter brought a choice outside of God's plan and destiny for humankind. It plunged Adam and Eve and their posterity into a need for the "refiner's fire."

God deals with his creation in two ways, individually and corporately. In the garden the Lord began with Adam, then Eve, and finally the Serpent. He then drove all three from the garden. The Serpent is brought low and eventually judged by the seed of the woman. Adam and Eve, and their descendants, entered into the refiner's fire through the individual judgments God placed on the man and the woman.

The cross of Christ became the place of God's judgment in dealing with mankind's sin. When we embrace the cross personally and by faith receive what Christ has done for us, we are raised up into the newness of His life and we begin a journey of experiencing the refiner's fire in the exchange of our life for His.

The primary way the Lord has chosen to refine us is through relationships. Nobody can refine themself. The main reason for this is that it is most difficult to recognize the areas in one's own life which needs refining. It takes external pressure. Marriage is the primary relationship the Lord uses in the refining process. Next are children that demand attention and cause us to refocus our time, energy, and resources. If we are not blessed with children, the Lord has no shortage of pressures to use in the refining process.

I cannot help believing that the refining process is what John the Baptist was prophesying when he said," As for me, I baptize you with water for repentance, but He who is coming after me is mightier than I, and I am not fit to remove His sandals; He will baptize you with the Holy Spirit and fire" (Matthew 3:11-12). The fire is the fire of "refinement." Even our Lord was led by the Spirit into the wilderness to be tempted by the devil. Jesus knew the fire before He experienced the glory.

Refinement is not a popular message. God's promise of blessing receives much more popularity, but the only way to true blessing is through the fire. Refinement may not sound encouraging, but it will bring the greater weight of glory if we will embrace God's purpose and His ways.

Father, I confess that Your ways are not my ways. By faith, I receive Your way of the refiner's fire. I ask to be baptized with the Holy Spirit and fire. Refine me Lord for Your glory.

## September 27 – I AM UNDONE

Isaiah 6:5 – Then said I, Woe is me! for I am undone; because I am a man of unclean lips, and I dwell in the midst of a people of unclean lips: for mine eyes have seen the King, the Lord of hosts (KJV).

The New American Standard Version translates Isaiah 6:5 "for I am ruined!" When one is undone they feel ruined. This is not a bad place to come before God. Job also experienced this deep sense of being undone in God's presence. His response was "I will ask You and You instruct me. I have heard of You by the hearing of the ear; but now my eyes see You; therefore I retract, and I repent in dust and ashes" (Job 42:5-6). Job had many opinions about God, especially in defending himself against the accusations of his four friends. Job was well established in his position of being right.

We must become undone before God before He can lift us up to the place He has prepared for us in Christ. Even Jesus, though He had no sin, He humbled Himself before God the Father. The Father lifted Him up and gave Him a name above every name. As we take the same position of Isaiah and Job, the knowledge of being "undone" and "retracting" all our conceited words through repentance, opens the door for a great experience with the Lord.

When the Lord touches our tongue, we will have something worthwhile to contribute. When we repent of our opinions and acknowledge that He alone has the right viewpoints, then God will deal with those who stand against us with their opinions. We are living in a time when many in the body of Christ are repenting of their strong positions which are rooted in self-exalted thoughts. The Lord is granting His body grace, through the power of the Holy Spirit, to lay down self and be united by pressing into the Lord Jesus Christ to know His plan and will.

It is unnecessary to "defend God" or "our positions." We are to represent His Word, what He has said, and let Him defend Himself through fulfilling His word, whether by judgment or by salvation. It is in His presence we will find fulfillment and not in the acceptance of people. God will give us acceptance through others, but they are not our source of fulfillment.

If we have been buried with Christ and raised up with Him by the power of the Holy Spirit, then our identity is in Him, side by side with one another for His purpose and glory. It is time to let go of anything that originates in us and spend time listening for the voice of God through His written word and the united word of the Spirit as He works through the body of Christ in the earth. Listen for the themes of Scripture and the themes being spoken in a united way to this generation.

Father, I come to You undone. I recognize that I am most opinionated. Help me, as You did Job, to become quiet before You. Speak to me of the areas You want to change in my life. Give me grace to receive Your correction. Cause me not to defend myself nor You. Help me to be a faithful representative of Your character and will.

## September 28 – GENUINE FAITH WILL BE TESTED

1 Peter 1:6-7 – In this you greatly rejoice, even though now for a little while, if necessary, you have been distressed by various trials, so that the proof of your faith, being more precious than gold which is perishable, even though tested by fire, may be found to result in praise and glory and honor at the revelation of Jesus Christ.

Peter knew what he was talking about, having been through the fire himself. You cannot talk about "fiery trials" if you have not been through them yourself. A known teacher in the body of Christ told the story about sitting with a young man who was talking about doing great things for God. The teacher was intently looking into the young man's eyes. The young man asked him, "Why are you looking so intently at me?" The teacher responded, "I am looking for the scars."

 The Christian walk is not for the faint of heart. Jesus was "a man's man." Peter spoke about being protected by the power of God through faith for salvation ready to be revealed in the last time (1 Peter 1:5). Peter went on to help believers understand that we greatly rejoice in what God has done, even though for a little while we go through various trials. Trials prove our faith. One can evaluate their maturity level based on how they handle trials. Peter teaches believers that the trials of our faith are "more precious than gold which perishes." Gold is a very precious metal. Peter says that the "trials of our faith" are more precious than gold. Even gold is tested by fire to remove impurities. Is it any wonder that our "faith" is also tested by fire?

It is important to understand that we do not bring glory to God through our success, but rather through our faithfulness. Paul taught us to remain steadfast, "having done everything, to stand firm. Stand firm" (Ephesians 6:13-14). Paul and Barnabas strengthened the souls of the disciples, encouraging them to continue in the faith, and saying, "Through many tribulations we must enter the kingdom of God" (Acts 14:22).

As I look back over my life, I am reminded of many trials and tribulations. I did not enjoy the times of testing, but I am grateful for what they produced. It is in pressing through that we find growth. It is similar to a weight lifter. One must learn how to use the weights to gain the greatest benefit. The weight lifter must push through the pain, not to the point of injury, but to the point of breaking down the tissues so they can be rebuilt to a greater strength. I can truthfully say that I increased in faith because of the various trials I have gone through. I rejoice in the Lord because He has proven Himself to be faithful.

Finally, Paul admonishes us, "to be strong in the Lord and in the strength of His might" (Ephesians 6:10). Aren't you glad you do not have to trust your strength? He is the source of strength, He is the supplier of all you need, and He is counting your faith more precious than gold, even tried gold that has gone through the fire.

Father, I thank You for all Your promises. I am weak, but You are strong. I give You the distress of trials. I pray that when Jesus returns, every trial I have known will be found to result in praise, glory, and honor to You.


## September 29 – FROM DARKNESS TO LIGHT

John 1:6 – There was a man sent from God, whose name was John. This man came for a witness, to bear witness of the Light that all through him might believe.

Two thousand years ago "Light" came into the world. Not ordinary light, but light that lights every man. This verse strongly implies that before "The Light" there was only darkness. Men were filled with darkness. The prince of darkness ruled throughout mankind.

John was God's prophetic instrument who pointed to the Light. The Light was a man, Jesus. John testified of Jesus as "the Light". Later, Jesus testified of Himself as being the light of the world. "Then Jesus again spoke to them, saying, 'I am the Light of the world; he who follows Me will not walk in the darkness, but will have the Light of life'" (John 8:12). Only through Christ is it possible to have light. It is only in the following of Jesus that one can walk in light. To the world this is an offensive view.

"You are the light of the world. A city set on a hill cannot be hidden; nor does anyone light a lamp and put it under a basket, but on the lamp stand, and it gives light to all who are in the house.  Let your light shine before men in such a way that they may see your good works, and glorify your Father who is in heaven" (Matthew 5:14-16). The Holy Spirit was sent to indwell each believer as the source of this light. When Jesus told His disciples that they "are the light of the world," He was not saying light originated in them, but by being joined to Him, they too became "the light of the world." The Holy Spirit has raised up lights in each successive generation. Today, those who follow Jesus are "the light of the world."

"We must work the works of Him who sent Me as long as it is day; night is coming when no one can work. While I am in the world, I am the Light of the world. When He had said this, He spat on the ground, and made clay of the spittle, and applied the clay to his eyes, and said to him, 'Go, wash in the pool of Siloam' (which is translated, Sent). So he went away and washed, and came back seeing" (John 9:4-7). "We must work the works," Jesus included His disciples in this statement and He also included us. Christianity is rooted in doing the works of God. Light is manifested in the works! Jesus said, "Believe Me that I am in the Father and the Father is in Me; otherwise believe because of the works themselves" (John 14:11-12). It is in doing the "works of God that faith is stirred in the hearts of those yet in darkness.

Church, it is time to arise and do the works of the Father as Jesus modeled. The Holy Spirit has come to empower each believer in the works of God and manifest light to a dark world. Let us say with Jesus, "We must do the works of Him who sent us." Father, let Your light shine in me. Use me in good works as a light in a darkened world to bring glory to Your great name. Holy Spirit, come and have Your way in me for Jesus' sake.

## September 30 – GREATER THAN JOHN THE BAPTIST

Luke 7:28 – I say to you, among those born of women there is not a greater prophet than John the Baptist; but he who is least in the kingdom of God is greater than he.

John pointed to the greater, Jesus. John recognized his call and purpose in God. John said, "He who is coming after me is mightier than I" (Matthew 3:11). Jesus was the mightier one. John went on to recognize that Jesus would baptize believers with the Holy Spirit and fire. John only baptized to prepare the way, but Jesus *was* the way. He who is the way has equipped each believer to manifest His life in the world. Believers, filled with the Holy Spirit are the greatest witness to the fact that light has entered the world.

We can be critical of the church and perhaps there is much to be critical about, but reality is, without the Lord's church in the earth, this world would be steeped in unimaginable darkness. That is not an excuse to be at ease, but a call to rise up and be "greater than John the Baptist." The greater than John, Jesus, is living in us through the Holy Spirit. Throughout history, the church has been the greatest witness to the fact that light is in the world. Individually and corporately we are to testify to Christ's resurrection life and power. "Even when we were dead in our transgressions, He made us alive together with Christ (by grace you have been saved), and raised up in Him" (Ephesians 2:5).

Many of God's people are slumbering. Many churches are focused inwardly rather than outwardly. The church can be more like a theater than the model Jesus gave, which was a Vine (John 15). It is time to awake from slumber. It is time to throw off the theater mentality. It is time to become "greater." As the people of God, let us come back to God's original intent, "In Him, you also, after listening to the message of truth, the gospel of your salvation—having also believed, you were sealed in Him with the Holy Spirit of promise, who is given as a pledge of our inheritance, with a view to the redemption of God's own possession, to the praise of His glory" (Ephesians 1:13-14).

Week after week, God's people listen to the message of truth, but are they filled with the Holy Spirit in order to do the message? The greater is not in the listening, but in the doing. The Spirit of God is calling to the church of today, be the light of the world. He is calling to God's Shepherds, preach the word and be instant in season and out. He is manifesting His power and making us know that we do not have to go it alone. He is with us to equip and reveal the greater than John. He is with us as we witness Jesus, the Christ, alive from the dead who delivers from darkness and fills all who will believe with His Holy Spirit, dispelling darkness and manifesting light.

Father, awake me from slumber. As I listen, fill me with Your Holy Spirit of promise. Cause me to be greater than John as Jesus declared. Thank You for making me part of the vine. I ask You to allow me to bear much fruit and that the fruit will remain and multiply.

## October 1 – A BELIEVING PROBLEM

John 5:46-47 – "If you believed Moses, you would believe Me; for he wrote about Me. But if you do not believe his writings, how will you believe My words?

Israel had a believing problem. Their problem of believing was ingrained in their core being as a people. Throughout their history, unbelief was at the forefront of the nation's problems. Unbelief of their leaders kept them out of the Promised Land for a generation. They spent forty years wandering in the desert. Part of Jehovah's purpose was that they might learn to believe and trust Him as their King.

Throughout Israel's history, they rejected the words of the prophets. They not only rejected their words, they killed many of the prophets. Jesus charged His generation, "Woe to you! For you build the tombs of the prophets, and it was your fathers who killed them. So you are witnesses and approve the deeds of your fathers; because it was they who killed them, and you build their tombs. For this reason also the wisdom of God said, 'I will send to them prophets and apostles, and some of them they will kill and some they will persecute,  so that the blood of all the prophets, shed since the foundation of the world, may be charged against this generation'" (Luke 11:47-50).

It is very important to understand all that took place in the generation in which Jesus was born. Truly, it was "the fullness of time" (Galatians 4:4). The Lord brought everything to a head in one generation. Even though the covenant people had done despicable things throughout their history, God had been merciful to them. Now, in a final attempt, He reaches out by sending His own Son in the likeness of sinful flesh in order to redeem those under the law. He first sent John the Baptist to witness of His coming Lamb who would take away the sins of the world (John 1:29). Jesus came in the power of the Spirit. He healed, He delivered from demonic powers, He fed them, and He taught them, but still they did not believe. Their leaders were determined to kill Jesus, the Christ.

In one final attempt to draw Israel into a relationship, God's wrath was poured out on His own Son for their unjust deeds. This time He included all the nations through His redemptive work. The Father gave Israel a generation of time to believe Him. Only a remnant believed, which left Him no other choice than to fulfill His word through His Son, "This generation will not pass away until all these things take place" (Matthew 24:34).

Through the power of the Holy Spirit, the Father and the Son continue to reach out to this present generation with the redemption invitation and promises. Will we believe what He has declared and all the prophets gave testimony concerning? What the apostles witnessed and testified? What history itself witnesses? Jesus is Lord! His Word is absolute! He loves us and wants to fill us with His precious Holy Spirit so He can have daily fellowship with His redeemed people, Jews and Gentiles, who believe on Him. He is the one who rose from the dead and is coming again in power and glory.

Father, I thank You for all Your promises that are Yes and Amen to Your glory of God. I believe, Lord, help my unbelief. Give me grace to trust You in all things.

# October 2 – THE GOSPEL IS MOVING LIKE THE SUN

Psalm 113:3-4 – From the rising of the sun to its setting the name of the Lord is to be praised. The Lord is high above all nations; His glory is above the heavens.

Jesus told His disciples that they would receive power when the Holy Spirit came upon them. He also told them they were to begin the mission in Jerusalem and from there go to Samaria, Judea, and to the remotest parts of the earth (Acts 1:8). Jerusalem was filled with the Good News as multitudes received the Gospel of the kingdom of God. It spread to Samaria, then throughout all Judea and began the journey westward reaching to Spain during the lifetime of the apostles. Eventually all of Europe received the gospel of the kingdom. The Pilgrims and others took the Good News across the Atlantic Ocean. Part of God's purpose for America was to be used to spread the Good News everywhere.

Europe and America have left their first love and become materialistic and filled with the pleasures of the world. The Gospel has continued to move like the sun and today is hovering over Asia where the greatest kingdom expansion is taking place. I fully expect the Gospel to eventually spread to the Arab nations and be the instrument of God in defeating the false religion of Islam, as multitudes hear the gospel and turn to the Lord Jesus Christ through the power of God. As the nations of the Middle East turn to Jesus as Lord, Israel will be moved to jealousy just like Paul said in Romans 11:13-14. I am convinced that the gospel is heading back to Jerusalem.

The Bible speaks of two separate outpourings of the Spirit, called the former and latter rain. "He has poured down for you the rain, the early and latter rain as before. The threshing floors will be full of grain, and the vats will overflow with the new wine and oil" (Joel 2:23-24). The last two thousand years has been the first or former outpouring of the Holy Spirit. There is coming another outpouring of the Holy Spirit called the latter rain which will see the reaping of the nations. The pouring out of the Holy Spirit is associated with the harvest of the nations. In the natural, the former or first rain prepares the soil for the seed. If there is little rain, afterwards a harvest will be reaped, but it won't be the full potential. When the latter rain comes in the time of harvest, it produces a "bumper crop." A principle of Scripture is the latter will be greater than the former.

The coming of the Lord is "the blessed hope" (Titus 2:13). Before He comes, there is work to be done. The Lord is going to have a large harvest. Even now, our Lord is aligning the nations for His own purposes. God is calling His body to prepare themselves for a fresh outpouring of the Holy Spirit. Once again, we are reminded that the harvest is white and ready to be reaped. It will take God's power to accomplish God's purpose among the nations.

Pray for the lost. Pray for the nations. Pray for workers. Pray to know your part in the time of harvest.

## October 3 – MULTIPLICATION BY CREATING A TIPPING POINT

Matthew 8:29 – They cried out, saying, "What business do we have with each other, Son of God? Have You come here to torment us before the time?"

A tipping point has been defined as "the moment of critical mass, the threshold, and the boiling point." It is clearly revealed in the New Testament that the enemy knew more of God's plans than God's people. The Lord has always given His word so His people could know what He expects, what He is going to do, and how they are to respond. God's prophets held a special place in revealing God's works. "Surely the Lord God does nothing unless He reveals His secret counsel to His servants the prophets" (Amos 3:7). The prophets had prepared God's people for the coming of their expected King. The people knew He was coming, but they did not receive Him. "He came to His own, and those who were His own did not receive Him" (John 1:11).

Matthew 8 gives us the story of the believing centurion. Jesus said of him, "I have not found such great faith with anyone in all of Israel" (Matthew 8:10). Jesus found unbelief with the covenant people. He experienced demons giving testimony of who He was, but He would not receive their words. Instead, He drove them out of individuals and set the captives free.

Matthew 8:28 begins the report of Jesus' ministry in the country of the Gadarenes. There He found two men who were bound by demons. The demons who spoke to Jesus were afraid that Jesus He had come to torment them. They entreated Jesus, "If You are going to cast us out, send us into the herd of swine" (Matthew 8:31). Jesus said to them, "Go!" Jesus did not cast them into the swine because He did not like swine, but rather for the sake of the man. There was a lot of demonic power there that could have hurt or killed the man. Jesus had mercy on the man.

The enemy thinks out of selfishness and cannot think in terms of eternal love. It was the love of God that created a tipping point in Jesus' generation. People reacted to the tipping point Christ brought because of their hardened hearts. The tipping point was rooted in love, power, and authority. Jesus brought a critical mass. He brought things to a boiling point. This love has never been duplicated in one man. It can be manifested through multitudes of believers indwelt by the Holt Spirit. Power that has not been duplicated is available to those filled with the Holy Spirit. Jesus had authority which had not been demonstrated by anyone in human history. His authority came from the throne of God. Each believer can operate in God's authority by the Spirit of God who lives in every son and daughter of God.

Jesus has been given all authority in heaven and in earth. He delegates that authority to faithful believers through His resurrected life. The greater effectiveness of Jesus' authority is demonstrated through a united church in localities and in regions. No believer carries all authority. The body of Christ is God's delegated authority in the earth. Each believer can bring a tipping point into their sphere as they are led by the Holy Spirit. A greater tipping point can be created by a united body in each community, as the church is led by the Spirit of God.

Father, I pray to be made a tipping point in my sphere of responsibility. I pray for a united church in my locality which makes it possible for advancement of the kingdom of God. Advanced against everything that resists Your plan and purpose. I ask You for increased love, power, and authority to be manifested in my life.

# October 4 – ONENESS WITH THE FATHER

John 14:12 – Truly, truly, I say to you, he who believes in Me, the works that I do, he will do also; and greater works than these he will do; because I go to the Father.

As Jesus partakes of His last meal with His disciples, He shares some of His most intimate thoughts. He knows the events which are about to take place would shake their world to the very core. The chapter begins with Jesus saying, "Let not your heart be troubled." He points them to His Father as the source of belief. He assures them that He is going to prepare a place for them in the Father's house. He also assures them that as He goes, He will also return for them so where He is, they might be also.

Jesus assures them that He is the way to the Father. No man can come to the Father except through the Son. He says, by knowing Him one should know the Father. Everything we see in Jesus is what the Father is like. He is full of compassion. He loves the unlovely. He is a provider. He is a protector. He heals and delivers from evil. He forgives the vilest of sinners and transforms their lives.

Jesus reinforces the fact that the words He speaks are not His, but they originate from the Father. He also makes it clear that the works He performs are not His works, but the Father's works through Him (John 14:10). He gives them two options for belief. "Believe Me that I am in the Father, and the Father in Me: or else believe Me for the very work's sake" (John 14:11).

Some have trouble believing the words of Christians because they do not see or experience the reality of those words in the life of the confessing Christian. Jesus modeled how we are to live out the believing life. He modeled this for us by allowing the Father to fill Him with the Father's life both in word and deed. He gave us the Holy Spirit who is the Spirit of the Father and the Spirit of the Son. This is the greater works Jesus promised we would do. We are not just to model the Father and the Son, but we are to pray for others to receive the Holy Spirit, even as we have received Him.

God did not intend that we should try to be like Jesus in our own effort. He fills us with His Holy Spirit so His life can be lived through us. This is why Paul could say, "We offer ourselves as a model for you, so that you would follow our example" (2 Thessalonians 3:9). Paul was a model to the saints, as we too should be a model for others. Not in our own effort, but by the power of God.

Daily, we need to be filled with the Holy Spirit. It is only the Holy Spirit who can produce the life of the Son and the subsequent life of the Father in us. In the natural, one's identity comes through their father. The Scriptures reveal that Jesus came for a number of reasons, one of which was to reveal His Father to Israel. Their identity was wrapped up in Abraham as their father. Jesus came to reveal the one in whom Abraham trusted. Through the Spirit of God, Abraham saw Jesus' day by faith. Jesus wanted Israel to find their identity in the heavenly Father. He wants the same for each of us. Allow the Holy Spirit to reveal more of the Father to you. Let your full identity be in Him.

Father, I believe in You and I believe in Jesus whom You sent. I choose to receive my identity from You. I pray for Your life to be revealed in me, the fruit of the Holy Spirit. I ask the Holy Spirit to make me a model for others, as You did with Paul.

## October 5 – WHAT IS THE FATHER LIKE?

John 14:9 – He who has seen Me has seen the Father

The four Gospels give us wonderful understandings about the Father. Today, we will devote our selves to the Gospel of John and examine what he reveals about the Father through the Son who is the expressed image of the Father.

Jesus is the only begotten from the Father, full of grace and truth (John 1:14). Jesus is full of grace and truth because the Father is full of the same. The Father loves the Son and has given all things into His hand (John 3:35). The Father loves His sons and daughters in the same way He loves Jesus. The Father seeks those to be His worshipers (John 4:23). The Father knows that it is through worship we enter into His presence, His liberty, and His peace.

"My Father is working until now, and I Myself am working" (John 5:17). The Father has always been a worker. He worked the six days of creation and then He rested from His work. He created Adam as a worker in the Garden. Jesus relates the Father's work with His work. He calls each believer to enter into the work of the Father and the Son through the power of the Holy Spirit.

"For the Father loves the Son, and shows Him all things that He Himself is doing; and the Father will show Him greater works than these, so that you will marvel" (John 5:20). It is marvelous how the Father loves the Son and gave Him all things. Here, Jesus tells us that the Father shows Him all things. He also tells us that the Father will show greater things to the Son. The greater things are:

> ➢ The ability to give life to whomever He wills.
> ➢ The ability for the Son to have life in Himself.
> ➢ The Father gave all judgment into the hands of the Son.

We can see by these few verses that the Father delights in His Son and loves to give Him things. Our heavenly Father loves us as well. As we live in the center of His love, He will choose to give us those things from His riches in glory. "My God will supply all your needs according to His riches in glory in Christ Jesus. Now to our God and Father be the glory forever and ever. Amen" (Philippians 4:19-20).

Many have been disappointed with earthly fathers because of their sin and neglect. Our heavenly Father wants to heal any brokenness we might carry from past relationship with a father. Father God will help us enter into His abundant love through His only begotten Son. The Holy Spirit has come to reveal the love of the Father through the kindness given to Christ and now available to all who will believe.

Father, I thank You for Your goodness that was revealed through Your Son, Jesus. Thank You for sending the Holy Spirit to give me the experience of Your love. Your love that forgives me, Your love that grants me eternal life, and Your love that gives me the security of Your grace. You are a good Father!

# October 6 – THE ROLE OF THE SPIRIT

John 14:16 – I will ask the Father, and He will give another Helper, that He may be with you forever; that is the Spirit of truth.

The Father sent Jesus to redeem mankind from the curse of the Law (Galatians 3:13). When Jesus fulfilled the Father's plan, He then asked the Father for the Holy Spirit to be given to all those who believed on Him. Jesus refers to the Spirit as the "Helper." Jesus and the Father have not left us alone to fend for ourselves. It is marvelous how the Holy Spirit has been given to indwell each believer. It is incredible to know that the Father and the Son are in us by the presence of the Holy Spirit who was given to be with us forever.

The Holy Spirit is our life source in Christ. The Holy Spirit is the one who continues to reveal the Father to us. It is worth our time to read through the gospels, paying special attention to what the Scriptures teach us about the Father. The more I have learned about the Father, the more I have grown in security, confidence, and faith. The Holy Spirit wants to help us be able to say from our heart, Abba Father or "Daddy, dear Daddy."

When we learn about the "fruit of the Spirit," we are learning about the very nature of God. Love, joy, peace, patience, kindness, goodness, faithfulness, gentleness, and self-control all proceed from the Father. Each of these aspects of God is seen in the Lord Jesus. They can now be seen in our life as a manifestation of the Holy Spirit's work. We know the Father is living through us by the evidence of the fruit. When Scriptures speak about maturing in Christ, they are referring to the development of the fruit of the Spirit.

The Holy Spirit's role is to draw us to Christ, and then reveal to us the nature of Christ which always points to the Father. Paul says it beautifully. "For you have died and your life is hidden with Christ in God. When Christ, who is our life, is revealed, then you also will be revealed with Him in glory" (Colossians 3:3-4).

We will be in the presence of the Father and the Son in glory. The Holy Spirit will still be in us. We won't see the Father and the Son and the Holy Spirit, just the Father and the Son. "I saw no temple in it, for the Lord God the Almighty and the Lamb are its temple" (Revelation 21:22). Yes, the Holy Spirit is leading us to that day in eternity when we will be consumed by the glory of God. We don't have to wait for that day. Even now, we can move from glory to glory as we allow the Holy Spirit to reveal the Almighty and the Lamb in an ever-increasing way.

Father, I pray for the Holy Spirit to take me deeper into Your love. As the old hymn declares, "Deeper, deeper in the love of Jesus, deeper let me go – Higher, higher in the school of wisdom, more of Christ to know – Deeper yet I pray, higher every day, wiser, blessed Lord in Your precious holy Word."

## October 7 – THE FAMILY OF GOD

Ephesians 2:19 – You are no longer strangers and aliens, but you are fellow citizens with the saints, and are of God's household.

Within the body of Christ, our basic relationships can be expressed in terms of family. We are part of God's extended family. God is our Father and we are brothers and sisters through Christ. There was a time in each of our lives that we were strangers and aliens to God's household. Through the power of the Holy Spirit we were born again. He made us "fellow citizens with the saints." The Spirit is the one who is charged with the work of connecting us in Christ's body. If you have been born again, you are in the household of God.

As families join to families, a kinship is developed. People from many walks of life are joined together in covenant love. Covenant love is God's kind of love and happens within committed relationships; Love which is rooted in relationship, established under pressure, and developed through servanthood.

This is God's plan for maturing His sons and daughters. It all begins as "little children" (Matthew 18:3). Life in Christ grows inward to bring forth a "godly seed." At the same time, new lives are added from without. While we grow in numbers and organizational complexity, we must also grow in our call to be family. If either of these is ever lost, we have missed God's purpose.

Jesus said, "Come unto Me all you that labor and are heavy burdened, and I will give you rest." As each one comes to Jesus, we receive forgiveness and acceptance from the Father. We in turn are to give the same to others.

The chorus of an old gospel song (Words and Music by William J. Gaither Copyright 1970) goes like this:

> I'm so glad I'm a part of the family of God.
> I've been washed in the fountain, cleansed by His blood.
> Joint heirs with Jesus as we travel this sod,
> I'm so glad I'm a part of the family of God.

The family begins in God the Father. God the Son has made it possible for you and me to be joined into this eternal family. The Holy Spirit uses the seed of God's word to join us to the Father and the Son, but also to each other in this incredible eternal plan.

Father, I thank You for joining me to the family of God. I celebrate You as my heavenly Father. I thank You for Jesus, my Redeemer King and my Elder Brother. I thank You for giving to each believer the Holy Spirit, who applies the blood of Jesus to cleanse me, who then nurtures me and reveals that my identity now comes from You.

# October 8 – DISCERNING THE BODY OF CHRIST

1 Corinthians 11:31-32 – If we judged ourselves rightly, we would not be judged. But when we are judged, we are disciplined by the Lord so that we will not be condemned along with the world.

This is a very powerful and important portion of Scripture. Paul helps the church at Corinth to examine their approach to the "Lord's table." Every congregation should read and study carefully what Paul writes. Verse 30 answers the question why many are sick in the body of Christ and why some have died prematurely. Paul says it comes from three things:

1. Eating and drinking the bread and the cup of the Lord in an unworthy manner

2. Failure to examine oneself, causing judgment on oneself
3. Not judging the body rightly

Close examination of these passages and, in fact, the entire book of Corinthians reveals how they address relationships within the body of Christ. When there is broken relationship among believers, it opens the door for the kingdom of darkness, reproach from an unbelieving world, and hinders the Lord's purposes.

Jesus said, "If you are presenting your offering at the altar, and there remember that your brother has something against you, leave your offering there before the altar and go; first be reconciled to your brother, and then come and present your offering (Matthew 5:23-24). The Lord puts a very high premium on relationship within His body. We must examine ourselves regularly to make sure our hearts are right toward our fellow believers. Paul informs us that not "judging the body rightly" causes sickness and even premature death. Our scripture today says that "if we judged ourselves rightly, we would not be judged." The Father wants His children to learn how to examine their own hearts. The Holy Spirit enables us to do this if we will ask for His help.

"When we are judged, we are disciplined by the Lord so that we will not be condemned along with the world" (1 Corinthians 11:32). We know that we are sons and daughters because the Lord disciplines His children (see Hebrews 12:5).

A true father disciplines his children. Today, many children have not known the loving discipline of a father. Many are self-centered because of not experiencing a father's love through discipline. Some have known only anger from their father. The loving discipline of a father helps to produce respect for authority and a respect for others. Father God disciplines His children for their good. The writer of Hebrews says, "All discipline for the moment seems not to be joyful, but sorrowful; yet to those who have been trained by it, afterwards it yields the peaceful fruit of righteousness" (Hebrews 12:11).

Father, cause me to be discerning about how I treat my spouse, my children, other believers, and those outside Your kingdom. Make me aware when I have offended another and grant me humility to ask forgiveness of the offended one. When

You must discipline me, cause me to be open and willing to receive Your discipline, for I know it will produce in me the peaceful fruit of righteousness.

## October 9 – THE PEACE OF DISCIPLINE

Hebrews 12:11 – All discipline for the moment seems not to be joyful, but sorrowful; yet to those who have been trained by it, afterwards it yields the peaceful fruit of righteousness.

In our devotion yesterday, we concluded with the biblical statement of Hebrews 12:11. What the writer of Hebrews is stating is so important that it requires we look deeper into the truth it contains.

The Almighty God, who spun off worlds with His Word, is our heavenly Father if we have trusted His Only begotten Son for our salvation. His Holy Spirit resides in us and bears witness to this fact. "You have not received a spirit of slavery leading to fear again, but you have received a spirit of adoption as sons by whom we cry out, 'Abba! Father!' The Spirit Himself testifies with our spirit that we are children of God, and if children, heirs also, heirs of God and fellow heirs with Christ, if indeed we suffer with Him so that we may also be glorified with Him" (Romans 8:15-17).

The child of God is not a slave, but an adopted son. The child of God can cry out Daddy and Father.  My oldest son Paul is adopted. He has known this fact from his earliest childhood. Immediately, his mother and I thanked God for him and declared his adoption to legally settle his sonship in our family. I declared he had a father and a mother who loved him and would never abandon him.  Paul received the same blessings, but also the same discipline as our natural children. I can truly say we did not treat any of our children differently.

Paul the apostle said, "Indeed we suffer with Him so that we may also be glorified with Him" (Romans 8:17). The suffering is our identity with His cross. Because of the cross, God raised Christ up and glorified Him. Our access to the family of God is through the cross of Christ. We have been raised up in newness of life and as joint heirs of God's grace.

The Father's training comes through discipline. Discipline is not the wrath of the Father, but His love to produce the fruit of peace and righteousness. God's wrath concerning sin was settled at the cross of Christ. Father God is not angry at mankind and especially those who have been adopted into His family through the redemptive work of Christ. He trains His children through various types of disciplines. We should pay special attention to how Jesus trained His disciples in order to know how God wants us to be trained.

Jesus modeled the Father's love. He first showed the Father's nature "full of grace and truth." He taught through words with love and authority. He reached out to the weak and needy. He demonstrated the Father's love through direct action. He told His disciples to go do as he was doing, and gave them the authority to accomplish the assignment. He corrected their misunderstandings, bickering, and wrong heart motivations. He promised them another Helper just like Him so they would not have to go it alone.

Father, I want to be corrected and rebuked by You when necessary. I know it won't be pleasant, but I also know it will mature me and produce the peace of righteousness in my life.

## October 10 – BE CAREFUL HOW YOU JUDGE

John 7:24 – Do not judge according to appearance, but judge with righteous judgment.

One Sunday morning, an old cowboy entered a church just before services were to begin. Although the old man and his clothes were spotlessly clean, he wore jeans, a denim shirt, and boots that were very worn and ragged. In his hand, he carried a worn out old hat and an equally worn out old Bible.

The church he entered was a very upscale and in an exclusive part of the city. It was the largest and most beautiful church building the old cowboy had ever seen. It had high cathedral ceilings, ornate statues, beautiful murals, stained glass windows, plush carpet, and velvet-like cushioned pews. The building must have cost many millions of dollars to build and maintain.

The congregation was all dressed in the finest and most expensive suits, dresses, shoes, and jewelry the old cowboy had ever seen. As the poorly dressed cowboy took a seat, the others moved away from him. No one greeted him. No one welcomed him. No one offered a handshake. No one spoke to him. They were all appalled at his appearance and did not attempt to hide the fact. There were many glances in his direction as the others frowned and commented among themselves about his shabby attire. A few chuckles and giggles came from some of the younger members.

The preacher gave a long sermon and a stern lecture on how much money the church needed to do God's work. When the offering plate was passed thousands of dollars came pouring forth. As soon as the service was over the congregation hurried out. Once again no one spoke or even nodded to the stranger in the ragged clothes and boots. As the old cowboy was leaving the church the preacher approached him. Instead of welcoming him, the preacher asked the cowboy to do him a favor. "Before you come back in here again, have a talk with God and ask him what He thinks would be appropriate attire for worshiping in this church." The old cowboy assured the preacher he would do that and left.

The very next Sunday morning the old cowboy showed back up for the service wearing the same ragged jeans, shirt, boots, and hat. Once again, the congregation was appalled at his appearance. Again, he was completely shunned and ignored. The preacher noticed the man still wearing his ragged clothes and boots, and instead of beginning his sermon, stepped down from the pulpit and walked over to where the man sat alone.

"I thought I asked you to speak to God before you came back to our church." "I did," replied the old cowboy. "If you spoke to God, what did he tell you the proper attire should be for worshiping in here?" asked the preacher. "Well sir, God told me that He wouldn't have the slightest idea what was appropriate attire for worshiping in your church." He said He's never been in here. That church family sounds rather "dysfunctional." They are obviously more concerned about what is seen on the outside rather than what is unseen on the inside.

"We are not again commending ourselves to you but are giving you an occasion to be proud of us, so that you will have an answer for those who take pride in appearance and not in heart" (2 Corinthians 5:12). Those who judge after appearance are judging from "pride" and not the Spirit of the Lord. The story above illustrates how both individuals and church bodies can be filled with pride and arrogance, rather than the love of God.

Father, give me eyes to see as You do. Create in me righteous judgment as the Lord Jesus instructs all His disciples to have.

## October 11 – LOVE, FORGIVNESS, AND ACCEPTANCE

Romans 15:7 – Accept one another, just as Christ also accepted us to the glory of God.

While we accept each other as we are, we do not remain as we are. As each one comes to Christ, forgiveness and acceptance are given by the Father. We then become part of one another on the very common ground of His power of love to forgive and accept each one as we are. For each believer, this is the starting point in Christ Jesus.

From this starting point, we grow together in an atmosphere of love, hope, and encouragement, no matter what difficulty or devastation we face. Of course, people enter the kingdom of God and are baptized into the body having come from many backgrounds. Our life together in the body begins a process of healing and growth which can take a very long time. An atmosphere of love, forgiveness, and acceptance is necessary to help in assisting people to receive, what in many cases has never before been communicated or experienced.

In the body of Christ, we esteem the covenant of marriage, we honor singleness, and we support the single parent. Marriage is under attack as perhaps it has never been before. The marriage covenant is the sure foundation we must build upon. If the marriage foundation is destroyed, the whole culture will collapse. We must first learn how to love, forgive, and accept in our homes before we will be successful in our relationships within the church.

We must reach out to singles, who many times feel displaced from family. The single person can more fully give themselves to the cause of Christ because of less time constraints. Many singles would love to be used within the family of God, both in church activities and within families belonging to a congregation.

It is important for the church body to give support to those who have found themselves single again through divorce or death. Many times, we form groups of people with similar life experiences, but their deeper need is family. They need to know the love of fathers and mothers within the body of Christ.

We must treasure and affirm children, including them in our worship, in our ministry moments, and social events. They are our future! The Lord has always been focused on the generations. Our children will carry the torch in the future. Now is the time of their training.

In the body of Christ we will always find diversity of personality and lifestyles, each adding something valuable to the whole. I suggest including each group I have mentioned in your prayers.

Father, I pray for the families of my congregation, fathers and mothers and their children, that Your kingdom rest on their lives. I pray for the singles as they seek to know how they fit into the family of God. I pray for those who have found themselves single again. I pray for healing in their lives and for the development of healthy relationships.

## October 12 – OUR PERSONAL GROWTH

2 Corinthians 3:18 – We all, with unveiled face, beholding as in a mirror the glory of the Lord, are being transformed into the same image from glory to glory, just as from the Lord, the Spirit.

While we are to accept each other as we are, we do not remain as we are. The Spirit of God is at work bringing change as Scripture reveals. The change into Christ's image is an expression of God's love to the world. You are sent to others as a love letter from God. The Father accepts us just as we are, but He is also at work to change us to be like Him. The change happens in the context of family and as we interact with those who are yet unreached for God's kingdom.

Acceptance does not promote sin. Acceptance empowers people to risk facing and confessing their sin and moves us toward wholeness. It is important to realize that each person has the right to become who God intended them to be. At the same time, we must guard against selfishness, always putting the interest of family before the interests of individuals. Acceptance and opportunity to grow is what each of us needs most in life.

Our understanding of God's will for the body of Christ is not centered around buildings or religious activities, but family relationships and environment—a relationship with God as Father, Jesus as our elder brother, and the Holy Spirit as the one who nurtures us by revealing the Father and Son in greater depths. Our commitment in Christ is to other believers to whom we have been joined. They are to be seen as our brothers and sisters in His family. As members of His family, we extend His love and power to the world. Our life in a church family is expressed in multi-dimensional relationships.

The writer of Hebrews gives clear instruction concerning our relationships within the body of Christ. "Therefore, strengthen the hands that are weak and the knees that are feeble, and make straight paths for your feet, so that the limb which is lame may not be put out of joint, but rather be healed. Pursue peace with all men, and sanctification without which no one will see the Lord. See to it that no one comes short of the grace of God; that no root of bitterness springing up causes trouble" (Hebrews 12:12-15). What wonderful counsel for each member of the family of God.

Father, I ask for the Holy Spirit to work in my life that I never come short of the grace of God in any of my relationships. Give to me a love for family as You love family, both natural and spiritual family. Help me to nurture each relationship that You have given me and use them to bring change in my life for Your glory.

# October 13 – POSSESSIONS OR JESUS

Luke 18:22 – Sell all that you possess and distribute it to the poor, and you shall have treasure in heaven; and come, follow Me.

When Jesus walked this earth, he admonished folks to lay down their possessions and follow Him. The rich young ruler asked how he could receive salvation. When Jesus told him to go and sell everything and give it to the poor and follow Him, the young man decided that the price was far too high for him to pay. He did not realize the price Jesus would pay for his sin.

I am bought with a price, Jesus' blood. I am covered thoroughly with the robe of righteousness which the Father has placed upon me. Jesus lives in me through His Spirit. What joy to know my heavenly Father loves me, and gives me a relationship with Him through Christ Jesus. When the Father looks at me, He sees not what I used to be, but He sees the righteousness of the Lord Jesus Christ. Nothing I possess compares to the price which was paid for my salvation.

It is important for the child of God to walk the tightrope between possessions and our treasures in heaven. Possessions, in and of themselves, are not evil or wrong. In the case of the rich young ruler, Jesus was challenging his heart. He was attached more firmly to his possessions than what was healthy. It cost him eternity. The Lord might have chosen to return all or more than what he would have given to the poor. He needed to be free from the bondage to his possessions.

Jesus told the church at Laodicea, "Because you are lukewarm, and neither hot nor cold, I will spit you out of My mouth" (Revelation 3:16). The issue with the members of the church in Laodicea was not eternal life; it was their commitment to the Lord's purpose and His ability to use them. They felt content in their prosperity and became "lukewarm" in their commitment to Christ and His kingdom purpose.

We must examine our hearts to see if we too are "lukewarm" because of materialism. As a Christian, there must be a tension between wealth and our commitment to a Christ-like lifestyle. While on earth, Jesus had all He ever needed, but was not wealthy by the world's standards. Paul, the apostle said he suffered the loss of all things for Christ (Philippians 3:8). Yet he always paid his own way. He paid for the care of his team members; he used the school of Tyrannus in Ephesus, no doubt renting its use for two years, and he paid for his own rented house in Rome (Acts 28:30). The issue for the rich young ruler and the church at Laodicea was a "heart issue." It is an issue for many in the Lord's church today.

Father, help me search my heart to know if I am in bondage to possessions. Give me grace to be free from any bondage which prevents me from totally being committed to You and Your kingdom. Grace me to follow Jesus by giving away everything to which my heart is attached, knowing You will give me all I need to fulfill Your purposes and plan in my life.

## October 14 – PRIVILEGES WE ENJOY

Hebrews 12:22-24 – You have come to Mount Zion and to the city of the living God, the heavenly Jerusalem, and to myriads of angels, to the general assembly and church of the firstborn who are enrolled in heaven, and to God, the Judge of all, and to the spirits of the righteous made perfect, and to Jesus, the mediator of a new covenant, and to the sprinkled blood, which speaks better than the blood of Abel.

In these passages, we can identify seven privileges believers enjoy through our relationship with the Father and the Son in the power of the Holy Spirit.

> ➤ We *have come* unto Mount Zion, (God's Hill) His permanent resting place in heaven where God reigns as KING of Kings and LORD of Lords.
> ➤ We *have co*me into God's city for which Abraham searched. In fact, Galatians 4:26 indicates that Jerusalem above is the place of our new birth. All who have been "born again" can say, "I was born in Mount Zion," Jerusalem, the city of my God."
> ➤ We have come unto an innumerable company of angels. The Scriptures indicate that we are surrounded by angels looking into what God has done. "Do not neglect to show hospitality to strangers, for by this some have entertained angels without knowing it" (Hebrews 13:2). "It was revealed to them that they were not serving

themselves, but you, in these things which now have been announced to you through those who preached the gospel to you by the Holy Spirit sent from heaven — things into which angels long to look" (1 Peter 1:12).

➤ We *have come* to the General Assembly and Church of the First Born which are written in heaven. Presently, the name of every believer is written together with all the names of those who are members of His church. It is important to be reminded we are not alone. Those who have gone before us are present before the Throne of God and the saints on earth are present through the indwelling Holy Spirit.

➤ We *have come* to God the judge of all. The blessing for the true believer is that judgment has already taken place as Jesus became God's sacrifice for our sins. God's judgments come through the Lord Jesus Christ. As a believer we receive what Christ has done for us. The unbeliever will have to answer for their sins before God because they did not trust Christ who took their judgment upon Himself.

➤ We *have come* to the spirits of just men made perfect. In the spiritual realm, we have been joined with all those who have died and fully entered into His rest. I believe they are cheering for us to finish our course. In the natural, this is hard to understanding, but by faith we receive the insights that God's Word reveals.

➤ We have come to Jesus, the mediator of the "new covenant." We have legal rights in heaven to receive salvation. Everything Jesus did on our behalf would hold up in a court of law. By the "Law of Sacrifice," that is, "the innocent dying for the guilty," Jesus destroyed what Satan held over us and the judgment which the Law of God brought, declaring all guilty before God.

Father, I thank You for Your Throne of Grace. I rejoice in the place of Your rest. I pray for the continual help of the Holy Spirit in my daily life to abide in the place of rest where all the spirits of just men reside for eternity. I receive by faith all the privileges of a child of God.

# October 15 – SEE THAT YOU OBEY HIM THAT SPEAKS

Hebrews 12:25 – See to it that you do not refuse Him who is speaking. For if those did not escape when they refused him who warned them on earth, much less will we escape who turn away from Him who warns from heaven.

An individual may consider himself a Christian for numerous reasons. One can have a thorough knowledge of the Scripture and be true in their beliefs of what the scripture teaches. The directive of the writer of Hebrews in verse 25 is the real issue. "See to it that you do not refuse Him who is speaking."

"God, after He spoke long ago to the fathers in the prophets in many portions and in many ways, in these last days has spoken to us in His Son, whom He appointed heir of all things, through whom also He made the world" (Hebrews) 1:1-3). The study of the "Gospels" is vital to our growth and development. Jesus represented His Father in heaven perfectly. He never spoke from His own initiative, only what He heard His Father saying. It is important for every believer to evaluate their viewpoints and their actions against what Jesus taught and did.

The Holy Spirit has been given to every believer as "the Helper" of their "new life" in Christ. He is not given to help us develop our own ideas and lifestyle. He is given to lead us to the death of self and into the resurrected life of Christ. Our life in Christ is completely in the "Spirit," lived out through our everyday natural life.

Simply stated, do we hear through our natural ears or through a spiritual ear? One can listen to a sermon and process with their natural mind, accepting or rejecting what was taught. On the other hand, the spiritual person will listen through the ear of their spirit in order to have the mind of Christ.  "He who is spiritual appraises all things, yet he himself is appraised by no one. For who has known the mind of the Lord, that he will instruct Him? But we have the mind of Christ" (1 Corinthians 2:15-16).

Our thought for today is: "See to it that you do not refuse He who is speaking." Jesus spoke in His earthly ministry and gave us "the word of the Father." He has given each believer the

Holy Spirit who is commissioned to reveal God's Word to us. We must choose to hear through the spirit rather than through our natural reasoning.

"I pray that the eyes of your heart may be enlightened, so that you will know what is the hope of His calling, what are the riches of the glory of His inheritance in the saints, and what is the surpassing greatness of His power toward us who believe" (Ephesians 1:18-19). Paul's concern for believers was that they would "know". We can only truly know if we chose not to "refuse" the one speaking from heaven.

Father, I choose today, to hear Your Son who came from heaven and spoke. He then returned to heaven and continues to speak through Your life-giving Spirit. Give me ears to hear what the Spirit is saying today so I can obey.

## October 16 – THE WORD OF GOD IS SETTLED

Hebrews 13:8 – Jesus Christ is the same yesterday, and today, and forever.

There is one human who never changes, Jesus Christ, God's Son, Savior. The Word of God manifested in the Word made flesh. That Word dwelt among us, full of grace and truth. That Word is now seated at the right hand of the majesty on high. From the very beginning, God purposed the Word to be made flesh. "In the beginning was the Word, and the Word was with God, and the Word was God" (John 1:1-2). "The Word became flesh and dwelt among us, and we saw His glory, glory as of the only begotten from the Father, full of grace and truth" (John 1:14-15).

In all the Scriptures, there is nothing more profound than "the Word was made flesh." Because God's Word is forever settled, Jesus is the same yesterday, today, and forever. In Jesus' earthly ministry, He expected God's covenant people, the Jews, to receive His word because it is the word of the Father. Jesus came in fulfillment of the Old Testament prophecy. The Jews had been given the responsibility of the oracles of God. "They were entrusted with the oracles of God. What then? If some did not believe, their unbelief will not nullify the faithfulness of God, will it?" (Romans 3:2-4).

The Jews were the carriers of God's Word for all of mankind. Some did not believe. This was especially true during the ministry of Jesus. Their unbelief did not hinder God's faithfulness. The whole Jewish nation might have rejected Jesus, but God would still be faithful to His Word. All that we read in the Scriptures concerning Jesus is true today as well. He still ministers in truth and grace through the power of the Holy Spirit. The promises which Jesus fulfilled in His earthly ministry are available to us because "He is the same". God's people are to be a people of "hope" because the Lord has given us a sure expectation of our future.

God's Word never changes. God's Son is always the same. All truth is eternal. God the Father and God the Son are full of truth and grace ministered in the power of the Holy Spirit. God has done all that He said He would do. Jesus utterly fulfilled the Father's will. As sons and daughters of God, we are called not only to believe, but to live out the word of God in our daily lives. We too, are called to be faithful carriers of God's promises. We are called to demonstrate the settled word of God by the conduct of our lives. Not all will believe, but some will glorify God for what they experience in us. All will give an account to God for what is demonstrated as we walk in righteousness and the power of the Holy Spirit.

Father, I thank You for Your settled word. I firmly put my faith in Jesus Christ, the same yesterday, and today, and forever. Help me demonstrate Your truth and grace through how I choose to live my life in the power of the Holy Spirit.

## October 17 – WHAT GUIDES US?

Ephesians 4:15 – We are to grow up in all aspects into Him who is the head, even Christ.

This clear purpose of our heavenly Father is outlined throughout the New Testament. Many believe or at least live like God's purpose is to bless them, making them a success, and answering all their prayer requests. That viewpoint was the mistake God's people made when Jesus walked the earth, teaching and preaching the kingdom of God.

In the Book of Ephesians, the apostle Paul clearly outlines the will and purpose of God in the life of every believer. Paul pens what should be guiding the believer. "We are to grow up in all aspects of Christ." Everything the Father is doing is about His only begotten Son. He has included us, intending that we will grow up into Christ. The Father is looking for those who will freely surrender everything to Christ and give control of their life to His Spirit.

Some important questions to be asked are:

1. Am I allowing the Holy Spirit access to every area of my being?
2. Can I see areas in my life that have Christ at the center?
3. Am I aware of specific areas in my life where the Lord is dealing with me?

It is important for each believer to examine himself and determine if "Christ is the head" in their life. It is impossible to grow up into Christ if we are not allowing Him to be head in all things. Through our free will, we say yes to the Lord, first in every clear command given to us in His Word. And secondly, as we learn to recognize His voice as He guides us through life's decisions.

In order for the Lord to guide us, we must first allow the Holy Spirit access to our thinking processes. Regularly ask the Father to give you the mind of Christ. Identify areas of the past which you have surrendered to Him and evaluate how well you are letting Him be in control. Ascertain specific areas which the Lord has spoken to you about where He wants control.

As believers, we must be active in the growth process. The Psalms teach us how to actively interact with the Lord in both the good and difficult times. David actually commanded his soul to bless God and not forget His benefits. "Bless the Lord, O my soul, and all that is within me, bless His holy name. Bless the Lord, O my soul, and forget none of His benefits; who pardons all your iniquities, who heals all your diseases; who redeems your life from the pit, who crowns you with loving-kindness and compassion; who satisfies your years with good things, so that your youth is renewed like the eagle" (Psalm 103:1-5).

Father, I desire Your guidance in every area of my life. I choose to give the Holy Spirit access to my whole being. Thank You for those areas of my life where the Holy Spirit presently has control. Show me specific areas You currently want to help me surrender to the Holy Spirit.

# October 18 – GOALS

1 Timothy 1:5 – The goal of our instruction is love from a pure heart and a good conscience and a sincere faith.

Paul identifies three necessary components in order to fulfill the goal of his instruction. The stated goal is "love." In order for God's love to operate through us, we must have "a pure heart" and "a good conscience" and "sincere faith." God's love is first pure. The world knows many types of so-called love, but "divine love" is pure beyond our ability to comprehend. The Father sent His only begotten Son to demonstrate "pure love."

It is impossible to understand pure love by just having someone tell you about it. It is impossible to comprehend pure love by reading about it. Pure love has to be lived! Jesus of Nazareth lived the pure love of the Father. It is one reason He could say to His disciples, "When you have seen Me, you have seen the Father" (John 14:9). As we develop our relationship with the Lord Jesus, we will experience the development of His love in us. The believer is "joined to the Lord." "The one who joins himself to the Lord is one spirit with Him" (1 Corinthians 6:17). God's love in the believer is present because the believer has become "one spirit" with Him.

The second component necessary for pure love to operate through us is found in a "good conscience". The conscience is a critical part of our mind. It regulates our sense of "right and wrong". Before we came to Christ, the conscience was a moral guide to our fallen nature. It is a sensitive part of our human-make up which can easily be damaged and quit working. "Speaking lies in hypocrisy; having their conscience seared with a hot iron" (1 Timothy 4:2 KJV). Through the blood of Christ, our conscience is made clean. "Let us draw near with a sincere heart in full assurance of faith, having our hearts sprinkled clean from an evil conscience and our bodies washed with pure water" (Hebrews 10:22).

The third component is sincere faith. When I think of sincere faith, the word "humility" comes to mind. A sincere faith is a faith that operates through the spirit of humility. Love is an operation of faith. Pure love is an action of our love toward others before they demonstrate any kind of love toward us. This requires faith. Jesus is our example of "sincere faith." He always operated in the spirit of humility. His actions always had others in mind. True faith causes us to keep our eyes on Jesus, who is the author and finisher of our faith.

As we read the Scriptures and the instruction of the apostles, let us make "love our goal". Remember, God so loved the world that He gave His only Begotten Son. The Son demonstrated the Father's love. Now, we have been joined to God by the Holy Spirit and His Love is within our being. Let us love others as He loves us!

Father, I ask for the power of Your love in me to dominate my heart, my conscience, and my faith in all my relationships with others, believers and unbelievers alike.

## October 19 – BY A GOOD CONSCIENCE AWARENESS OF GOD COMES

Hebrews 9:14 – Cleanse your conscience from dead works to serve the living God.

A good conscience is necessary for the believer to be able to navigate with the guidance of the Holy Spirit. If one's conscience is dull from not being listened to, it produces an inability to hear the guidance of the Spirit. The writer of Hebrews makes the contrast between the Old Testament sacrifice of the blood of goats and bulls and the New Testament sacrifice of the blood of Jesus. In Hebrews 9:13, he states that the sacrifice of animals was "sanctified for the cleansing of the flesh." In verse 14, he asked the question, "How much more will the blood of Christ, who through the eternal Spirit offered Himself without blemish to God, cleanse your conscience from dead works to serve the living God?"

Your conscience gives you an awareness of God's will. Thirty five years ago, I walked through a very difficult period in my life. Because of hurt, I made some poor decisions. In my choices, I disobeyed God when I ignored my conscience. I found that it became easier and easier to serve a dead work over obeying God. One day, I came under deep conviction and turned loose of my will and declared "I only want Your best, Lord." Immediately, I experienced the "blood of Jesus cleansing my conscience from dead works to serve the living God." My conscience was back in full operation and once again I was able to make difficult, but correct decisions. Thank God for the cleansing blood of Jesus! That experience taught me that the word of God is true regarding a "seared conscience" (1 Timothy 4:2).

The conscience becomes the believer's guidance system as it is cleansed by the blood of Jesus and surrendered to the Holy Spirit. I believe the conscience was part of the "Divine DNA" given to man when God breathed into man's nostrils the breath of life as recorded in Genesis 2:7. When man fell, the divine life departed and man was left with a natural life. The conscience remained and carried a sense of right and wrong. It helped give man a moral guidance, but was very deficient without the Spirit of God. Man was left to his own devices. Through the new birth, the conscience once again is connected to the "Divine DNA" through the Holy Spirit.

In our awareness of God's presence and His will, the Holy Spirit can release spiritual gifts. A good conscience is vital for us to be sensitive to the Spirit's guidance through gifts like wisdom, knowledge, and discernment of spirits. Ask the Lord to search your heart and show you any areas in your conscience that need cleansing. Allow the Spirit to apply the blood of Jesus to any areas which He reveals to you. A fully operating conscience will cause you to be more sensitive to the Holy Spirit's will in guiding your life.

Father, I ask for the searchlight of Your Spirit to examine my conscience and make me aware of any non-functioning parts. Show me any compromise I have made that restricts my conscience from being fully operational. I pray for the ability to hear Your Spirit's guidance at all times.

# October 20 – THE INNER AWARENESS OF CONFORMING TO GOD'S WILL

Psalms 32:5 – I acknowledged my sin to You, and my iniquity I did not hide.

A good conscience is instrumental in having an inner awareness of conforming to the will of God. A good conscience will also let us know when we have departed from God's will. The conscience gives both a sense of approval and judgment. The term, "a good conscience" does not appear in the Old Testament, but the concept does.

In Psalm 32, David was smitten in his heart because of his lack of trust in the power of God (2 Samuel 24:10). His guilt turned to joy when he sought the Lord's forgiveness (Psalm 32). In the New Testament, the term conscience is found most frequently in the writings of Paul. Some people argue erroneously that the conscience takes the place of the external law in the Old Testament. The conscience is not the ultimate standard of moral goodness. "I am conscious of nothing against myself, yet I am not acquitted by this; but the one who examines me is the Lord" (1 Corinthians 4:4). Paul examined his life, including his motivations and could not find any problems. Paul understood the Lord would be the final judge.

Under both the Old and New Covenants, a good conscience is formed by doing the will of God. Under the Old Covenant, Israel received the Law of God and it was inscribed on the hearts of the covenant people. In the New Covenant, God's will is inscribed on the hearts of believers by the Holy Spirit. He reveals the will of God through the Word and the conscience becomes sensitized to that will. The believer is then able to discern God's judgment against sin. "When the Gentiles who do not have the Law do instinctively the things of the Law, these, not having the Law, are a law to themselves, in that they show the work of the Law written in their hearts, their conscience bearing witness and their thoughts alternately accusing or else defending them, on the day when according to my gospel, God will judge the secrets of men through Christ Jesus" (Romans 2:14-16).

The conscience of the believer has been cleansed by the work of Jesus Christ. It no longer accuses or condemns. Part of a believer's responsibility is to live to maintain a pure conscience. Equally important is not encouraging people to act against their conscience. The reason it would be wrong to encourage actions against one's conscience is that it would not be an act of faith. "He who doubts is condemned if he eats, because his eating is not from faith; and whatever is not from faith is sin" (Romans 14:23).

Father, I thank You for the inner awareness of conforming to Your will. Help me maintain a pure conscience as I walk in faith, doing Your will.

## October 21 – THE GUIDANCE OF THE HOLY SPIRIT

Romans 8:1 – All those who are being led by the Spirit of God, these are sons of God.

Through the conscience, the Holy Spirit guides believers by giving a sense of direction, a sense of purpose, and a sense of pleasing God. The Scriptures declare our position in Christ through faith, as sons of God. This includes you ladies as well, like men being part of the bride of Christ. The evidence of sonship is manifested in the guidance we receive from the Holy Spirit and confirmed in our conscience as we receive direction, purpose, and knowing we are pleasing God.

It is important to understand that growth takes time. One begins by coming to a sure knowledge of salvation. We have a sense of acceptance by God the Father, not because we have done anything to earn it, but Christ Jesus has done all to purchase salvation. Because of what Christ has done one can have confidence in their conscience of the assurance of salvation. One then grows in Christ, being guided by the Spirit of God. As the Holy Spirit guides, He leads the believer to a sense of the purpose of God.

When we seek the Lord for direction, it is appropriate to say, "Your will be done." James speaks of those who say, "Today or tomorrow we will go to such and such a city, and spend a year there and engage in business and make a profit" (James 4:13). James goes on to say, "You do not know what your life will be like tomorrow. Instead you ought to say, If the Lord wills, we will live and also do this or that" (James 4:14-15). The Spirit of God will help us in our choices as we request His involvement. Through His guidance we will know our direction.

Direction will lead to purpose. The Lord wants to establish a sense of purpose in us. Purpose is connected to growth in Christ. Early in our Christian walk, we may have a sense of purpose, but over time we should come to know our purpose. In our conscience, we should have both knowledge and a peace about God's purpose in our life. For some, it may be family commitment, vocational calling, a specific task to be accomplished, and a particular assignment in the local church, or a variety of other things.

However the Spirit of God may lead our life, one thing is for certain; His leading will produce knowledge of pleasing God. The Spirit only leads in a direction that pleases the Father. Practice the instruction which James gives, "If the Lord wills." Form the habit of committing every day to the Lord. Expect the Holy Spirit to guide you, directing your path. Just as Solomon instructs, "Trust in the Lord with all your heart, and do not lean on your own understanding. In all your ways acknowledge Him, and He will make your paths straight" (Proverbs 3:5-6).

Father, I commit my ways to You. I want Your guidance in my direction and in my purpose to know I am pleasing You.

## October 22 – FAITH IS

Hebrews 11:1-2 – Faith is the assurance of things hoped for, the conviction of things not seen. For by it the men of old gained approval.

The writer of Hebrews establishes the fact, that "without faith it is impossible to please Him" (Hebrews 11:6). There are a number of different kinds of faith. We will consider three types in our devotional.

Natural faith is simply a mental assent. I have faith that my car will be in the location where it was parked. I have experienced a time when it was not where I parked it because it was parked illegally. Natural faith operates within the realm of natural reasoning. It is a reasonable expectation of a particular outcome.

Self-motivated faith falls into the category of "metaphysics." Some call this kind of faith "mind over matter." That is, if I can just believe hard enough, my circumstance will change. This kind of faith originates in the soul of an individual. It is self-generated and self-imposed on a particular area, which one believes for change to take place.

God-breathed faith is biblical faith. True faith is an operation of the Spirit of God. When the writer of Hebrews says, "Without faith it is impossible to please Him" he is not speaking of a manufactured faith. He understands it is God who gives faith. When one looks up into the heavens and acknowledges God as creator one has an open heart where faith can operate. The essence of faith is rooted in the cross of Christ. Paul states, The life which I now live in the flesh I live by the faith of the Son of God" (Galatians 2:20 KJV). It is not only faith in Christ, but His faith lived out through the believer.

The Father is raising up a body of believers who will demonstrate Christ's faith to an unbelieving world. Many try to generate faith in the things they do for God, but the Father is looking for those who will open their hearts and allow the Holy Spirit to breathe Christ-like faith into their being. In essence, this is what being filled with the Spirit is about. It is the life of God filling the believer with the presence of the Godhead so that the faith of Christ may be manifested in the life of a believer. "Not I, but Christ"! This kind of faith captures the meaning of "sincere faith".

Father, I thank You for opening my heart to receive Your kind of faith. First, to trust You for salvation through the cross of Christ and then to receive Your Spirit so I might fulfill Your intended purpose. Daily breath Christ-like faith into my being I pray.


## October 23 – THE MEASURE OF CHRIST

Ephesians 1:15-16 – Having heard of the faith in the Lord Jesus which *exists* among you and your love for all the saints, do not cease giving thanks for you, making mention of you in my prayers.

Others should hear about our faith because we have a testimony established among people who see the results of Christ's life in us. It is the Holy Spirit's work to produce Christ in us. Remember, it is "Christ in you, the hope of glory" (Colossians 1:27). Paul understood he had been made a minister to the church. He saw it as a "stewardship from God." He also understood this stewardship as a benefit to those who belonged to Christ. Paul felt an urgency to fully carry out the preaching of the word of God. He knew he carried the mystery of God in his being, a mystery that had been hidden to past generations. That mystery was now being revealed to Christ's church. The mystery was the riches of God's glory among the Gentiles, which is "Christ in you."

This is the faith Paul says he heard of in the Ephesians. Their faith in Christ produced a love for all the saints. The glory of God is rooted in the love of God. Glory is not simply a cloud like Israel experienced on the mountain. It is the all-encompassing "Love of God." God intends for His love to be manifested through His creation man. It was manifested in Christ and spreading in His church as these Gentile believers began to demonstrate God's love among themselves and to others.

The love of God causes us to proclaim Christ to every man. Paul's calling caused him to admonish and teach every man with all wisdom so he could present every man complete in Christ (Colossians 1:28). This was Paul's purpose in his labor for God. The bottom line for Paul was to be used by the Lord to bring every man to the "measure of Christ." The measure of Christ is to love as he loved. "This is My commandment, that you love one another, just as I have loved you. Greater love has no one than this, that one lay down his life for his friends. You are My friends if you do what I command you" (John 15:12-14).

Father, I pray that the measure of Christ be revealed in my life. I thank You that Christ is in me as the hope of glory. I pray for faith and love to increase in my life as demonstration of Your presence. Grant me influence that will lead others to desire relationship with You.

# October 24 – STRIVING ACCORDING TO HIS POWER

Colossians 1:29 – For this purpose also I labor, striving according to His power, which mightily works within me.

Paul tells us in Colossians 1:29 that he was laboring and striving (fighting) according to the Lord's power which was at work in him. There is a work to be accomplished (labor) and a fight to be fought (striving). The labor is comparable to the one at work in the field preparing for the day of harvest. This includes plowing, sowing, watering and reaping. It is a full time job. There is also warfare, which is "striving" to attain the victory over the enemies of the gospel who want to hinder and destroy the harvest. Our victory is rooted in the Lord Jesus Christ and manifested in the believer by the Holy Spirit.

"Only conduct yourselves in a manner worthy of the gospel of Christ, so that whether I come and see you or remain absent, I will hear of you that you are standing firm in one spirit, with one mind striving together for the faith of the gospel" (Philippians 1:27). The Gospel calls believers to a certain kind of conduct. It is in our conduct that we reflect the control of Christ in our life through the power of the Holy Spirit. What do people say about our life? Are we convicted of being a Christian or would many be surprised to hear that we are trusting Christ? Paul lists four areas of the believers "striving."

- ➢ Standing firm in one spirit (a unified body)
- ➢ Having one mind as the body of Christ in your location
- ➢ Striving together (you do not go into battle alone)

Paul pulls these three areas together around "the faith of the gospel." As believers, we must contend for the faith. "Beloved, while I was making every effort to write you about our common salvation, I felt the necessity to write to you appealing that you contend earnestly for the faith which was once for all handed down to the saints" (Jude 3).

"You have not yet resisted to the point of shedding blood in your striving against sin; and you have forgotten the exhortation which is addressed to you as sons,"

'My son, do not regard lightly the discipline of the Lord, nor faint when you are reproved by Him; for those whom the Lord loves He disciplines, and He scourges every son whom He receives" (Hebrews 12:4-6).

As believers, we must resist sin. For some it has cost them their lives. That is not so with us yet. In the battle, we strive to please the Lord. At times, it is necessary for the Lord to discipline us because we are "sons," whom He is developing into mature men and women of God.

Father, I ask for Your help as I labor, striving according to Your power, which mightily works within me. Help me to stand firm in one spirit. Help me to have one mind in Your body. Join me in the battle with other faithful believers. Cause me to be strong and faithful when corrected by You.

## October 25 – WITNESS OF THE SCRIPTURES

John 5:39 – You search the Scriptures because you think that in them you have eternal life; it is these that testify about Me.

John 5 mentions four witnesses regarding Jesus. They are: the witness of John the Baptist, the witness of works, the witness of the Father, and the witness of the Scriptures. Jesus declares, He can do nothing on His own initiative and if He alone testifies about Himself, His testimony is not true (John 5:30-31).

What Jesus says about Himself is also true for every believer. As a believer, I can do nothing on my own initiative. One of the great challenges of the Christian walk is learning to live out of the life of the Spirit as opposed to drawing from our natural life. Many believers initiate good works, the problem being "they initiate them." The works which Jesus performed came from the Holy Spirit, not Jesus' own ideas of how to serve His Father. The witness of Jesus came from other sources. Jesus knew who He was, but He let other sources testify concerning Him.

The witness of John pointed toward Jesus and away from John. The witness of works demonstrated God's power through Jesus' life. The witness of the Father is that He sent His only Begotten Son. He spoke many times, through many individuals, and in many different ways concerning the coming of Jesus. The witness of Scripture is in the miraculous way the Law and the Prophets testified of Christ.

The fallacy of the religious leaders was they thought life was contained in the Scriptures. They did not recognize the One of whom the Scriptures spoke. To receive life is not a matter of conversation, but action. The action required in this case was to believe Jesus. Believe not only His words, but His works.

After Pentecost, the witness of all that Jesus did was witnessed in the coming of the Holy Spirit. Eternal life is obtained through the Spirit. As we believe the witness of others pointing to Jesus, as we believe the work of Jesus in the cross, as we believe the Father's declaration that He sent His only Begotten Son, and as we believe the Scriptures.

As we receive Christ, His life is firmly rooted in us through the power of the Holy Spirit, and then we become part of the witness. The transformation of our life, the witness of our faith through how we now live and share with words, God's love becomes a conduit of God's grace.

Father, thank You for the witness You have given of Your will revealed in Christ. Thank You for sending the Holy Spirit to draw me to Christ and the life You made possible through faith in Jesus, the Christ, my Savior, and my Lord. Use me to testify of Your Son that others also may know His life.

## October 26 –THE WITNESS OF JOHN

John 5:36 – He was the lamp that was burning and was shining and you were willing to rejoice for a while in his light.

It cannot be emphasized too greatly how important John the Baptist was to the introduction of Jesus and His kingdom reign. John was the prophetic bridge from the Old to the New Covenant. The last verses of the Old Testament recorded in the book of Malachi spoke of John when it said, "Behold, I am going to send you Elijah the prophet before the coming of the great and terrible day of the Lord. He will restore the hearts of the fathers to their children and the hearts of the children to their fathers, so that I will not come and smite the land with a curse" (Malachi 4:5-6).

These verses reveal the heart of our heavenly Father. Elijah was the premier prophet of the Old Covenant. He represents the total prophetic revelation of the Old Covenant. John came in the spirit of Elijah. We know these scriptures speak of the time of Jesus' first coming because Jesus calls John Elijah. Elijah is coming and will restore all things; but I say to you that Elijah already came, and they did not recognize him, but did to him whatever they wished. So also the Son of Man is going to suffer at their hands" (Matthew 17:11-12).

Prophets are anointed to be lamps to God's people. John was that lamp, lighting the way for Jesus to enter His ministry. In those days, a lamp was fueled by oil which caused the wick to burn. As John "burned" for Jesus, those hearing him rejoiced for a time. Through the power of the Holy Spirit, we too are called to burn for Jesus and to point to the "Lamb of God" who takes the world's sin away. John's light revealed Jesus. The light of the Holy Spirit in us reveals Jesus to a dark world as well. People rejoice in that light until they find out what is required to have the light in them. Many reject God's love because, in order to receive what God has done in Christ, they are required to give up their life and receive His. This is why Jesus said "Many are called, but few are chosen" (Matthew 22:14).

For the one who receives the testimony of John, they become "greater than John." "Truly I say to you, among those born of women there has not arisen anyone greater than John the Baptist! Yet the one who is least in the kingdom of heaven is greater than he" (Matthew 11:11). Wow! We are greater than John! How can this be? The greatness of the least in the kingdom of God comes through being joined to Christ in the power of His resurrection and His indwelling Holy Spirit. John was part of the last covenant which looked forward to Christ's first advent. We are those who are part of the "new" who live in the present reign of the Lord Jesus Christ. We are waiting for His glorious return, when at His appearing we will be joined with all those who have gone before us.

Father, I thank You for what You have done in Christ. I pray for the oil of the Holy Spirit to fill my life so I might burn like John, filled with light that points to Your great love in Christ.

# October 27 – THE WITNESS OF WORKS

John 5:36 – The testimony which I have is greater than the testimony of John.

Most would agree that John the Baptist had a powerful testimony of God's power used to introduce the ministry of the Lord Jesus Christ. Jesus declares that His testimony is greater than John's. Jesus' greater testimony came through the works which the Father gave Him to accomplish. The greatest of the works is found in the cross. Before the cross, Jesus revealed the Father's work in His ministry to God's covenant people, Israel.

One of the first works took place in a Synagogue as a man manifested demons. Jesus cast out the demon by rebuking him, saying, "Be quiet, and come out of him" (Mark 1:25). The demon had said to Jesus, "What business do we have with each other, Jesus of Nazareth? Have You come to destroy us?" Jesus would not receive the testimony of the demon, but the work spoke for itself. The people were all amazed and debated among themselves, saying "What is this? A new teaching with authority! He commands even unclean spirits, and they obey Him" (Verse 26).

Another work was the healing of a paralytic through forgiveness of his sins. "Jesus seeing their faith, said to the paralytic, 'Son, your sins are forgiven'" (Mark 2:5). Of course, this made the religious leaders angry because they counted it as blasphemy, thinking in their hearts, "Who can forgive sins but God?"

Finally, Jesus raised the dead. Lazarus had been dead four days, when Jesus prayed saying, "Father, I thank You that You have heard Me. I knew that You always hear Me; but because of the people standing around I said it, so that they may believe that You sent Me. When He had said these things, He cried out with a loud voice, 'Lazarus, come forth'" (John 11:41-42).

The Father also equipped His people through the power of the Holy Spirit to do the "works of God." God has called us to good works. This is why the gifts of the Holy Spirit are made available to believers. The Father has not commissioned us to go and proclaim the good news without also supplying what is needed to accomplish the task. As believers, we have authority and power in Jesus' name to proclaim the good news of the Gospel and demonstrate the power of the kingdom of God.

Jesus was given the full measure of power to do the works of His heavenly Father. Each believer is authorized to move in the portion of power the Father chooses to give. The works of God usually need to be developed in a believer's life. Don't be disappointed the first time you pray for someone to be healed and they're not healed. Just keep praying for the sick and trust God.

Father, I ask to be used by You to minister Your love to others. I pray for the works of God to be manifested in my life. I pray that Your works through me would witness to others of Your greatness and help lead them to a relationship with You.

## October 28 – THE WITNESS OF THE FATHER

John 5:37 – The Father who sent Me, He has testified of Me.

The Father gives testimony to all He does. If the Father has called you and sent you, He will bear witness of you. The Father sent Jesus and testified about Him through the prophets of the Old Covenant. All the prophets spoke of Christ, pointing to His coming. Daniel even pinpointed the exact time of Christ's ministry in his seventy year prophecy in Daniel 9. Isaiah described His suffering perfectly in Isaiah 53. John the Baptist, the last Old Covenant prophet, actually pointed out Christ declaring, "The Lamb of God who takes away the sin of the world" (John 1:29).

The Father begins His witness in our lives as we respond to His Son through faith, just as the Father testified of Jesus when He spoke from heaven. "This is My beloved Son, in whom I am well pleased" (Matthew 3:16). He witnesses of His love for us. He declares it in the Scriptures, He bears witness in our regenerated spirit, and He encourages us through others.

The enemy of our soul tries to discourage us through feelings of unworthiness and rejection. He is a liar! We are not unworthy; for the Son has made us worthy, even though we are in the process of growing up into Him. The Father declares us "accepted"! Our past may try to haunt us through the statements of others. Statements filled with rejection, worthlessness, and failure. Those views of others are under the blood of Christ who declares we are beloved, accepted, worthwhile, darling, successful, purposeful, and important. We are His prize, His darling, and His beloved bride.

Jesus was very direct with the religious leaders whose hearts were hardened and controlled by the devil. Jesus declared, "You have neither heard His voice at any time nor seen His form. You do not have His word abiding in you, for you do not believe Him whom He sent" (John 5:37-38).

Today, believe His word and His witness about you. Receive His love, acceptance, and forgiveness. The Father is ecstatic over you. We are in Christ and cannot be separated from His love. Rebuke the lies of the enemy that say you're not worthy. Reject any negative comments from the past. Release those who have spoken poorly of you. Accept the Father's love and favor. Then allow the Holy Spirit to reveal what He has done for you and in you that others might hear the witness of the Father through you.

Father, thank You that I am loved and accepted by You because of what Jesus has done on my behalf. I receive Your witness of me and want to tell others how You love them because of Your beloved Son, the Lord Jesus Christ.

## October 29 – CHRIST LEFT US AN EXAMPLE

1 Peter 2:21 – For you have been called for this purpose, since Christ also suffered for you, leaving you an example for you to follow in His steps.

As Peter states, "we are to follow in His steps." What steps did the Lord leave us and how is it possible for us to walk as He did? He committed no sin (1 Peter 2:22). We start out with a major problem, even after the regeneration of the Spirit of God; we have a sin nature which must be put to death. In Romans 6 he deals with the problem and answers the question of how it is possible to walk as He walked. There was no "deceit" in His mouth. I certainly would like it said of me, there is no deceit in my mouth. What is deceit? "That which gives a false impression, whether by appearance, statement or influence." (Vine's Expository Dictionary of Biblical Words, Copyright © 1985, Thomas Nelson Publishers.)

The Christian life is a process. It begins with the mindset, "our old self is being crucified with Christ" (Romans 6:6). This is why we are no longer "slaves to sin." The work of salvation has been done in our spirit, but we must form a mindset in our soul of considering ourselves dead to sin. "Consider yourself to be dead to sin, but alive to God in Christ Jesus" (Romans 6:11). Christ suffered for us and we join His sufferings, by choosing "death to self."

The Scripture uses the word "sanctification," which speaks of being separated to God. Our flesh is weak and hinders us from serving Christ. Before we gave our life to Christ, we were slaves to sin. Christ set us free from that master called sin. We now have a new master, called righteousness. "Now present your members as slaves to righteousness, resulting in sanctification" (Romans 6:19). This is the new mind which Christ wants each believer to possess; I am dead to sin in Christ, no longer a slave to sin. I am alive unto righteousness, to serve righteousness. All of this is made possible through the Lord Jesus Christ. We are now to ask the Holy Spirit daily for His life to sustain us in our entire decision-making process.

"Now having been freed from sin and enslaved to God, you derive your benefit, resulting in sanctification, and the outcome, eternal life" (Romans 6:22). Jesus freed us from sin's domain. We must not only believe, but apply Christ's life in our daily walk. Salvation was secured in Christ, but the application is our responsibility. Assurance of our position in Christ is rooted in His work of redemption, but confidence to walk as He walked comes through obedience to the power of the Holy Spirit. The Spirit leads to "sanctification" with the final outcome of "eternal life."

"While being reviled, He did not revile in return; while suffering, He uttered no threats, but kept entrusting Himself to Him who judges righteously; and He Himself bore our sins in His body on the cross, so that we *might* die to sin and live to righteousness; for by His wounds you were healed. For you were continually straying like sheep, but now you have returned to the Shepherd and Guardian of your souls" (1 Peter 2:23-25). I find myself returning again. How about you? I know of none who have obtained sinless perfection, but I know many who confess day by day their weakness and ask for Christ's power to help in pleasing the Lord.

Father, I thank You for the Shepherd and Guardian of my soul. I need Your daily help for me to walk in Christ's example. Fill me afresh with Your Holy Spirit so I might die to sin and live to righteousness.


## October 30 – EVERY ONE WHO PRACTICES RIGHTEOUSNESS IS BORN OF HIM

1 John 2:29 – If you know that He is righteous, you know that everyone also who practices righteousness is born of Him.

The context of John's writing is to encourage the children of God. In verse 24, John says to "let that abide in you which you heard from the beginning." What was it that they heard from the beginning?

- ➢ God's love for them.
- ➢ He had promised eternal life to those who believed.
- ➢ The anointing, which is the Holy Spirit.

John told the believers that he was writing to them because of those who were trying to deceive them. He is addressing the same problem Paul had to address, the Jews who distorted the Gospel. They were teaching the believers that they had to practice certain Jewish customs in order to be saved. John tells them, "You have no need for anyone to teach you; but His anointing teaches you about all things" (1 John 2:27). John was establishing the fact that the Holy Spirit was given to them to teach and clarify the gospel they had received. John was not saying to reject teachers. He recognized the "anointing" was the obvious final word. The anointing was in them, and not external.

John gave believers wise counsel when he said, "Now, little children, abide in Him (1 John 2:28). Today, many run after all the different teachers and doctrines that are being represented. Some are leading God's people away from a healthy relationship with the Father and the Son. People run after doctrines, supernatural manifestations, and charismatic personalities. Abiding in Christ is no doubt the wisest decision one can make. Waiting on Him, proving all things, and holding fast to what is true. As we abide in Him, we will have confidence when He appears.

John is not questioning the believer's position regarding eternal life. He knows all believers will stand before the judgment seat of Christ. In that day, he does not want the believer to be ashamed, but to have confidence because of practicing righteousness. It is not the practice of the works of the law, but the practice of righteousness through faith in Christ that matters.

Father, I thank You for the confidence to stand before You and not be ashamed. Thank You for the anointing that is in me through the Holy Spirit. I pray for You to protect me from false teaching and instruct me by Your Spirit in righteousness.

## October 31 – DOING THE WILL OF GOD

Matthew 7:21 – Not everyone who says to Me, Lord, Lord, will enter the kingdom of heaven, but he who does the will of My Father who is in heaven will enter.

This is a very clear word from our Lord about entering into the kingdom of heaven. The subject which Jesus is addressing can be found in verse 23, "You who practice lawlessness." The lawlessness which Jesus is addressing is that of the religious leaders and their followers. They claimed to be followers of God and part of His kingdom, but they had established their own rules and were lawless and not submitting to the Law of God.

Jesus fulfilled God's Law and was the only means to a right standing before His heavenly Father. Faith in the work of Christ gives us access to the Father and acceptance in His kingdom. Those who have trusted Christ are in varying degrees of development in terms of their daily obedience. "When the kindness of God our Savior and His love for mankind appeared, He saved us, not on the basis of deeds which we have done in righteousness, but according to His mercy, by the washing of regeneration and renewing by the Holy Spirit" (Titus 3:4-5).

God richly poured out His Spirit through Jesus. He justified us by His grace so we would be made heirs in our hope of eternal life. Through belief in what God has done by justification we should be careful to engage in good deeds. It is to our profit to be fruitful in good works and obedience to our great God and Savior.

It is vital to understand that no one person can obtain access into God's kingdom except through Jesus Christ. It is He, and He alone, who justifies every believer. It is equally true that He did not save us simply to go to heaven, but as "heirs according to the hope of eternal life . . . we should be careful to engage in good deeds." There is the great tension of the scriptures regarding salvation. It is not by works which we have done that we trust, but by His work alone. The expected result of the Father is through the power of the Holy Spirit, we do the work of God by engaging in good deeds.

Paul says to Titus, "I want you to speak confidently, so that those who have believed God will be careful to engage in good deeds" (Titus 3:8). It is with confidence I speak as well. God has secured your salvation, believe Him for what He has done on your behalf and do good works. Each day, ask for a fresh infilling of the Holy Spirit to do God's works. In order to do those works, we must have God's power.

Father, I thank You for Your kindness and love for mankind. Thank You for saving me not based on my deeds, but Your mercy. Now Lord, fill me with Your Holy spirit, that by Your power I might do deeds of righteousness.

## November 1 – TAKE UP THE FULL ARMOR

Ephesians 6:10 – Finally, be strong in the Lord and in the strength of His might. Put on the full armor of God.

Paul uses the word "finally" as he wraps up his teachings to the church at Ephesus. He was not correcting any error in this letter as he does in many of his writings. He gives the saints strong foundational teaching with redemption in the first chapter. Paul lays out eight themes in his letter:

- ➤ The blessing of redemption
- ➤ We are alive in Christ
- ➤ Stewardship relating to God's Grace
- ➤ Unity of the Spirit
- ➤ The Christian walk
- ➤ Be imitators of God
- ➤ Marriage and family relationship
- ➤ The armor of God

Paul teaches that our battle is not in the natural realm, but in the supernatural. His message is an important message for believers today. Many come to a church service for the wrong motivations. Let's consider three so we might search our own hearts concerning our own motivation. If necessary, repent and come into alignment with God's Eternal purpose.

First, many go to a church service to receive a "pep talk," something to help get them through the week. There are those who need to be encouraged. That is not wrong. It is part of the reason Christians gather. God's purpose and desire goes much deeper than pep-talks.

Second, some come as a sense of duty. Their heart is not fully engaged. They attend from a need to have religious activity. Many feel a need to "appease God" by their attendance. God is not looking for appeasement, but obedience to His calling.

Third, there are those which attend a church service when their soul moves them on special occasions or when other activities don't interfere. You could say it is obeying God on their terms.

The purpose of our gathering is primarily for corporate worship, equipping, and instruction. Of course, this includes receiving the Lord's Supper. Within these areas, the Spirit of God wants to manifest His presence among the body and minister His gifts to meet needs in the lives of God's people.

"Put on the whole armor of God, so that you will be able to stand firm against the schemes of the devil" (Ephesians 6:11). When Paul writes, "put on the whole armor of God," it is a clue there be warfare. The armor of the Lord provides for both offense and defense in the battle. This armor is intended to be worn by those who have received God's salvation. His salvation is greater than most realize. Tomorrow, we will enlarge on this thought.

Father, thank You for the armor You supply for Your saints. Please give me wisdom and understanding for the spiritual battle in which we are engaged. Cause me to be strong in the power of Your Holy Spirit. Teach me how to effectively wear the armor and be effective both offensively and defensively in the battle against the enemy.

## November 2 – WE ARE IN A BATTLE

Ephesians 6:12 – For our struggle is not against flesh and blood, but against the rulers, against the powers, against the world forces of this darkness, against the spiritual forces of wickedness in the heavenly places.

At times, it takes a number of English words to adequately communicate the meaning of the one Greek word. Words such as: deliverance, healing, safety, and wholeness bring a larger view of the salvation our God has provided. They also give us a larger view of the areas of attack from the enemy, areas such as demonic strongholds, sickness, disease, and persecution. Each one of these represents areas of battle in which the believer engages. Then there are the daily challenges of the flesh and dealing with temptation.

The armor must be put on daily. The practical application of God's armor is to help His warring church conquer evil. Our verse today clearly identifies the forces behind the battle. Do I believe the word of God concerning the battle? The proof of my belief is found in obedience through application. "Put on the whole armor of God." This is not a suggestion, but a command.

"Take up the full armor of God," (are you?) so that you will be able to resist in the evil day, and having done everything, to stand firm" (Ephesians 6:13). Have we done everything? "Stand firm therefore having girded your loins with truth" (Ephesians 6:14). The armor begins with truth. The belt of truth holds all the armor together.

Consider what Jesus said about truth. "Jesus was saying to those Jews who had believed on Him, 'If you continue in My word, then you are truly disciples of Mine; and you will know the truth, and the truth will make you free'. They answered Him, We are Abraham's descendants and have never yet been enslaved to anyone; how is it that You say, you will become free?" (John 8:31-33).

Deception can be ruthless. Throughout Jewish history, they were in bondage to the nations around them. For seventy years, the Israelites were captive to the Assyrians. Presently, they were captive to Rome. They really were slaves and the one speaking to them was "the Son of the house." "Jesus answered them, 'Truly, truly, I say to you, everyone who commits sin is the slave of sin. The slave does not remain in the house forever; the son does remain forever'" (John 8:34-35). We are no longer slaves, but sons. We must put on the truth every day, exercising our position in Christ against the enemies of our soul. Gird yourself with truth every day. All truth is eternal. In this case, truth is a man. Paul said, "Put on the Lord Jesus Christ, and make no provision for the flesh in regard to its lusts" (Romans 13:14).

Four elements of entering into truth are: honesty, confession, repentance, receiving and giving forgiveness. Releasing others who have sinned against us opens the prison door and sets the captive free!

Father, I thank You for the freedom You have made possible in Christ. I chose to put on the "full armor of God." Thank You for the girdle of truth I wear which holds all Your provisions together in my life.

## November 3 – WEARING THE ARMOR OF GOD

Ephesians 6:14b – Put on the breastplate of righteousness, and having shod your feet with the preparation of the gospel of peace; in addition to all, taking up the shield of faith with which you will be able to extinguish all the flaming arrows of the evil one.

The breastplate of righteousness covers your heart region. Righteousness is a heart issue. The enemy shoots his arrows at our hearts to try and kill the life of God. Many have received arrows from others, from childhood through adulthood.

Believers can have great difficulty in their Christian growth because of wounds to their heart from the past. The Lord wants to heal us from the inside out. As we are healed, it is important to put on the breastplate of righteousness to stay well in one's heart.

Putting on the shoes of the gospel of peace is for our daily walk. We are to walk in peace and bring peace wherever we go. Just as we take time to prepare our natural feet for walking, we must take time to prepare for our walk in Christ. It begins with intimacy with our heavenly Father. As we experience peace in the morning with the Lord, we are readied for the day and our experience with others.

Paul says, "Taking up the shield of faith." It takes effort to put on the armor, but it is a necessary daily activity. We are called to walk in faith. It is the person of faith that overcomes the world. It is the person of faith that advances the kingdom of God. It is faith that pleases God (Hebrews 11:6). The devil hates people of faith because they cause his kingdom great problems. Only through faith do we "extinguish" his flaming arrows. The picture Paul is illustrating is that of a Roman soldier. The Roman soldiers would stand together with their shields interlocked. As believers we are to interlock with other believers against the enemies attacks. We do not have to go into the battle alone.

The "evil one" has a very ordered kingdom; he rules his domain with control and oppression. His purpose is to cause chaos for God's plans. Satan is ruthless in his attack on God's kingdom purposes and God's covenant people. Paul outlines what we are up against in this battle. Many Christians try to meet the challenges they face through their own natural reasoning. The wisdom of man is not sufficient to deal with the kingdom of darkness. It is important for the believers to understand the warfare in which they are engaged. The armor is very important to our success in the battle.

It cannot be emphasized enough how important righteous living and a life of faith becomes as it relates to the subject of "spiritual warfare." Allow the Holy Spirit to search your heart daily and expose any area that has not been cleansed by the blood of Jesus and surrendered to His kingdom rule. Invite the Holy Spirit to establish your life habits in an atmosphere of faith. Repent of any areas He reveals that are not motivated by faith. Paul reminds us, "Whatever is not from faith is sin" (Romans 14:23).

Father, I thank You for both the breastplate of righteousness and the shield of faith. Grant me grace to put on both these essential parts of the armor that You have supplied. Strengthen me in the battle of advancing Your kingdom on earth.

## November 4 – THE HELMET OF SALVATION AND THE SWORD OF THE SPIRIT

Ephesians 6:17 – Take the helmet of salvation, and the sword of the Spirit, which is the word of God.

Paul says that we must "take" both the helmet and the sword. They are not placed in our hands; rather we must take the responsibility for picking them up. The helmet of salvation covers our heads. Salvation is holistic in its nature and is intended to minister daily to our souls. The soul has three main areas that need to experience God's salvation daily: the will, the emotions, and the mind. All three areas need to be brought under the control of the Holy Spirit. The mind has at least five areas which the Lord wants to bring into conformity to the mind of Christ. Satan has his designs on each of these areas.

The five areas of the mind are described by Paul. We read in Colossians 3:2 about the affections of the mind. "Set your affection on things above, not on things on the earth." Paul mentions our imaginations in 2 Corinthians 10:3, "Casting down imaginations, and every high thing that exalts itself against the knowledge of God, and bringing into captivity every thought to the obedience of Christ." He writes about the conscience in 1Timothy 1:19. "Keeping faith and a good conscience, which some have rejected and suffered shipwreck in regard to their faith." Paul describes the use of the memory in 1 Corinthians 15:2. "Keep in memory what I preached unto you." Finally, Scripture illustrates our ability to reason in Acts 19:8-9 when Paul "entered the synagogue and continued speaking out boldly for three months, reasoning and persuading them about the kingdom of God."

We must "take up the sword of the Spirit." The sword of the Spirit is the word of God. It is two-edged and can be dangerous if mishandled. One edge cuts away the fleshly nature of my own heart. The word of God is essential in changing my perspective and helping me see from God's point of view. The other edge is the side of the blade for helping free others. When the sword is handled properly, bondages can be cut off those to whom you are ministering. It is important to read, study, memorize, and meditate upon the word of God. When we give ourselves to these four areas, it will cause us to become skillful with the sword of the Spirit.

Father, I thank You for these two important pieces of armor. Help me to put on the helmet of salvation daily, and to take up the sword of the Spirit. I ask You to make me a skillful warrior in Your army. I want to walk in the victory of the Lord Jesus Christ every day.

## November 5 – WITH ALL PRAYER IN THE SPIRIT

Ephesians 6:18 – With all prayer and petition, pray at all times in the Spirit.

Prayer is one of the most important disciplines of a believer's walk in Christ. Prayer is our means of communication with our heavenly Father. Prayer is what we have been called to as priests of God. The authority Jesus has given to His church to overcome the kingdom of darkness is implemented by prayer. Prayer is not our thoughts being expressed to God, but rather through relationship with the Holy Spirit we receive God's desires, "Your will be done, on earth as it is in heaven" (Matthew 6:10).

Paul used the word all – "With all prayer and at all times." When writing the Thessalonians, Paul admonishes them, "pray without ceasing" (1 Thessalonians 5:17). Prayer is not a ritual, but rather a lifestyle. Prayer must be Spirit-led to accomplish God's purpose, and not from one's own soul life. "God's house will be a house of prayer for all peoples" (Isaiah 56:7).

The New Testament gives us an expanded dimension of prayer. "To pray" is always used of "prayer" to God. "Now I pray to God that ye do no evil; not that we should appear approved, but that ye should do that which is honest, though we be as reprobates. We can do nothing against the truth, but for the truth. For we are glad, when we are weak, and ye are strong: and this also we wish, even your perfection" (2 Corinthians 13:7-8 KJV). I site the KJV because the quote uses the word "wish." Paul is praying his desire or wish to God for the Corinthians.

Paul's injunction in 1 Thessalonians 5:17 is "to pray without ceasing." This describes his burden for the Lord's Church to enter into her calling of prayer at all times. Paul's prayer for the Philippians is most insightful when he says, "This I pray, that your love may abound still more and more in real knowledge and all discernment, so that you may approve the things that are excellent, in order to be sincere and blameless" (Philippians 1:9-10). Locating the prayers of Paul and the other apostles is a profitable study. Incorporate them into your prayer life. This prayer in Philippians is a powerful prayer which truly identifies the Father's heart for His sons and daughters.

In tomorrow's devotion, we will discuss a number of meanings for prayer. I will include: proper prayer and how faith relates to prayer. The Holy Spirit is present to help us enter into Paul's encouragement to the Saints at Ephesus, "With all prayer and petition pray at all times in the Spirit." Daily, ask the Father and the Son to fill you with their Holy Spirit. The Holy Spirit will lead you and direct you throughout the day. You will find yourself praying more as the Spirit of God gives you insights and direction in the day's activities.

Father, I thank You for inviting me to partner with You every day through prayer and petition. Fill me with Your Spirit as often as needed so that I might be alert to Your will and guided in my daily decision making. Use me to pray for others in their walk, that by faith I would see Heaven's will brought to pass.

## November 6 – BE ON THE ALERT

Ephesians 6:18b – Be on the alert with all perseverance and petition for all saints.

Throughout the New Testament, the verb "to pray" carries a number of meanings. A few examples are to ask, make request, to desire, beseech, and to call to one's aid. The word "intercession" is used often in today's church. It speaks of requests made on behalf of others. The Scriptures do not speak of an office of "intercessor." The Holy Spirit leads individuals to make petition on behalf of others. Some are led by the Spirit to pray on behalf of nations. Nations include people groups coming to a revelation of the Lord Jesus Christ.

The Holy Spirit is the sole interpreter of the needs of the human heart. He makes intercession on behalf of the saints. Prayer is impossible to man apart from the Spirit's help: "The Spirit also helps our weakness; for we do not know how to pray as we should, but the Spirit Himself intercedes for us with groaning too deep for words" (Romans 8:26). Believers are exhorted to pray at all seasons in the Spirit (Ephesians 6:18; cf. Jude 20). "The effective prayer of a righteous man can accomplish much" (James 5:16).

Paul teaches that prayer is made from two sources. "For I will pray with the spirit and I will pray with the mind also; I will sing with the spirit and I will sing with the mind also" (1 Corinthians 14:15). When Paul speaks of the mind, he is speaking of his understanding. Paul is saying that there are areas of need of which we are aware in our minds. We don't need a special revelation to pray. Just pray! There are other needs of prayer which come by revelation through the gifts of the Holy Spirit. Paul is speaking of "his spirit" praying and singing. In the context of the chapter, he is addressing the subject of the private use of tongues.

Just as Paul said in Ephesians 6:18, be on the alert with all perseverance and petition for all saints. This is one of our assignments, beloved. As we put on the armor of God daily, let us make sure we do not neglect this exhortation. This would be a good time to commit or recommit yourself to a lifestyle of prayer. Prepare for the battle! The war is on with the kingdom of darkness. The saints of God must be engaged in the battle or suffer loss.

Father, I pray for Your help to cause me to be on the alert with all perseverance and petition for all saints. Grant boldness to all

Your servants throughout the world to be given utterance to make known the mystery of the gospel. Give me that boldness as well to witness Your love revealed in Jesus Christ our Lord.

# November 7 – DO NOT LOVE THE WORLD

1 John 2:15 – Do not love the world nor the things that are in the world. If anyone loves the world, the love of the Father is not in him.

What a great verse of scripture to remind us of how easily we can become separated from the love of the Father. The Father does not forsake us, but we can be drawn away from His presence as we are filled with things. Some years ago, I began to change a habit of saying I loved a particular item. I realized that habit nurtured "things" rather than a person. The Father is concerned about persons. Love is meant to be organic and not about objects.

The world is corrupt through sin. Sin gave Satan a right to rule the nations and corrupt the world through systems. Jesus conquered Satan and made it possible to bring the nations under God's government. The work of salvation in the life of a believer destroys the works of the flesh with its lust and gets the love of the world out of the saints of God. Jesus made it clear when He prayed to the Father saying, "I do not ask You to take them out of the world, but to keep them from the evil one" (John 17:15). Jesus prayed these words because He understood, while the disciples were in the world, the attacks against them would be rooted in Satan and his domain.

It is not wrong to have possessions as long as the possessions do not possess us. There is an expression I learned many years ago, "Hold on to things loosely." I enjoy restoring old radios and transmitters. I continually need to practice not becoming emotionally attached to a nice piece of equipment. I am grateful for all that the Lord has blessed my wife and me with, but I know I can be satisfied with little because I have known both little and abundance.

The Holy Spirit wants to develop a kingdom culture in us. That is, everything we own, time we spend, and places we go must have a foundation in the kingdom of God. Whether or not I am purposely involved in a particular kingdom activity, the kingdom of God is to be my first priority.

Father, reveal to me if there is any worldliness in my life. Help me, by the power of the Holy Spirit, to be free from any love of the world. I choose to only make room for the love of the Father in my life.

## November 8 – REMAINING FAITHFUL

1 John 2:24 – If that which ye have heard from the beginning shall remain in you, ye also shall continue in the Son, and in the Father (KJV).

Abiding is an important topic of the New Testament. In the last hours of His earthly life, Jesus taught His disciples what it meant to abide in Him. "Abide in Me, and I in you. As the branch cannot bear fruit of itself unless it abides in the vine, so neither can you unless you abide in Me. I am the vine, you are the branches; he who abides in Me and I in him, he bears much fruit, for apart from Me you can do nothing" (John 15:4-5).

For some, John 15 can be a difficult chapter because of the illustration of removing branches and casting them away. It is important to understand that Jesus is speaking to His apostles. They are the ones He is sending into the world to lay the foundation of His Church by preaching the "goodness of His kingdom." Judas, who was named among the apostles, was really an agent of the devil. The Jewish people saw themselves as the "special people of God." Jesus is now defining who the people of God really are. Apart from Jesus, nothing can be done that has eternal significance.

The sum total of what Jesus came to accomplish is found in the Father and the Son taking up a place of residence in the believer through their indwelling Holy Spirit. In John's gospel account, he calls this "abiding." In John's letter to the church, he again calls this work of God "abiding." God's will is to abide in every part of the believer's life. The Father and the Son desire for the believer to come and know as much of their nature as one can contain.

The word abiding speaks of fellowship. "What we have seen and heard we proclaim to you also, so that you too may have fellowship with us; and indeed our fellowship is with the Father, and with His Son Jesus Christ. These things we write, so that our joy may be made complete" (1 John 1:3-4). Abiding in Christ is what produces fellowship with the Father and the Son. It also is the foundation of relationship among believers. There is a wonderful joy when one learns about an individual they know who has entered into a fellowship with the Father and the Son. The other day, a friend was sharing with me his recent experience with God. I was filled with joy and it allowed me to share with him deeper things in Christ than I had previously shared.

Father, I want to grow in my relationship with You. Lead me to abide in You so that Your will might be established fully in my life. I have determined to press into You. I ask You to supply the needed grace in my life to be Your faithful servant.

## November 9 – FAITH, HOPE, AND LOVE – THE KEY TO VICTORY

1 Corinthians 13:13 – Now faith, hope, love, abide these three; but the greatest of these is love.

Normally you do not think of spiritual warfare when reciting 1 Corinthians 13:13. These three pillars of the Christian walk are essential to our battle against the enemy. These three weapons have power to destroy the enemy's entrenchment in the mind of believers and will pull down strongholds of arguments against Christ.

We begin with faith, not only because it is mentioned first, but because "without faith it is impossible to please God" (Hebrews 11:6). Jesus would often declare that one's faith had made the individual whole. The biblical definition of faith is that "Faith is the assurance of things hoped for, the conviction of things not seen" (Hebrews 11:1). Faith operates out of assurance. Assurance comes by the promises of God's word. "Faith comes from hearing, and hearing by the word of God" (Romans 10:17). The context of Romans 10 begins with Christ as the end of the law for righteousness. Righteousness has its root in Christ alone.

Romans 10:6 quotes Deuteronomy 30:14, stating that the righteousness based on faith speak of the word of God being near us, that is in our mouth and in our heart. Faith operates by the word of God taking root in our heart and then being formed in our mouth. Both our mouth and our heart are connected with righteousness. We think in righteous terms and we speak with righteous words.

When we were in the flesh, our heart and mouth produced works of the flesh. Jesus said, "The things that proceed out of the mouth come from the heart, and those defile the man. For out of the heart come evil thoughts, murders, adulteries, fornications, thefts, false witness, and slanders" (Matthew 15:18-19). In Christ, our heart and mouth are to be used as instruments of righteousness producing life.

In his letter, James connects "faith and works." James asks the question, "If someone says he has faith but he has no works, can that faith save him? Faith is spoken, but the kind of faith that brings about results is the faith of Christ which always produces works of righteousness. Christ- like faith will reach out into the community and set the captives free from sin, sickness, demonic oppression, and to serve the Lord Jesus Christ. Faith is the first pillar of three. Today, why not believe God for an infilling of His Holy Spirit in the realm of faith? Let the Holy Spirit search your heart and cleanse any areas needing washed in the blood of the Lamb. Trust the Holy Spirit to put "the word of faith" into your mouth. Saints, be established in a lifestyle of faith!

Father, search my heart and see if there be any wicked thing in me. I ask to be made wholly consecrated Lord, to Thee. I pray to be established in faith and be used of the Holy Spirit to set others free from every stronghold of the enemy binding up their life.

# November 10 – HOPE THAT WILL NEVER BE MOVED

Psalm 31:24 – Be strong and let your heart take courage, all you who hope in the Lord.

Strength and courage come from a "hope in the Lord." This is because the Lord never changes. "I the Lord, do not change; therefore you, O sons of Jacob, are not consumed" (Malachi 3:6). We can have confidence because the Lord is the hope of our salvation.

Our minds need to be trained in a hope that is rooted in God the Father. The world teaches us to hope in ourselves and become self-reliant. David learned to hope in the Lord. "For You are my hope; O Lord God, You are my confidence from my youth. By You, I have been sustained from my birth; You are He who took me from my mother's womb; My praise is continually of You" (Psalm 71:5-6). This is the kind of mind-set we must develop in this matter of hope. It begins by knowing the Lord had an important part with our birth. Before we were converted, the Lord was already at work in His purposes for us. Some of us experienced times when our lives might have been shortened, except the Lord "sustained" us. I am grateful to have the same testimony as David, "You are my confidence from my youth." Regardless of what stage of life we came to know the Lord, it is important to understand He had His hand upon us.

Hope is developed from a love for God's word. "I hope for Your salvation, O Lord, and do Your commandments. My soul keeps Your testimonies, and I love them exceedingly. I keep Your precepts and Your testimonies, for all my ways are before You" (Psalm 119:166-167). The hope David possessed was not a maybe hope, but a sure knowledge of God's faithfulness and enduring mercies. His confidence came from his relationship with God. Even in his failures, he trusted the Lord based upon God's character and not his own perfection. "Be gracious to me, O God, according to Your loving-kindness; according to the greatness of Your compassion blot out my transgressions. Wash me thoroughly from my iniquity and cleanse me from my sin" (Psalm 51:1-2).

Solomon learned from his father, King David. He learned to hope in the Lord and trust His commandments. "Hope deferred makes the heart sick, but desire fulfilled is a tree of life. The one who despises the word will be in debt to it, but the one who fears the commandment will be rewarded" (Proverbs 13:12-13). In his later years, Solomon forgot his own counsel. He experienced the "debt to the word." Solomon began to depend on his own human wisdom. He was not able to transfer to his son what he had received from his father David.

Biblical hope affects more than our own life. It affects the generations. David's hope in God has had a profound effect on millions down through the ages. David's greater Son, the Lord Jesus Christ, came to establish hope for mankind. Because of the cross and the resurrection, the Holy Spirit is able to impart an eternal hope that will fully be revealed at the Lord's appearing. Tomorrow, we will consider "hope" as a New Covenant believer in Christ.

Father, I thank You for Your servant David, who laid such a wonderful foundation of hope through his words and his life testimony. I pray You will help me be established, day by day in the hope which the Holy Spirit imparts.

## November 11 – FAITH, THE SUBSTANCE OF HOPE

Hebrews 11:1 – Now faith is the assurance of things hoped for, the conviction of things not seen.

Hebrews 11:1 – lays the foundation for faith. The eleventh chapter of Hebrews has been called "the honor role of faith." Note how the writer begins verse 1, "now faith is." What a powerful expression of absolute trust. The writer does not say faith might be, but is! Is what? It is the assurance of the things hoped for. I like the way the King James expresses this passage. "Now faith is the substance of things hoped for, the evidence of things not seen" KJV. I appreciate the word "substance" because it speaks of the spiritual material from which hope is formed. Material objects have "molecules", whereas biblical faith is the substance of "hope." This expectation of hope means "an absolute confidence." It is so real it is made of the "evidence of things not seen".

The rational mind has great difficulty with this kind of thinking. The spiritual person knows this kind of thinking is what causes miracles to take place through a believer. As a believer in Christ, our hope is in His resurrection power. "We had the sentence of death within ourselves so that we would not trust in ourselves, but in God who raises the dead; who delivered us from so great a peril of death, and will deliver us, He on whom we have set our hope. He will yet deliver us" (2 Corinthians 1:9-11). This is New Testament Christianity! Listen how Paul expresses hope to the Roman believers. "May the God of hope fill you with all joy and peace in believing, so that you will abound in hope by the power of the Holy Spirit" (Romans 15:13).

Jesus, when quoting Isaiah 42:2 declares "He will lead justice to victory" (Matthew 12:20). The Pharisees had gone out to conspire against the Lord how they may destroy Him. Jesus, aware of their plans, withdrew Himself and then healed the sick and gave the people warnings. He quoted Isaiah 42:2-3 so the people would know He was the one fulfilling Isaiah's prophetic declaration. Our hope is rooted in Jesus because He fulfilled the prophetic words given by the Prophets of old. God's word has proven true. Christ's resurrection established God's covenant forever. As we trust in Christ, we are brought into a place of "assurance and conviction" that makes up our faith. Faith is the substance of our hope. We can experience peace and joy presently, while waiting for His return. "Looking for the blessed hope and the appearing of the glory of our great God and Savior, Christ Jesus" (Titus 2:13).

Our faith flows out of our hope in the resurrection. We are to work His works in faith as we wait for His return and the glory that will be revealed. Pray to grow in the substance of faith that your hope may be firm and increase unto His coming. Let hope be settled about who you are in Christ. Grow in faith that will move mountains of resistance. By faith see the victory over sin, sickness, demonic strongholds, and anything else that would dare to resist God's purpose in your life.

Father, by Your Spirit, I ask You to help me be one who moves in faith. Cause hope to increase in me as the substance of faith enlarges and my confidence grows. Give me courage to resist doubt and unbelief. Use me to bring others to faith and hope through the power of Your Holy Spirit residing in me.

## November 12 – HOPE AGAINST HOPE

Romans 4:18 – In hope against hope he believed, so that he might become a father of many nations according to that which had been spoken, "So Shall Your Descendants Be."

This is an interesting Scripture. Abraham "hoped" because he believed. All the evidence was against such a position. The Scriptures indicate that Abraham gave consideration to his body and his age, but he did not become weak in his faith. Abraham trusted the "promise" of God. He did not waver in unbelief, even though all evidence suggested he should just accept his physical condition at the age of 100. Physically speaking, he could not produce children. "Abraham grew strong in faith giving God the glory" (Romans 4:20). Abraham was fully persuaded that what God had promised, He was able to perform. Is it any wonder he is called the "father of the faithful"?

As believers in Christ, it is important to realize that we received our introduction by faith into this grace in which we stand. Our greatest expectation is hope of the glory of God. At the same time, we glory in tribulation. The reason we are to glory in tribulation is because it produces a number of attributes. "Tribulation brings about perseverance; and perseverance, proven character; and proven character, hope; and hope does not disappoint, because the love of God has been poured out within our hearts through the Holy Spirit who was given to us" (Romans 5:3-5).

Abraham knew tribulation, but faith grew because he believed God's promise over rational reasoning. This kind of language and suggestion is an offense to the natural man. It is why the scriptures speak of the cross as an offense. How can belief in the death of Christ bring about eternal life for individuals? It just does not make sense to the rational man. On the other hand, the natural man does not receive the things of the Spirit because they are spiritually understood. It takes the Holy Spirit to reveal Christ. It takes the Holy Spirit to give us faith and hope. Through the Holy Spirit, love is poured out within our hearts.

Faith, hope, and love are three cords that cannot be easily broken. The greatest of the three is love. It is love that undergirds everything else. As a believer, it is important to nurture these three attributes. They find their greatest development in a believer's life through challenges which create an atmosphere for their development. What challenges are you facing today? Inquire of the Lord about developing faith for those challenges. Let faith become the substance of hope toward your challenge. Trust the Holy Spirit to help you walk in faith by love.

Father, grant me grace to live a life of faith, producing hope, and working by love. As Abraham of old had hope against hope, I pray that I too, might live in a high level of hope when facing impossible circumstances in my life.

## November 13 – THE LOVE OF GOD HAS BEEN POURED OUT WITHIN OUR HEARTS

Romans 5:4 – The love of God has been poured out within our hearts through the Holy Spirit who was given to us.

Imagine, the God of all creation has poured out His love in the heart of every believer. The Lord does this through the Holy Spirit when He is given to the believer. We have been devoting ourselves to the subject of faith and hope. We now will consider love and how it is the foundation to faith and hope.

"In Christ Jesus, neither circumcision nor uncircumcision means anything, but faith working through love" (Galatians 5:6). A major issue which Paul had to address was the question concerning the need to be circumcised in order to legitimately be a Christian. Paul is clear on the subject. Only faith working by love matters.

Paul wrote to the Corinthians and listed many things that confirmed his calling and apostolic ministry. Within the list he cites, ". . . in purity, in knowledge, in patience, in kindness, in the Holy Spirit, in genuine love" (2 Corinthians 6:6-7). Every believer has been called to freedom in Christ. This freedom empowers us to serve others. The heart of the gospel of the kingdom is in "serving others." This involves reaching out to another who is hurting, broken, and trying to find their way to God. We are to use our freedom for their benefit. We are to never take advantage of a brother or sister to benefit ourselves. Paul says, "Through love serve one another."

The love of God is difficult to grasp. It is foreign to the various types of human love. The love of God requires one to give up their life for the sake of another. It is impossible to operate in God's love without the Holy Spirit's participation. He has to impart the Love of God and then we must receive His love. Finally, we choose to administer His love to another.

In John 21:15-19, the Lord sought to help Peter come to know the love of God by asking him, "Do you love me more than these?" Jesus did this three times. Each time, as Peter answered in the affirmative, Jesus directed him to take care of His lambs. In Acts 13, Paul and Barnabas were called by the Holy Spirit to go to the Gentiles and proclaim the love of God. They experienced beatings and stoning in their ministry. In spite of the despicable way they were treated, they pressed forward in faith and hope motivated by the love of God revealed in the Lord Jesus Christ.

Father, I ask You to fill me day by day with Your love, drawing me ever deeper into intimacy with You. I pray to know more and more of the love of God found in Christ Jesus, my Lord. I ask You to help me to grow up into a fuller manifestation of Christ's love for others, and to come closer to loving as You love.

## November 14 – IN THE CROSS, LOVE IS BIRTHED

John 13:3-4 – Jesus, knowing that the Father had given all things into His hands, and that He had come forth from God and was going back to God, got up from supper, and laid aside His garments; and taking a towel, He girded Himself.

The thirteenth chapter of John brings together a number of important insights for our own development in the love of God. Before the Feast of Passover, Jesus knew His time had come to die, passing from this world to the Father. The scripture says of Jesus, "Having loved His own who were in the world, He loved them to the end" (John 13:1b). As Jesus partakes of His last meal with His disciples, He knows that the devil already put it into the heart of Judas to betray Him. He knows that the Father had given all things into His hands. With that knowledge, He prepares to wash His disciple's feet.

Once again, Peter becomes an example for us. His human nature is so much like all of ours. I thank God for Peter. Jesus came to Peter to wash his feet. Peter responded in a way which was typical for him when he said, "Never shall You wash my feet!" (John 13:8a). Jesus was very clear with Peter, "If I do not wash you, you have no part with Me" (John 13:8b).

The love of God was being demonstrated in the upper room toward these disciples. Jesus the Servant, modeled the love of God to each one of His disciples, even with the knowledge that one of them was about to betray Him. He told His disciples, "You are clean, but not all of you" (John 13:11). The love of God was about to be demonstrated to the whole world as Jesus, God's Servant, hung on the cross for our sins. He took the punishment for sin and death. He went to hell in our place. He overcame death and hell and now reigns in victory over all. By faith, as we embrace what the Lord accomplished for each one of us, the love of God is born in our hearts.

In his letter to the church, the Apostle John is very clear about the operation of God's love in the believer. "The one who does not love does not know God, for God is love. By this, the love of God was manifested in us, that God has sent His only begotten Son into the world so that we might live through Him" (John 4:8-9). The manifestation is in the transforming work of God's love in us. The world can only know the "love of God" by what is manifested in our lives. When someone is "born again," they are born into the love of God. The true sign of God's rule in our life is God's love.

Maturity in Christ is evaluated by the manifestation of God's love. "In this is love, not that we loved God, but that He loved us and sent His Son to be the propitiation for our sins. Beloved, if God so loved us, we also ought to love one another" (John 4:10-11). Jesus came to bear our sins. We then, must forgive others. Forgiveness demonstrates the love of God in our hearts. Let me be clear, the believer is in a state of growth. Some have worked through their issues of unforgiveness more than others. Our salvation is witnessed by God's love manifested in us. The Holy Spirit wants to show us the areas we have not yet developed in His love. If You are aware of issues in your life where you do not have God's love manifested in you toward others, the Holy Spirit wants to help you.

Father, I thank You for Your love poured out at the cross through my Lord Jesus Christ. Because of the cross, I thank You for the Holy Spirit who is now poured out in the hearts of believers such as myself. Fill me with the love of God, especially towards those who are difficult to love.

## November 15 – PERFECTING THE LOVE OF GOD

1 John 4:12 – No one has seen God at any time; if we love one another, God abides in us, and His love is perfected in us. By this we know that we abide in Him and He in us, because He has given us of His Spirit. We have seen and testify that the Father has sent the Son to be the Savior of the world.

The subject of the love of God is enormous. John reminds us that no one has seen God at any time. Jesus was the manifestation of God in human form. "He who has seen Me, has seen the Father" (John 14:9). John goes on to say that "God abides in us." If we have repented of sin and received God's love in the person of Jesus Christ through the power of the Holy Spirit, God is abiding in us. If that is true, then His love is being perfected in us as well. In Christ, we are in a state of growth and development that has its manifestation in God's love. He gave us the Holy Spirit for the purpose of developing in us the same love of Christ revealed in Jesus' earthly life and ministry.

John writes, "If we love one another, God abides in us, and His love is perfected in us." How can we reconcile the divisions and sometimes mean-spiritedness seen in the body of Christ? First, we need to understand that John is giving us the ideal. The goal of maturing is the "love of God manifested in a believer's life. God's love is being perfected in us. Second, it is understood that believers are in a state of development, "working out their own salvation with fear and trembling." There are some who deal with the brokenness of their lives for many years. The important factor is an effort to press into God's love and allow His love to be expressed through the stages of growth.

Many wrestle with their own security in the "love of God" because they have difficulty receiving His love for themselves, let alone abiding in His love, and then releasing it to others. This is why it is so important to take time in the initial process of coming into the Christian faith. It is tempting to hurry people through the process like cattle, rather than leading them like sheep. We make joining the organization the greater importance, when healing of their past wounds and receiving God's love for specific areas in their life should be our objective. As the believer learns to die to "the old" self and embrace "the new" in "the Holy Spirit," they can learn to abide in God's love and His sustaining power.

Father, I ask You for help in perfecting Your love in my life. I ask for the same love to fill me that worked in Jesus throughout His earthly ministry. Show me anything which blocks Your love from growing in me. Help me to repent and forsake any obstacles that are in the way.

## November 16 – HOLD FAST YOUR CONFESSION IN CHRIST

Hebrews 3:1 – Holy brethren, partakers of a heavenly calling, consider Jesus, the Apostle and High Priest of our confession.

The book of Hebrews has been called the "Royal Book." It addresses the royalty of Christ. He is the One every true believer confesses as King of kings and Lord of lords. He is our High Priest. Jesus is the One "He ever lives to make intercession for us," We can draw near with confidence to the throne because our redeemer has passed into the heavens. He is able to understand the weakness we have because of sin. He was tempted in every way as we are, yet without sin.

The book of Hebrews was written to Jewish believers who had been experiencing severe persecution. The intended readers were thinking of abandoning their faith and of lapsing back to Judaism. The author exhorts them to hold fast to their confession of Jesus Christ as Savior and Lord. Hebrews 10 is a powerful portion of scripture that establishes what Christ has fully done for each believer. "Let us hold fast the confession of our hope without wavering, for He who promised is faithful; and let us consider how to stimulate one another to love and good deeds" (Hebrews 10:23-24).

In the past, these believers followed the Law of Moses which instructed God's Covenant people to bring continual sacrifices for sin. The author wants these Jewish believers to understand the Law was only a shadow of the good things to come. Further, the sacrifices they once offered year by year could not make them perfect. If the Law could have produced perfection, the worshipers would no longer be conscious of sin. Instead the law was a constant reminder of their need to receive God's forgiveness. In Hebrews 10, he writes of the impossibility of the blood of animals to take away sin. Those sacrifices atoned or covered up sin so God could have mercy upon His people. The Father looked ahead to the better sacrifice which He would offer on behalf of lost humanity. Only one sacrifice was needed now, the sacrifice of Christ. The one sacrifice of Christ is sufficient.

A new and living way has been established. Through the blood of Christ, we have confidence to enter into the holy place. "A new and living way was inaugurated for us through the veil, that is, His flesh" (Hebrews 10:20). Because we have a great high priest over the house of God we can draw near with a sincere heart in full assurance of faith because our hearts have been washed in His blood. Our confidence is in these facts. The writer says, "Let us hold fast the confession of our hope without wavering, for He who promised is faithful" (Hebrews 10:23). From this position, we are to stimulate one another to love and good deeds.

The writer encourages these Jewish believers in what God accomplished through the faithfulness in Christ when he exhorts, "Not forsaking our own assembling together, as is the habit of some, but encouraging one another; and all the more as you see the day drawing near" (Hebrews 10:25). Tomorrow, we will consider why it is important to encourage one another as the Day of Judgment draws near.

Father, I thank You for Your ultimate sacrifice on my behalf, Your own Son. Thank You that my conscience has been cleansed through the blood of Christ so I can have confidence to enter into Your presence. I commit myself to hold fast to my confession, drawing near with a sincere heart in full assurance of faith.

## November 17 – CHRIST OR JUDGMENT

Hebrews 10:26 – If we go on sinning willfully after receiving the knowledge of the truth, there no longer remains a sacrifice for sins.

The writer of Hebrews gives this severe warning based upon what he had previously written concerning the "one-time offering of the sacrifice of Christ." Remember, these Jewish believers considered returning back to their Judaism because of the severity of the persecution they were experiencing. The writer of Hebrews established the "one-time sacrifice of Christ" as the finished work of God. There remains no more sacrifice, only a fearful looking ahead to judgment.

The threefold purpose of the will of God can be seen in a summary of the New Testament:

> ➤ Christ's sacrifice and the power of His resurrection
> ➤ The coming of the Holy Spirit to bring forth God's new creation in the earth through believers in Christ's eternal work. The result being Christ revealed in each believer as a witness to the world of the truth of the Gospel of the Kingdom of God
> ➤ The return of Christ when He judges both the "quick and the dead." In other words, the living and those who had died.

There is no more sacrifice to be offered, only what Christ has already done. The only thing remaining is Judgment Day.

Hebrews 10:26-31 are difficult scriptures for some to understand, especially if they are not read in the context of the writer's letter. "If we go on sinning willfully after receiving the knowledge of the truth, there no longer remains a sacrifice for sins" (Hebrews 10:26a). The emphasis is on "willfully." In his letter, the Apostle John gives the thought, "continues to practice sin" (1 John 3:9). Receiving the knowledge of the truth does not mean born again. It implies that one has heard the truth and understands its implication: Christ is the end of sacrifices. "There no longer remains a sacrifice for sins (no more sacrifices will be offered), but a terrifying expectation of judgment and the fury of a fire which will consume the adversaries" (Hebrews 10:26b–27). The issue here is going back to the Law as a means of salvation. In the Law, there were continual sacrifices offered for sins. Christ became the end of the Law for dealing with sin. This is why the writer says that there is no more sacrifice. The one and only acceptable sacrifice is Christ's death.

For these Jewish believers, going back under the Law would be trampling underfoot the Son of God. It would be regarding the blood of the sacrifice as unclean and would be an insult to the Spirit of grace. If the sacrifice of Christ is rejected then the only expectation is judgment. The Lord will judge His people. The writer uses the Law as his example. "Anyone who has set aside the Law of Moses dies without mercy on the testimony of two or three witnesses" (Hebrews 10:28). He then says, "How much more severe punishment do you think he will deserve who has trampled underfoot the Son of God, and regarded unclean the blood of the covenant by which he was sanctified and has insulted the Spirit of grace" (Hebrews 10:29).

The writer is making this point: don't go back, because only judgment will lie ahead. He then reminds these Jewish believers of the entrance into the kingdom of God beginning in verses 32-34. "Therefore, do not throw away your confidence, which has a great reward" (Hebrews 10:35). Tomorrow we will devote ourselves to this great exhortation.

Father, I thank You for the blood sacrificed in Christ's death. I plant my confidence firmly in His blood. My sins have been cleansed, and I am sanctified through Your covenant in Christ.

# November 18 – YOU HAVE NEED
# OF ENDURANCE

Hebrews 10:35-37 – Therefore, do not throw away your confidence, which has a great reward. For you have need of endurance, so that when you have done the will of God, you may receive what was promised.

Confidence comes from trusting in the Lord no matter what our circumstances look like. These Hebrew Christians needed to be encouraged in God's absolutes because of the severe persecution they were enduring. It is difficult to keep your eye on the prize when you are being beat up on every side. Every believer goes through difficulties in their spiritual journey. Some have more challenges than others. Some believers have become discouraged and quit trying; others have been pulled into a fringe type group not teaching the gospel of the kingdom of God.

As believers, we have been given promises by God. We all need endurance to keep going until we receive the promise. This is the life of faith. In the case of these Hebrew believers, the promise the writer is addressing is the return of Christ. "Behold, I am coming quickly, and My reward is with Me, to render to every man according to what he has done. I am the Alpha and the Omega, the first and the last, the beginning and the end" (Revelation 22:12-13).

The Scriptures declare that the righteous live by faith. "Behold, as for the proud one, his soul is not right within him; but the righteous will live by his faith" (Habakkuk 2:4). Hebrews says, "If he shrinks back, My soul will have no pleasure in him" (Hebrews 10:38b). The Lord's pleasure is in righteousness. The author of Hebrews writes, "We are not of those who shrink back to destruction, but of those who have faith to the preserving of the soul" (Hebrews 10:39).

God's desire for each believer is "persevering faith." It is from this base of exhortation we read of the honor roll of faith in Hebrews 11. What a list of "by faith" people we find.

> ➢ By faith, Able offered to God a better sacrifice than Cain
> ➢ By faith, Enoch was taken, so that he would not see death

- By faith, Noah . . . prepared an ark for the salvation of his household
- By faith, Abraham when he was called, obeyed
- By faith, even Sarah herself received the ability to conceive, even beyond the proper time of life, since she considered Him faithful who had promised
- Many more are listed who lived by faith

Hebrews 11:39, "All these, having gained approval through their faith, did not receive what was promised, because God had provided something better for us, so that apart from us they would not be made perfect." Beloved, in Christ we are being made perfect by faith.

Father, I call on You to help me be preserved in faith. I thank You for all those who have gone before me that lived a life of faith. I pray that I might grow in my ability to abide in Your love and press toward the prize that is in Christ Jesus my Lord.

## November 19 – JESUS, MY EXAMPLE

Hebrews 12:1 – Since we have so great a cloud of witnesses surrounding us, let us also lay aside every encumbrance and the sin which so easily entangles us, and let us run with endurance the race that is set before us, fixing our eyes on Jesus.

The writer of Hebrews pulls all of his thoughts together in this verse. The fact is, many have gone before us, which walked through challenges, temptations, and impossible circumstances. If they overcame, we can overcome too, because the one they were looking for has come. Sin is a nuisance for the believer, but it can be conquered in the power of Christ's life giving Spirit. Jesus Christ overcame sin and the devil. He overcame in His flesh. When He was tempted by the devil, as recorded in Matthew 4 and Luke 4, He overcame by the Word of God. The devil tempted Him in the three major areas of human's life. He overcame in His spirit, His soul, and His body.

Jesus, the author and finisher of our faith, set an example for us in how He resisted the evil one and served the purpose of His heavenly Father. Jesus was able to overcome through the power of the Holy Spirit which has been poured out for all flesh.

God the Father, through faith in Christ's finished work, has given us the promise of the "Gift of the Holy Spirit" (Luke 24:49). It will take the "power of the Holy Spirit" to overcome the flesh and the devil (Acts 1:8).

In the Book of Hebrews the cloud of witnesses were all Old Testament saints who looked for Messiah's Day by faith. As we look back, the cloud of witnesses has greatly increased. It includes the saints of the first century and many others down through the centuries to our present time that are with the Lord and will come with Him when He returns to judge all unrighteousness.

Clear instructions have been given to each one of us throughout the Scriptures that we too are to overcome by faith. The writer of Hebrews speaks to each of our lives, as referenced in our devotional scripture, "Let us also lay aside every encumbrance and the sin which so easily entangles us, and let us run with endurance the race that is set before us, fixing our eyes on Jesus." What are the encumbrances you face? What is the sin that dogs your feet? As we approach the end of another year, prepare your heart before the Lord to let go of encumbrances and sin. Allow the Holy Spirit to search your heart and reveal where He would be pleased to help you find freedom through Christ and His overcoming life.

The enemy of our soul has as his objective "entanglements." It is entanglements which hinder our race. Each of us needs endurance to finish the course and stand before the Lord Jesus Christ confident we have finished well. Only as we "fix" our eyes on Jesus can we stay untangled and filled with endurance. Today, if you hear His voice through the writer of Hebrews, commit your life to the race. Begin now to remove the "entanglements." Allow the Holy Spirit to search your heart for any areas of sin. Repent and let the blood of Jesus cleanse you. Be filled afresh with His Holy Spirit, asking for endurance in the race.

Father, search me and see if there are any hindrances to the race I am called to run. Let all encumbrances and any sin, whether or not I am aware of them, be repented of and cleansed. Help me, daily, to fix my eyes on Jesus. I pray that the year ahead will be the best yet in my pursuit of Your will and purposes.

# November 20 – THE AUTHOR AND PERFECTOR OF OUR FAITH

Hebrews 12:2 – Fixing our eyes on Jesus, the author and finisher of our faith; who for the joy that was set before Him endured the cross, despising the shame, and is set down at the right hand of the throne of God (KJV).

Do we see Jesus simply as a part of history or perhaps an important religious figure? Is he a theological figure in the New Testament to us, a great teacher? Perhaps we have embraced Him as our personal Savior. In our scripture today, the writer says we are to "fix our eyes" on the Lord Jesus. Further, He is the "author and finisher of our faith." Everything begins with Him and ends with Him. In the book of Revelation, Jesus calls Himself, "the Alpha and the Omega" (Rev. 1:8). John the Apostle calls Jesus, the faithful witness, the firstborn of the dead, and the ruler of the kings of the earth" (Rev. 1:5).

Consider the instruction, "fixing our eyes on Jesus." How often is He looked to first? How much time do believers spend thinking about Jesus and His human expression of God's love lived out in our midst. He is our example. More than that, His life resides in the believer through the power of the Holy Spirit. A believer has a moment-by-moment choice: draw from the old self or receive from the new life rooted in Jesus Christ.

Fixing our eyes means more than to look upon. Obviously, we do not physically see Jesus, but we can look upon Him as the one who completely lived out the Father's will. We can read and meditate on His word, and we can see the results for those who have trusted Him throughout their life.

Jesus authored our faith. The word finisher in the KJV means "perfected." In order to fix our eyes on Jesus, we must read, study, and meditate upon the Word of God. We must learn what the author of our faith has said. Because He has already run the course and finished it, we can receive faith that leads to hope as we now run the course by His life that dwells in us. As He finished well, we too can finish well if we stay fixed upon Him.

Our verse says Jesus endured the cross because of joy. How can this be? He offered His life as a ransom for many that He knew would trust God for redemption. He despised the shame of the cross, but accepted it because He knew it was the only means to man's redemption. When His work was finished, He sat down next to His Father. Being seated speaks of rest. Jesus is at rest having done the will of God. You and I might be anxious about many things, but our rest is found in His completed work of our salvation.

Fix your eyes on the risen Lord. Receive His rest for your life today. Be anxious for nothing, but by prayer and supplication make your requests known to Him. Endure hardships, letting the Holy Spirit work maturity in your growing life found in Christ.

Father, I choose to fix my eyes on Your Son and not on the circumstances of this life. I confess today that greater is He that is in me than he that is in the world. I know that Your Son is the author and finisher of my faith. I receive the help of the Holy Spirit to finish well.

## November 21 – CONSIDER HIM

Hebrews 12:3 – Consider Him who has endured such hostility by sinners against Himself, so that you will not grow weary and lose heart.

When life becomes difficult through many trials and tribulations, especially personal attacks because of your faith in Christ, it becomes easy to grow weary and lose heart. This was the case for these Jewish believers. These believing Jews were the "remnant" who trusted Christ. The majority of their fellow Jews rejected Messiah's Day. That majority made it very difficult on the remnant that trusted the good news of the Gospel of Christ's overcoming kingdom.

As believers, we have faith in Christ's finished work through His cross. We also trust in the promised future resurrection of all believers and His glorious return with His saints to judge all unrighteousness. By faith, we receive the Gift of the Holy Spirit, the promise of the Father. When persecution and resistance comes to our faith, it can be shaken. When our expectations are delayed, this too can cause us to lose heart as these precious saints were experiencing. "Hope deferred makes the heart sick, but desire fulfilled is a tree of life" (Proverbs 13:12). The life of faith walks between these two tensions, "hope deferred and desire fulfilled."

Our author speaks to us as he says, "consider Him." Jesus' life is our example. Jesus' life in us is our hope. Paul exhorts each believer, "Put on the new self who is being renewed to a true knowledge according to the image of the One who created him" (Colossians 3:10). Read Colossians and receive Paul's instructions and his understandings of our battle. We must take action and "put on the new self." His life is present, but by faith we must put it on day by day. In each new challenge, make it your habit to turn to God your Father and in Jesus' name through the power of the Holy Spirit, put on the mind of Christ. You might ask, "How is that done?".

> ➤ When you are faced with difficulties, stop and ask for God's presence.
> ➤ Recommit your entire life to Christ and surrender your thoughts, emotions, and will to Him.
> ➤ Ask the Father, in Jesus' name, for the guidance of the Holy Spirit.
> ➤ Forgive those who are causing you trouble and thank the Lord for the opportunity to experience the sufferings of Christ.
> ➤ Ask to learn obedience through this time, even as Christ learned obedience through sufferings.
> ➤ Renew your faith in the hope of His glorious return with all His saints.

This will be a good start in putting on the mind of Christ. The Lord has called us to partnership with Him. He did the hard work, now we are to live out what was accomplished through His finished work at Calvary.

Father, in Jesus' name and through the power of Your Holy Spirit, I ask for the mind of Christ today. As I consider Him who has endured such hostility by sinners against Himself, I know it was for me and all who believe that He suffered. Strengthen me in the hope of my calling as I journey toward that expected day of Christ's return.

# November 22 – THE FATHER'S DISCIPLINE

Hebrews 12:5 – My son, do not regard lightly the discipline of the Lord, nor faint when you are reproved by Him.

This section of scripture is one of the strongest affirmations of the Father's love toward every believer. The phrase "my son" carries with it a very strong commitment of love. For Father God to address us as sons puts us on an equal level with Christ. Because of Christ's sacrifice of His life for our sins, we have access to the Father as sons of God. This includes believing women in much the same way as believing men become part of the bride of Christ.

The writer begins his thoughts early in verse 4 saying, "You have not yet resisted to the point of shedding blood in your striving against sin." In short, he is saying that Jesus shed His blood to deal with the issue of sin. You have not lost your life battling sin. Then he reminds his readers of the Lord's exhortation found in Proverbs 3:11: "My son, do not reject the discipline of the Lord or loathe His reproof." Do we understand that hardships are really opportunities for the Lord to develop us as mature sons of God? As one grows older, it becomes easier to identify how the Lord used difficulties to develop a Christ-centered maturity in our life. The difficult times were really instruction times from God used to train us.

Solomon reminds us, "If you are slack in the day of distress, your strength is limited" (Proverbs 24:10). The word slack means "to give up." Weakness would be to not understand God's purpose in the times of trouble which prepares us so that we will endure to the end. The Lord does not discipline our lives in order to cause us to give up, but rather for us to learn how to endure. Because He loves us, He instructs us by the pressures and trials of life. Even when He finds it necessary to punish us, it is always with a view toward our benefit.

Beloved, God deals with believers as "sons." Even in the natural realm we know that a good father will discipline his son. A believer is subject to the Father of spirits and through discipline, the believer grows to maturity. Discipline for the moment is never enjoyable; in fact, it can really feel uncomfortable and perhaps sorrowful. If we receive it for its intended purpose, it will produce "the peaceable fruit of righteousness" (Hebrews 12:11).

"Therefore, strengthen the hands that are weak and the knees that are feeble" (Hebrews 12:12). As we become strong in the Lord through His disciplines, we can turn our attention to others to be a conduit of His grace to help in their time of weakness. Rejoice in correction, learn to appreciate rebuke, and learn in humility. His favor is on you when He applies divine discipline. Many times it comes through others. Don't resist, but allow His Holy Spirit to sanctify you through the process.

Father, I thank You for Your great love revealed in Christ and continued through Your wonderful disciplines used to mature me in Christ my Lord. Fill me with gratitude for Your favor upon me as a son of God through corrections and reproofs.

## November 23 – GRATITUDE IS THE BEST ATTITUDE

Hebrews 12:28-29 – We receive a kingdom which cannot be shaken, let us show gratitude, by which we may offer to God an acceptable service with reverence and awe; for our God is a consuming fire.

The writer of Hebrews had been speaking of "the unshaken kingdom." He admonishes the reader not to refuse the Lord who is speaking from heaven like those of old refused the one who spoke from earth, chiefly Moses and the Law. The ground shook when God spoke from the mountain to Israel. God promised to shake not only the earth, but heaven as well. The Lord indicates the removing of things that can be shaken. He also declares there are things which cannot be shaken. It is in this context the writer assures us that we are receiving a kingdom which cannot be shaken.

As a believer our attitude should be one of gratitude. If we are in Christ Jesus through faith in His finished work at the cross, then we have been made partakers of an "unshakable kingdom." No matter what happens around us, we are firmly established in Him. Shaking will take place. There are those things which will be consumed, "for our God is a consuming fire." His eternal plans for His kids are settled. From this truth and our understanding, gratitude should dominate our life. From that gratitude flows – "an acceptable service." The service the writer is addressing is a life of praise and worship.

Gratitude cannot be worked up, but is an attitude of the heart that comes from the knowledge of who we are in Christ Jesus the Lord. It is knowledge that we have a heavenly Father who has given us all things that cannot be removed for His praise and glory. With that knowledge firmly established, praise and worship becomes a constant in our life.

This is a season when Americans celebrate what God has given us, principally "freedom and liberty" rooted in a strong faith in God through the Gospel of the Kingdom of God. Many have lost vision regarding the true meaning of the first Thanksgiving the Pilgrims celebrated. There is a great shaking happening in both the nation of America and throughout the nations of the world. Nevertheless, God's kingdom cannot be shaken. Only our wrong concepts of His purposes can be consumed.

Let gratitude fill your heart today for all that our great God and King has done. Regardless of what is happening around us, what we see on the television news of the shaking of our culture; we must know that our God reigns! His promises are sure. He never changes! For that reason His eternal plans will be accomplished. "Walk in Him, having been firmly rooted and now being built up in Him and established in your faith, just as you were instructed, and overflowing with gratitude (Colossians 2:6-7).

"For everything created by God is good, and nothing is to be rejected if it is received with gratitude; for it is sanctified by means of the word of God and prayer" (1 Timothy 4:4-5).

Father, I thank You that You are good. Fill me with gratitude for all You have done in Christ Jesus. From that gratitude, open my spirit so that heavenly praise and worship might flow from my innermost being. Give to me a true heart of gratitude.

# November 24 – FILLED WITH THANKSGIVING

Psalm 100 – "Shout joyfully to the Lord, all the earth. Serve the Lord with gladness; come before Him with joyful singing. Know that the Lord Himself is God; it is He who has made us, and not we ourselves; we are His people and the sheep of His pasture. Enter His gates with thanksgiving and His courts with praise. Give thanks to Him, bless His name. For the Lord is good; His loving-kindness is everlasting and His faithfulness to all generations."

What an expression of praise and thankfulness! When it comes to the Lord, a quiet thank you does not seem sufficient. Shout to the Lord. There have been times when I just had to lift my voice to a loud level and shout to the Lord. Not shout at the Lord, but to the Lord. It was not because He was hard of hearing, but simply because He is worthy to receive my praise and thanks with all my strength.

Part of being filled with the Holy Spirit is being filled to overflowing with praise, thanksgiving, and gratitude for all our great God and King has done for us. Truly, there is no one like our God! Consider how our God humbled Himself and became as one of us. God, who is Spirit, took on our form in the person of the Lord Jesus Christ. The God of all creation allowed His created man to crucify His flesh on the "Old Rugged Cross," the cross stained with the blood of our Creator and now our Redeemer. What utter shame, complete rejection, and absolute cruelty He endured. Love beyond imagination, love so sublime was poured out all for you and me.

It is difficult to comprehend this kind of love! It is a love for individuals, a love for communities of people, and a love for the nations. The entire world has known His love. God's love spread from Israel to Asia Minor and Europe and then across the Atlantic Ocean to what became America the Beautiful. The Gospel spread from Europe and America to the nations of the world. The message of God's salvation is so rich and so free. The Gospel continues to impact the nations as Asia is filled with men and women born into the kingdom of God. The Gospel is not static. It is a dynamic force in the earth bringing transformation to those who will believe what Christ has accomplished in His death, burial, and resurrection.

Like the Sun that moves across the sky from east to west, the Gospel is moving back to Jerusalem. Its power will transform Arab nations to trust in Christ. Eventually, a great company of Jewish people will come to know the Messiah who died for them, as the nations are harvested for Christ. Rejoice O Saints of God! We are victorious in the end!

As Americans celebrate the National Day of Thanksgiving, let us remember what God has done for all mankind. Here are a few scriptures to encourage us as we express personal gratitude to the Creator and Redeemer of our souls.

"Now He who supplies seed to the sower and bread for food will supply and multiply your seed for sowing and increase the harvest of your righteousness; you will be enriched in everything for all liberality, which through us is producing thanksgiving to God" (2 Corinthians 9:10-11).

"Be anxious for nothing, but in everything by prayer and supplication with thanksgiving let your requests be made known to God" (Philippians 4:6). "Devote yourselves to prayer, keeping alert in it with an attitude of thanksgiving" (Colossians 4:2). "Amen, blessing, and glory, and wisdom, and thanksgiving, and honor, and power, and might, be to our God forever and ever. Amen" (Revelation 7:12).

## November 25 – THE CHANGELESS CHRIST

Hebrews 13:5 – I will never leave you, nor will I ever forsake you.

With confidence we can say the Lord is my helper, I will not be afraid. We are living in questionable times. Many of the certainties we have known in the past have disappeared. More and more uncertainty grips the hearts of people. As we have spoken of before, God is shaking everything. Only the unchangeableness of Christ cannot be moved. It is in His promises every believer can depend. We must draw near to the Lord through the indwelling presence of the Holy Spirit to receive the confidence necessary in these challenging days.

As we move toward the Christmas season, it is vital that we seek the wisdom of God regarding finances. The world will be working hard to draw people into debt. The world will play on our emotions, both through guilt and greed. The Scriptures state, "Make sure that your character is free from the love of money, being content with what you have" (Hebrews 13:5a). Perhaps this is a time for simplicity rather than extravagance in terms of material things. During this season, I want to seek the Lord for a greater simplicity in my lifestyle and an increase of extravagance in terms of consideration and love of others. Would you join me in greater expressions of gratitude to our heavenly Father for His blessings and increased expressions of love toward others?

The Lord desires to draw closer and closer to us. The willingness of our heart to give the reigns of our life to Him is what draws the Holy Spirit into increased intimacy with us. He is waiting for our invitation for Him to draw near. There are times when it feels like the Spirit of God has taken leave. He really has not, for He promised to never leave us nor forsake us. He waits for us to be desperate for His presence. It is a prepared heart that the Lord desires, not a need for a momentary fix.

As we prepare for the Christmas season, be reminded how the Lord spoke through the prophets of old concerning the day He would dwell among His people. He looked forward to the time He would be among those who named the name of the Lord. His desire has not changed. He sent His Holy Spirit to indwell our lives, filling us with the presence of the Lord. He so desires to draw close during this time of remembrance of His birth long ago. Let us first remember to seek Him and invite His presence among us. Next, let's remember others above ourselves. Finally, let us reach out to those less fortunate, even as the Lord reached out to us.

Father, again I give thanks to You for all Your multiplied blessings in my life. Your love to me is so undeserved, but I receive it with gratitude. Work deeply in me that I might communicate Your love to others. I stand in the knowledge that You will never leave me nor forsake me.

# November 26 – BE EQUIPPED IN EVERY GOOD WORK

Hebrews 13:20-21 – Now the God of peace equip you in every good thing to do His will, working in us that which is pleasing in His sight.

The Scripture above is part of the benediction the writer of Hebrews gives as he brings his letter to an end. The benedictions of the Apostles emphasize "peace." True peace can only be found in "the God of peace." Men have sought to establish peace in the earth, but it has been a peace on their terms. True peace can only become reality when the "Prince of Peace" is received. The true peace of God was brought about when He raised Jesus from the dead. He is the great Shepherd of the sheep through the blood of the eternal covenant.

Jesus equips His saints in every good thing to do His will. By the power of the Holy Spirit dwelling in us, we are given the mind of Christ. The Lord Jesus Christ was equipped in His life and ministry to do the Father's will. He now is equipping His followers to do the same. Through gratitude and thanksgiving, we should pursue the Father's will to do what is pleasing in His sight. This is a great conclusion as we approach the end of one year and prepare for the new.

Equipping implies training. Training begins with personal responsibility and discipline. Throughout the year we have examined numerous disciplines that should be in every believer's life. As a believer, we have been called to the fellowship of prayer with our heavenly Father. As we open our hearts to Father God through the pattern of prayer Jesus gave us in Matthew 6:9-15, we are continuously brought to the Throne of Grace. As we develop the discipline of reading the Word of God, including memorizing scripture, meditating upon truths, and writing down what the Lord shows us, we prepare ourselves for "every good thing."

As we develop our relationship with Father God, we become prepared to relate the Good News of the Gospel to others that come across our paths. This happens mostly by how we live our lives, but also by taking every opportunity to share God's love. Every day, ask the heavenly Father "what is pleasing in Your sight"? Ask to be filled each day afresh and anew with the Holy Spirit so you can do the will of God.

Father, thank You for the peace You have made possible through Jesus Christ. Thank You for the blood of the eternal covenant making it possible for Jesus Christ to equip me in every good thing to do Your will. Strengthen me in the disciplines of the faith so I might bear witness of Your love to others. Fill me today with Your Holy Spirit to be empowered as Your witness.

## November 27 – A FOOT LAMP TO GUIDE ME

Psalm 119:105 – Your word is a lamp to my feet and a light to my path.

I have some solar foot lamps to guide along a path in my yard. Each lamp only puts out enough light for a few steps. The word of God is like the foot lamps. We need light for each step we take. This is why it is important to be in God's Word regularly. The word of God profits us more than anything else in life. It is profitable for teaching, reproof, correction, and instruction.

The Scriptures give us the principles of the kingdom of God. They teach us about God's design of how to live successfully. The Scriptures teach us how we must rightly relate to authority. We learn of various areas of responsibility God has assigned to us. We are responsible for our words, our actions, our thoughts, and our attitudes. The scriptures teach us about ownership, motivations, freedom, and success.

The word of God is profitable for reproof in areas of our key relationships such as relating to God, self, family, friends, and preparing for the future. It is especially helpful for a young person in learning how to relate to the opposite sex. Reproof is not negative unless we choose to respond negatively. The wise person loves reproof. "Poverty and shame will come to him who neglects discipline, but he who regards reproof will be honored" (Proverbs 13:18).

The word of God teaches responsible steps of action in our relationship toward God and others. An example would be, "making the most of your time, because the days are evil"

(Ephesians 5:16). A responsible "action" would be to budget time as one ought to do with money. How much free time do I have? How do I presently use my time? What could be eliminated, what is of the utmost importance? Another example would be speaking "kind words." "Do not let kindness and truth leave you; bind them around your neck. Write them on the tablet of your heart. So you will find favor and good repute in the sight of God and man" (Proverbs 3:3-4). The insight is to not let kindness become separated from you. The action would be to keep kindness in your thoughts and habits.

Finally, God's word is profitable for instruction. Deepen your commitment to God's word as your means of instruction in righteousness. Pray, asking for "specific instructions" from the Lord on applying biblical principles in your daily walk. As the Lord helps you to grow in spiritual maturity, share what you have learned with others.

Father, help me increase in basic steps of spiritual maturity. I pray for Your word to illuminate steps along the pathway of my walk. Help increase my love of teaching, reproof, correction, and instruction.

## November 28 – BEING QUICK AND SLOW AT THE SAME TIME

James 1:19 – You know this, my beloved brethren. Everyone must be quick to hear, slow to speak, and slow to anger.

What a great word from James, the brother of Jesus! Every believer should know this principle of truth, but at the same time we all need to be reminded. The principle of quick hearing and slow speaking is especially needed this season of the year. Most will spend time with close friends and family members as we celebrate the birth of our Lord Jesus Christ. Whenever we spend close time with others, sharing responsibilities and conversation, there is opportunity for misunderstandings to occur.

The saying, "think before you speak" is especially helpful in preserving peace. Listening carefully to another not only provides one with information about their reasoning or opinion, but an opportunity to keep one's emotions under control. It is important to respond to differing views with respect and as few words as possible. Well thought out responses can provide for interesting and stimulating conversation. I have determined not to be pulled into emotionally driven political talk. If the discussion is not supported by an educated view, I am not interested in plunging into heated emotional opinions.

When I first began secular work, I realized I would see my follow workers daily. I did not need to reveal everything I thought at one setting. I prayed daily for the Holy Spirit to guide me in my conversation with my fellow employees. I can testify that God was faithful. Over the years, I had opportunity to lead some to Christ. Others were interested in what I had to offer and would seek me out in conversation; there are always those who reject your views no matter how you approach the conversation.

As believers, we need to give a listening ear for the voice of the Holy Spirit. He knows both how to nudge us forward and to hold us back from quick responses that could lead to anger. It takes discipline to stop and pay attention to His impressions. I have found more times than not, the Holy Spirit will have us listen a great deal more than having us speak. Early in my ministry life as I began to relate with pastors from many different streams and traditions, I practiced being the last one to speak. I wanted to hear what the others had to say and listen for the voice of the Holy Spirit to instruct me in what I should bring to the conversation. It was a difficult challenge, but it proved to be helpful.

As we celebrate the Prince of Peace and His birth, let us take the lead in peaceful conversations and helpful participate in activities of the day. As James instructs, "Be slow to speak and slow to anger," celebrating, not only Christ, but others and their life in relationship with you. You are Christ's servant and a representative of His kingdom.

Father, I thank You for this season of the year. I ask for this to be the most peaceful and enjoyable Christmas my family has ever known. I pray for the Holy Spirit to be my constant guide and helper as I relate with others in this season. I pray for Your presence in all my holiday activities, all for Your glory.

# November 29 – KEEP ME FROM
# PERSONAL FAVORTISM

James 2:1 – My brethren, do not hold your faith in our glorious Lord Jesus Christ with an attitude of personal favoritism.

Favoritism was a problem in the early church, especially as it related to social class. It is a basic human problem that has followed man down through the centuries. As a pastor, one of the complaints I would hear from individuals is that people in the congregation are "cliquish." As believers, we must guard ourselves from isolating others. We are called to be a family built together in community. Jesus told His disciples, "By this all men will know that you are My disciples, if you have love for one another" (John 13:35).

It is not wrong to have some people you count as favorite friends. There is a difference between "favorite" and "favoritism." Favorite could relate to an individual's personality, their upbeat attitude, and general likability. Favoritism addresses paying more attention to one person over another where there should be equality. Paul experienced this with Peter as recorded in Galatians 2. Peter knew that the Lord had accepted the Gentiles as equal to the Jews. Peter was fellowshipping with a number of Gentiles until a group of Jewish believers arrived from Jerusalem. Peter separated himself from the Gentiles to gain favor with the Jewish brothers. Paul, observing this, rebuked Peter openly for his hypocrisy.

Part of our development as followers of Christ is to learn how to accept others in spite of personality oddities or even distasteful language. Love, acceptance, and forgiveness are goals for each believer. The Lord wants to equip His church to be truly Christian in a non-Christian world. Many attitudes held by church-going people are counter to the attitude of Christ who "so loved the world that He laid down His life for the most offensive among us.

In this Christmas season, let us not only remember the babe in a manger, but the risen Christ who desires all men be saved. "The Lord is not slow about His promise, as some count slowness, but is patient toward you, not wishing for any to perish but for all to come to repentance" (2 Peter 3:9). Make sure, when you are out in the world shopping or just enjoying the season, that your life gives witness of the risen Christ.

Father, I pray to be filled with the love of Christ during this Christmas season. Especially help me in regard to those who are not filled with Your love. Help me grow toward others in a way that is pleasing to You. I pray for the Holy Spirit to remove all manner of favoritism from my life. Help me be respectful toward all, even those who do not respect me.

## November 30 – DEMONSTRATING LOVE, ACCEPTANCE, AND FORGIVENESS

1Timothy 1:15-16 – It is a trustworthy statement, deserving full acceptance, that Christ Jesus came into the world to save sinners, among whom I am foremost of all. Yet for this reason I found mercy, so that in me as the foremost, Jesus Christ might demonstrate His perfect patience as an example for those who would believe in Him for eternal life.

The Kingdom of God is all about love, acceptance, and forgiveness. In the kingdom of God, we first love, and then move into acquaintance. This is different than the world's perspective where we get acquainted then we move toward love. Usually people have many acquaintances; they have some friends, but are in need of real love and acceptance.

The love of God is not based on what I do or do not feel. His love is rooted in the Lord Jesus Christ who died freely before anyone sought Him out. God's love is commitment and is independent of feelings or knowledge of what another has or has not done. By God's grace, we should be able to love and accept people before we really know them. Once we come to know a person, God wants to supply the necessary grace to love and accept them in spite of what we have come to learn about them. This is not by human effort, but through the grace that God supplies.

Consider how the Lord Jesus spent His time. He hung out with the outcasts of His society. He ate with sinners who had robbed their own people to become rich. He ministered to prostitutes and tax collectors. He was known as a friend of sinners.

Today, the church is filled with broken people, people who need to be loved and accepted. Some of these believers have come from heavily damaged pasts. Some have had a life of trauma beginning in their childhood. Others have had marriages that produced severe wounds and have left many scars. Others brought injuries upon themselves through addictions and poor choices relating to sexual involvements. Each person is precious in the Lord's sight. The blood of Jesus is more than sufficient to cleanse and heal broken lives. The other healing factor is people, who themselves have experienced God's grace in their life, reaching out in the spirit of love, acceptance, and forgiveness to those in need.

The Christmas season is the ideal time to express love. It is that special time of the year to demonstrate real acceptance. Examine your heart and see if there is anyone you have failed to forgive from your heart this past year. If so, choose to forgive that one now. If appropriate, let them know how you have chosen to forgive and accept them in your heart as one you love and care about. Ask them how you can pray for them in the New Year.

Father, I ask You to help me to be a person that lives in Your power to love, accept, and forgive with my whole heart. Fill me with the Holy Spirit to demonstrate Your power by extending my life to serve another who is in need.

## December 1 – FAITH AND WORKS

James 2:14 – What use is it, my brethren, if someone says he has faith but he has no works? Can that faith save him?

Some have thought James preached a different Gospel than that of Paul. Paul laid the foundation of believing faith throughout his letters. "For by grace you have been saved through faith; and that not of yourself, it is the gift of God; not a result of works, so that no one can boast" (Ephesians 2:8-9). How do we reconcile what James says with Paul's teaching?

There is a difference between saying you have faith and actually demonstrating that faith. I knew a man some years ago that evidenced a knowledge of Scripture. He told me he believed the Bible, but his life did not demonstrate a "believing faith." Saying "I have faith" is one thing, but living that faith is totally another. The evidence of faith should be expected from one who says "I have faith." As we grow in faith a greater demonstration of our faith will be evidenced.

Paul taught, "God saved us, not on the basis of works which we have done in righteousness, but according to His mercy" (Titus 3:5). Redemption came through Jesus Christ and His sacrificial work. We had nothing whatsoever to do with that work. He went to the cross for you and me while we were dead in our trespasses and sins. All that is required of us is to receive what Christ has accomplished. What James is addressing in his letter is the attitude that all I need to do is to say "I have faith." Saying it and believing it are two totally different spheres. Believing what Christ has done will produce a demonstration of faith. Do others know your faith by what you say or by what you do?

It is the Holy Spirit who gives us the ability to believe. He grants the gift of repentance. He reveals to us the need for the work of Christ to be applied to our lives. He regenerates us, causing the life of Christ to be lived out through us. Through believing faith, we can be filled with the Holy Spirit daily and live out Christ's life, demonstrating faith by our works. Trust Christ totally for your salvation through the work of His cross. Don't talk about your faith; demonstrate your faith by allowing the Holy Spirit to work through you in serving others.

In this season of the year, there will be many works of good deeds toward others. It is the "Spirit of Christmas" to give! All that giving is not related to personal salvation.  On the other hand, the true believer should be in the forefront of giving. There are many opportunities to allow your faith to operate in the Christmas season. Some examples are to help feed the homeless, taking gifts to the children of prisoners through Angel Tree Ministry, and sharing thoughtful gifts with your neighbors. Perhaps you will also be able to speak of your faith and help another receive the greatest gift in their life, Christ the Lord.

Father, I thank You for sending Your Son to die in my place. My faith is centered in all You have done in Christ. I ask for the

Holy Spirit to fill me with Your life. Cause me to demonstrate saving faith by works pleasing to You.

## December 2 – THE TONGUE IS A FIRE

James 3:6 – The tongue is a fire, the very world of iniquity; the tongue is set among our members as that which defiles the entire body, and sets on fire the course of our life, and is set on fire by hell.

In this verse, James goes straight to the heart of human problems. James says, "No one can tame the tongue" (James 3:8). Only Jesus was able to control His tongue, He did this by only saying what He heard His Father saying. The Holy Spirit was given to bring forth the life of Christ in each believer. He begins with the heart because the issues of life flow from the heart. Next, He wants to control our tongue. It is profitable for believers to give themselves a personal evaluation. Consider what changes have taken place with your words since you believed. Have there been changes such as cursing, taking the Lord's name in vain, or harsh comments toward or about others? Then think about what changes still need to take place, such as a soft answer, more positive conversation, and words for encouraging others around you.

The fire of the tongue can be quenched by the "water of the Word of God." It is through the Holy Spirit that the tongue can be controlled. "Let the words of my mouth and the meditation of my heart be acceptable in Your sight, O Lord, my rock and my Redeemer" (Psalm 19:14). What a great prayer that David gave us! Why not daily ask the Lord for His help regarding your words and the things you think about? Invite the Holy Spirit to be in charge of your conversation. Freely give your heart and mind to Him day by day so He has your permission to assist you in what comes out of your mouth. It might take a while to break old patterns of speech, but He will faithfully help if you will be persistent.

"Who may dwell on Your holy hill? He who walks with integrity, works righteousness, and speaks truth in his heart. He does not slander with his tongue" (Psalm 15:1-3). The Psalmist lists a few things that God cares about. Walking in integrity speaks of values and wholeness. The first step in quenching the fire of the tongue is to be established in the value of relationship. That is, caring about the feelings of others. Next is experiencing your own wellness. This means coming to a place of wholeness through Christ. Another area that concerns our Lord is works of righteousness. Works of righteousness are rooted in what pleases God and what affects others in a positive way for their good. A third area is learning to speak truth from the heart. A healthy heart, spiritually speaking, becomes a fountain of kind words that cleanses others. Last, is guarding your tongue from slandering another individual. Make it a habit to not uncover another person's weaknesses in front of other people.

Father, I ask for the power of the Holy Spirit to tame my tongue. I trust You to help me with the words of my mouth and the meditations of my heart. I pray that both will be acceptable to You.

## December 3 – WISDOM FROM ABOVE

James 3:13 – Who among you is wise and understanding? Let him show by his good behavior his deeds in the gentleness of wisdom.

As you begin to read the third chapter of James' letter to the church, you read of comparing the gentleness of God's wisdom to bitter jealousy and selfish ambition of the heart. The old nature can easily become filled with jealousy and selfish ambition. Both jealousy and ambition are products of the sin nature and represent the old self. They are focused on serving self as opposed to serving others. Certainly this is a great contrast to the life of Christ, which was filled with gentle wisdom as He served the needs of others around Him.

Through faith in the power of Christ's resurrection and His life-giving Spirit we too can be filled with gentle wisdom. Conversion, as it relates to Christianity, is about drawing our life from Christ's life which has been given to the believer by the Holy Spirit. Many Christians continue to live from the old life and habits rather than the new life contained in the new birth. Jealousy and selfish bitterness can be entangled with many other sins. The danger of these sins is that they create arrogance and lies. The world system is filled with this type of arrogance and deceit. The world sees this type of nature as wisdom. It is not a wisdom that comes from God. James calls it "earthly, natural, and demonic (James 3:15). Where you find jealousy and selfish ambition, you find disorder and evil.

God's wisdom is pure. It has no hidden motives, just a desire to relate and help others. It is peaceable. It is filled with desire to produce peace in the life of believers. It is gentle. God's wisdom seeks to help resolve problems with a gentle voice and a gentle hand. God's wisdom is reasonable. The wisdom of God does not reason from emotions, but rather from truth. The wisdom of God is filled with mercy and good fruits. When God's wisdom is administered and received, it is productive. God's wisdom is neither double-minded nor filled with hypocrisy. It is unwavering in its nature and always has the best interests of others in view.

As we celebrate the birth of the "Prince of Peace," make it your ambition to sow peace into the lives of others. Ask the Holy Spirit to fill you with the wisdom of God. Ask Him for the life of Christ to be manifested in all you do. Seek His life of peace, gentleness, mercy, and good fruits. Make it your ambition to be known as a person of wisdom because of your relationship with the "God of wisdom" through His Son, Jesus Christ. Develop a more intimate relationship with the Holy Spirit by listening carefully for His promptings and knowing His word through the Scriptures.

Father, I ask for the help of the Holy Spirit in drawing my life from the new birth and not the old natural life I had before Christ. I pray for Your gentle wisdom to control me and to produce good behavior that is pure and peaceable. Help me, Your servant, to be unwavering without hypocrisy in all I say and do.

## December 4 – THINGS TO AVOID

James 4:1 – What is the source of quarrels and conflict among you?

James proceeds to answer his own question by identifying numerous sources of conflict. He begins with "pleasures that wage war in your members" (James 4:1b). Pleasures speak of lust. Lust can be manifested in numerous ways. Sexual sins, material wants manifested in things, and any other worldly possessions that come from fleshly desires. These things produce jealousy, competition, and covetousness. This is contrary to the exhortation of learning to be content in whatever state we are in.

Quarrels and conflicts, for the most part, are rooted in the attitude of insisting on having things my way. It is really the same root that is found in lusts. James continues his thoughts by saying, "You lust and do not have; so you commit murder" (James 4:2a). James is giving a tough message to the church. A familiar saying is, "I would kill for that." Can you recognize the source of James' comment in the more modern day expression?

"You are envious and cannot obtain; so you fight and quarrel" (James 4:2b). No wonder James deals with the subject of faith and works. It sounds like those to whom he is writing are not living the life of faith, but still living by the lust of the flesh from which they had been redeemed. The life of the flesh and the life of the Spirit are in direct enmity. James goes on to deal with the subject of wrong motivations of prayer. "You ask and do not receive, because you ask with wrong motives, so that you may spend it on your pleasures" (James 4:3). James likens this motive to "adultery." He calls it "friendship with the world." Friendship with the world is hostility toward God. If one wishes to be a friend of the world, then that one becomes an enemy of God.

These are rough Scriptures to wrestle with, but important ones. At this time of the year, the world begins to put pressure on consumers to spend, spend, and spend. The world will make you feel guilty when you don't spend a lot of money on gifts and other things at Christmas time. The world does not have our best interest in view. The world appeals to our lusts and pleasures. The Spirit of God in us is jealous for our life to not be drawn to worldliness. He wants to give us great grace as we humble ourselves before God. "Submit therefore to God. Resist the devil and he will flee from you. Draw near to God and He will draw near to you" (James 4:7).

Avoid lusts, pleasures, envy, and jealousness. Avoid quarrels and conflicts. Draw close to God. Learn to be content with what you have. Give away and bless others, especially those who are lacking the basics. Nurture the presence of the Spirit of God who has come to indwell your life with His gracious presence. Long for fellowship with God, and not the friendship of the world.

Father, I ask You to help me avoid those things that are not pleasing to You. I ask for the Holy Spirit to show me when I am demanding my own way, so that I can repent. I desire to draw near to You, Father, and I thank You for Your promise to draw near to me.

## December 5 – DO NOT SPEAK AGAINST ONE ANOTHER

James 4:11 – Do not speak against one another, brethren.

The Gospel has as a major focus on relationship. Relationship is rooted in care for another. Mature relationship is the willingness to put another person's welfare above your own. The greatest demonstration of this is revealed in Christ Jesus. God put His love for us first when He gave His Only Begotten Son to mankind. As Mary carried the "the Prince of Peace" in her womb, she carried the greatest expression of love that creation has ever known.

Jesus taught His disciples about God's love when He said, "By this all men will know that you are My disciples, if you have love for one another" (John 13:35). The men the Father gave Jesus were about as diverse a group as one could find within the Jewish culture. In the natural, they did not have much in common. There were brothers in the mix, but even brothers many times have deep-rooted issues in their relationships. It was the love of the Father in Christ that provided the spiritual substance for a new kind of love among people.

James instructs the body of Christ not to speak against one another. He helps us to understand that when we speak against our brother or sister, we are speaking against the law and judging the law. He goes on to say, if we judge the law, we are not a doer of the law, but a judge of the law. We need a proper biblical view. "There is only one Lawgiver and Judge, the one who is able to save and destroy; but who are you who judge your neighbor?" (James 4:12). Making judgment about others is a dangerous proposition for kingdom people. According to 1 Corinthians 11, the wrong judgment of others in the body of Christ caused some believers to die an early death, while others were weak and sick as a result.

When a person is judgmental and critical, the spiritual circulation system among believers becomes clogged. Having a loving and accepting attitude of others opens up communication and an opportunity for a deeper development of love and respect. There are times when a person needs a word of correction or reproof, but it is important to understand the depth of the relationship we have with the individual before bringing either one. It is also important to have invested time and care in the relationship because it creates a platform for a corrective word.

Many times a relationship breaks down because of speaking behind another's back. I believe this is what James is addressing in his exhortation to not speak against one another. If you find that you are having a relational difficulty with a family member or a brother or sister in Christ, go to that one and gently seek to resolve the problem. Do not go to others in an attempt to try and figure out what to do. The Scripture is clear, go first to the person where there is offense and try to resolve the problem. You may win your brother or sister as you exercise Christ' love toward them.

Father, keep me from being a judge of the law and help me be a doer of Your word. Keep me from a critical spirit and give me a sincere love for family members and my brother and sister in Christ. Preserve me as Your disciple through love for my fellow believer. In this Christmas season, help me to be a witness of the Prince of Peace.

## December 6 – DON'T BE A PROCRASTINATOR

Proverbs 15:19 – The way of the lazy is as a hedge of thorns, but the path of the upright is a highway.

My father taught my brothers and me, "Don't put off till tomorrow, what you can do today because tomorrow never comes, it is always today." Delay in one's responsibilities will cause a pileup of things to be done which will have a strong effect on your ability to think clearly. Procrastination causes great pressures in an individual's life such as pressures in relationships, pressure regarding scheduling responsibilities, and pressure in one's own emotional make-up.

Planning is vital for our spirituality. "Commit your works to the Lord and your plans will be established" (Proverbs 16:3). Planning begins with a life committed to God's eternal purpose. Our time belongs to the Lord. We must learn not to be careless about how we use our time. As you plan your day, do it with the Lord. Ask the Father to be in charge of your plans. When you write down the things you need to accomplish, ask the Holy Spirit for His guidance. This is a sure way for your plans to be established. It is also good to ask for "divine appointments." As we plan those natural appointments, know that the Lord may have some divine appoints He has prepared for you.

Planning is vital to our emotional well-being. When our mind is filled with confusion, it produces emotional stress that can affect every other area of our life. God's will is for our emotions to be in a state of peace and rest. It is in that rest we find our greatest productivity. The Holy Spirit has been given to lead us into the rest of God.

Planning is vital to our physical health. Spiritual and emotional inconsistency is at the root of many physical problems. "A joyful heart makes a cheerful face, but when the heart is sad, the spirit is broken" (Proverbs) 15:13. God made man a triune being after His own image. "Now may the God of peace Himself sanctify you entirely; and may your spirit and soul and body be preserved complete, without blame at the coming of our Lord Jesus Christ" (1 Thessalonians 5:23-24).

Planning is vital relationally. Procrastination can be very difficult on relational health. It puts others in a difficult position as their scheduling is affected by another's procrastination. Procrastination is selfish because it neglects to take into consideration this effect on other people's time. The Holy Spirit is our helper. He is present to help us overcome procrastination.

Father, I commit my ways to You. I ask for the Holy Spirit to lead me in my busy schedule. Help me not to procrastinate, but be responsible regarding the things I need to accomplish in my daily life. Show me what my priorities are and what is not important. I claim the peace of God for my whole spirit, soul, and body that I might be a witness of godly order in a busy world.

## December 7 – BE PATIENT UNTIL THE COMING OF OUR LORD

James 5:7 – Be patient, brethren, until the coming of the Lord.

In the month of December, believers turn their attention toward celebrating the birth of the Savior. What a tremendous time of the year, as we remember all that the Lord has done for His people. James, in the 5<sup>th</sup> chapter of his letter, addresses the misuse of riches in verses 1-6. In the 7<sup>th</sup> verse James exhorts God's people to be patient until the coming of the Lord. What James is addressing is relevant today.

There is a misery coming on those that are rich who do not regard our Lord and Savior. James makes a sobering statement when he says, "You and your silver have rusted; and the rust will be a witness against you and will consume your flesh like fire. It is in the last days that you have stored up your treasure!" (James 5:3). Gold and silver don't rust, so obviously the statement is an exaggeration to make a very important point. We now know that for that generation, the last days referred to the destruction of the Temple, the city of Jerusalem, and the Jewish society as a whole. Men were putting their confidence in "riches," but those riches were about to perish.

The application is vital for our generation as well. We do not know precisely when the Lord will return, but it is evident we are closer than when we first believed. The culture we have known is on shaky ground. The world economic picture is changing and will continue to change as we approach the end of all things. The exhortation of James to be "patient" is a worthy thing to meditate upon. "Do not complain, brethren, against one another, so that you yourselves may not be judged; behold, the Judge is standing right at the door" (James 5:9). In all we do, let the return of Christ be fully central in our minds. Judge your actions as believers, knowing that one day all our actions will be judged by Christ.

The return of Christ is the great filter for our motivations. Our faith is evaluated, not only on trusting Christ in His first coming, but on our confidence in His return. His first coming through His death on the cross provides us with the gift of salvation through repentance and trusting in His shed blood. Our patience toward His return helps us walk in righteousness before God and towards others.

Those who have preceded us, namely the prophets who spoke in the name of the Lord, are examples to us of suffering and patience. There are many throughout the world walking in that kind of endurance. Consider Job and his endurance. Also consider the outcome of Job's endurance. The Lord was merciful and compassionate toward Job. He will also be merciful and compassionate toward us as we endure through difficult times, waiting for the coming of our Lord Jesus Christ who has His reward with Him.

Father, strengthen my patience by helping me be continually focused on the coming of the Lord. Help me to not trust in riches that will parish, but in the true riches of Christ. During this Christmas month, help me, through the power of the Holy Spirit, to bear witness, both of Your first coming as the Babe of Bethlehem, but also the Judge who will return to judge the hearts of all. I pray that I might be faithful in difficult times.

## December 8 – HEALING AND FORGIVENESS THROUGH CHURCH ELDERS

James 5:14-15 – Is anyone among you sick? Then he must call for the elders of the church and they are to pray over him, anointing him with oil in the name of the Lord; and the prayer offered in faith will restore the one who is sick, and the Lord will raise him up, and if he has committed sins, they will be forgiven him.

The Holy Spirit has anointed elders for the body of Christ. True elders carry many responsibilities regarding the care of God's people. The early church ordained a number of men in each city who gave shepherding oversight to the Lord's flock. James writes, the sick one "must call for the elders." This calling for the elders does not seem to be optional. By the same token, the elders have a responsibility to pray over the individual. This seems to have been an ordinance in the New Testament church. The Holy Spirit has been restoring the healing ministry to the church for some time. Many local churches make it a practice to pray for the sick. In those churches where eldership is practiced, the elders lay hands on the sick and anoint with oil.

The anointing with oil is a very old custom which was practiced and adapted in the New Testament churches as they developed in the first century. Oil is seen throughout the Scriptures as a representation of the Holy Spirit. The elders are to pray the "prayer of faith." Only prayer offered in faith has authority to bring results. To pray in faith means praying according to the instruction of scriptures. Note the strong assurance that their prayer "will restore the one who is sick." James goes on to say, "the Lord will raise him up." There is not only the promise of restoration, but forgiveness as well.

Based on James' instruction and the promise given, we should confess our sins to one another. Sin should be minimal in the life of any believer. The practice of sin is a sure sign that one has not been born again. Open confession of sin provides a twofold benefit. First, there is to be accountability within the community of the believers. Second, it gives a chance of conviction in the hearts of others. Both of these benefits provide an atmosphere for healing, both physically and spiritually.

Whether one is an elder in the Lord's church or an individual seeking simply to obey and serve their Lord, "the effective prayer of a righteous man can accomplish much" (James 5:16b). As God's people, let us pursue righteousness, confess sin, and be faithful in prayer.

Father, I thank You for Your provisions outlined in the Book of James. Fill me with the Holy Spirit that I might walk in righteousness fulfilling Your will. If there is any sin in my life, cause me to become aware and willing to confess openly. Renew me in the ministry of prayer along with Your people who are called to intercede on behalf of the lost and the hurting.

# December 9 – COVERING A MULTITUDE OF SINS

James 5:19 – He who turns a sinner from the error of his way will save his soul from death and will cover a multitude of sins.

I believe this to be one of the most profound Scriptures in the Bible. There is nothing more valuable than a soul. We know this because God gave His absolute best to redeem the souls of men. Once we have received redemption, the Lord makes us part of the solution to sin by enabling us to help other sinners become aware of God's wonderful love. When one embraces the truth of God's word, they begin to have an eternal perspective.

According to our verse, straying from the truth happens within the body of Christ. Persecution can tempt a large number of people to stray. There is always the enticement of the flesh. The influence of others can draw us away from our first love. It is important that we cover one-another's backs. This is one reason why it is so important to be part of a small group. In the small group setting, we can share our challenges, temptations, and even our faults through confession.

James encourages those reading his letter that whoever turns a sinner from the "error" of his way saves a soul from death and will cover a "multitude of sins." Let us never forget, Jesus came to save sinners. He did the work of redemption, but has chosen us to share His redemptive grace. I love the old hymn titled "I Love to Tell the Story." Christmas time is such a great occasion to share with others the story of Jesus' love. It is important for us to be reminded how many around us are perishing. As a believer, the power of God is in us to be used to turn the lost around. We have gotten away from that kind of thinking and speaking because of our sophisticated world. The Gospel is that simple: Christ came to save sinners.

The sin nature is singular, but it is multiplied in the sinful practices it produces. When the blood of Christ is applied, it becomes like a flood, washing away everything in its path. Thank God for His cleansing power given through the blood of Christ! James chose to end his letter to the churches with this thought of turning a sinner from the error of his way. It is a good thought for us to think about as we wind down the year and prepare for the next. As we remember the gift of God, let us be mindful to share His gift with others.

Father, I thank You for saving my soul. I thank You for making me whole and giving me Your salvation so rich and free. Fill me with the Holy Spirit and share with others Your great love that turns sinners from the error of their ways.

## December 10 – FOUND WITH CHILD BY THE HOLY SPIRIT

Matthew 1:18 – Now the birth of Jesus Christ was as follows. When His mother Mary had been betrothed to Joseph, before they came together she was found to be with child by the Holy Spirit.

People from previous ages had looked forward to this moment in time, when the woman's seed mentioned in Genesis 3:15 would bring forth a Savior. From that time in the garden until this special generation, known as "Messiah's Day," there had been "enmity" between the seed of the woman and the serpent. In a very short period of time, this was all about to change. A man was about to be born who would fulfill God's word given in Genesis 3 regarding, "crushing the head of the serpent."

The Holy Spirit waited during the first creation for the Word of God so that He might bring order from the chaos of the elements. The Spirit was now moving again as the fullness of time had come. "When the fullness of the time came, God sent forth His Son, born of a woman, born under the Law, so that He might redeem those who were under the Law, that we might receive the adoption as sons" (Galatians 4:4-6).

The fullness of time had come as the Holy Spirit moved upon Mary and created the Holy Child Jesus in her womb. God's means of salvation was being brought to birth. It is amazing to think about that glorious time. The world continued on as normal. Nobody in the Roman government knew what was about to happen. Some prophetic people in Israel knew the time was near for Messiah to be revealed.

Mary, holding in her heart what had been told her by an angel, went to be with her cousin Elizabeth, who also was with child. The baby in Elizabeth's womb leaped when Mary and the Holy One within her entered the room. Elizabeth was filled with the Holy Spirit and "cried out with a loud voice" and said, "Blessed are you among women, and blessed is the fruit of your womb! And how has it happened to me that the mother of my Lord would come to me?" (Luke 1:42-44). She knew by the Spirit that Mary was carrying the Messiah in her womb.

In our time, as the world goes on its way, the Lord is at work among His people, as well as in the midst of the nations. The Lord transcends time and space and works among us by His Holy Spirit. It is important for us to wait upon Him with listening ears so we, like Mary and Elizabeth, are in a place for the Lord to call us and use us for His eternal purpose. We too, carry something holy inside us. God gave us the promise of His Spirit for simply obeying the Gospel. Every believer is called to represent the Holy One of heaven.

Jesus' birth is more than an event to celebrate. It is the only answer for mankind and his lost condition. As Mary went to share with Elizabeth, let us be ready to give others the reason for the hope that lies within us. We serve the living God who dwelt among us as the babe in his mother's womb.

Father, I thank You for sending Jesus. I thank You for having a prepared vessel in Mary who was obedient to Your word saying, "Behold the bondslave of the Lord; may it be done to me according to your word" (Luke 1:38). I ask You to create in me that degree of a submissive heart.

## December 11 – THE MAGNIFICAT

Luke 1:45 – Blessed is she who believed that there would be a fulfillment of what has been spoken to her by the Lord.

One of the great declarations ever and one of the clearest prophetic words given came through the mother of our Lord. It is called the "Magnificat." As you read Mary's glorious pronouncement let the Holy Spirit minister to you from every word she spoke.

Mary said, "My soul exalts the Lord, and my spirit has rejoiced in God my Savior. He has had regard for the humble state of His bond slave; for behold, from this time on all generations will count me blessed. For the Mighty One has done great things for me; and holy is His name. His mercy is upon generation after generation toward those who fear Him. He has done mighty deeds with His arm; He has scattered those who were proud in thoughts of their heart. He has brought down rulers from their thrones, and has exalted those who were humble. He has filled the hungry with good things; and sent away the rich empty-handed. He has given help to Israel His servant, in remembrance of His mercy, as He spoke to our fathers, to Abraham and his descendants forever" (Luke 1:46-55).

As we walk through this Christmas season remembering the birth of our Savior, exalt the Lord with your soul, and rejoice in your spirit in God your Savior just as Mary did. The Lord has regarded each one who has put their trust in Him. Trusting Him takes humility on our part, a humility that recognizes that He chose us to be His Servant.

Mary prophesies that God's mercy will be upon each succeeding generation toward those who fear Him. She declares what the Lord has accomplished in this great act. He scattered those who were proud, He has brought down rulers from their thrones, He exalted the humble, and He filled the hungry with good things, and gave help to Israel, remembering His mercy.

Mary had the right focus. She was pregnant with the child. She did not focus on her pregnancy, but rather, she looked ahead by faith to the purpose of God.  As we celebrate Christ's birth, let us remember His commands, primarily love one another as He loved us and to take the Gospel to the nations declaring the great things our God has done for us.

Father, I thank You for the Magnificat that came from Mary's heart and mouth. Fill me with the Holy Spirit that I might magnify Your name and Your deeds before this generation. I thank You for Your mercy upon all those who fear Your name. Help me, Father, to point some toward You during this Christmas season that they too mighty glorify You.

# December 12 – ZACHARIAS' PROPHECY

Luke 1:67 – Zacharias was filled with the Holy Spirit, and prophesied.

Zacharias, the father of John, prophesied at the birth of his son. Later John, who introduced the ministry of Jesus to Israel, became known as "John the Baptist." In the very beginning of the Gospels, we observe how Zacharias was filled with the Holy Spirit. Elizabeth, John's mother, was also filled with the Spirit. Even John, in his mother's womb, was filled with the Holy Spirit. Mary was overshadowed by the Holy Spirit in the conception of Jesus. There was a lot of Holy Spirit activity around the birth of Christ. I believe the Father was anticipating the day when He would pour out His Spirit upon all those who believed.

The Spirit of God caused Zacharias to prophesy a powerful word in preparation for Messiah's appearing. Luke 1:68 – 79 records Zacharias' prophetic word to Israel. He began by declaring the Lord God of Israel as "Blessed." He looked ahead to what the Lord would do and proclaimed in the present tense, "He has visited and accomplished redemption for His people." He went on to speak of God's horn of salvation in the house of David. Because the horn is used by animals as a weapon, it came to symbolize power and might. Zedekiah, a false prophet in Ahab's day, made horns of iron to portray how Ahab was going to defeat the Syrians (1 Kings 22:11). God lifts up the horn of the righteous but cuts off the horn of the wicked (Psalm 75:10). Probably as an extension of this meaning of the word, horns in the visions of Daniel and John symbolized kingdoms and individual kings. David spoke of God as the horn, or strength, of his salvation (2 Samuel 22:3; Psalm 18:2). (Nelson's Illustrated Bible Dictionary, 1986, Thomas Nelson Pub.).

Zacharias went on to mention that the prophets of old had spoken about God's deliverance appearing to bring salvation from Israel's enemies. The Apostle John wrote, "The one who practices sin is of the devil; for the devil has sinned from the beginning. The Son of God appeared for this purpose, to destroy the works of the devil (1 John 3:8-9). Luke records in the book of Acts, "You know of Jesus of Nazareth, how God anointed Him with the Holy Spirit and with power, and how He went about doing good and healing all who were oppressed by the devil, for God was with Him" (Acts 10:38).

Praise God for His horn of salvation, who by His might alone overcame the works of the enemy, putting the devil to an open shame. As we celebrate the birth of Christ, declare with Zacharias, "Blessed be the Lord God of Israel, for He has visited us and accomplished redemption for His people, and raised up a horn of salvation for us" (Luke 1:68-69).

Father, I bless and thank You for Jesus, the Lord. Each day, fill me with Your Holy Spirit that I too might declare Your wonderful salvation and prophesy of the good things to come in Christ the Lord.

## December 13 – THE GOD OF MERCY WHO REMEMBERS HIS HOLY COVENANT

Luke 1:72 – To show mercy toward our fathers, and to remember His holy covenant, the oath which He swore to Abraham our father, to grant us that we be rescued from the hand of our enemies.

Today, we continue looking at the prophecy of Zacharias. God is the God of "mercy" and the God who makes a "covenant" with His people. He never fails in mercy and He never breaks His covenant. What He promised Abraham hundreds of years before, now is coming to pass. Zacharias was His instrument to declare the time had come. Zacharias' son, John was God's chosen servant to introduce the One who would establish mercy and a New Covenant sealed in Christ's blood.

Beloved, God never forgets what He promises. Zacharias spoke of God "showing mercy toward our fathers." Although the fathers of Israel failed again and again, the holy one of Israel did not. So Zacharias looked back saying "our fathers." This new thing God was about to accomplish was not only for the present generation and those to come, but also for those who had gone before. The record is clear concerning this. "The tombs were opened, and many bodies of the saints who had fallen asleep were raised; and coming out of the tombs after His resurrection they appeared to many" (Matthew 27:52-53).

Again we note what Paul wrote, "When He ascended on high, He led captive a host of captives, and He gave gifts to men" (Ephesians 4:8). Paul referred to the fact that Christ first descended into what the Jews called "paradise," where the righteous dead were waiting His appearing and the hope of resurrection. He led them to heaven with Him. Some gave testimony before ascending to the Throne of God.

God's mercy, which has been given to us through the New Covenant in the blood of Christ, is the means by which we are rescued from our enemies. These include the spiritual enemies of Satan's kingdom and the enemies of the gospel in human form, who have rejected God's means of salvation and persecute God's redeemed people. Many times, we are privileged to see victories in the now through salvations, through deliverance from evil spirits, through healing of sick bodies, and the overcoming of circumstances. There are yet greater victories to be experienced when Christ returns with His saints and those who remain are caught up with Him in the air forever to be with the Lord. Together with Christ, judgment will be poured out on all those who have rejected His offer of salvation and mercy.

Now is the acceptable time to receive salvation and mercy. God is pouring out His Spirit around the world. The individuals who will trust Christ and receive God's gift of salvation will also receive God's mercy, both now and in the future. This includes the nations. The nation of Israel rejected the mercy of God provided through Christ and experienced God's judgment at the end of the first century. Today, God's mercy is being offered to Jew and Gentile, and many are receiving the Gospel. We trust for many more to receive God's mercy and grace in our generation. We look forward to the day of the Lord's return when those who have trusted Christ will experience the fullness of God's blessings in His Son.

Father, as I celebrate the birth of Christ with family and friends, I give You praise for Your great mercy and faithful covenant. I pray for my family and friends, who yet need to know You by receiving Your offer of salvation. I pray that this season will provide opportunity for them to consider Your offer of mercy and grace.

# December 14 – SERVE THE LORD IN HOLINESS AND RIGHTEOUSNESS

Luke 1:74-75 – Grant us to serve You without fear, in holiness and righteousness all our days.

Abraham was committed to serve the Lord all his days in holiness and righteousness. God honored Abraham because He believed God. Abraham believed God for the future because he saw by faith what God had promised. "Abraham believed God and it was credited to him as righteousness" (Romans 4:3). Abraham is known as "the father of the faithful." He is the example of a faith-filled life. He did not experience everything God had promised him, but he saw it by faith, knowing God was faithful to all His promises.

Abraham served God without fear.  It was faith that allowed him to serve God, trusting Him throughout his entire life. There were moments when Abraham wavered, but he did not camp in fear, but overcame through faith. He received God's corrections and changed his way of thinking when reminded of God's eternal promises.

Abraham was a man that served God in holiness. When we look at Abraham's life, we could view some decisions he made as not being holy. God sees things differently because He sees the heart of an individual. The holiness of God is closely connected to the life of faith. The life of faith is lived out in the weakness of our flesh. Faith is judged ultimately by how we respond to holiness. When we do not live a "separated life" to God's purpose, we are not walking by faith. Faith takes us beyond our rational thinking. Faith causes us to make decisions based on future expectations. Holiness is the present evidence of our faith in operation.

The result of faith and holiness is "righteousness." Holiness is our actions of faith; righteousness is our state of being. We can be holy and live righteously all our days because Messiah has appeared and overcome the world on our behalf. Zacharias anticipated God's salvation in his prophetic word. Up to this time, Israel was under the hand of its enemies. Through Christ, in the power of the Holy Spirit, Israel could now fulfill God's plan, living the way the Lord had purposed.

Let us be renewed in faith, holiness, and righteousness during this Christmas season as we remember all that the Lord has done through Christ. The babe of Bethlehem is now the reigning King of the nations. Yield to Him in your life and give Him the control He rightly deserves. Receive the power of the Holy Spirit daily and overcome the enemy of your flesh, the enemy of your soul who is the devil, and the enemy who empowers this world's systems. We are more than conquers through Jesus Christ the Lord!

Father, I thank You for the overcoming life I have in Christ Jesus. Let faith, holiness, and righteousness fill me. As I remember the babe of Bethlehem, I bow to the risen Christ who is seated far above all His enemies. I look forward to His glorious appearing when all those who have trusted Christ will be together to celebrate Your awesome salvation.

## December 15 – THE PROPHET OF THE MOST HIGH

Luke 1:76 – You, child, will be called the prophet of the Most High; for you will go on before the Lord to prepare His ways.

John the Baptist was the greatest of all the Old Testament prophets. Jesus testified of John saying, "This is the one about whom it is written, Behold I send My messenger ahead of You, who will prepare Your way before You" (Luke 7:27). Today, we hear the term "forerunner." John was the "true forerunner." John had a powerful anointing of the Holy Spirit upon him and when he spoke, great conviction came upon the people. Many responded to his call to be baptized. His ministry of baptism was a preparatory response to the coming Messiah. Some thought that John was the Messiah, but he was only preparing the "way" for the Lord.

One reason for the confusion about John's prophetic ministry was that Moses had spoken of a prophet like himself. "The Lord your God will raise up for you a prophet like me from among you, from your countrymen, and you shall listen to him" (Deuteronomy 18:15-16). Some were questioning whether John was "that prophet" of which Moses spoke. John was chosen by God to point out the "true prophet," the Lord Jesus Christ.

It is interesting to note in Zacharias' prophetic word, that he speaks of the Lord's ways. Jesus fulfilled the purpose of God in many different respects. One of which is that He is the true Apostle, Prophet, Evangelist, Pastor, and Teacher. All those ministries come from the Lord Jesus Christ. In the New Testament, it is Christ who is the true prophet. If one is called to the office of "Prophet," Jesus takes of His prophetic anointing and places a portion on the one He has called. Jesus' ways are altogether righteous. He makes the one who believes on Him, altogether righteous. Jesus is our High Priest who is ever-living to intercede on our behalf. When a believer enters into the ministry of intercession, the anointing of Jesus for intercession comes upon that one.

John the Baptist was the first forerunner in the New Testament. He prepared the way for our Lord's entrance into ministry. Jesus speaks of the "least" in the kingdom of God as being greater than John. "Truly I say to you, among those born of women there has not arisen anyone greater than John the Baptist! Yet the one who is least in the kingdom of heaven is greater than he (Matthew 11:11-12). Each believer is a forerunner as they live a kingdom lifestyle before a Christ-rejecting world. Some are called, like John, to live lives that are separated from the world in a profound way. Some give up the comforts of the culture they have known and go to live among people from a completely different culture to bear witness of Christ and His love.

The Holy Spirit has come to show us the "ways" of the Lord. He leads individuals into various experiences and expressions of Christ's life and love. The Spirit of God is the One who prepares us for the life He has chosen to reveal in us. He gives gifts to enable us to more accurately represent the Lord Jesus and His love for people. Accept the call of God to be His representative in your sphere of influence. John fulfilled his call to present Christ to Israel. I choose to accept the call of God in my life to reveal Christ and His love to those around me.

Father, I ask for the Holy Spirit to anoint me to be a forerunner. Let my life represent Christ in such a way that Your ways are manifested through me. I pray for the love and compassion of Christ to be evidenced in my daily walk before others, that they might be drawn to the Savior.

## December 16 – THE BIRTH OF A SON

Luke 2:7 – She gave birth to her firstborn son; and she wrapped Him in clothes, and laid Him in a manger, because there was no room for them in the inn.

Luke records the greatest event in all human history. Mary, a virgin, gave birth to the Son of God. Of all things, He was laid in a manger because there was no room in the inn.

Isaiah the prophet, 700 years earlier, prophesied Jesus' birth. "Ask a sign for yourself from the Lord your God; make it deep as Sheol or high as heaven . . . The Lord Himself will give you a sign: behold a virgin will be with child and bear a son, and she shall call His name Immanuel" (Isaiah 7:11, 14). The Old Testament prophet Micah pinpointed the place of Immanuel's birth. "But as for you, Bethlehem Ephrathah, too little to be among the clans of Judah, from you One will go forth for Me to be ruler in Israel. His goings forth are from long ago, from the days of eternity" (Micah 5:2).

The creator of the worlds was laid in a manger because there was no room for Him. To think about the events of the first Christmas defies all the rational thinking of man. Christ, who created all things, came as a baby and lay in a manger. "He is the image of the invisible God, the firstborn of all creation. For by Him all things were created, both in the heavens and on earth, visible and invisible, whether thrones or dominions or rulers or authorities — all things have been created through Him and for Him. He is before all things, and in Him all things hold together" (Colossians 1:15-18).

From the fall of man in the garden, there has not been room for the living God. He has had to break into human history. He has had to reveal Himself through signs and wonders. He chose to hide Himself in human flesh and reveal His love through humility and brokenness. Only by His Holy Spirit can one see who He is and embrace His love.

At this particular season of the year, it is good to ask ourselves, "Will I make room for the risen Christ in every area of my life"? He not only wants to be in the inn of your heart, but He wants ownership because He bought your spirit, soul, and body with His precious blood spilt thirty-three years after His birth. You cannot truly celebrate Christmas without celebrating His resurrection from the dead and His habitation among humans through His Holy Spirit. The complete story is that He is coming again in bodily form for "We know that when He appears, we will be like Him, because we will see Him just as He is. And everyone who has this hope fixed on Him purifies himself, just as He is pure" (1 John 3:2-3).

Father, I thank You for the babe in the manger, Jesus Christ the Lord. I thank You for His willingness to be rejected of men. I thank You for Your love that has drawn me to the Savior and enabled me to partake of His sufferings. I thank You for Your precious Holy Spirit and for the promise of Christ's return and our gathering unto Him.

## December 17 – JESUS PRESENTED IN THE TEMPLE

Luke 2:30 – My eyes have seen Your salvation.

Simeon was a resident of Jerusalem. The Scriptures record that he was righteous and devout, looking for the consolation of Israel. The Holy Spirit was upon him. Israel had been in difficulty for centuries. From the days of the Babylonian captivity, they had been under the domination of a number of nations. For a couple hundred years, they had experienced the cruelty of Roman rule. The nation was looking for and expecting the promised Messiah. They knew that the Messiah would bring comfort through deliverance to the covenant people.

The Holy Spirit came on Simeon, and He revealed to him that he would not see death before he had seen the Lord's Christ. "He came in the Spirit into the temple; and when the parents brought in the child Jesus, to carry out for Him the custom of the Law, then he took Him into his arms, and blessed God" (Luke 2:27-28). Simeon knew he could now die in peace because his eyes had seen God's salvation. He prophesied saying, "You have prepared in the presence of all peoples, a light of revelation to the Gentiles, and the glory of Your people Israel" (Luke 2:30-32).

Under the anointing of the Holy Spirit, Simeon blessed Joseph and Mary. He spoke to Mary, "Behold this Child is appointed for the fall and rise of many in Israel, and for a sign to be opposed—and a sword will pierce even your own soul—to the end that thoughts from many hearts may be revealed" (Luke 2:34-35).

The fall of many speaks of those whose hearts were evil. In His earthly ministry, Jesus revealed the evil hearts of many of Israel's religious leaders. In Matthew 23, Jesus condemned these evil men and pronounced eight woes upon them. In the Book of Revelation, Jesus, in symbolic language, speaks of these religious leaders as "the false prophet" (Revelation 19:20). The rise of many, speaks of the new creation man that Jesus is bringing forth, first in Israel and then among the Gentiles. It is those who were dead in their trespasses and sins, but are now raised from the dead and made alive in Christ through the power of the Holy Spirit.

What a powerful word Simeon gave to Mary! Jesus was opposed, but overcame all His enemies through death on the cross. Indeed, Mary was pierced in her soul as she watched her Son die on the cross for the sins of the world. Overwhelming joy must have filled her heart when she beheld Him after the resurrection.

Father, I thank You for the consolation of Israel. I thank You for the rise of all those who have put their trust in Christ. I pray for the salvation of many during this Christmas season as they hear of the Savior's birth and learn of His death on the cross for their sins and the gift of eternal life.

## December 18 – A SAVIOR IS BORN

Luke 2:11-12 – Today, in the city of David there has been born for you a Savior, who is Christ the Lord.

Heaven truly came to earth on the day of Christ's birth. Not only was the Son of God born in Bethlehem, but a multitude of angels filled the skies and revealed themselves to many who were waiting for the expected Messiah. As shepherds were watching over their sheep, the glory of the Lord appeared as an angel spoke to the shepherds and those shepherds were filled with fear.

The angel said to them, "Do not be afraid; for behold, I bring you good news of great joy which will be for all people; for today in the city of David there has been born for you a Savior, who is Christ the Lord" (Luke 2:10-11). Man is normally fearful of the supernatural. Angels appearing and talking certainly qualify for supernatural activity. The heart of the Lord is revealed through these angelic words, "Don't fear." The Father sent His Son because He wanted a relationship with man. You cannot have a healthy relationship with another if there is "terrible fear." God's word to mankind is "Don't be afraid because I have provided salvation".

The angel goes on to explain that he had come to bring "good news." It was news of "great joy" and this news was "for all people." The Gospel is the Good news of Jesus Christ. It starts with His birth, but grew to include His death, burial, and resurrection. As Jesus hung on the cross, He gave up His life for all people.

Real joy is found in a relationship with God the Father, through faith in His Son Jesus Christ, and the abiding presence of the Holy Spirit whom the Father has given. Wouldn't you love to have been around the fire that evening as the shepherds talked about what they had just experienced on their watch? Their minds must have gone back to the many passages of Scripture they heard from their religious leaders over the years.

Our God is the God of Victory! There had been no prophet to bring the Word of the Lord for over four hundred years. The religious leaders of Israel had become dull of hearing and filled with lust for power. Things looked rather bleak for the "covenant people." But on this night, the sounds of victory rang through the skies. Declarations of "peace on earth" and proclamations of "goodwill toward men" rang out through the quiet stillness of the night. God is a God of the immediacy. "An angel of the Lord suddenly appeared" (Luke 2:9).

For over two thousand years, the message the angel brought to these shepherds has been ringing out in the earth. From Jerusalem, men began to carry the good news until the entire then-known world had heard "Jesus is Lord." The message has continued down through the centuries to our day. Christmas is a wonderful time to be renewed in the Gospel through Christmas carols and Christmas plays. It is also a great time to be renewed in God's will. Each of us can share the good news with another or perhaps with many.

The gift of God in Christ was never meant to be held privately, but is intended to be shared with as many people as is possible. Tell someone about Jesus before the year's end. Pray for divine appointments and allow the Holy Spirit to lead you.

Father, anoint me with the Holy Spirit to share Your Good News to as many as You would lead me. Release through me the message of freedom from fear, and the blessing of peace and joy from the presence of the Lord.

## December 19 – GLORY TO GOD IN THE HIGHEST

Luke 2:14 – A multitude of the heavenly host appeared praising God and saying, Glory to God in the highest, and on earth peace among men with whom He is pleased.

At the birth of Jesus the whole of heaven's hosts joined in the celebration. The angel of the Lord appeared many times throughout the Old Testament to bring to men messages from the throne of God. Daniel the prophet experienced numerous occasions when Gabriel the archangel appeared to him with messages from God. Never before did a multitude of the heavenly host come declaring words from God as recorded in the book of Luke.

The Scriptures can be so clear at times and this verse is one of those occasions, "Glory to God in the highest." God is Spirit and His throne is in heaven. We cannot comprehend either God or His throne. God is mystery to man, so God revealed His nature by sending His Only Begotten Son in human form. Not only did He do this, He has made it possible, through Christ, for His Holy

Spirit to live inside every believer. In this verse the angels say, "In the highest," there is no height higher than the Throne of God.

The angels also made it abundantly clear concerning God's will: "On earth peace among men with whom He is well pleased." As we look back in scripture, there was a time when God was not pleased. "Then the Lord saw that the wickedness of man was great on the earth, and that every intent of the thoughts of his heart was evil continually. The Lord was sorry that He had made man on the earth, and He was grieved in His heart" (Genesis 6:5-6). What an indictment against mankind! God's heart is fully revealed in Luke's record of Christ's birth. He reconciled His grieving over creating man as revealed in Genesis with His "Great Love" revealed through His Son Jesus and the "new creation" in the Spirit He was bringing forth.

God the Father is pleased with man, not because man is good, but because of "the man Christ Jesus." "For there is one God, and one mediator also between God and men, the man Christ Jesus, who gave Himself as a ransom for all, the testimony given at the proper time" (1 Timothy 2:5-6). Now was the proper time. The angels began the proclamation that awesome night. The Apostles continued the proclamation as they preached Christ in "faith and truth" (1Timothy 2:7).

It is now our turn! As we celebrate His birth and remember what the angels declared, make sure you represent heaven well. God wants peace among men. God is well pleased with us as He sees Christ revealed in all men and women who have put their trust in God's first new creation man.

Father, I thank You for Your declaration of peace and pleasure of man. Thank You for Your heart of love and mercy shown toward fallen man who had no hope. You have given hope to the world through the birth of Your Son Jesus. Help me to be joined with the angels in proclaiming Your great love.

# December 20 – SO THEY CAME IN A HURRY AND FOUND HIM

Luke 2:15 – Let us go straight to Bethlehem then, and see this great thing that has happened which the Lord has made known to us.

The shepherds did not hesitate to seek out Jesus once informed of what the Lord had done for them. The Scriptures tell us that they came in a hurry and found their way to Mary, Joseph, and the baby as He lay in the manger.

The Lord has many ways of informing people of what He has done. The shepherds responded correctly by immediately searching out the Christ child. Some people want to get more information, while others need to think about their experience for a while to decide whether to believe it or not. When the Lord reveals Himself, He expects an immediate response. The degree of the revelation is not the issue. Some may think if God revealed Himself to me like He did to the shepherds, I too would believe and immediately respond. Human nature is strange and sometimes hard to figure out in terms of how one might respond under similar circumstances.

There are many distractions in life to keep us from running hard after God and His purpose. Even supernatural experiences can be a momentary excitement. I have been in many gatherings over the years and have watched the power of God touch people dramatically. It has always been curious to me how quickly and easily the excitement of the Lord's presence can be forgotten and the normal routines of life are simply picked up as if nothing had taken place. These shepherds were transformed by their encounter.

After seeing the babe in the manger, they immediately made known what the angels had declared to them about this child. Those who heard the shepherds wondered at the things told them. Mary treasured those reports in her heart. The shepherds went back to tending their sheep, but glorified and praised God for all that they had heard and seen.

The spirit of Christmas is in telling others the wonderful story of God's love for man and His provision of salvation through Jesus the Christ. We give gifts as a symbolic gesture as we remember the greatest gift ever given. Reflect on the many occasions the Lord revealed Himself to you in some supernatural way. Ask Him to remind you of the times He has made His presence known. Like the shepherds of old, you knew the joy of the Lord's presence. Glorify and praise God for He is altogether worthy.

Father, I thank You for the message of Your grand love for all mankind. Help me to run hard after You to discover Your treasures in Christ. Cause me to be as the shepherds, a witness of the things I have been told and have seen.

## December 21 – THE VISIT OF THE MAGI

Matthew 2:1 – After Jesus was born in Bethlehem of Judea in the days of Herod the king, magi from the east arrived in Jerusalem, saying, "Where is He who is born King of the Jews"?

The magi were known as "wise men" from Persia. They were like the magicians or astrologers of the Prophet Daniel's time. These men were guided by a star in the east toward Jerusalem. They suddenly appeared in the days of Herod the Great, inquiring for the new-born king of the Jews, whom they had come to worship.

The role of the star in Matt 2 suggests a connection with astrology. These astrologers, pursuing their observations of the stars in the heavens, encountered a sign of God (Matt 24:29-30). God broke through their misguided system to make the great event known. The joy, rejoicing, worship, and gifts which mark the response of these wise men to the birth of Jesus is quite a contrast to the troubled state and murderous intent of Herod and his Jewish advisers in Jerusalem (Matt 2:1-12). (Nelson's Illustrated Bible Dictionary, Thomas Nelson Publishers.)

Why should the new star lead these wise men to look for a king of the Jews? These wise men from Persia were more like the Jews, in religion, of all nations in the world. They believed in one God, they had no idols; they worshipped light as the best symbol of God. Everywhere throughout the East, men were looking for the advent of a great king who was to rise from among the Jews. It had fermented in the minds of heathen as well as Jews, and would have led them to welcome Jesus as the Christ, had he come in accordance with their expectation. Virgil, who lived a little before this, wrote that a child from heaven was looked for, who should restore the golden age and take away sin. This expectation arose largely from the dispersion of the Jews among all nations. They carried with them the hope and the promise of a divine Redeemer. Daniel was a prince and chief among this very class of wise men. His prophecies were made known to them. The calculations by which he pointed to the very time when Christ should be born became, through the book of Daniel, a part of their ancient literature. (Smith's Bible Dictionary, PC Study Bible formatted electronic database, 2006 by Biblesoft, Inc.)

Isn't our God good? He prepared the entire world for the advent of our Savior, who is King of kings and Lord of lords. As we celebrate His first advent of 2,000 years ago, let us not forget His Second Advent is before us. The Lord is even now preparing the modern world for the greatest event in all of history, the return of the Lord Jesus Christ in bodily form to receive His redeemed people and judge all who have rejected His gracious offer of salvation and eternal life.

Celebrate the newborn King as the magi did, but keep your eyes on the east as they were doing, for He is coming again with great glory and triumph! The Holy Spirit not only witnesses in us the reality of His first coming and redemptive work, but also His return for His saints and the final judgment of systems that have rejected Him from the beginning of man, including the devil and all his angels.

Father, I thank You for the record of the magi who were also seeking the promised King. Thank You that today, as then, there is a hope growing in the earth for the return of King Jesus. Fill me with Your Holy Spirit that I might be a strong witness of Your first coming that provided salvation, and of Your glorious return in Your chosen timing.

## December 22 – HEROD'S SECRET PLAN

Matthew 2:7 – Herod secretly called the magi and determined from them the exact time the star appeared.

The magi came first to Jerusalem in their pursuit of finding the newborn King of the Jews. Sometime had transpired since the birth of Christ; remember they had travelled from Persia, east of Israel. The first thing they did was to seek out the present king. Herod was only a pawn of Rome and had no real authority. They inquired of Herod the whereabouts of the newborn King because they saw His star. I am reminded of what the Scriptures say, "The heavens are telling the glory of God; and their expanse is declaring the work of His hands" (Psalm 19:1).

God's first Bible was in the heavens. Consider the story of the gospel told through the constellations. The constellation of "Leo the Lion" speaks of the "Lion of the tribe of Judah." The constellation of "Virgo" speaks of the "virgin birth." The constellation in the southern hemisphere known as the "southern cross" reveals the method of redemption. Adam and Abraham could see God's story in the heavenly skies. The world and false religion distorted the meaning of God's story in the heavens. The magi knew the stars from a distorted perspective, but God opened their minds to understand that "this star is different and speaks of the long awaited King of the Jews."

Herod's evil heart is revealed as the magi's request and statement disturbed Him and he called together all the chief priests and scribes of the people, inquiring of them where the Messiah was to be born. These men told Herod that it was Bethlehem, reciting the prophet, "You, Bethlehem, land of Judah, are by no means least among the leaders of Judah; for out of you shall come forth a ruler who will shepherd My people Israel" (Micah 5:2). Herod then used the magi as his instrument to locate Jesus. As they left Herod, the star they saw in the east, went on before them until it came and stood over the place where the child was. This was not an ordinary star. They saw it in the "east" while Israel was to their west. In other words, the star led them all the way to Bethlehem and the house where the holy family lived.

When the magi found Jesus with His mother, they worshipped Him. They then presented gifts of gold, frankincense, and myrrh (Matthew 2:11). The Lord appeared to Joseph in a dream and said, "Get up! Take the child and His mother and flee to Egypt, and remain there until I tell you; for Herod is going to search for the child to destroy Him" (Matthew 2:12). Herod's secret plan was not secret to the God of heaven. Again, the Lord was fulfilling His prophetic word: "Out of Egypt, I called My Son" (Hosea 11:1). It appears the gifts from the magi were used over the next couple of years to provide financially for the chosen family. The magi returned home without going back to Herod with their findings

Father, I thank You for Your great power revealed in the heavens through the star that led the magi. I thank You for Your awesome provisions for the holy family. I thank You for the protection You provided them until the evil of Herod's heart was ended. I know Your Holy Spirit was mightily at work and continues to work with and through Your people today.

## December 23 – THE ENEMY IS ENRAGED, BUT RESTRICTED

Matthew 2:16 – When Herod saw that he was tricked by the magi, he became very enraged, and sent and slew all the male children who were in Bethlehem and all its vicinity, from two years old and under.

For a devotional, this Scripture is not encouraging, but it is reality. God's enemies hate Him and all that is His. God is good and gives good gifts to His creation man. For someone to hate God, they must be evil in their core. Satan's nature is evil in its depth. Those that are filled with pride and hate to the point of mass murder are a manifestation of Satan's core. Herod was evil as he sought to kill Jesus through the genocide of the male children less than two years of age.

Satan tried to stop the purpose of God through mass murder of Hebrew children twice in history, when God was providing a deliverer through Moses and when Christ was born. At other times, he has tried to kill the Jewish people through genocide. During the first century, Satan tried to kill off the Lord's church through the Roman emperor Nero.

We know the history of the twentieth century as Hitler tried to exterminate the Jewish people prior to the Lord returning them to the holy land. The enemy has used numerous nations in modern times to murder God's people to stop the growth of

Christianity. In more recent times the enemy has used the radical Islam to attack God's people. The hatred of Jews and Christians throughout the world has grown in volume and incidents of murder.

The enemy is scared because he knows his time is short. "The demons believe and shudder" (James 2:19). All is not dark and evil. The Spirit of God is being poured out in these days in preparation for a great harvest of souls. Just as in the time of Christ, terrible things happened, but God overcame terrible things with His goodness through Jesus the Lord. When the Holy Spirit was poured out on the Day of Pentecost, a great awakening took place and multitudes were saved and set free from the devil's power. "You know of Jesus of Nazareth, how God anointed Him with the Holy Spirit and with power, and how He went about doing good and healing all who were oppressed by the devil, for God was with Him" (Acts 10:38).

This same Jesus is pouring out His Spirit with the same old time power around the world today. Rejoice, saints of God, for the devil is defeated and Christ is victorious! Light has come as Christ declared in the gospels and His saints are to be that light through the power of the Holy Spirit. Evil things may happen, but God is at work. "So then, my beloved, just as you have always obeyed, not as in my presence only, but now much more in my absence, work out your own salvation with fear and trembling; for it is God who is at work in you, both to will and to work for His good pleasure" (Philippians 2:12-13).

Father, I thank You for Your overcoming life that lives in me. I rejoice in Your Son who has defeated the evil one through His cross and in the power of the resurrection. Help me, Lord, to stand strong in the battles and also to overcome by the power of Your Holy Spirit who is in me.

## December 24 – GO INTO THE LAND

Matthew 2:19-20 – When Herod died, behold, an angel of the Lord appeared in a dream to Joseph in Egypt, and said, "Get up, take the Child and His mother, and go into the land of Israel; for those who sought the Child's life are dead."

Christmas Eve is a wonderful time for celebrating the new life which was about to be birthed in the earth. The exact date is not all that relevant, but the reality of this occurrence changes the perspective of eternity. Our Scripture for today is filled with hope and encouragement that the Lord's enemies will be silenced and the land is our possession. The early church experienced how the enemies of Christ became His footstool with the death of Nero and the destruction Jerusalem and the Jewish religious system that had persecuted the early saints.

Life is a journey. Joseph journeyed to Egypt by divine direction. After Herod's death, the Lord led him back to the place of his heritage. The enemy does all he can to hinder the purpose of God, but our God is sovereign and quiets His enemies so his people can accomplish their purpose. Joseph once again obeyed the divine leading and entered into a new season for his life, the life of Mary and the Child Jesus.

Even though Herod was dead, his son Archelaus was reigning over Judah. This caused Joseph to be afraid. I am certain that he sought the Lord to know what he should do. Many times, the Lord gives great victories to His people, but circumstances arise that can cause us to fear. Fear is natural, but must be overcome. God did not give us fear. "God has not given us a spirit of timidity, but of power, and love, and discipline" (2 Timothy 1:7). Timidity is translated "fear" in the KJV. The spirit of fear or timidity has caused many to stumble and not fulfill God's intentions. When fear raises its ugly head, we need to seek God's help immediately.

God warned Joseph in another dream and he left for the region of Galilee to live in Nazareth. Throughout the ministry of Jesus, He was known as a "Nazarene." Nazareth was an obscure, insignificant place. Nathanael asked, "Can anything good come out of Nazareth?" (John 1:46). Thus the word Nazarene was a fitting title for the One who grew up "as a root out of dry ground, despised and rejected by men" (Isa 53:2-3).

Father, I thank You for how You lead each life chosen to fulfill Your will. Thank You for giving us the details of the birth of Your Son, Jesus of Nazareth. Thank You for Joseph, Mary's husband, and the sold-out life He demonstrated. Help me, through the power of Your Holy Spirit, to also live a sold out life for You, reflecting Your will in all I do.

# December 25 – CHRISTMAS, CHRIST'S DAY

John 1:4-5 – In Him was life, and the life was the light of men. The light shines in the darkness, and the darkness did not comprehend it.

The Gospel of John does not give us the details of the Christmas story, but sums up in these two verses what the Christmas story is about. The earth was filled with death and darkness. There was no real hope, except in the "promises of God" of the One to be born who would free humanity from the chains of death and darkness.

The time had come! "When the fullness of the time came, God sent forth His Son, born of a woman, born under the Law, so that He might redeem those who were under the Law, that we might receive the adoption as sons" (Galatians 4:4-5). God promised that the deliverer would come as the "seed of the women" (Genesis 3:15). The entire Law of God given through Moses, pointed toward the coming deliverer. The Law could not save us because of the weakness of human flesh, "What the Law could not do, weak as it was through the flesh, God did: sending His own Son in the likeness of sinful flesh and as an offering for sin, He condemned sin in the flesh, so that the requirement of the Law might be fulfilled in us, who do not walk according to the flesh but according to the Spirit" (Romans 8:3-5).

God the Father has summed up everything in His Son Jesus, the Christ. Today, we are free to receive all the Father has promised and prepared for those who are willing to abandon their own life for new life in Jesus. Presently, it is spiritual. By faith, we choose Christ and His life over our natural life and its resulting death. By faith, we receive His Holy Spirit, who gives us the Life of Christ through the "new birth." We are empowered to live a life free from sin and share with others God's Good News of life and light. God will use each believer, who allows Him, to lead others into a relationship with the living God through faith in Christ the Lord.

We look forward to the next great advent of our Lord, which is His Second Coming. No man knows the day nor the hour of the Lord's return, but we are to live entirely for Him, waiting in expectation of that glorious day.

Most were not prepared for His first advent. Multitudes missed out on the great benefits of His first coming. Since that time, many have believed and have prepared themselves for His return. Those who died in Christ did not see their hope fulfilled in this life. They are now with Him in heaven and will return with Him as a great company of faithful ones to receive those who remain on earth. Together we will ever be with the Lord. The Apostle John puts it this way, "Beloved, now we are children of God, and it has not appeared as yet what we will be. We know that when He appears, we will be like Him, because we will see Him just as He is. And everyone who has this hope fixed on Him purifies himself, just as He is pure" (1 John 3:2-3).

Merry Christmas in the worship of the Newborn King!

## December 26 – THE RETURN OF OUR GREAT GOD AND KING

Titus 2:13-14 – Looking for the blessed hope and the appearing of the glory of our great God and Savior, Christ Jesus, who gave Himself for us to redeem us from every lawless deed, and to purify for Himself a people for His own possession, zealous for good deeds.

Isn't our God good? He prepared the entire world for the advent of our Savior, who is King of kings and Lord of lords. As we celebrate His first advent of 2,000 years ago, let us not forget His Second Advent is before us. The Lord is even now preparing the modern world for the greatest event in all history, the return of the Lord Jesus Christ in bodily form to receive His redeemed people and judge all who have rejected His gracious offer of salvation and eternal life.

Every believer should be looking for the blessed hope. The world does not have such hope. The world only possesses ideas of trying to produce utopia, peace among men, and a better world system. The problem is deeply rooted in man, mainly his heart that is filled with selfishness and pride. Even in democracies, it is observable how corrupt the heart of man has become. Political campaigns are filled with ego and pride. It is a proven fact that negative campaigning is effective.

The answer to man's dilemma is rooted in our Scripture. Christ Jesus gave Himself to redeem us from every lawless deed. Humans cannot help themselves when it comes to being lawless before God. We just can't keep His laws, no matter how hard we try. We can discipline ourselves to be as good as possible, but there is no hope of attaining God-like righteousness without Christ. The Holy Spirit redeems us and imparts a right standing before God because of what Christ has done. The Holy Spirit is always at work in our lives to purify and set us apart to be zealous for every good deed. Christ's work in us is not only for today, but that He might present us to God His Father in eternity. He is coming back for a spotless bride, not resulting from our efforts, but rather His cleansing blood.

As we leave this Christmas season and walk toward a New Year, let us move our eyes from the babe in a manger to the ascended Lord who is seated at the right hand of the Majesty on High. He is the one who is preparing to return for His blood-washed people and judge all those who refused His Gospel of Peace. This year, allow the Holy Spirit to work deeper in your heart. Embrace His plan and purpose of producing more of Jesus in all you do and say.

Father, I thank You for the redemption that has freed me from lawlessness unto good deeds. I pray for daily infillings of Your Holy Spirit to help me grow into Jesus' image and likeness. I pray for Your church to be prepared for Your glorious return to take place, in Your perfect timing.

## December 27 – KEEPING YOUR EYE ON THE PRIZE

Hebrews 12:2 (KJV) – Looking unto Jesus the author and finisher of our faith; who for the joy that was set before Him endured the cross, despising the shame, and is set down at the right hand of the throne of God.

Jesus is the prize!

Joseph kept his eye on Mary and then Mary and Jesus after the Lord's birth. He knew His responsibility in serving the God of Israel. While God, who is in heaven, was the Father of the Lord Jesus Christ through the power of His Holy Spirit, Joseph provided earthly fathering of Jesus. Jesus was known as "the carpenter" (Matthew 6:3), one could surmise that He worked with Joseph in the carpenter shop.

John the Baptist looked for the "Lamb of God." His eyes were looking for the one who would take away the sins of the world. With the information we have about John, we know he was filled with the Holy Spirit while in his mother's womb. We know he separated himself from society and spent time in the wilderness, no doubt seeking God about the assignment which had been given to him.

All of the disciples of our Lord were engaged in the society and culture of that day. They had jobs. They were integrated with family and their immediate culture. The twelve saw Jesus and followed Him at His call. Eleven kept their eyes on Christ and fulfilled their calling. One turned out to be a "traitor," selling out to the Lord's enemies for a few pieces of silver.

Down through history the story is told of multitudes whose spiritual eyes were drawn to Jesus and followed Him. Some followed Christ to martyrdom. Many others have stories that will not be told until eternity. All those who followed the Lord in this life found fulfillment in their obedience to His leading.

Along with these saints, we are looking for the glorious return of our Lord and Savior in bodily form. The scriptures tell us that when He comes "His reward is with Him" (Revelation 22:12). The prize is Christ, but He is a "rewarder of those who diligently seek Him" (Hebrews 11:6). We are called to keep our eyes "fixed upon Jesus" (1 John 3:3). All our hope, our absolute certainty, is rooted in the promise of His return for His own. It is important day by day to remind ourselves, He is coming again and His reward is with Him. Keep your eyes fixed upon the Savior. The things of this life will soon fade away, but He is our steadfast hope.

Father, I thank You for all those who have demonstrated that their eyes were fixed on Jesus. Help me to keep my eyes on the prize. Protect me from the distractions of the world and the challenges in life that can cause me to take my eyes off the Lord and His reward.

## December 28 – THE HARD ROAD BEFORE THE DISCIPLES

Matthew 10:23 – You will not finish going through the cities of Israel until the Son of Man comes.

Chapter ten of Matthew is the clearest expression of Jesus to His disciples that He would return before they had finished their mission of taking the Gospel to every city in Israel. At the time of Jesus' statement they did not comprehend what He meant. Throughout their ministry they looked for His return. They truly desired to be with Him. Throughout history, believers hoped for Jesus' return. They interpreted the events of their times as the certainty of His return. It is no different in our day.

Beloved, it is important to understand what Jesus was saying to His disciples before we try to understand how these scriptures apply to our generation. In Matthew 10, we read of Jesus sending His disciples out to the towns of Israel with power to heal and cast out demons. They went with a clear word of the good news that the Messiah was present. They were sent only to the "lost sheep of the house of Israel" (Matthew 10:6). They "proclaimed that the kingdom of heaven was at hand and to prove it, they healed the sick, raised the dead, cleansed the lepers, and cast out demons" (Matthew 10:7-8). Jesus gave them many other instructions as well. He warned them that there would be wolves among the sheep that would try to harm them.

Jesus defined the clear meaning of discipleship for His disciples. "A disciple is not above his teacher, nor a slave above his master (Matthew 10:24). I encourage you to read the whole tenth chapter. Jesus spoke very clearly of that generation and the mission He was giving to His disciples. It was a mission to the House of Israel. In the book of Acts, we see that the Samaritans and Gentiles were brought into God's plan as well. The first and primary mission of these disciples, who became apostles, was to the lost sheep of Israel.

Jesus was saying to them, "You will not finish the mission before I come." They fully expected Christ's return before the end of the century. When Jesus spoke of His return, it is obvious He was not speaking of His physical appearance. To have a better understanding of the glorious return of Christ, it is important to understand what took place in first century Christianity.

As Jesus spoke of the "Son of Man coming," He spoke of His return to judge unbelieving Israel at the end of that generation. He is not speaking of the end of the world, but the end of an age. The age of Moses, or the age of the Law, was about to be brought to an end. It had served its purpose and now all of Israel was called to be reconstituted through and under King Jesus. The message went out to every city of Israel. All of the tribes of Israel heard the message that the kingdom of God was present among them. The message was confirmed with signs following. Tomorrow we will see the contrast of what Jesus said to His disciples in Matthew 10:23 and His return at the end of the world to receive His church and judge the nations who reject His offer of salvation.

Father, I thank You for the Scriptures that speak of Your plans and purposes. I thank You for the blessed hope of Christ's return and pray that I will be filled with Your Holy Spirit daily in order to represent You well with whom I come in contact.

## December 29 – GOD'S SON HAS SPOKEN IN THESE LAST DAYS

Hebrews 1:1-2 – God, after He spoke long ago to the fathers in the prophets in many portions and in many ways, in these last days has spoken to us in His Son, whom He appointed heir of all things, through whom also He made the world.

These words were written to Hebrew believers who were being persecuted and had become discouraged. The author wrote, "In these last days has spoken to us in His Son, whom He appointed heir of all things, through whom also He made the world (Hebrews 1:2). And again he wrote, "How will we escape if we neglect so great salvation? After it was at first spoken through the Lord, it was confirmed to us by those who heard,

God also testifying with them, both by signs and wonders and by various miracles and by gifts of the Holy Spirit according to His own will" (Hebrews 2:3-4).

The Gospel was preached and confirmed in the generation of the disciples. Part of the message was a coming judgment on the Jewish nation that rejected two things. They did not accept the New Covenant in the blood of Christ and the presence of the kingdom in the person of the Holy Spirit. The writer of Hebrews identified the last days as beginning in the ministry of Jesus. For that generation, it was the end of the Jewish religious system as they knew it. The city of Jerusalem along with the temple was destroyed in 70 AD, just as Jesus had warned throughout His earthly ministry. The Apostles gave the same message of warning throughout their ministry.

Just before His arrest and crucifixion, Jesus entered the temple and judged the religious leaders with very harsh words (Matthew 23). He went on to share with His disciples in Matthew 24 concerning the events which would transpire in their generation before His return when He would finish the apocalyptic judgment on the Jewish religious system which had rejected His Messianic message and the gift of His Holy Spirit. Once we understand the "Gospels" and the message of the apostles to their generation, we can inquire of the Lord of our generation. We can look forward to His bodily return for His church and the eventual judgment of the Gentile nations who reject His Lordship in the earth.

The early church was created at the beginning of the last days, as represented by Peter in his first sermon recorded in Acts 2. Our generation exists at the end of those last days when we are to be looking for the literal and physical return of our Lord. The message of His return is a vital message needing to be preached in our times. Unfortunately, men have scrambled the message of Christ's return with their own ideas, making it difficult for people to receive. The message is clear and not as complicated as it has been made out to be. In the very same way Christ fulfilled all His words to His disciples when He came in judgment of the Christ-rejecting Jewish system. This time, He will come to judge the whole world, but this time His saints will be with Him.

Paul described the "mystery of the resurrection in 1 Corinthians 15:50-57. "In a moment, in the twinkling of an eye, at the last trumpet; for the trumpet will sound, and the dead will be raised imperishable, and we will be changed." Just as Mary's boy was born and brought redemptive hope to all of Israel and eventually the entire world, hope continues as we wait for His victorious return.

Father, I thank You that You sent Your Son to speak in these last days. I put my faith in all He has spoken and wait for Your promises to be fulfilled in my Lord's return. Help me speak clearly and plainly of Your return in the hopes of many coming to Christ.

## December 30 – YOUR BROTHER WILL RISE AGAIN

John 11:24 – Martha said to Him, "I know that he will rise again in the resurrection on the last day".

The eleventh chapter of John gives us one of the greatest messages of hope. Mary and Martha had expected Jesus to immediately come when hearing of their brother's sickness. He did not, and Lazarus died. He was buried before the Lord arrived. Their hopes were dashed and they were only left with the hope of the future resurrection. Life is filled with dashed hopes and expectations for many. Some people experience more than others.

When Jesus arrived, Martha appealed to Him by saying, "Even now, I know that whatever You ask of God, God will give You" (John 11:22). Jesus assured Martha that her brother would rise again. Martha responded that she knew he would rise again in the resurrection on the last day. This is an important statement that helps us to understand the next great event. Martha's statement is consistent with both Old and New Testament scriptures that indicate the resurrection is the final event of human history, happening on the "last day," as Paul said, "at the last trumpet" (1 Corinthians 15:52).

Jesus then gave Martha the cornerstone of our Christian Faith. "I am the resurrection and the life; he who believes in Me will live, even if he dies, and everyone who lives and believes in Me will never die. Do you believe this? (John 11:25-26). "Never die," is the greatest guarantee we possess. That promise contains all the promises of God. "They are yes; therefore also through Him is our Amen to the glory of God through us" (2 Corinthians 1:20). For the believer, life is settled in the "I am." Our life is hidden in Christ, who is in God.

Martha was contending with human emotions in the passing of this good man, Lazarus. She was confused and broken, yet abiding in her was faith concerning the future resurrection. As you prepare for the New Year set your eyes on Jesus, the resurrection and the life. He alone provides hope and stability as we weather difficult seasons in life. There is no promise made of an easy life void of hurt and difficulty. But there is the promise of both His presence and His physical return. Jesus' presence made the difference in Lazarus' case. The resurrection of Christ sealed the future for all those who put their trust in Him.

As the early church faced Great Tribulation and the future destruction of Jerusalem, Jesus instructed John to write down what he saw and send it to the seven churches mentioned in the Book of Revelation, which is the Revelation of Jesus Christ. Jesus spoke saying, "Do not be afraid; I am the first and the last, and the living One; and I was dead, and behold, I am alive forevermore, and I have the keys of death and of Hades" (Revelation 1:17-18).

Christ Jesus rules the nations, directing events for His purposes. He revealed to John how He was about to direct the events at the end of that generation who first heard the Good News of His Gospel, events of judgment against His enemies. Beloved, be encouraged, regardless of what may happen in your life or in the nations, Jesus is Lord! He is the Resurrection and the Life. He is the Coming King who will judge all those who have rejected His Covenant. Hope in God! Trust in Christ! Be filled again and again with the Holy Spirit. Enjoy your life in God.

Father, I thank You for Your promise given to Martha, "he will rise again". I thank You that Your promises are Yes and Amen to Your glory. Help me bring glory to Your name throughout the coming year.

# December 31 – THE FINAL VICTORY

Revelation 22:7 – Behold I am coming quickly. Blessed is he who heeds the words of the prophecy of this book.

Eight times in the first three chapters of Revelation Jesus speaks of events which will quickly take place. In the last chapter of Revelation, Jesus declares these events "must soon take place" (22:6), I am coming quickly" (22:7), "the time is near" (22:10), and "I am coming quickly) 22:12. Is it possible there might be a clue for John and the churches of that day that something apocalyptic was about to take place?

Today, many hold to a popular view about the Book of Revelation that all the symbolism in the book is about future events that are yet to take place. In this brief devotional, we do not have time to explore the entire book of Revelation, but consider the ten times Jesus strongly implies, "soon to take place." This great prophetic book establishes the absolute victory of Christ over His enemies. There are three enemies which are symbolized. They are the false religious leaders among the Jews, Jerusalem with its governmental structure which had killed the prophets, where Jesus was crucified, directed the persecution of believers, and the world systems and philosophies represented in the Roman Empire.

"I, Jesus, have sent My angel to testify to you these things for the churches. I am the root and the descendant of David, the bright morning star" (Revelation 22:16). Jesus states that this writing is for the seven churches mentioned in chapter 2 and 3. He was preparing them for the soon-coming events symbolized in Revelation when He would come and judge all His enemies. What hope and blessing is ours as we look back on history and see the fulfillment of all that Jesus declared. We look forward with great hope and expectation of His physical return after finishing His Great Commission, "Go into the entire world and preach the good news." The devil does not win, we do!

The sign of the Kingdom was seen in the first century church as Christ judged His enemies in 70 AD. The present day outpouring of the Holy Spirit being experienced around the world is preparing believers for the harvest of the nations. Jesus' literal return is the next great event on God's calendar when time will be no more.

Let us devote ourselves fully to the Lord and His agenda. There are many books that help to define God's purposes in clear terms. The most important book is the Bible. The enemy tries to keep us from immersing ourselves in the Scriptures. He tries to confuse our minds with natural reasoning. He has always tried to divide Christ's body in order to suppress the power of heaven manifested in a united redeemed community filled with the Holy Spirit. Remind yourself of what our Lord accomplished through first century believers and His judgments upon His enemies. Remember saints that the final victory lies before us and the Holy Spirit is our Helper who will never leave us. AMEN!

# DAILY DEVOTIONAL INDEX

## DEVELOPING YOUR RELATIONSHIP
## WITH THE HOLY SPIRIT

December 11 - THE MAGNIFICAT
12 - ZACHARIAS' PROPHECY
13 - THE GOD OF MERCY WHO REMEMBERS HIS HOLY COVENANT
14 - SERVE THE LORD IN HOLINESS AND RIGHTEOUSNESS
15 - THE PROPHET OF THE MOST HIGH
16 - THE BIRTH OF A SON
17 - JESUS PRESENTED IN THE TEMPLE
18 - A SAVIOR IS BORN
19 - GLORY TO GOD IN THE HIGHEST
20 - SO THEY CAME IN A HURRY AND FOUND HIM
21 - THE VISIT OF THE MAGI
22 - HEROD'S SECRET PLAN
23 - THE ENEMY IS ENRAGED, BUT RESTRICTED
24 - GO INTO THE LAND
25 - CHRISTMAS, CHRIST'S DAY
26 - THE RETURN OF OUR GREAT GOD AND KING
27 - KEEPING YOUR EYE ON THE PRIZE
28 - THE HARD ROAD BEFORE THE DISCIPLES
29 - GOD'S SON HAS SPOKEN IN THESE LAST DAYS
30 - YOUR BROTHER WILL RISE AGAIN
31 - THE FINAL VICTORY

# CONTACT INFORMATION

George Runyan is available as a guest speaker for Sunday Services, Conferences, Bible Schools, and Leadership Development Seminars. You can contact George via e-mail or by writing him.

E-Mail: grccm@cox.net

Ministry Address:

City Church Ministries
c/o George Runyan
PO Box 152388
San Diego, California 92195

## Other Resources Available from the Author:

MANDATED, Promise of Greater Works Fulfilled
ISBN: 1-59352-213-4

SALVATION TRUTHS – God's Salvation Plan for His Threefold Creation Man

HIGHWAY to HEALING – A God Given Ministry

CONCERNING SPIRITUAL GIFTS

LAYING FOUNDATIONS


## RECOMMENDED RESOURCES:

Charles Simpson Ministries – www.csmpublishing.org

Mark Hoffman – On Earth as it is in Heaven and The Joshua Principle (Changing the world by reaching children) Dave Hoffman – Prayer Will Change Your World and Fear of God – www.foothillschurch.org   (go to resources then store)

Jerry Ray – Kingdom Royalty – www.perpetualKingdom.com

Nathan Daniel – Freedom through Forgiveness – www.ftfmin.org

George Kouri – Sign of the Kingdom – www.signofthekingdom.com

Vision Publishing with many helpful books – www.booksbyvision.com

CPSIA information can be obtained at www.ICGtesting.com
Printed in the USA
BVOW041150251012

303879BV00001BA/6/P